Y0-ELU-710

*Many of the merits and none of the
defects of this translation are owing to Dr. Henry Beets, who carefully read and edited the manuscript.*

—*The Translator.*

FOREWORD

The first volume of Dr. Schilder's work on the suffering of our Lord met with an unusually favorable reception from every section of the American Protestant press. In the *Lutheran Standard,* we read: "It is a thorough-going exposition of pertinent Scripture passages, a determined effort to penetrate beneath the form of words and to establish in the believing heart the glory of our redemption in Christ and His eternal sufficiency for us in all things." Other Lutheran papers agreed.

The *Presbyterian Guardian* commented, "This treatment of the Passion probably never has been surpassed in its combination of acute reflection upon the sacred text and fresh, stimulating form of expression." The *Christian Observer* called the book "an outstanding contribution to the Christian literature of the day."

"It is hard to write of this volume in measured terms," wrote the *Evangelical Christian;* "in each chapter will be found spiritual treasures that will bless, inform and delight the mind." "A great book," agreed the *Sunday School Times,* and *King's Business* commented, "The Scriptural penetration of this unusual mind and spirit will challenge the most informed student of the Word, and nourish the humble believer."

Summing it all up, the London *Service* stated: "This book is a masterpiece, not merely because of the considerable literary ability displayed, nor even because of the reverent, devotional spirit manifested, but as the publisher states, 'distinctive of the book are the richly suggestive flashes of exegetical insight, and the welcome specific detail brought to bear upon the study in the effort to present the sublimely organic unity of the Saviour's awful passion.' This is easily the finest book on the subject that we have yet seen."

We trust that this second volume, CHRIST ON TRIAL, will be welcomed with equal heartiness by the English speaking world. These chapters cover our Lord's Passion from Gethsemane till He was condemned to be crucified. Mr. Henry Zylstra, who translated the first volume, continued his work with this second book. The publishers have not spared any effort to make the exterior of the volume as attractive as its contents.

HENRY BEETS, LL.D.

Grand Rapids, Mich.
Dec. 7, 1938

CONTENTS

CONTENTS—Continued

Christ Being Led To Annas

CHAPTER ONE

Christ Being Led To Annas

> *And (they) led him away to Annas first; for he was father in law to Caiaphas, which was the high priest that same year.*
>
> JOHN 18:13.

GETHSEMANE lies behind us now.

Christ is about to meet *the judge*.

At this point, accordingly, the gospel of the suffering of Christ passes into a second stage. The Christ of God who can proclaim justice in this world by virtue of His inherent authority is to come into contact with "judges" who will pass judgment on Him by virtue of an authority they have received from God. For, in spite of the fact that they flagrantly abused it, their authority had its source in God. And this first contact between Christ and these judges introduces a new element into His passion and represents an abrupt transition in the gospel of His suffering.

The transition is clearly delineated.

Up to this time Christ was permitted to move around freely. He could go where He pleased. He could enter Jerusalem, or He could stay out of it. Had He wanted to, He could at the close have tried to rediscover the combination of the beginning, the beautiful beginning in which He had united a reformation of the temple with a wedding. Or else He could have prepared Himself for that different combination — a reformation of the temple issuing in death. Which of these was it to be? Temple and wedding march, or temple and funeral dirge? Which shall it be? The temple and the power of working miracles, or the temple and degeneration, a degeneration, mark you, under the cover of heavens which withhold their forces and conceal their light.

15

That question was put to Him by the world which surrounded Him and especially by the struggle which His ever-active thoughts were carrying on in the depths of His heart. From all sides He was being bound by the law and by the evangelical will. But as yet there were no bonds which restricted His body. There was no authoritative coercion other than that of God. And God was concealing Himself more and more by the hour.

Not so now. Now the Man of sorrows enters upon a new phase. He is put into bonds. The *judge* begins to play a rôle. External authority is to have a hand in the matter. Moreover, this new authority does not conceal itself; on the contrary, it imposes itself upon Him. Christ is no longer allowed to go His own way. Malice becomes His portion; humiliation and disdain seek out their worldly means to oppress Him, and we know that the world has many means which it is glad to lend to those who wish to give the essence of humiliation and disdain appropriate external shape and form.

Hence all those who think on Him in reverence will acknowledge that Christ now enters upon a new and narrower way.

In everything that took place heretofore, Christ governed the situation and was *victorious* over it. Gethsemane represents a victory won. But who among men recognized that this was so? Who, pray, lifted up paeans of praise in His honor, or even thought of doing so? Not one, of course; not even one.

Accordingly, the Son must act as though Gethsemane had never existed, and must carry the conflict which He first experienced in His soul into the public market-place and into the world's tribunal, there to begin that struggle anew. He bears the essence of His victory within Him, but that too must be put into hiding. He must appear before the judge. And the judge gets his authority from God. In fact, God puts Christ into contact with two kinds of judges: the judge who represents temporal authority; and the judge who is the symbol of spiritual jurisdiction.

It is before the second of these that He appears first. Christ is led into the presence of Annas. Now Annas, by reason of tradition and family relationship, belongs to the *priestly* court of justice. It is not surprising to learn that Christ was first brought into contact with the spiritual court of justice of His own people. It is true that the Jews were fettered by the chains of Roman dominion. But the Romans followed the tactics of very enlightened despots. They allowed the peoples whom they conquered to retain as many of their customs and usages as possible. In matters affecting religious life, Rome gave those she vanquished an almost entirely free hand. Thus it was that the Sanhedrin, being a tribunal of justice in religious affairs, still exercised great authority under Roman rule.

The president of the Sanhedrin was the high priest. At this time the incumbent of the presiding officer's chair was Caiaphas. And Annas, his eminent father-in-law, was a prominent figure of the day.

These two, Annas and Caiaphas, had, before time began, been given by the foreordaining God the horrible mandate of speaking the first word in the trial of Christ. May they tremble at the responsibility of that terrible mandate . . . But, alas, they have never learned to tremble. A weightier mandate was never given than these two received when God told them: *Let this ruin be under thy hand* (Isaiah 3:6); let the crumbled ruins of Israel's wasted life be subject to thy rule.

No, never were those who were called to a heavy burden farther than these two officious ones from replying with that suitable cry of despair: *I cannot be an healer; do not make me a ruler of the people* (compare Isaiah 3:7). These two suppose they are still doing very well in their office even in these last days. As a matter of fact, who is thinking about "last days"? Surely, as long as Rome continues to send out her credentials to these spiritual judges, the world will continue on its way.

Caiaphas and Annas, then, are seated in their authoritative seats. They sit in judgment on the case of the Nazarene. Annas has the first word. For He *must be put to death.*

He must be put to death. And Annas and Caiaphas must have a hand in it. True, the Romans have not given the Jews the authority to carry out a death sentence; it was a formal requirement that the Roman governor had to grant his permission before a death sentence could be executed. Nevertheless, the Sanhedrin, which for the most part is Caiaphas, plays an important rôle in this drama. The Sanhedrin has the authority to judge in spiritual questions and in matters pertaining to religion and to traditional rights and usages. Hence Caiaphas and his Sanhedrin have the advantage of knowing that when they give a religious color to an issue carefully prepared beforehand, the Roman government will not easily take exception to any death sentence which they recommend. For it was precisely in religious affairs that Roman authority wished to give the people of the provinces free rein.

Thus it happens that the Sanhedrin and its diligent president feel that they are under the burden of a responsible assignment. They must, if we may put it that way, provide the substructure to the sentence which Pilate can later pronounce valid by his seal. They feel that if they make an error tonight—for "it was night"—or if they fail to find suitable arguments, or if they do not succeed in satisfactorily defining and formulating their charges against this revolutionist, it will be unusually difficult for them to get the sentence confirmed. Particularly is this true in the case of so wonderful and popular a hero as the Nazarene happens to be. Accordingly, they must carefully employ every means at their disposal; they must be sure to gather and arrange carefully all available evidence in time to use it for proper litigation.

It is exactly for this reason that Jesus is immediately placed before Annas, the father-in-law of Caiaphas. That Annas, also called Ananos, was the first to be given the "privilege" of seeing Jesus before him is a circumstance which cannot definitely be said to issue from his official position, for he was, as a matter of fact, no longer the high priest. It is true that Annas had been appointed to the office of high priest by Quirinius the governor and that he had served in this capacity from the year 6 to 15 A.D. But he had been removed from his position by the Roman procurator Valerius Gratus. When Valerius came into power in the year 15 A.D., he put Ishmael in the seat of the high priest. After Ishmael, Eleazar and Simeon followed in rapid succession. And thereupon Joseph Caiaphas was given the reins of office.

Officially, therefore, Annas had no right to demand a hearing of Jesus, or to have that hearing entered upon the record as a legal step in the official litigation against the Nazarene. Anything Annas could do could never have the character of an official action. He was simply giving Jesus a preliminary hearing. The official session of the Sanhedrin would come later. Hence, in our thinking about this matter, we must keep that later session distinguished from this antecedent hearing which Annas gave Jesus.

How did it happen, then, you ask, that Jesus was led before Annas first? Perhaps Annas was staying in the house of Caiaphas; it may be that the two shared the same home; or it is possible that each lived in a separate apartment of the same palace. Some observers suppose that Annas, informed of Caiaphas' plans and curious to know how these would develop, made it a point to be present just for this "occasion" in order to see what the result of the movement against the Nazarene would be. The supposition is not an implausible one, for it would explain what would otherwise be a rather singular circumstance: namely, that the captain of the Roman soldiers gave permission to take Jesus into the presence of a person who had no official position. For if Annas and Caiaphas were together at this time, there could be no objection to such permission, and granting it would require no special discussion on the part of military and spiritual authorities.

We can easily understand why these spiritual authorities, these masters of theology, were much in favor of having Jesus appear before Annas first of all. Several reasons can be indicated for this. Or perhaps we can say that things simply drifted that way of their own accord. To summon the Sanhedrin, with its more than seventy members, required time. An official session of that body would have to be called and that could not be done in a moment. Hence those who were working behind the scenes took advantage of the opportunity to make use of this necessary interim by placing Jesus before Annas for a so-called preliminary hearing. These tactics would certainly prove beneficial. In the first place, this would be making "productive" use of time. Besides, Annas was a man having a seasoned experience; he had been called upon to act in difficult cases before, and had developed a technique in the art of finding official formulas and procedures. This man, surely, would be invaluable to Caiaphas in defining the arguments, formulating the charge, striking out irrelevant matters, and, in short, quickly directing the litigation to the main issues. The old man's advice would make the work of Caiaphas just so much easier. We are not surprised, therefore, when we consider the various information given us in the Bible, to receive the impression that Annas and Caiaphas *co-operated* in preparing for the coming session of the Sanhedrin. Naturally, this procedure would make the work of Caiaphas, the president, easier. But another advantage, not to be disdained, is that it would help him in his efforts to offset the objections raised by the Sanhedrin —and objections there were—to a death sentence. In short, it would help him to make the point that the law *required* the death of the Nazarene. Caiaphas, you see, could then quote an authority: the venerable Annas himself had said so.

To these considerations must be added the fact that Annas undoubtedly took delight in seeing Jesus bound before him. He had followed the various exhibitions of hatred which had been directed against Jesus with a sympathetic interest; in fact, he had taken an active part in these. Hence it was a source of grim pleasure to the old aristocrat finally to see the man before him who—in his estimation—had almost started a revolution against the authority of the priesthood. This old aristocrat and Sadducee, this noble man "who had grown gray in the service" inasmuch as he was the father of a generation of priests and even the founder of a dynasty of high priests, could not keep back the thought that the ever-growing popularity of the name of Jesus spelled a declaration of war by the masses against the priesthood. His lips gave expression to the grimness with which he deigned to use the word—the *masses,* the *vulgus.* Now that uncrowned king was standing before him. Indeed he was uncrowned, and unanointed. And he had hurled curses about recklessly, not the least of which were directed against the priestly caste.

We can easily appreciate his situation. His priestly dignity had been forced into an attitude of evasive indifference towards the madding of the people who were being carried away by the Nazarene—those masses, the *'am-ha-arets.* In spite of the haughty imperviousness of his demeanor, however, the soul of the decorous old master was greatly perturbed. Think, he had been the high priest himself, the father of five other high priests, the father-in-law of still another high priest, and the grandfather of a seventh. Accordingly, every disdainful speech which Christ directed against the high priests and the leaders of the people had come to Annas as a personal insult to the honor of his family.

Now Jesus is standing before him. Moreover, they are a private company here—no need here of the decorous restraint required by an official setting. Indeed, this for Annas is a realization of a desire he had nurtured for a long time. It is his greatest gratification. It may be that he paused for thanksgiving because of it. Was not God giving him "grace and honor"?

For Christ, however, this is *suffering*. The fact that his litigation begins with an "informal" action is an insult to Him. It is an indication of the kind of mentality that is to judge Him, and it bodes no good.

However, that is not the worst aspect of it. Worse for Jesus than this formal violation of law is the fact of the coerced meeting between him, the true High Priest, and this representative of the ancient priesthood. Annas, who, as we observed, opened the way to a whole family of priests, manifests in his person the decadence of the priestly office in Israel. The rights of the generation of Aaron, although guaranteed inviolable by law, had been violated frequently in the course of the years. But the later authorities ignored as much as possible the privileges of priestly families.[1]

Now the fact that Annas had seen five sons, besides a son-in-law and a grandson, enter into the office of the priest, and had also held the office himself, was in itself a forthright unmasking of the deplorable condition of the generations of priests and of their crowned heads in general. For, if the ancestral law had still been in force, Annas would have worn his purple robe until his death.[2] He would not have seen a single successor take his place. From another point of view, of course, it is also true that the given circumstances do represent a singular honor. "God gave grace and honor . . . ." This was a time in which priests were succeeding each other all too rapidly. Not seldom corruption led to murder and to a change of dynasty. Arbitrary Roman administrators did the rest. Therefore the fact that Annas was able to keep the honor in his own generation as long as he kept it there is evidence of the respect accorded him, not so much by the people who sometimes spoke disparagingly of his dynasty, as by the official leaders of the people. And the days were still far away in

---

1. Holtzmann, *Neutestamentische Zeitgeschichte*, 1906, p. 102.
2. Holtzmann, p. 164.

which the crowd would venture to murder his son, Ananos, the second.

Indeed, the honor accorded him was a great honor. We cannot but think in this connection of the Jewish woman who had seven sons, each of whom was admitted to the offiice of priest. She was allowed to regard this as an honor so great that her admirers applied to her the words of Psalm 45, verse 13: *The king's daughter is all glorious within; her clothing is of wrought gold.* So evil an application of a text shows us the quality of the spiritual climate in which Annas also lived. Many continued to bow in reverence before him. As father of the dynasty of priests, he was accorded so much honor that the incense offered to him was accompanied by texts drawn from the Bible.

God is not putting our Saviour into the presence of just one of the many decadent figures of that day, is not placing Jesus before the tribunal of just one of those transient and trivial priests of which there were all too many at that time — twenty-eight of them, in fact, in about a hundred years. No, God places His Son over against the founder of a *family* of priests in whom a little of the ancient dignity, pride, and glory had again been fanned into a flame.

Thus it happens that a contrast is most discriminatingly brought to light—the contrast, namely, between a priesthood according to the flesh and a priesthood according to the Spirit. True, such a contrast is imperceptible to anyone who looks solely at the external side of these circumstances. Externally observed, Annas seems to be the fruition of a new promise. He looks like a new shoot out of the stem of the priesthood, and who, indeed, can recognize in Christ Jesus anything but the tree which has been hewn down?

But God sees things with eyes other than those of the world. He points out the contrasts which inhere in the things which are not superficial and which are not visible. It is true that Annas personally would not have liked to see such a hymn of praise as the 45th psalm go out of fashion; nor would he, permeated as he was by the logic of the priests, have wanted any of the fragrances of the myrrh to be wafted towards the Christ who is standing before him. But in this which is his weightiest hour God judges quite differently. In God's eyes Christ is standing over against a priest and a generation of priests to which, not the 45th, but the

82nd, psalm is applicable: How long will ye judge unjustly, and accept the persons of the wicked? Or again: O thou tribunal, seated to do justice, dost thou speak justly? But to its Son who is in bonds, heaven now applies the words of psalm 45, and they are very rich in content:

> My heart is inditing a good matter: I speak of the things which I have made touching the king: my tongue is the pen of a ready writer. Thou art fairer than the children of men: grace is poured into thy lips: therefore God has blessed thee forever.

The dynasty of the priests of Annas may pride itself in a priestly caste which can point to an eminent father and mother as the founders of a family of priests. But Jesus Christ desires a higher thing; He wants to be priest according to the order of Melchizedek. Melchizedek, too, was a priest having no priestly father or mother; his coming was as inexplicable as that of a bolt of lightning. Annas represents a dynasty of priests which derives from the flesh its standards for determining succession in an office which augured unusual distinction for a few persons. Over against him stands Jesus. Jesus represents a mysterious priestly essence which, according to the Spirit, incorporates into the true priesthood, and ministers the grace of a priest to all those who know of it by reason of the fact that they are included in the Messiah through faith. The dynasty of Annas salvages from Israel's and Aaron's legacy what it thinks worth preserving, and steels its heart against the spirit of prophecy weeping at the ruins of Aaron. It is eager to cover the nakedness of Aaron, but it is unwilling to do so with its own cloak. It wants to throw a cloth, borrowed from Rome or from Babel, over the dilapidated furniture of the house of Israel. On the contrary, Christ would cover the nakedness of Aaron with His own garment of righteousness, or, failing in that, would exhibit that nakedness to the staring eyes of all the sons of Ham in the world. He would build a house for the bearers of the tradition of Aaron, provided that the architectural plans are according to the vows of Aaron. Should these find this house too revolutionary in structure to suit them, they can have the alternative of standing out in the cold of the universe. And the universe is cold . . .

The contrast is complete, is perfect. Therefore it is enduring. Accordingly, it is no mere coincidence that the dynasty of Annas, long after Golgotha, was still enraged against Christ's lambs of sacrifice. We know that the sword of the children of Annas was crimsoned later by the blood of James, the brother of the Lord.

This contrast, then, became the decadence of Aaron's wasting priesthood[1] in Annas, and the florescence of Melchizedek's fulfilled priesthood in Christ traces its genesis to the distant past. Moreover, its development extends far into the future. Hence it is that God, in order to make that contrast obvious to the whole world, allows the Priest according to the order of Melchizedek to be led as a captive into the presence of one who exacts tithes by the grace of Rome and Babel, the decorous old Annas.

Alas, Melchizedek: it is unfortunate that you are no longer here to bless and to demand tithes. How pitiable, Lord Jesus, is the fact that God has bound Thy hands so tightly that they cannot be extended in blessing or reach out to accept the tenth part of a tithe for Thyself. "Mein Jesu, was hast du getan; in was für Missetaten bist du geraten?"[2]

We see, therefore. that the drama of Jesus' trial is marked by a prologue in which the conclusion of the tragedy is plainly announced.

Has not Annas himself personally experienced what it means to suffer as Israel's priest under Roman authority? He may insist upon his dignity, but it is a fact, nevertheless, that he had had to suffer retrenchment, that one of Rome's satellites had first appointed him to the priesthood and had later taken that office away from him. This humiliating experience should have led Annas to ponder carefully the tragic conflict of Israel's rejected priesthood, the conflict of a *spiritual* office which had become subjected to a carnal authority. The riddle of the hewn-down tree affected Annas also; in fact, it should have served as a matter for lifelong meditation for the old priest. Or, in any case, it should have opened his eyes to the large, eschatological significance of Jesus of Nazareth, who, confronted by the same problem, experienced it in his body in a far more excruciating form of suffering than Annas, and who demonstrated it daily in his life from the time when He lay in His manger.

---

1. In the sense of a traditional connection, the genealogy is unknown.
2. Well-known theme of the *Passion of St. Matthew*: My Jesus, what hast Thou done; in what crimes hast Thou been involved.

What Annas objects to in Christ, of course, is that He gave a different solution to the riddle of the hewn-down tree, than the old priest wished. Christ's solution to it was not one of external power but of a life after the Spirit. Annas is so completely occupied with his own mocking misery, which he evasively tries to conceal, that he takes no notice of the preaching of the Nazarene. He chooses to let the stem of David and Aaron lie in all its nakedness and blunt misery and to send its stench up to heaven, rather than to notice the new shoot out of Nazareth. After all, this new voice which had risen had raised the old sound over Israel and its dynasty of priests.

Therefore the short scene presenting Christ before Annas is a compendium of a pronounced contrast between the flesh and the spirit which within a few years will divide Israel into a people living by faith together with Abraham and a people dying by reason of its own unbelief and hardening of heart.

This scene represents something else besides. It speaks to us of an Aaron and of a Levi who were unwilling to bow the knee before Melchizedek. Aaron bent the knee before Melchizadek and Levi gave him tithes, but they did so only when they were in the loins of Abraham. Now that they are standing on their own feet, they say to the successor of Melchizedek: give us tithes or perish. Not all of those who were included in the loins of Abraham live by the *faith* of Abraham. Hence, when God put the chair of judgment in position, and arranges the curtains behind which the session of the judges of His own Son will convene, the shadows deepen, and everything which happens is full of dramatic power and figurative significance. The gleanings of Aaron and the harvest of Melchizedek are placed in the balances of the world. Who dares to weigh them?

Annas dares. Now he is lost. This master in charge of the scales had no knowledge of imponderables; he had lived in vain.

Christ's Apology Before Annas

CHAPTER TWO

Christ's Apology Before Annas

> *The high priest then asked Jesus of his disciples, and of his doctrine. Jesus answered him, I spake openly to the world; I ever taught in the synagogue, and in the temple, whither the Jews always resort; and in secret have I said nothing. Why askest thou Me? ask them which heard me, what I have said unto them: behold, they know what I said.*
>
> JOHN 18:21.

INTERPRETERS differ in their opinions of how we are to think of the historical sequence of events at the beginning of the trial of Christ. John informs us in the 19th verse of our chapter that the *high priest* questioned Christ. Now some suppose that this is a reference to the same hearing that took place, according to the accounts of the other evangelists, before the Sanhedrin under the direction of Caiaphas. Obviously the Revised Version has regarded this interpretation a plausible one, for in spite of the fact that according to a simple rendering of the Greek text, verse 24 should read, "Annas *sent* him bound to Caiaphas," the Revised Version has "Annas *had sent* him bound to Caiaphas." Now it is plain that if this last translation is correct,[1] the report of the hearing before the high priest, which report immediately precedes this verse, is an account of the official hearing at the plenary session of the Sanhedrin, of which Caiaphas was the presiding officer.

This interpretation, which is supported by other arguments besides, is nevertheless objectionable for numerous reasons. We shall let it suffice to name only this one, that such an interpretation is possible only if one does some unwarranted manipulating of

---

1. It is identical with that of the King James Version.

the text. Only then can this reconstruction of the chronological order of events, (think again of verse 24, to which reference was made), be read into the text. Hence we prefer to agree with those who accord John the usual meaning, altering nothing, not even in the translation. We choose the interpretation which has it that the hearing spoken of in verses 19 to 23 took place in the house of Annas, to which, as we observed, Christ was first brought. When we read in the 19th verse that the high priest questioned Christ, we may believe that this high priest may very well have been Annas, inasmuch as he was the former bearer of that office, and was still functioning in that capacity in this instance. That consideration raises a second question, namely: Granted that Jesus was brought before Annas, who is the high priest that does the questioning recorded in the 19th verse? Annas himself? Or Caiaphas perhaps, who, being present, may have joined in the conversation? We shall not state which of the many interpretations of this point is preferable. The main issue involved in this matter inheres in the fact that, as is plainly the intent of the narrator, the hearing before Annas was of a *preliminary* character. It was designed to gather materials and to formulate specific charges for the plenary session of the Sanhedrin to come later. It is very likely, therefore, that both authorities, the father-in-law and the son-in-law, were present at this hearing.

Nor is it remarkable that this investigation makes it a point to probe into Christ's *doctrine* and to ask about His *disciples*. As a matter of fact, even that is not quite true. The narrative tells us *first* of the inquiries about the disciples, and only then of the investigation into the doctrine of Christ. It is not impossible that design and purpose are concealed beneath this order of events as given in the account. For, from the point of view of the status of the family of the priest, less depended upon the message Christ proclaimed than upon His disciples, upon the *influence* of His words, the so-called "success" of His preaching. We know that people who flutter about at the periphery of the realm of truth obstinately insist upon confusing "blessing" with "success." They have less respect for the principle of organic life which is illustrated by a seed which, falling into the ground, slowly unfolds itself, and gradually but surely evolves into a tree, than for the principle of mechanical things, illustrated by any structure representing a mere aggregation and juxtaposition of quantities. They fear a law which proceeds from an organic principle less than a myriad-faceted organization which clothes the multitudes of its disciples in the uniform of the voluntary enthusiasm of its Spirit or in the civilian's garb of the guerilla warriors of truth. Their first concern is not about the profundity or the truth of a given view or principle, but about the number of its devotees or propagandists. If this is a large number, they speak of a "success," but of the concept "blessing" in its unique Biblical sense they say not a word. Hence, when a person preaches some new doctrine, founds some new school of thought, and begins to get followers, and if it happens that this doctrine and school are unsympathetic to them, they will soon be asking how many followers there are. Only after that, if any time remains, will they investigate the substance of the doctrine which is being preached.

Irrespective of the ultimate purpose of our text, it is plain from the manner in which "the problem of the Nazarene" is raised for discussion in the conferences of the caste of priests that that method of approach is quite appropriate to the order of procedure indicated in the text. They first asked about the disciples, and only then devoted some attention to the doctrine of Jesus. Caiaphas himself said: *Behold, the world is gone after him* (12:19). And it is this same emphasis which moves them to act so relentlessly now.

They first ask Jesus about His *disciples,* yes. The first question officially put to Jesus concerned the number of His disciples. In contemporary parlance, we would say that Jesus was asked first of all about "the success of His organization." It is apparent that the ruling dynasty of the priests, as well as the faction represented by the Sanhedrin, was of the opinion that Jesus intended to begin a movement, making His starting point a small nucleus. They were of the opinion also that He had already begun this. At least, they create the impression that He is gathering a group of disciples around Him, and that it is very difficult to say just how large His school of followers is. This insinuation suggests that Jesus is preaching a secret doctrine to an exclusive circle, or at least that He is preparing plans for a surreptitious conspiracy against the existing authorities.

Accordingly, the questions put to Jesus by Annas are themselves imputations of guilt. The atmosphere in which Jesus is received is one of antithesis and antipathy from the very start. But we should be proving ourselves short-sighted if we could not say more about the spirit of these questions than that. Perhaps the queries which Annas addresses to Him do represent a hidden animosity. However, we may not stare ourselves blind by looking at that fact solely. It may also be that Annas' questions give expression to a kind of curiosity and to a typically human fear even though these particular motives were not openly expressed.

No, we must not begin by all too facilely casting stones at Annas; we must begin by seeing in him a man of like passions with us. Can we suppose that this old man, whose gray hairs are about to enter the grave without peace, is a greater deceiver than we? Dare we think that we would have spoken differently than this notable person of Jerusalem spoke?

Surely not. We may not take the tragic out of this tragedy by naming Caiaphas, Annas, Pilate, and Herod pure deceivers, men so very bad that it would be hard to find their equals in whole city blocks of respectable contemporary cities. Such an attitude would betray the fact that we have no real appreciation of the nature of the human soul, and of the nature of our own sin, which, together with Annas, dares to sit in judgment — upon Jesus.

In fact, every honest observer must pay Annas this tribute that in conducting the examination he proceeded authentically and in a manner which showed his familiarity with his times. Caiaphas had good reason to give the first word in this trial to this accomplished diplomat.

Annas asked Jesus whether He was secretly gathering a school of disciples around Him. And his question may be taken as an expression of that picture of the Messiah which was haunting the imaginations of the anemic minds of Jesus' contemporaries. Whoever is familiar with that picture of the Messiah which the Jews of Jesus' time preferred to conjure up before themselves — a picture clearly delineated in their writings — will know that they were confidently looking forward to a messianic *mystery*. Their Christology — that is, their doctrine of the Messiah, or the Christ —contained a very interesting chapter which treated of the messianic *secretiveness*.

The fact is that the Jews living in this "fulness of time" wanted to taste the flavor of mystery and secretiveness in their Messiah. They may put many questions to the Messiah, but they had better know that they wish no answer to these unless that answer is given in a piquant way. The true Messiah — as they would have it— must be of unknown origin. The real messianic movement must get under way under cover. *When Christ cometh no man knoweth whence He is* (John 7:27). The attitude was very generally current that the Messiah would be enveloped in mystery for a while before He made His public appearance. One Jewish writer thought it possible that at the time in which he was writing the Messiah had already been born but was temporarily keeping Himself aloof. The supposition was, then, that during this period in which the Messiah was living but was still unrevealed, He Himself was not yet aware of the nature of His future work. This last would not become clear to Him and to others until later. In short, the burden of this writer's message was that the great light might be breaking through at a time when nothing as yet pointed to its appearing.

Others supposed that the Messiah was *intentionally* holding Himself aloof *because of the sins of the people*. It was even thought possible that He was keeping Himself in hiding in Rome. Still others asserted that He would come from "the north." In any case, however, He would when He made His appearance step forth out of a condition of seclusion and of mystery. This popular notion had its resemblances to that arbitrary interpretation of later theologians who concluded similarly on the basis of Isaiah 7. We read there that the Messiah would eat "butter (thick milk) and honey." This these theologians interpreted as meaning that He would be found among the shepherds in the wilderness, far from the city. Culture, they said, would affect Him harmfully. You see, then, that many in Israel were looking forward to a *concealed* Messiah who would make His appearance suddenly in the nimbus of a paradoxical, wonder-working power. His appearing would be a mystery; there would be a careful underground preparation of armaments. Thereupon, the arsenals would suddenly be broken open.

No, do not cast stones at the aged Annas. Leave that to God. Is it impossible — a human soul is so unfathomably complicated, we know — that he unconsciously still reckoned with the possibility that Jesus was the Messiah? Do not reply that this possibility is barred by the fact that he bound Jesus. Think of Herod's many secret visits to the Baptist — in prison. And is not Herod himself secretly harboring the suspicion that a dark mystery may be lurking beneath the manacled Jesus? Then why should not Annas feel just that? The human heart attempts to evade so much of what it cannot face outright. Ah, *perhaps* the mind of Annas is haunted by the thought that the miracle, the long-awaited miracle, may possibly emerge suddenly from this Nazarene.

Note that we are advisedly italicizing "perhaps." For it may also be that this supposition ascribed to Annas is not correct at all. We cannot dissect his soul; God alone can do that. Moreover, just what have we to do with the secrets lurking in the soul of Annas? Our responsibility is simply to be honest in the matter, and to remember that, formally considered, the questions which Annas asks are in conformity with the tenor of the Jewish theology of his time. His conduct of the hearing directs it straight to the core of the messianic problem as the Jews of his day conceived of that problem. Viewing in this light, we are not much concerned to know whether some anxiety lurked in Annas' soul underneath the allegations of guilt which this priestly aristocrat flung into the face of the bound "Galilean" from the provinces.

It is enough for us to know that the logic of the facts and nothing else induced this spiritual judge to demand that Jesus answer two questions. One of these concerns His doctrine. Is His doctrine a sealed book, or His teaching open and above-board? The second question refers to His disciples. Are these people of the street, these former cripples, these dismissed publicans and but lately civilized sinners, these untutored ones — are they really His disciples? Or has He some other school of followers?

In short: Jesus, who are you?

And Jesus rises to report on His messianic mystery. *That mystery*, He says, *does indeed exist, but it is not what they think it is or can be.*

Listen to the apology of Jesus Christ. He asserts that He has never done anything or taught anything in secret. He says He has always done His work in the full light of day. He has preached daily in the temple and the synagogues. Yes, in the temple, where the leaders of the people were ever present and where the censor-ship was strict. And in the synagogues, where the masses went in and out continuously, and where, no less than in the temple, the doors were never closed during the services. The temple was the place where broad principles were exposed; there the rabbis as-signed chairs to those who proclaimed old and new doctrines and modes of thought. In the synagogues, however, new doctrines were not presented, but there new applications of current doctrines were discussed. In other words, Jesus states that He varied His methods of teaching sufficiently; and He adds that wherever He was He never turned His back to the community of the people. He says in effect: I have never wanted to found a secret cult; I have never been a prophet "of the desert" or of the "inner closet." To form a nucleus designed to work its way forcibly into the ex-isting body of the church, state, and community by way of intro-ducing an alien element into these, bent on eventually destroying them, is a law quite incompatible with the kingdom of heaven. I have done nothing, Christ means to say, other than to set free and to cause those seeds to sprout which God Himself has planted in the field of Israel. I have not planted two kinds of seeds, he as-serts; I have introduced no germinal properties alien to the body of the people, but have under the full light of the sun wanted to cause the seeds, which the God of truth long ago planted in Israel's soil, to germinate. Hence secret doctrines and esoteric organizations are none of mine. I come not to break down but to fulfill.

You observe that Christ's apology leads to this question: Just why are you examining me? You are asking, He says in effect, for that which you know very well already. In order to escape from the mercilessly searching condemnations which you have detected in my teaching, you act as though I used language designed to con-ceal my real purposes. You act as though you were perplexed about what is the real state of things; and as you ask me now to lift the veil for you, you present your petition in the guise of a *prayer* on the part of the *uninformed*. But that prayer is essential-ly a mask covering the *enmity* of the *unwilling*. Just why, indeed, are you interviewing me? So far was my preaching removed from secret and occult doctrine, that you may ask anyone who happens along and you will be able to get from him a "summary" of what I taught.

We must ask now what the meaning is of this dialogue being carried on between Christ and the high priest. We must ask what relationship exists between this apology and the whole history of the passion.

We believe we are touching on the real significance of this apology when we say that Jesus is here confessing His messianic office, and that He is confessing it precisely to those whose official life has wholly denied and completely outgrown its own messianic tendencies.

The office which was introduced into Israel at God's behest has gradually been turning its back to the people and more and more been standing aloof from them. The common people are being despised. The priests feast upon those who bring sacrifices. Single individuals, when they see a suitable opportunity, climb to the top of the ranks over the backs of the masses. The spirit of Michal has entered into the colleges of the priests and into their secret societies. The timbrel of David has become a mere monogram on their stationery; David's religious dance has lost its validity for bondmen and bondwomen.

Over against this delight in aristocratic isolation which tends to fix a gulf between the office and the people, Christ places His messianic obedience. The man of the street was never a stranger to Christ. He never acknowledges any antithesis between the official dignity inherent in Him and the people — those scurvy sheep who are in great need. It is true that His doctrine contains a mystery which no one can appropriate to himself except the man who is regenerated by the Spirit. But there is nothing avaricious about this secret. It has in it no jealousy at all except in the sense that God is jealous of the things which are God's. Life is life and it can never be anything else, and because the doctrine of Christ is a living doctrine, only he who lives by virtue of the regenerating Spirit can accept that doctrine in his person and in the "hidden man of the heart." In all other senses, however, Christ in the preaching of this life and in the offer of this living mystery never turned aside from the masses, from the many, from the communion. You must look for those who shut up the secret formulations of their subtilized theories among the Pharisees and Sadducees and also among the members of the priestly caste. These sealed up their choicest morsels lest some uninitiated ones should eat of and de-

light in them. Yes, they graciously kept their apothecary shops
open for the "rabble" — until sundown, you understand, and never on Sundays. However, Jesus never made an intellectual doctrine of the life which He preached, and accordingly never confused death and life in His preaching. Unstintedly and unrestrict-
edly He spread His offer of doctrine and of life abroad. He did
so with an "earnest calling" which proffered bread and medicine
without stint. This His inquirers must have noticed, for they often criticized Him for keeping His shop open on the Sabbath day,
and for delivering His bread on every day of the week.

Delivering His bread — yes, that is the word they wanted. They
wanted a neutral term. They refused to say that He had given
bread gratis; that would make it too obvious that their "delivering" had none of the connotation of "selling " in it. But surely
they could not have forgotten this. Again . . . why do they question *Him?* In this hearing the contrast between Christ and His
judges is fully revealed. Christ tears all the slips of paper on which
they have written their neutral terms into pieces. He puts that
contrast emphatically; He uses unmistakable terminology. He
says: "I spoke publicly; I always taught in the synagogue and in
the temple where all the Jews are accustomed to gather; they who
heard me know what I said." The emphatic thrice-repeated use of
the personal pronoun "I"[1] has in it the thrust of a criticism; for
the judges of Jesus did not use a searchingly accurate diction.
How much of what was in their heart did they actually proclaim
to the world? All that they have in mind at present is designed
to leave the people out in the cold. "Not on the feast day, not on
the feast day" — that is their cry. They are perfectly willing to
go through the regular routine of public worship the procedure
and order of which everyone can learn by heart; and they are quite
willing to carry out the regular schedule in the temple. But the important current issues, such as that of the eschatological preaching
of the Nazarene, for instance, they prefer to discuss behind closed
doors. A sombre secretivenes pervades their private discussion.

But Christ spoke His apology with forthrightness, and thus at
the very beginning of His contact with the law made the good confession boldly. Observe what He does. He immediately places

---

1. The Greek text indicates this very clearly.

the issue of His *office* before this *spiritual* tribunal, for the institution of any *office* in Israel is messianic in its purpose. Hence
a proper conception of the messianic problem was possible only on
the basis of a true appreciation of what the concept of *the office*
implied. In this respect also Christ proves to be the Obedient One,
for He wants to keep the litigation which is confronting Him pure
to the extent He Himself is active in it. In the day of the great
judgment — and that day has arrived now — Annas must not be
able to say to Jesus, "You used a language which was designed to
conceal your thoughts from me; I have therefore good reasons for
blaming you." Instead, Christ comes to Annas, and asks him, "Do
you not know the prescription? It is an old and tested one taken
from your own pharmacy . . . unless, indeed, you have robbed
your God of it."

Even that, however, does not conclude Christ's defense. His
apology not only proclaims His intention to come to everyone with
His word of revelation but also testifies to the power which resides in His word, enabling it actually to reach everyone. He said
nothing in secret; that is the first emphasis. It refers to His intention, to His purpose, but that is not all. He adds something. *Ask
them which heard me,* he says. That is the second emphasis. It
refers not to His intention but to the *effects.*

If we were to use the language of the church, we would say
that in this second emphasis Christ is touching on the problem of
the *manifest character* of revelation.

Christ's teaching may be foolishness and an offence to everyone who does not believe it, for life is always just that in relation
to death, but it must be borne in mind that Christ also declared in
His apology that He *attained* His purpose in His preaching. He
preached not upon the basis of the law of seclusion but upon that
of a will to communion. Christ spoke to the people of the street
with affection, yes, but also with effect. Now Annas may adopt
the pose which hints that the scroll on which Christ's real purposes
are written is so securely sealed that not even those who are
learned in the Scriptures, not even the scribes, can have access to
it. Annas may act as though an inquiry conducted among the people in an effort to find out the content of Jesus' teaching would be
futile, inasmuch as these untutored ones who after all, are not
scribes, cannot possibly know what this Nazarene's doctrine really

is all about. But, over against this double injustice, Christ puts the pronouncement that He has taught nothing in secret, that on the contrary He has presented His instruction in terms intelligible to the masses and in a way which enabled them to grasp the central significance of it. For Christ faithfully acknowledged the essence of His messianic calling, even in the method He employed in His pedagogy. Just as in the incarnation He affiliated Himself with their human condition, so He allied Himself with the thought patterns of the people in the means He employed for His teaching. He made use of their concepts, their modes of argument, their "mind-sets" now, just as in the incarnation He allied Himself with flesh and blood, and graciously worked His way into all the modes of expression common to our human life. Surely, Christ's pedagogy is an expression of the whole secret of the incarnation of the Word. Christ outspokenly testifies to the truth of this when He says to Annas: *"Ask them which heard me: behold, they know what I said."* Whoever gives some thought to these words will admit that this epilogue which was pronounced at the end of His life is in full conformity with the prologue in which, as is stated in the first verse of the first chapter of the Gospel according to John, He is announced as the Word made flesh. Just as He Himself was, so Christ's teaching was altogether divine, and was derived entirely from above, from another world; but again, just as He Himself was, so His teaching was also genuinely and entirely human; it used a language which was employed here below, and addressed its appeal to the needs of this world. The Word dwelt among us, and His own incarnation maintained the law of its being in reference to His messianic *message* also. For that reason Christ's apology was lifted high on this day as a torch of judgment over the house of Annas and Caiaphas.

At this point we cannot but remember Isaiah 29. In that chapter the prophet speaks of the straying people and of the faithless leaders. Fundamentally both of these are at enmity with the prophet. They close their hearts to the message he brings. Hence, by way of *judgment,* they are struck blind. Because they were unwilling at first they are unable later on, to grasp the message which comes to them.

You ask what course that judgment will take? You wonder how it will be realized? As the prophet thinks about the effect of

that judgment, he distinguishes two groups of people, each of
which in its own manner is actually experiencing that judgment
and is giving expression to the experience in words. These people
— and it is this consideration which compels our thoughts in this
direction — greatly resemble Annas and his questioning court of
priests.

The first form in which the judgment pointed out by Isaiah
overtakes these spirits is nicely delineated by means of a figure of
speech. He refers to the scribes; that is, to people who know how
to read, and are proud of the fact. But these say to Isaiah: "I cannot read, for the book in which the prophecy is written is sealed
(29:11); hence it is no fault of mine if these words are hidden
from me. If only they were accessible, I should understand them
at once. It is not my understanding or my will which is at fault;
it is because of its external character that I cannot appreciate the
book. It is sealed."

Mark how these children of death, these people who are struck
down by the judgment of God, struggle hard to vindicate themselves. If they are condemned, they say, it is through no fault of
their own, but is owing to the prophecy as it is, objectively. And
the ground of their vindication is the very one which Annas dares
to name against Jesus today. Annas is the first judge to give Jesus
a hearing. Listen to Isaiah, and note this: Annas is the last of the
learned among Israel, and the eldest of the people; and in the person of Jesus, a greater than Isaiah is here.

But the first thing Annas says is: *Your book is sealed.* If only
you would be frank and outspoken, O Nazarene, the whole matter
in all of its implications would be clear to me at once. I am learned
in the Scriptures, but that means nothing to me until you remove
the seals from your scroll. If only you would loosen the clasps
of the book, I would quickly state the meaning of this matter. I
can read, but you must break the seals.

Such, then, is the first charge. But the prophet Isaiah spoke
of a second group. He tells us also that the book of the prophecy
had been put into the hands of certain other people, and that it
had been unsealed and opened before them. But these make the
reply: "It is useless for you to give me the book, for I cannot read.
I am not learned. I am willing to do it; I am not opposed to the
book; nothing in my ethical practice would make me hesitate to

absorb its content, but the one thing that hinders me is this inade-quacy in my education. The thing that keeps me from the proph-ets and my soul from the Word is not animosity, but a difference of degree in intellectual attainment (29:12)."

In short, these people take the other way out. The first group denies the accessibility of the prophetic revelation. The second group simply remains untouched by a preaching which proclaims that prophecy is a power unto salvation. Isaiah may preach as loudly as he wishes that the Word of revelation is a hammer, a fire, a miracle in its potency. These people do not believe it. A person who because of temperament or intellectual capacity can-not "follow" such things, can hardly profit from such preaching. Now the plea of this second group also has its parallel in what Annas says to Jesus. What, Annas asks, could he possibly expect to find out by going to the masses who do not know the law? What could he expect to learn from the ignorant rabble? The people cannot read. In order to understand Jesus' teaching one must be able to grasp such things. According to this logic, and it is the very same which will put Jesus to death after a while, the question is not one of life or death, of peace with God or enmity against Him, of flesh or spirit, of this world or the other. The only rele-vant consideration is whether one has the intellectual capacity to grasp Jesus' teaching.

You see, therefore, that the case for the plaintiff against Jesus will begin by asserting that the doctrine of Christ is neither clear in its objective expression, nor effectual or miraculously influ-ential for the person who hears it.

We have already suggested that this double charge really repre-sents a twofold effort to escape from the divine judgment. Isaiah had said that a judgment of God would be effected in the form of a failure to understand the words of prophecy; but that judgment is not acknowledged as such by those who are included within it. They attempt to push the guilt—if indeed it can be called guilt under such circumstances—from their own shoulders and to place it upon those of God and prophecy.

Jesus had to take thought in replying to this charge which was flung at Him. He had to purge Himself of the blame entirely. For if He could not do so, He Himself would become the cause of the judgment which, according to Israel, was accruing to Israel's leaders in this moment.

Observe closely now. Christ opens His mouth to reply. He addresses His appeal in two directions. He speaks to Annas and says: I deliberately repudiate your criticism. At the same time He addresses God and says: For this tangible judgment of blindness and of hardening of heart, Lord, my God, I, the prophet whom Thou hast sent, am not responsible: Lord, do not let their hardening be charged to me as though I had known sin or had acted sinfully in my relationship to them.

You see, therefore, that Christ places a twofold repudiation over against the double charge they name against Him. In response to the first charge which had it that He certainly had sealed the book of His teaching He replied: I have kept nothing hid. My scroll is unclasped. True scholars of the Scriptures may never appeal to the secret character of my prophetic pedagogy, or to my love of seclusion as though these were the cause of their unbelief. If they do not know what I teach, it is because of their enmity that they do not know it. The natural man does not appropriate to himself the things belonging to the Spirit of God—and that is *his* lack.

Just so, over against the second charge, which had it that the simple must have reached a certain stage of intellectual development before they can appreciate what Jesus is doing, He mentions the fact that He counts His faithful disciples among "the poor," the untaught, the blind, the deaf, in short, among the common folk. Faith is not a question of more or of less knowledge but of self-assertion or self-denial over against God. The appropriate question to ask is not "What do you know?" but "In what is your life rooted?" Do you draw your sustenance from the Spirit or from the flesh?

Thus Christ, in this closed session, and in the presence of the priestly caste which existed in this fulness of time, declares that He stands in communion with Isaiah and with Him who sent Isaiah. This is the "day" whose coming Isaiah had prophesied (29:18). This is the messianic day in which the deaf hear the words of Christ and in which the blind see Him. This is the day in which the meek (whose life instead of being intellectually broadened is ethically renewed) shall rejoice, and in which the needy, those who frankly ask and seek instead of haughtily asserting themselves, shall see the dawning of a new light (19:19). Thus Christ proves that He does indeed present a revelation which comes from above and which can be appropriated only by those who have been born again (regenerated "from above"); but Christ proves also that anyone who hungers and thirsts for the Word and who opens himself to the Word can meet his Messiah in righteousness. The questionings of Annas are present at all times and at all places. Inasmuch as they are an expression of enmity, they call the sin of an unregenerate heart the piteous inadequacy of an inferior mind. But Christ tears the mask from the lie. His words at once point out and fulfill the judgment.

And how should we escape from so great a condemnation? Alas, we are included in it. It is a disturbing thought that Christ at the very beginning of His conflict with the law at once fully maintained His genuine Messiahship, for it is because of this fact that the dialogue between Annas and Jesus has a bearing upon us. We who calmly read these things are being taken from the street by Christ Himself and are being placed in the presence of Annas. Remember now that Jesus Christ is at this very moment saying to Annas, "You may ask him, you may ask her, what I said." Alas, in this Jesus goes so far as to dare to make His own death and life contingent upon the answer which we give to the question put to us by the tribunal of the world. The question being asked us is this one: What has Jesus in mind; what is His intention; what is the purport of His teaching?

No, do not reply that you beg to be excused from this matter. Simon Peter made the same request. But the very moment in which Jesus takes pride in the fact that the first hewer of wood and drawer of water who is casually snatched from the street is able to state the essence of Jesus' teaching, one of His great ones, one who had been with Him upon the mountain, with Him in the room of the Passover, and with Him in Gethsemane, arises, and swears with an oath: "I know not the man; the Nazarene means nothing to me." And this terrible culmination was the result in Simon Peter of the secret thought: I shall hold myself aloof from this matter.

Step out into the open now, son of man, whoever you are, you who are literally steeped in sermons, in calendar leaflets, in edifying books. Listen carefully, for this is the situation. Annas, i.e., Israel, i.e., the flesh, i.e., the natural world, is asking Christ this question: Who are you; what are you doing, what is the thrust of your preaching? And Christ *pointing to you* answers: *Ask him. He* can tell you if he wants to do so.

This is a very personal and a very perturbing issue, for it immediately involves us in the trial of Jesus. It involves us, together with all hewers of wood and drawers of water who have suffered the great misfortune (such is the language of the flesh) of having lived in Jerusalem. It is dangerous to live in Jerusalem, for to do so is to become involved in the great trial, in the great litigation.

Now cease looking for ways of escape. Do not, for instance, attempt to take this avenue out: Yes, I know, but I have not yet been thoroughly instructed; ask one of the older ones, one of the more seasoned Christians. No, do not attempt it. For Christ's apology stands or falls with the truth that everyone, the unlearned also, even the unconverted, can grasp enough of the clear teaching of Jesus to make it impossible for him to plead ignorance of it. Never, no, never say in your heart: The book is sealed; or, I cannot read.

How vehement, how forceful the Christ is! They draw Him into court, and by His first sentence He draws you and me into that court also, and involves us in His trial. How oppressive this is. To have heard a sermon of Jesus is to have become implicated in His trial. And that means that we have been brought before the tribunal which must sit on and satisfactorily solve the one great world-litigation.

But that too is grace. Yes, He implicates you in His trial, but He does that because He has first made your case His own in the presence of God. If you serve as a document entered as evidence in His apology over against Annas, you may know what Christ said beforehand about that which He would repeat in the great day: namely, that it would not be because of Him if any are left outside of the communion of life in that last judgment.

Reply now, and tell Annas, and say to Caiaphas, and to the whole world, that in reference to Christ there is but one appropriate thing to do: to surrender and to be willing to believe. Thereupon we shall see a great schism, a thoroughgoing separation made. And this separation will not be effected by the acute insight of Annas but by the genuineness of Jesus. It will take place at the door of the tribunal as the people come in.

This will be the nature of that separation; by these tokens you can know it. Two persons came into the court of the Nazarene to pray. The one strode boldly in, lifted up his eyes to heaven, placed one hand over his heart, and with the other pointed to Jesus, saying, while Annas and Caiaphas nodded their approval: There[1] is the Nazarene. His book was sealed. I had no chance to bring my mind to bear upon it. His message simply did not reach me. Father, if it be that Thou didst speak through Him, forgive me, for I pray the prayer of an unwitting one.

The other also came. Shamefacedly he crept into the corridor, fell to the ground, his eyes touching on the dust. Father, he groaned, here[2] is he who fulfilled the great mission. His scroll was unfurled; my eyes were opened; He taught me to read. Father, I believed; help Thou my unbelief. His giving and His preaching was mighty and conquering; but my guilt in taking it and in listening to it continues daily, and that is a great guilt.

Two men had prayed in the court of Christ Jesus. Behind the clouds the verdict was read. There the "prayer of the unwitting one" was named a declaration of war and an act of war on the part of "an unwilling one." This petitioner was dragged from the entrance to the exalted tribunal, lest he defile the sanctuary. The angels, as they bound him, sang: "Thou dost allow no *petitioner* to *stand*." And they sang that before God. They said: "Thou makest him to go forth from Thy presence if he is not one who prays; but none can stand in Thy corridors, O God."

As for the other, he came from his house justified. The angel of the Lord conducted him into the inner sanctuary. This angel as he led him on sang before God: "Thou dost let no petitioner stand before Thee; blessed is he whom Thou beckonest *to come* to Thee."

---

1. Iste: the accused, the alien, who does not belong with us, whom I do not recognize.
2. Hic: mine, the one I love.

The clarity, the manifest character of the messianic revelation is the shibboleth in the titanic war between angels and devils. It is the mark of genuineness which characterizes the bread of life. It was the first thing upon which the Son, as the messenger of God, insisted. Without it He has no free passage among angels, for these will accept only one who cares for the poor. Hence the manifest character of the messianic revelation was, through the man Jesus Christ, the theodicy of God in the presence of Annas. Hence it naturally became the first term in the apology which Christ presented to the high priest.

One day He will let the words of that apology be accompanied in the clouds by the organ tones of the judgment. *Ask them who heard me*—I am one of them. Alas, this word breaks open the sources of God's destructive, purifying winds. *Mea res agitur*; I have long ago lost sight of Annas. I hear Christ playing His mighty organ. He has drawn out all the stops. Ah, the overwhelming sublimity of that day.

Christ Condemns the Vicious Circle

CHAPTER THREE

Christ Condemns the Vicious Circle

> And when he had thus spoken, one of the officers which stood by struck Jesus with the palm of his hand, saying, Answerest thou the high priest so?
>
> Jesus answered him, If I have spoken evil, bear witness of the evil: but if well, why smitest thou me?
>
> JOHN 18:22,23.

THE apology which Christ addressed to Annas at the beginning of His trial was not concluded by the words considered in the preceding chapter. That apology is deepened by Christ's response to the blow, which, as a symbol and as a brutal revelation of the whole actuality of this sinful world, rocked the atmosphere when Jesus stood before the aged Annas. Christ was struck on the cheek. He was struck before the accusers were able to set on paper a single formulated charge. Moreover, the blow was dealt Him by one who had no authority to administer blows. A subordinate, a servant, whose business it was neither to determine nor to execute penalties, is the one who struck Christ.

We know approximately how matters went. When Christ replied to Annas by means of the words we pondered in the foregoing chapter, He placed this superannuated high priest—and Caiaphas also, if he was present—in a position of great embarrassment.

Had they wanted to convict Christ of a revolutionary attack upon the existing order, or at least of the fact that He was considering such forceful means and *coups d'etat* as were employed by this world, the proper procedure for them to follow would have been to question those who had been in direct contact with Christ's word. They could have called in any amount of witnesses from

49

the street, and Christ, by lightly touching on the fact that they
were not following this logically natural procedure, simply—if we
may use a current phrase—simply left Annas "without a leg to
stand on."

At this point the flame of self-assertion leaps from the master
to the servant. In their hearts Caiaphas and Annas have already
concluded what they want to do with Christ. The only question
which still concerns them is on what legal grounds they can best
base their proposed action. For that reason the penetrating light
which Jesus suddenly throws upon their strangely illogical procedure is doubly uncomfortable for them. Now it happens that in
this embarrassing situation one of the attendants has been so sym-
pathetically identifying his own with his patron's feelings that he
makes use of the "argument" which is the first resort of stupidity
and hate. He gives Jesus a sharp blow on the cheek. Perhaps the
blow was to the jaw. If one wants to, one can turn to a great deal
of material which has been written about the exact nature of this
blow and what name characterizes it best. At this time we shall be
content with the knowledge that Christ was struck while still
standing before Annas.

The attendant names as his motive for this brutal piece of business the fact that Jesus answered the high priest unbecomingly.
Well, this is not the first time that people in the effort to escape
from the content of a message, choose to criticize the form in which
it is given. Naturally, such response is always foolishness. It is
especially that when the message is one which comes from Christ.
Obviously, if I am to determine whether any given expression has
been clothed in a "becoming form," I must first determine what
its meaning, its content, its purpose is; I must appraise this in reference to the standard of the law of God. For it would be folly
to say that there is only one form which is appropriate to all possible messages in the world. The richer one's mind is, and the more
qualified one is in discriminating issues, and in enhancing their
meaning, so much richer will be the forms which give the argument
and testimony expression. As a matter of fact, each meaning must
have its own and peculiar form. Now Christ, also inasmuch as
the forms and manners of His replies and protestations are concerned, is infinitely rich, for He never makes hackneyed, stereo-
typed speeches. Every speech, every protestation, every testimony

which He makes, He makes but once. His spoken word always has its unique meaning, its peculiar place in the history of revelation, and it also has its peculiar purpose there. The dates of His letters determine their form, for each day for Him differs from the others, and each of His messages is appropriate to the day on which it is spoken.

For this reason, then, it was folly for the servant of the high priest to raise the question of the form, of the manner, of Christ's reply, in his effort to absolve himself and his patron of the content of that reply. No one may ever ask Jesus, "Answerest thou the high priest *so?*" as long as he has nothing to say about the *content* of Jesus' words.

Again Christ's majesty appears in the fact that he immediately refers the question of the manner, of the style, of His speaking to the content of His message. If I, he says, have spoken evil, go on and testify of the evil; and if I have spoken well, why, pray, do you strike me? By this rejoinder Christ does not allude to the speech He has just made in reply to the high priest, but He refers to all of His speaking, all of His pedagogy, all of His prophetic teaching as He conducted these throughout His public activity in Israel. Christ does not engage in discussion with this eye-servant about the manner and tone of His last words, but raises the question of the synthetic content of all of His teaching taken as a unit. If ever I have taught anything which was evil, you may point it out, He says. Have I not said just now that anyone who heard me can testify of my doctrine? If you were present at my addresses—very well, say on. Tell your patron by all means, then, what you know of the content and purpose of my prophetic teaching. Begin at the beginning, I pray you. The blow which you gave me is an expression of overbearing impetuosity. And if you cannot point out that my teaching is subversive of true obedience to the law, binding as it is upon all, who gives you the right to strike me?

Such is the record of what happened in the hall of Annas. The next question is whether all of this is suitable matter for more specific study. Some seem to think that it is not. These do their best to add a little color to the sombre data of the Biblical narrative.

It is well known that Chrysostom—a name meaning "golden-tongued orator"—wanted to make this story interesting by maintaining that this servant of Annas or Caiaphas was related to Malchus, the man whom Jesus had just healed and protected from injustice in Gethsemane. Similar efforts to make interesting that which really weighs as heavily as eternity can be detected in a few other preachers "with golden tongues" also. Nevertheless, these efforts remain essentially mean, and are a disparagement of what is really a weighty message of revelation. Similar worthlessness characterizes the assertions of others to the effect that the man who struck Jesus was Malchus himself. Those who make this claim ignore the fact that the Greek text uses very different words in referring to these two. Malchus is called a slave, and the second subordinate is named a servant.

In other words, we do not know who this man is. To go on, however. As we read this story we must be on guard against shaking our heads in amazement at the brutality of this uncouth man. For if we do no more than to shake our heads incredulously, and then pass on to the order of the day, we overlook the fact that the logic of this impetuous person is by nature characteristic of us all.

This narrative must also be related to a setting. If we separate this blow from the moment in which it was given, and pass judgment upon it from the outside only, it becomes lost among all the insults and disparagements of soul and body which will take place afterwards. But if we pause to consider what is taking place in this moment and at this place between Christ and the person who struck him, this apparently trivial episode becomes a definite subsidiary part of that extensive history of the passion in which everything has its special place.

Now if we were asked to say what to our mind appears to be the main issue in this matter, we should reply as follows. Christ at the very beginning of His legal process was, because of the course things were taking and because of the pathetic fate of the whole world-order, involved in the vicious circle to which our life is subservient. But He, asserting Himself in His strength, passes judgment upon that vicious circle, and, as a greater than Samson, He begins to deliver the world and Himself from it. In principle

He on this occasion already comes down from the cross and redeems Himself—Himself and us.

He begins to do so. For the process of the redemption is merely set in motion by this means. And we may remember that our Samson is not hesitant as was the other one.

If this is the main issue, our first duty is to point out that there is a vicious circle in the world in which we live. This we want to indicate in part by reference to the events of the day, and in part by allusion to the world-view which explains and sheds its light upon these events.

In the first place, the facts of the "trial" which is being carried on here speak an unmistakable language. We can put the message of that language in these words: *In the place of judgment, wickedness was there!* A legal process is in course of action. That process must be set in motion according to law. But unrighteousness enters into the place of justice. Certainly it was illegal for a servant to do what only a judge has authority to do. The law emphatically forbade that an accused person be treated as a convicted person before the charges had been investigated and sustained. Now if it be true, as it is here, that unrighteousness sits in the seat of judgment, and that this violation of law is the first step in the trial, then the circle which life is describing here must be named a vicious circle. By the use of such methods no one can ever escape from his own problems, and the provinces of justice and injustice can never be properly circumscribed. The unpunished blow which was given to Jesus, therefore, really amounts to an official placement of Jesus outside of the sphere of law. Essentially Christ is being regarded as an outlaw.[1] The trial has not even begun; there has been no opportunity to give the law a chance to express itself against Him, but already He has been placed outside of the sphere and the course of law.

That is why this blow, which Caiaphas and Annas are quite willing to countenance, represents a new phase in the suffering of Christ. Until now He has been an *exile*; now he becomes an outlaw. And there is a significant distinction between the two. Being an exile means that one is no longer in one's original dwelling

---

1. Used here and throughout this work not in the sense of a "rebel," but as "one having no rights."

place, that one is a man without a country. But of such a man it
can at least be said that the authority which drives him out of his
country is the authority of law. The law pursues him, the law exerts itself against him. Hence to be an exile is not the same as to
be an outlaw. An exile stands outside of the pale of his country,
but not outside of the bourne of the law.

But the outlaw? Alas, he is thrust outside of the sphere of law.
He is given up into the hands of arbitrary forces, of whoever
wishes to take him. He is not merely exiled; he is accursed. Such
is the vicious circle. The circle describes itself around the chair
of Annas.

Note the situation. Those seated here are the official executors,
the officially appointed bearers, the authentic proclaimers of the
law in Israel. We must remember that Israel, although fast decaying, is still, according to God's ancient ordinances and according to the "dispensation" of this particular phase of the history
of revelation, the people which peculiarly sustains and exercises
and proclaims the law. In the kingdom of heaven up to this time
this people has been entrusted with the laws of revelation, and
consequently also with the law of that particular proclamation of
justice whose fundamental principles of jurisprudence coincide
with the realm of heaven. Hence this place especially must everywhere reflect the light of the law. According to the dispensation
of the ages it must lead to the specific "case" of Christ. The law
must fan the flames prompting Caiaphas and Annas to action.
All things here must scintillate with the lights of the perfect commandment which alone can illuminate a lawless world.

But the tragedy of the blow which is dealt Christ in this room
arises from this that it proclaims aloud: We cannot sever the
knots of sin; we cannot and will not explain the riddles of human
life in terms of the law which God announced from above. Hence
this body of officials proceed to take the shortest route. Here is
the Lawgiver Himself, One who professes to be the expressed
Image of the Highest Lawgiver, and the Reflection of His legislative glory. And this one is named an outlaw, is beaten and insulted
as such, and is thrust outside of the pale of legal procedure. Says
Christ: I am the expressed Image of the Lawgiver of heaven and
earth. In me you will find an expression of law a thousand times
stronger, a thousand times more moving and alive than were the

tables of Moses, though these were written with the finger of God. I am the law, and I am the one who both interprets and fulfills it. But before Caiaphas and Annas can say whether the law is compatible or at variance with Christ, they have "in the place of judgment," that is, in the place dedicated to the law, thrust Him outside of the sphere of jurisprudence altogether.

That is what prompted us to say that the repercussions of this blow were felt in all the worlds. This is the last self-defense of a lost mankind: a curse, an impetuous stroke of the sword upon the knot which God has tied in the rope, the rope of the Forbidden Admission. It represents a departure from the unique office of justice at the very moment in which that office should have made itself felt most effectively.

All this is sad enough. Nevertheless, it can also be very easily understood. That statement referred to above, *"In the place of judgment, wickedness was there,"* can readily be explained by the truth which underlies it: namely, In the place of knowledge, blindness was there; at the place of insight into the hidden essence of things, a superficial sense of externalities was there. Or, if we wish, we can put it even more directly: In the place of insight into the essence of the *Messiah* (Christ), we find only a superficial sense of the exterior *Jesus* (the man as He appeared in history).

This much, at least, is certain: *Justice* whirls around in a vicious circle because *knowledge* does. Significant, therefore, is the question put to Jesus by the high priest, a question which we have already illuminated from another side. Annas asks Jesus, you remember, to inform him about His *disciples* and His *doctrine*. In other words, two matters require his attention: Christ's *influence* and Christ's *teaching*.

Now it is plain that this question is put to Jesus too soon. Surely, before I can say anything about the disciples which Jesus has and about the teaching which He gives I must know about his hidden *essence*. *Who art thou?* That is the first relevant question. And the second question, "What art Thou revealing to me?" (the doctrine), as well as the third, "With what success art Thou influencing others and me?" (the disciples), may never be separated from the first question. Only when I have seen the essence of Christ, the reality of the Messiah, the basic significance of the Son of man, the real meaning of God become flesh—only then can I have a proper perspective and true knowledge of His teaching and of His success. As long as I look only at the externalities of the number of His disciples and of His doctrine, as long as I fail to believe and appreciate the deep mystery of His being, I must continue to be an embarrassed or an arrogant fool. For externalities can never explain externalities. "Jesus" is not the explanation of "Jesus." The historical manifestation of Jesus does not explain itself. That which the externalities explain and make tangible must be illuminated by the light of the concealed essence, of the inner being. Jesus and His historical appearing must be understood in reference to Christ (the messianic being foretold long ago, and conceived in God's eternity). The historical manifestation of the Word of Life can be understood only in relation to the superhistorical, external decrees of God, arrived at in the council of peace and derived from the mystery of His trinity.

Inasmuch, therefore, as Annas limits his investigation to those two externalities, Jesus' success and Jesus' propaganda, he, in spite of the fact that he is standing on ground which by special revelation had been prepared for receiving the hidden meaning of the God of the Messiah, remains entangled in the vicious circle of purely natural knowledge. He remains oblivious to the great blessing of special revelation. He nonchalantly overlooks all of the Scriptures, for these point only to the hidden essence of the Messiah. He is perfectly willing to look upon Jesus the Nazarene in the light of his own impoverished theology, of his own Sadducean party-interest, and of his Jewish ideal of nationalism. But he refuses to look upon Jesus in the light of special revelation. He explains time in terms of time, externalities in terms of externalities, and historical phenomena in terms of historical phenomena.

Such is the tragedy of the events of the day. We have said already that as a judge Annas *cuts* the knot which was tied instead of *untying* it. This also applies to him as a seeker of the truth. As a *thinking* man also he cuts the knots into pieces instead of unravelling them according to the wisdom of the Scriptures. Hence Caiaphas and Annas become enmeshed in the same snare which trapped Pilate later. Just as Pilate degenerates from sinning against truth ("What is truth?") into sinning against justice ("What is justice?"), so Israel's priests at this time degenerate from a false approach to the problem of truth to a false solution of the great problem of justice.

Such is the vicious circle as it was drawn by the *events of the day*.

Can it be, then, that the events of this day are so much different from those of other days in the world? No, not at all. If you fit the trial of Christ Jesus into the whole course of the world you will come to recognize the fact that this is all that could possibly be expected to take place. Jesus must be condemned by the world at all times, for the world simply cannot escape from the vicious circle. How, indeed, can circles and straight lines ever get on together? How can the flat planes of the world and the intervention of God's lightning harmonize? Can we suppose that there will be no more friction, no more nameless antagonism between the sons of men included in the vicious circle and the Son of man who is of the line of transcendant revelation?

But for this purpose came Christ into the world, that He might break the cycle of the vicious circle. And because He came into the world for this purpose, I must learn to appreciate the seriousness of this session which is being conducted by Annas. In other words, I must learn to correlate the events of the day with the whole scheme of the Biblical world-and-life-view.

We may be sure that the events of this day (and this night), in other words, that the events as they concern Annas, are appraised aright only if related properly to the world view which teaches us the essential despair of that vicious circle. For it is only from such a viewpoint that we can see in that circle in which both knowledge and justice are spinning around, not only an incident in the life of Annas and Caiaphas but also a symptom of all purely natural life.

Who, indeed, can teach us the nature of that circle? Which philosopher, which philosophy can teach us its secret or point out its laws? Surely, no philosophy, no world-view which observes things from a human vantage point can do so. For all things human and all things mundane in so far as these are not vanquished and blessed by the God of special revelation and of special grace are included in and cannot escape from the viciousness of it. Every philosophy, every "theology," every system of morals, every body of jurisprudence which is built up solely on a base of human wisdom and is worldly in its origin, is and remains natural and carnal. Each of these is included in the maelstrom of the world; each is another effort to explain time in terms of time, to regulate the world by means of the world, and to proclaim justice by means of those who themselves are unjust. In short, every world-view not derived from special revelation is itself included in the fatal cycle.

That world-view alone which comes from above and not from below will be able to discover the vicious circle of our human life as it really is and to reveal to us that God may deliver us from it.

Such a world-view chants its lamentation in the book of Ecclesiastes. We must pause to consider it. The book of Ecclesiastes occupies a unique position among the books of the Old Testament. It is one of the last of all those Scriptures which, taken together, constitute that Old Testament. Formerly this fact was denied by many. It was thought that Solomon was the writer of Ecclesiastes. Were this true, the book of the preacher would by no means be one of the latest of the Old Testament writers. In recent times, however, the conviction is becoming firmer that Solomon was not the author of the book. As a matter of fact, the original text of Ecclesiastes indicates nowhere that Solomon wrote it. On the contrary, this book was written after the time of Nehemiah and Malachi. It dates from a period in which Israel's glory had long waned and in which alien despots were treading upon the vestiges of her proud past.[1] And the sole and ever-repeated theme of this wonderful book is the vicious circle.

Its author has observed that Israel's glory has departed from her. The empire of Solomon has been trodden upon and broken; first by his epigones, and later by the enemies of Israel. Now Solomon himself, after many centuries, arises from his grave—for Ecclesiastes, embodying a well known rhetorical device, introduces Solomon to us as the speaker—in order to declare that everything associated with the great king, his wisdom, his might, his culture, amounted to nothing save vanity and the tedium of endlessly cyclical movement. That is what the glory of Solomon amounted to, *observed solely from a temporal point of view*. Solomon does

---

1. Compare Dr. C. van Gelderen, *De boeken der Koningen*, Volume 1, J. H. Kok, Kampen, 1926, pp. 241-242.

not suffice to explain Solomon. He had great power, but his power was broken. He had great wisdom, but his philosophical system was mocked by succeeding thinkers—other philosophers succeeded him in the world. Solomon issued books of law and outlined a system of legal procedure, but what has remained of these? As for Solomon's culture? In all of its splendor it also had to give way to destruction, bit by bit. The whole of Solomon's artistically evolved life is part and parcel of the vicious circle. And what, alas, can be done about that? Who, pray, can push back its ever-moving wheel? No one is capable of doing it. The wheel of history is ever turning, to and fro, up and down. *Nature* and *history,* these two acts in the drama of *general* revelation, never reveal the hidden mystery of the eternal, immovable things of God in a way which gives peace to human hearts, always being hurtled to and fro as they are. Just as nature is ever repeating itself, in an endless, expansively cyclical process, so is the history of men. Everything goes but to return, rises to fall again. The one breaks down what the other has begun. No lecture room, no court of justice, no seat of culture, no conference group devoted to a discussion of war and peace, is fixed and sure. What exists today will return tomorrow and the tedium of such interminable repetition is fatiguing even to the point of death.

So says the Preacher about general revelation. He demonstrates to himself and to us how pitifully wanting this general revelation is when it is separated from special revelation.

But he says more. Next to the general *revelation* stands *general* or *common grace.* Of that the Preacher also speaks. He points out how meagre common grace is when it is independent of special grace. Of these two the Preacher is constantly talking: of nature, and of the busy and multiple historical life of man. These are the two domains of general revelation and of common grace. And these two are a part of that deterministic cycle which we have called the vicious circle, *unless* . . . .

Unless? Yes, *unless the domain of general grace is governed by a living and quickening power derived from special grace, and unless the domain of general revelation is illumined by the special revelation of God which intervenes from above.*

You see, then, that the book of Ecclesiastes has a beautiful significance for the Old Testament. This book laments the meagreness, the essential poverty, the insufficiency of general revelation and of common grace. That is the value of the book. Yes, that is its peculiar value. The old covenant must die with a lamentation, must pass out with a cry, because of the insufficiency of general revelation; for thus a sound of rejoicing may break out later when Christ appears in the New Testament to give Himself to the victims of God's vicious circle as the great gift of special revelation and of special grace. True, these were found in Israel before this time also, but in the New Testament they reach their fulfillment, their pleroma.

This Preacher, then, stands at the very end of the weeping wall of the Old Testament, mourning. He raises his bitter cry. And this is the burden of his lament: outside of the pale of the messianic light, eye (in nature) has not seen, nor ear (in history) heard, nor heart (in general philosophies of life) conceived the great mystery of final knowledge, redeeming insight, of absolute certainty, and *eternal* life. Only when that cry has been uttered, only when the sound of the dirge of all God's bondmen has been heard, will it be the time for the New Testament to point out to us the tower of the Lord's redemption standing behind the weeping wall of the Old. Then only will it be the time for Christ, the Chief Prophet, to drive out by means of intervention from above the uncertainties of the spirit of Solomon, the spirit which in itself was unable to sustain life. That will be the time for Paul to answer the Ecclesiast by pointing to Christ, the Messiah who has come. Then Paul can say: Eye hath not seen, nor ear heard, nor heart conceived (that which could not be obtained from general revelation), what God hath prepared for all of them that love Him. The great mystery is not discovered by a science which subsists on general revelation only, and builds its conclusions up on that, climbing from below upwards, but is revealed from above to those below by the authentic Word of God. For in the *beginning* was the Word, and the Word was with God, and the Word was God. And that Word by its own sovereign sharing of itself has *become flesh*.

Those are a few of the main ideas in the book of Ecclesiastes; such is the essence of its life. That is why this book in which the Old Testament breathes its last breath is the book of the vicious circle. It is in this book that the thought to which we alluded before was raised: In the place of judgment was wickedness, and in the place of knowledge was doubt.

No, no, he who speaks in this book is not a rebel clenching his fist against the palace which keeps the keys of the Bastille. He who speaks and voices his plaint in this book is a son of man who has shared in the misery of the world. For he, too, knows that without God and outside of the temple which is subject to that law of the world which says that wickedness is in the place of judgment, license in the place of law enforcement, he is in the place in which law is thrust aside at the very time when it should let its light shine upon the events of life.

No, the Preacher was not satisfied to say that the vicious circle was present even in the hall of justice. The awful merit of the Preacher is that he describes the whole of natural life, the whole of life not blessed by special revelation, as being subservient to the yoke, to the fate, of the vicious circle. Take nature, for example. In every respect and in every place nature describes a complete arc. The sun rises and sets again; clouds absorb water and release it again; hidden springs supply the rivers, but the sea is never so full that it overflows and smothers the springs. The whole of nature represents a continual vacillation, an endless repetition. Just such a cycle, says the Preacher, characterizes the life of culture, as long as it is not healed and redeemed by the temple, by special revelation, by the special law which is revealed by God. That which the one builds, the other breaks down; that which past generations evolve the future generations destroy; positions of rank shift from one to another; the leaders of today are the slaves of tomorrow. Thus it becomes apparent that the whole life of the world is subject to the law of rotation. Who is there that teaches a philosophy from one point of view and does so authoritatively? The wise teach us wisdom; tomorrow a wiser comes to destroy the wisdom of yesterday. Who can lay down a binding system of morals? That which is named right today is called wrong tomorrow. Virtue and vice continually exchange places with each other. Alas, when life is really left to itself, it is a mere merry-go-round of futility. It turns and turns, *et l'on revient toujours a ses premiers amours.* And even as history does, so men return to their first antipathies also. Today hordes of slaves assume the ranks of aristocrats, tomorrow others take their place.

Not one of the world's classes is assured of its status forever. Just as the servant of Annas arrogates to himself the function of a judge, just as Annas lowers himself to the status of a servant, so the whole world. The world would propel itself by its own ears, but it moves in a circle, and the circle is a very vicious one. On earth man walks in a medium of mystery, and there is no priest to explain God to him, no priest, at least, trained in the schools of nature and history, and in those two alone. Such is the vicious circle.

Fortunately, the Preacher said more than this. To that we shall refer later.

Pausing here, however, we ask ourselves: But is not this the core of the matter? And must we not return to this real issue as often as we undertake to say something about that blow given Christ, the great outlaw? Remember, that blow was a *demonstrative* blow. Accordingly, instead of hurling invectives against the servant of the aged Annas, we must acknowledge that he fits perfectly into the scheme of a world which wants to live outside of the pale of special revelation.

What we have here is a secularized house of priests which will have nothing to do with "the" law and which, accordingly, shuts out the law and the lawgiver. This is the vicious circle: to know nothing, and to act as though everything was perfectly clear—in short, to administer a blow. This is the pathetic state of things: to fail to place Christ the lawgiver over against Jesus the accused, to fail to measure and to judge Jesus by the standard of God who is the highest lawgiver, and yet to allow the meanest servant to take upon himself the prerogative of the most assured among the people. Such is the world: to refuse to see God in the man Jesus, but to punish the devil in him nevertheless — although this last act is an eternal impossibility. An eternal impossibility, for he only can discern the devil who can discern God. Only the spiritual man, says Paul, judgeth all things — the spiritual man, he who is nourished by the bread for which the Preacher hungered.

When the palace of the spiritual court of justice has been secularized, when all the windows looking out on the everlasting east, on God the lawgiver, have been walled up, that court cannot possibly deal justly with Christ. By such conduct it begins to look up on Him as upon a man among men, and upon His teaching as one among many teachings, upon His influence in procuring disciples as just another manifestation of a recurring phenomenon in the world. But it does not succeed in really explaining Him. Life can never explain life. History cannot lay history bare. And this inadequacy which refuses to confess itself is quite willing to cut the knots it cannot untie, is perfectly willing to smite the Wonder on the cheek. Such is the feeble gesture of victory on the part of the defeated. Moreover, this is the tragedy of us all. Every high priest who forgets God, every slave who forgets God, every zealot, be he serious or frivolous, who wants to explain the world in terms of the world will smite Jesus on the cheek in just this manner. They all strike Jesus; all strike the Wonderful, the Counsellor, the Mighty God, the Prince of Peace. Every philosophy, every theory, every so-called orthodoxy, and every heresy, which is not derived from special revelation, is a blow against the cheek of God, the sole Interpreter of the world, the sole Giver and Proclaimer of the law. The house of Annas has not properly evaluated the mind of the ranking person in this place. But by means of the fist of the meanest person, it frankly and facilely acts as though it had come to the right conclusion. That is the meaning of the blow on the cheek. You and I were born in this same house, and were expertly brought up in its traditions. Left to ourselves, we too would not have known the one lawgiver. The blow on the cheek means that we are attempting to argue Him out of existence. Every court of law in the world witnesses the gruesome injustice of the man who does not believe in God. The blow dealt in the hour of his trial demonstrates the folly and the vicious character of sin — of the sin, that is, which has separated the activity of the creature from the Logos of God. Because it has done that, it can never, never be logical again.

As this blow echoes through the air, I think of Ecclesiastes 1:15: *That which is crooked cannot be made straight.* Such is the empirical fact. The crooked line which follows a circular course cannot be made into a straight line by life itself. And I tremble when I read next to it the statement recorded in Ecclesiastes 7:13: Consider the work of God: for who can make that straight which He hath made crooked? Alas, in these words that which I experience empirically is laid down as the inescapable lot of the whole world, for it tells me that God Himself has created the world so that it can never solve its own problems nor unravel its own knots. If "God" does not become the "covenant God," if "God" does not become "the Father," if the Almighty does not say "I am Jaweh," if the voice of general revelation is not drowned out by the thundering approach of special revelation, then the rashness of the weary circuit-rider of time will ever again deal the blow against God's own Son. The tragedy of the matter certainly is that Annas and Caiaphas lagged behind; they came late and they came crippled. They searched, but could not find. Now they literally take the law into their *hands,* they resort to the blind solution of force. They take recourse to *blows.* But they do not know the Son of God. Shall I condemn them? Indeed, not. For who can make straight that which God has made crooked? Who can carry the straight line of all-conquering truth into the world, and who can break or bend into shape the crooked line of the vicious circle, if God Himself does not do so? Unless God is very gracious to me, unless He reveals the secret of Himself and the world to me, I, together with the whole world, will raise my hand to smite God on both cheeks. The act will be the most pious gesture in the prayer of the unwitting. In that terrible prayer the fatigue of the world, and its tedium, will be unaware of itself though unmistakably clear to all who have spiritual eyes to see . . .

Bind the hands of the man who smote Jesus just now, and look into the eyes of the Smitten One. He is your Lord and your God. As such He comes to point out the vicious circle to you. Mark how He reveals Himself as the Mediator just when that revelation is necessary. Christ answers the man who struck Him. If I, He says, in my public teaching, in my discourses, ever said anything evil, bear witness of the evil. But if not, if you can testify of nothing against me, why do you smite me?

By this reply Christ at once gets at the heart of the issue. The vicious circle, ever moralizing, argues: plead — or smite. The Mediator demands: bear witness — or believe.

Has the man who strikes Him, possibly, some critical ability in reference to the Christ whom he strikes with such dispatch? Has he mastered the difficult teaching of Christ? Has he some authoritative standard, some touchstone, according to which he can appraise what Christ has said? If so, let him speak. He who wishes to judge must be able to refer to his sources of law, and if he has no such standard, how can he administer the blow? That blow is a false front designed to enhance the mask behind which is concealed the face of an ignorant man. Christ merely asks a question but in that question the Messiah asserts Himself and swears that the legal process begun by the world against Him can take but one course. It must long for and bow before absolute authority. Whoever has not the capacity to criticize Christ may do nothing, may not even say anything which assumes that he knows what it is all about. Whoever has not discovered the sole relationship between Christ and the Chief Lawgiver of heaven may not summon Him into his court or reject Him from the sphere of law. The man who is ignorant simply may not deal with Christ as a problem which he has personally solved.

By pointing to and condemning the vicious circle at the beginning of His trial, Christ, therefore, remained the true Mediator. He enmeshed us in our own snares, entangled us in our own skeins. He proved to us that the only way to evaluate Him is to accept Him on His own authority. To every discourse He gives He appends the same introduction: Why did you strike me just now? Ah, how He embarrasses us. But what do we want? What do we expect outside of the pale of His authority? Imagine for a moment that Christ's absolute authority does not exist. Then we can never escape from our own difficulties, never elude the vicious circle. The servant may not smite, and the high priest can not bless. For Jesus of Nazareth passed by. Did He really pass by? No, if only He had. He is so very troublesome to the flesh. Who that has listened to His "Why did you smite me?" can fail thereupon to fold his hands in prayer? If I want to evaluate Christ without regard to His own claims to authority, what can I possibly expect to do? The blow represents folly; and a prayer is not wisdom. Nevertheless, up to this time those are the only two things to which I can resort.

Therefore I must let Christ reprimand me as He reprimanded the servant who struck Him. He strikes at the very manner in which I put the problem. My flesh was unwilling to listen to the Preacher, unwilling to attend to the book of Ecclesiastes. For the Preacher had declared that life could never explain itself, that a worldly court could not establish its own moral code, as long as it refused to subject itself to special revelation. So much my flesh would never grant the Preacher. And "Nazareth" does not explain my flesh. Heaven must explain the Nazarene, and His own deep heart — so large that it can contain the heaven of heavens — must interpret Him. Thou fool of Annas, the highest wisdom is to bow before authority. To appropriate the revelation which comes from above is the first principle of reasonable religion, thou mercenary hireling, thou who art continually breathing out blasphemy against the temple. Nature (including Jesus' food and drink, Jesus' life and death) is not explained by nature, but solely by special revelation. And today it is this special revelation which is addressing itself to thee. History (including Jesus' stay in Nazareth, Jesus' preaching in Galilee, and His being captive in Jerusalem) is not explained by history, but by special revelation. Today that revelation is addressing itself to thee. That, also, the Preacher knew.

Can it be that any among us sometimes thought that the Preacher knew only how to complain about nature and about history? Remember, we can truly and canonically lament the phenomenon of doubt when we look down upon it from the vantage point of the achieved certainty of faith. The insufficiency of the vicious circle is apparent only to the person who has reached that vertical course which leads upward from below. Only he can lament the relative inadequacy of general revelation who has learned to rejoice in special revelation. No, the Preacher is not a member or a guardian saint of that group of doubters which teaches that one can strike Jesus on the cheek without incriminating one's self. The Preacher, too, had drunk the clear waters which flow from the fountains of the Highest Wisdom.

When He had done so, He saw the temple rising out of and standing above nature. He saw the venerable temple rise out of the vicious circle of natural life, of natural wisdom, and of natural reason. That temple does not deign to discuss its authority but makes its authority binding. It does not argue in mundane terms about the right of God to demand sacrifice, but simply makes sacrifice a binding requirement. It does not make man the measure of good and evil but makes the standard of the temple of God absolutely authoritative. Those are the three articles of the basic law of the temple. Without consulting any of his ministers, the King is exalted far above the need of counsellors.

The first article of that fundamental law, then, was that the temple simply imposes its authority. Hence the call is sounded on all sides: *Keep thy foot when thou goest to the house of God.*[1] Freely translated that means: Go cautiously, be on guard, do not let your impulse dictate your steps, "keep your foot" for it is bound, keep your hand lest it smite the cheek, for you are bound. Keep thy foot, keep thy hand, restrain thy tongue, for the beginning of all wisdom is to bow before special and absolutely authoritative revelation. Nature will never teach you to restrain your foot: what difference does your conduct make to it? Nor does history make anything binding upon your conscience: what, pray, is good and what evil? But the temple, special revelation, that it is which really knows, which dictates the law, and does so without asking whether it suits you. The temple only can inspire caution.

The second article of the fundamental law of the temple has it that God's right to demand sacrifices — sacrifices instead of blows to the cheek — is not based on legal argumentation which is of earthly origin. The question "What must I do and what must I not do?" can be answered solely by the Chief Lawgiver Himself in His special revelation. That is why the Preacher says — and he hears the temple itself sounding the cry: *bring not the sacrifice of fools.* Liberally translated, that means: do not dally in the place of seriousness, and do not play idly with sacrificial blood, for everything you do and do not do must be governed by special law-giving revelation. Nature and history tell you to follow your own impulses, to bring sacrifices in the company of fools. Nature and history teach you that there is no absolute command. But the temple binds your hands and does not ask you whether you like it. Special revelation teaches the sacrifice of the wise.

The third article of the fundamental law of the temple maintains that I may never regard myself as my own standard of conduct. My subjective inclination can never be a sufficient authority in itself. Accordingly, the temple advises: *say not in the presence*

---

1. Ecclesiastes 4:17.

of the angels that you made a mistake,[1] *when you promised a great sacrifice and substituted for it a small one.* For, even after you have begun to bring sacrifices, even after you have become obedient in a general way, even then you have by no means been given the privilege of determining what is good and what is evil. Not only the fact that you must bring sacrifices but also the kind of sacrifices you must bring is governed by the commandments. In the temple everything is revealed with authority. Sovereign authority, then, is at the bottom of our lives. And that sovereign authority is absolutely binding for all of the efforts and results of our conduct.

You see, therefore, that the blow which insulted heaven in the house of Annas was not condemned in human terms based on expedience, or good taste, or natural love, but in the terms of the law of God. Christ disciplined the man who struck Him in terms of the same wisdom which informed the Preacher's temple-discourse, a discourse which sharply sets the temple off from nature and from history.[2] But Christ disciplined in order that He might heal. He who spoke in reprimand is the very same for whom the Preacher yearned. He is the bearer of absolute authority and its proclaimer. He is the sole revealer and preacher of the true law of the temple. In fact, He is the Temple, for God dwells in Him bodily. Destroy this temple, and within three days it will be built up again.

Christ, then, at the beginning of His trial immediately pointed Israel's judges back to the book of Ecclesiastes, in which the Old Testament was reaching out its hands to that great exponent of authority who would place the life of nature under the full rays of heavenly revelation, who would convert the merry-go-round of world history into a straight path to God — or into a straight road to Satan — and who would by the grace of the Lord make straight all the crooked lines of "God." For God is present in the general, and the Lord (Jaweh) is present in the special revelation. We must let Christ tell us this truth. The blow with which the last legal session of the Jews concluded its preliminary action is the

---

1. Ecclesiastes 5:5. As though you had mistaken the value of your sacrifice and are now, just as when you made the offer, following your own whim and fancy.
2. Ecclesiastes 4:17-5:5. According to some (with or without other texts) a *Zwischenstück*

confirmation of the tragical conflict expressed in the book of Ecclesiastes. But the word which Christ spoke on this occasion is
the maintenance and fulfillment of the solution which the Preacher discovered when he saw that no human norm, but only the
Word which was in the beginning, is warranted in proclaiming
the truth.

This Word which was in the beginning and which was with
God, is here. It is no wonder that John, the same evangelist who
wrote the well-known prologue about the Word which was made
flesh and which could put the weariness of the Preacher of the Old
Testament to rest, is the one who brings together the blow given
by the servant of the priest and the reprimand given by Christ.
The problem raised in this late book of wisdom in the Old Testament is solved in the prologue to John's gospel. And Christ was
willing to suffer for that solution. He offers His cheek to those
who would strike Him today in this terribly vicious, terribly ma-
lignant circle. Today all the ennui and tedium which the Preacher
suffered accrues to Him. The blow "grieves His spirit" so severely and makes Him so weary that no one can hope to give expression to it. Have courage, my Saviour, for "the conclusion of the
whole matter is this: Fear God, and keep His commandments."

No, do not ask whether all this constituted *suffering* for the
Christ. Was there no pain in this labor? Indeed, the worst of it
was not that the blow hurt Him physically. That again is but the
external side of the matter, although it has significance for those
who recognize the inner, hidden side. But the main thing also in
this instance is the *soul-suffering* of the Son of man. We can put
it thus: a blow dealt Him by the *Greeks* hurts Him less than a
blow given Him by the *Jews*. For, up to this time the Greeks have
been left to heathendom, have been allowed to stay in the vicious
circle; to them the oracles (special revelation) of God have not
been entrusted. The Greeks have only general revelation. But
Israel is a people of special revelation. To *Israel* the holy Scriptures came and with these the book of Ecclesiastes. The whole of
the old covenant closes with the summons: Look to the Messiah;
keep your foot when you go into the temple; restrain your hands
when you meet with the image of God; and know that the world
cannot explain itself, that the external side of things, be it of Solon
of Athens, of Solomon of Jerusalem, or of Jesus of Nazareth,

cannot account for itself. Tremble in the presence of the great mystery. And begin with the beginning, with the Word which was in the beginning.

However, in spite of the fact that Christ is the great goal to which the Preacher longingly looked forward, and in spite of the fact that the attention of the dying Old Testament pointed to the distant horizon on which the Messiah would sometime dawn, Christ as He appears here today stands as a smitten one. Darkness — also the darkness dwelling in His people — prefers the vicious circle to the straight line of the Messiah, that line of revelation which extends from above downward. They ask about His disciples and about His doctrine, but not about the essence of His being.

Because of its frightful inadequacy, therefore, this question becomes the downfall of Israel. It was a denial of the yearning of the Preacher; it was an outspoken abnegation of that which wounded the Ecclesiast even unto death. In short, it was an acceptance of the external, the empirical, the historical side of things, and of that side only. Ah, but this was suffering for the Christ! Think — to be the bread of heaven, for which the Old Testament had hungered because the scraps of nature could never satisfy. And to be rejected now, now when He is lying on Israel's display table as the bread of heaven! To be rejected because no one would look upon this bread in the light of heaven! Men placed it in the scales of earth and found it too light — and used it later as the bait by which to entice death to come.

The blow on the cheek — it is an outright denial of the burden of the Preacher. The dog returns again to his own vomit. The Preacher himself said so . . .

In view of what has been said now, it is a futile pastime to set up labored arguments about the weighty question of whether Christ, by reprimanding the man who struck Him, was practicing what He had preached on the mount. There are those who raise that question. They call attention to the fact that in His sermon on the mount He said: Whosoever shall smite thee on thy right cheek, turn to him the other also. Christ said that, these critics aver, and then tremulously add: But as a matter of fact He does not practice the theory Himself; instead of keeping silence, He pronounces a sharp reprimand.

Those who say this, however, are mistaken. For it is precisely in this that Christ fulfilled the sermon on the mount. The great fundamental idea underlying that sermon is that everything in the kingdom of heaven, everything, including the least significant detail of life, moves in a medium of infinite earnestness. Everything is subject to the law. Nothing is insignificant. And, although Christ in the sermon on the mount includes everything within the pale of the law, Annas and Caiaphas, and the servants attempt to thrust everything outside of the circumference of law. They find an outlaw in the very place where the Chief Lawgiver takes his stand. The vicious circle dresses the Chief Lawgiver in the ragged burlap of the outlaw, just as it dispatches the Chief Wisdom to Rome in the motley garb of a fool. In short, they place the whole trial outside of the sphere of Christ's sermon on the mount. When they did so, Christ restored things to their proper place by proclaiming to the man who struck Him that He must not exert a single muscle of his clenched fist before he has pondered upon and reached a conclusion about the problems of absolute authority, of the law and gospel, of the Word and eternity.

The impulsive reaction of our "natural" life, such as the blow to the cheek doubtless was, must be interpreted in the light of the absolute seriousness of life. If that is done, we will see that Christ who first pressed Himself and His judges against the high wall of the kingdom of heaven, now proceeds to offer the man, who struck Him on the one cheek, the other also, by way of giving him the right to testify of the evil if he can. "If I have spoken evil, testify of it." Christ does indeed turn His other cheek to all orators and all authors who manipulate their pen without reference to the sphere of revelation, and to all theological faculties who have humanized revelation. He says, Testify against me, lest you speak some word which shows that you do not understand God and eternity. If you cannot do this, bow before authority, acquiesce in it as the first principle of life, and then see whether I am not always what I say I am, to all who believe; then see whether I will not kiss you upon both cheeks.

Christ's reply, therefore, to the blow on His cheek is a messianic self-revelation. He reveals Himself to the fatigued people of the Old Testament and hears the prayers of the Preacher, in whose momentous book prophecy approached its culmination. In that book prophecy was awaiting its great First. A blow on Jesus' cheek without the word with which Christ accompanies it, would have left the court of Israel in the helpless condition of the Preacher, would have left it in the tragic conflict of the vicious circle. If Jesus had held His peace He would have been unfaithful to the house of Israel, He would have failed to respond to the duty of active obedience, He would indeed have failed to turn the other cheek. But now we know that He speaks the Word, that He ministers the Word, and that He has done well in this. He has done it for us, as an example to us. He has also done it in our stead.

This is a marvellous discovery. I am the one who by nature am ever trying to rid myself of this great Representative of authority by means of a blow to His cheek. Every word hastily spoken, every doubt-prompted leap to a false serenity, every flight from the pain of the absolute to the sedative of my accursed relativism, is but another blow which I am giving Christ, the great bearer, and the holy content of God's most special revelation. Alas, how often have I not struck my Saviour on His cheek! Alas, alas again — for now He comes to offer me the other. He hurls His lasso around me, He throws that evil circle of His condemning Word around my flesh. He tells me: If I have spoken evil, testify of it. This He says to me now. His patience is very frightening, for He inducts me into the world of His sermon on the mount. In that world I may strike Him on both cheeks if I feel like doing that — He swore with an oath that I could. Alas, Annas, you and I stand next to each other, next to each other and almost pressed to death against the High Wall of the kingdom of heaven. There He will offer me His cheeks — He has sworn that He would with an oath. His bonds wound me terribly. I cannot oppose this man whom you suspect, Annas. What must I do with your prisoner?

Annas does not answer. The High Wall is dumb. I know of only one thing which I can do. I shall tell Him that in this other world in which He offers me His other cheek and in which He offers me the right to speak out my cogitations aloud — that in this world I cannot breathe. I shall ask Him whether He will not first carry me into that world, receive me in grace, transfer me to the realm of His Spirit and teach me to breathe the atmosphere of eternity. When I open my eyes there, I shall not accuse Him, for He will have drawn me with the cords of love, and brought me to the place where I might reach His cheeks. I shall kiss His cheeks; I shall kiss Him whom my soul loves. Strike Him? Behind me, insane Satan; for who would strike Him? I shall sing hymns of praise in His honor, for faith is the substance of things hoped for and the evidence of things which cannot be seen in the vicious circle. I have read the sentence which my blow to His cheek has pronounced upon me; I read it from I Corinthians 2. The natural man cannot discern the things of the spirit; he has not the critical capacity to explain the things of time in terms of time, for these are all distorted. But he that is spiritual "judgeth" all things, even though he himself is "judged" of no man. Hence I must suffer the affliction of the blow on the cheek together with my Saviour from now on. I must do that as soon as He has bound my hands lest I should strike my Lord and my God. But I will bear the blows. I shall offer Annas both my cheeks. Thou art great, O Lord, and greatly to be praised, and our hands tremble restlessly at our sides until such time as Thou dost bind them, dost bind them with cords of love.

The Vicious Circle
Condemns Christ

CHAPTER FOUR

The Vicious Circle Condemns Christ

● *And they led Jesus away to the high priest: and with him were assembled all the chief priests and the elders and the scribes. And the chief priests and all the council sought for witness against Jesus to put him to death; and found none. For many bare false witness against him, but their witness agreed not together. And there arose certain, and bare false witness against him, saying, We heard him say, I will destroy this temple that is made with hands and within three days I will build another made without hands. But neither so did their witness agree together.*

MARK 14:53 and 55-59.

OUR preceding chapter was an exposition of the thought that the vicious circle in which, according to the Preacher, the whole world is ensnared as long as it shuns the Christ, is pointed out and condemned by Christ. It was His privilege and it was His duty to do so. Hence He presents Himself to us in the hall of Annas as the one solution to all questions. Moreover, His solution is not only the closing speech of all human argument, but also the *beginning,* the first contention, the word "which was from the beginning," proceeding as it did from the revealed God.

Now the Gospel turns the tables around. It shows us that darkness prefers itself to the light. Christ who would break through the vicious circle is in turn broken by it Himself.

For in the session of the Sanhedrin that which demands the death of Christ, God's great Answerer, is its obstinate clinging to an unsolvable riddle. We shall investigate precisely that in greater detail now. It will be a piteous story about the wrath of the vicious circle.

77

Jesus is taken from Annas to Caiaphas. The preliminary hearing in the presence of Annas has produced no results. They did not know what to do with the Nazarene there. Accordingly, Annas rids himself of this great burden. He can do this very easily because his time has already been served. Thus Christ is led to the Sanhedrin. This body was present in toto (Mark 14:53-55; Matthew 26:59). By that we do not mean to say that every last member was present, for it is also possible that the constituent colleges of the Sanhedrin were present in sufficiently adequate numbers to constitute a quorum. The assembly meets in the palace of Caiaphas. That is not surprising. It was night and the gate of the hill of the temple, accordingly, was closed, so that they could not meet in their official assembly hall. The work of darkness was in a hurry.

This was a very tragic spectacle, this opening of the session. They knew just what they wanted. Caiaphas said as much at the time. All they needed now was a formal basis for the sentence, a kind of formulation of the charge which could be made public to God and men. But that was not easy. We say again, that the preliminary hearing had proved fruitless and the Sanhedrin virtually was turning around in the same impotent situation. The Gospel according to Mark, particularly, points out very clearly how they must coil and twist themselves about in their attempt to arrive at some legal version of a charge and of a condemnation. At first all the members of the assembly set themselves to work at the task. All of the respectable gentlemen together try to find some testimony against Jesus. However, they find none. True, there were false witnesses enough but these contradicted each other badly. At least no one could find a harmony in the several testimonies which they presented.

Then, at long last, there were a few who found something. From the variety and abundance of the testimony heard, the subject they wished to discuss comes into the foreground sharply accentuated. Among this group, too, there is still some difference of opinion about the exact formulation and the precise phrasing of what Jesus has done amiss. But, after all, one cannot be too particular in a situation like this one. An argument which really carries weight has now been brought to the fore. It concerns a certain statement which Jesus made long ago when He had been challenged by the Jews to authenticate His *messianic rights*.

Now the fact that the issue concerned messianic rights tells us that it was indeed one which could legitimately be raised here. For Christ's messianic qualifications are indeed the major consideration in any trial which the world engages in against Him. Everyone should sit at attention now, for it seems that the main issue has finally been reached.

Just what is it that they have found? Well, let them tell it themselves. Everyone remembers that Christ once purged the temple. He found all kinds of traders there who were teaching the people to play with the law of sacrifice. A false desire for comfort had made God's commandments impotent by means of caricatured human promises. Everywhere the doors of the temple had the superscription, "Open for business." That holy zeal which gives God what is God's due was gone. The temple had been turned into a den of murderers.

When Christ noticed that, He had arisen in opposition. He had arisen by virtue of His authority as the Messiah. He had said to Himself — as He did so He was employing the logic of the *Son* thinking about His *Father's* house — that they had no right to defile or profane the house of His Father. If they persisted in doing that the task of the Son was clear. And thereupon Christ had whipped these people out of His Father's splendid palace. He had driven those out who had defiled the temple and whose conduct sent its foul stench up to heaven.

After this zealous business had been completed, the *authorities* had come to Jesus. Just what had He taken into His hands? Who had given Him the authority? Where were His credentials? Naturally, Jesus did not have these, at least no credentials written by men. Neither the political nor the spiritual authorities had qualified Him for such or for any other conduct. Nevertheless Jesus insisted that He was qualified to act as He did. His credentials, He suggested, came from above.

Well, if that were true, there was only one thing to do: to demand a *sign*. If He as a worker of miracles could exhibit some convincing token (just what kind they would consider in greater detail afterwards), they might be willing to consider the fact that indeed Jesus did get His rights from above.

In response to the request to show some sign by way of proving His qualifications, Jesus gives a very fitting answer. On the other hand He anwers the fools according to their folly, for He suggests a sign which not one of them is willing to challenge. He tells them that they can go ahead and *break the temple down, and within three days He will build it up again.*

Naturally Christ knew very well that they would not proceed to break down the stone temple in the shadow of which this dispute was being carried on. To that extent, therefore, His answer begs the question, and rules out of consideration the request they have put to Him. Why does He do it? Why? Because Christ is willing to show a sign only when it is accompanied by the *Word*. A sign which does not come accompanied by the Word cannot possibly convert anyone. A sign cannot in itself convince anyone. True, it makes its appearance in the phenomenal world, but if it is not explained in terms of the prophecy of special revelation, the sign is the exact equivalent of anything else in that world of phenomena. Then the sign also is but a part of the vicious circle of all natural, mundane life. Unless the sign is accompanied by the Word, it cannot help one to escape from the circle. One can never explain the sign with certainty, unless one has first been taken captive and vanquished by the Word of God. If that has not taken place, if *faith* is not present, the sign will have nothing to reveal, but will remain a conundrum which one explains this way, and another that way. A sign proves to be a sign only to those who beforehand, and without it, have believed solely because of the Word. To this extent, therefore, the answer which Christ gave the dignified gentlemen at the side of the temple who asked Him for His credentials was a true answer, replying to the fool in terms of his folly.

On the other hand, however, Christ also answered *not* the fool according to his folly (and that, too, is advised in the Proverbs). In other words, Christ presents a new folly by way of an answer to the other. In this He is quite serious. The answer which He gives contains a profound, a hidden meaning, a sublime and sacred seriousness, a sovereign and messianic sensitiveness, an awareness of His own worth; and it contains, besides, a judgment, a distinction between good and evil, between faith and unbelief.

That becomes apparent to us the moment we listen carefully to Christ's reply. For when He says, "Feel free to break down the temple, and I shall build it up in three days," He is giving expression to a riddle, to what in the Hebrew tongue is called the maschil. Such a riddle, or maschil, accordingly, is an intentional concealment of the truth. A concealment, yes, and to what end? Simply to keep something away from the auditor? No, but, on the contrary, to make him want a further explanation. The maschil is not a temptation designed to drive a person from the truth to the lie; but it is a testing, a proving designed to give him an opportunity to say what he wants. Does he want to be content with a concealed truth, or does he want to ask for the full revelation? The maschil does not dull the point of truth, but does indeed cover it. Especially in the instruction of Jesus does the maschil make a remarkable impression. It is a riddle in His prophetic instruction in which He presents a problem in such a way that all those to whom He speaks about it must be hurt by it, inasmuch as they will never escape from it in their own strength. After the maschil one can say which of those who heard Jesus desired further assistance, and which of them shut themselves up within the limits of their own pride.

All of these considerations hold true of the riddle which Christ spoke in reference to the breaking down and building up again of the temple. Who, indeed, would be able to say exactly what that statement meant? The enigmatic element was certainly conspicuous enough in this maschil of Jesus. His speech was full of obscurities.

For instance: Christ knew very well that no one would undertake to break the temple down. In fact, if anyone should have undertaken this work at His behest, He would thereby have been taking responsibility for something which He on other occasions definitely opposed. Very often, we know, Jesus assured those who heard Him that He did not desire the destruction of the temple. Moreover, such a "sign," if some one, for instance, had accepted the challenge to break down the temple, would no longer be a genuine sign. The question which was being touted here between Christ and the Jews was whether or not Jesus had the right to take any initiative inside of this stone temple. His right to do that was highly disputable to the Jewish guardians of the temple. Now imagine that they had broken the temple down simply in an effort to see whether Jesus could restore it before the next Sabbath day. Then they would have indicated that they had so much respect for His words that they needed no "sign" to convince them. The sign, then, would no longer have constituted evidence, which Jesus, as an alleged craftsman of unusual qualifications and extraordinary ability, had been asked to present. Instead of "seeing," of "testing," they would have been trusting. Then they would have had to take the responsibility entirely upon their own shoulders, even though they had begun by emphatically placing it upon the shoulders of Jesus.

Well, you see that no matter how they may twist about and contort themselves, people cannot escape from this answer. This is so completely true that we also would have been unable to escape from it, if we had been present at the occasion. Even if we had absorbed the whole Bible, even if we had absorbed the whole truth of the Scriptures, we would have learned nothing about the hidden meaning of this maschil, if Jesus had not told each of us in particular what He meant by His reply. However, He told His disciples what He meant, and by means of the Scriptures gave us the right interpretation of His riddle. It is to that we owe the knowledge of what Christ meant by His answer and of how He could fulfill it in Himself. We are told that the temple of which He spoke is His own body. Just as the Jewish temple was a house in which God dwelt, just so Christ's human nature is filled with the presence of God. The stone temple is stationary; it is the immobile property of God; it is the dwelling place, the domain of the great King. But Christ is the wandering temple. In Him God begins to move, comes to the world, makes His approach to the people and the powers here below. Therefore Christ may bear the name: the temple of the Lord. He knew this by virtue of His messianic consciousness; and from that He derived, as the greater than the stone temple, the right to proclaim the laws of the lesser temple. From that He derived the right to proclaim and apply, also by means of the purging, those laws of the lesser temple which grieved the Jewish authorities so sorely. Now it is this greater temple which the Jews are to break down (as they proceed to crucify their Saviour). But He will Himself, as the wandering dwelling place of God, restore that temple again, making it more glorious than it ever was before. He will make it translucent with the majesty which is in the highest heavens. This He will do by means of His resurrection from the dead.

So much for the hidden significance of this maschil pronounced by Christ. We return now to the point of our departure. And if we give our thoughts a natural and a free reign, we too will ask ourselves in astonishment: How in the world can this maschil be regarded as a sublime answer? How can we seriously maintain that by means of this maschil Christ answered the fools among the Jews not according to their folly, but according to His messianic wisdom? Is it true that the messianic majesty and dignity express themselves fully in this riddle? Surely, the Messiah is called, not to the great concealment, but to the manifest revelation; He is sent not to be secretive, but to be a discoverer of reality.

In reply to this, we would answer that the highest revelation also has the right to be the profoundest concealment. The most powerful love has the right to express the most powerful wrath. He who gives most can also take most. He who always hastens when he comes to me, has the right to detain me as long as he pleases. And such is the right of the maschil — of the maschil of my Lord Christ.

For a maschil, a riddle, without Christ is nothing more than the pain of the Preacher, that late writer of the Old Testament.[1] It is a fatal suffering, a brutal interference with my roving through the thoroughfares of the carnival of vanity. Of course, the maschil in the mouth of Christ Himself also causes acute pain, but it is a pain which the physician inflicts upon us not to put us to death but to heal us. It is an ingenious excitement of the sense of hunger in order that we may at the right time ask for bread.

We must not fail to take careful notice of the maschil as one of the ways used by Christ to reveal Himself. It does not commend our Christian thinking that we, in speaking of the means of revelation which God employs, write extensive articles about the *dream,* about the *deep sleep,* about the *vision,* and about the *theophany,* as being so many means of revelation of God in the Old Testament, and then leave no room in our thoughts at all for

---

1. See the preceding chapters in which the book of Ecclesiastes was discussed in connection with the vicious circle, and in connection with the insufficiency of nature and of historical phenomena to explain themselves.

the maschil of Christ. We say that this does not commend our
thinking. If we follow that course, the maschil will remain a riddle. That holds true not only for its content, but also for the fact
of its existence. However, if we leave the maschil uninvestigated,
it condemns us; for it is designed precisely to excite us to investigation. Why, it asks us, why does Christ speak in "parables;" why
does He use riddles instead of forthright speech — riddles which
involve people in attempts at explanation without ever providing
the possibility of a solution? Is Christ not the highest prophet?
After all, He is the one person in the whole world who in the most
absolute sense of the term is *called* to use a language which makes
His thoughts and the thoughts of God clear to us. Why does He
speak in parables that cannot be understood; why does He use
riddles which give no one a key to their explanation?

Christ alone is able to answer these questions. Moreover, He
has answered them. Once when His disciples challenged Him for
the intentional concealment of His thoughts in the form of parables, He told them that He did this in the sense of Isaiah: to reveal the thoughts of each man's heart. He used the parable, the
riddle, in order to make manifest a hardening of the heart where
that was already latent, and to effect conversion wherever a human
heart was susceptible and willing to listen to the pure words of
God. Consequently there is a double task here. On the one hand,
there is the calling "to make the heart of this people fat." Note
that it is a question of *this* people. In other words, the question
concerns a fleshly people, a people which already has a heart which
is "fat," a people which already is unbelieving. On the other hand,
there is also another people, and that people is very willing to take
Christ at His word. This people allows the layer of fat — to retain the Biblical figure of speech — to be melted away, gives itself
up to Christ without reservation, and then, in proportion to the
measure of its faith, sees in the Christ not a concealer of thoughts
but a revealer of them.

He must Himself provide the key for the explanation of all
His parables to this people. The children of this spiritual seed look
at the details of His instruction in the light of the main issue. They
look at the periphery from the viewpoint of the center of truth.
The unknown drives them to the known and to that which they
love. If they have discovered a particular statement which weighs

heavily upon them because they cannot account for it, they take it to the Word, to Christ Himself, and pray: "Do Thou explain this further." And can you believe that He will fail to hear their prayer? Indeed, He hears them, and answers them. The embarrassed children who come to the Master of riddles for a solution have their reward. He gives them an even clearer revelation, one which disclosed the riddles that went before; He gives them a revelation which puts the key of wisdom, fashioned by God Himself, into their trembling hands, so that the doors of God's house and of the palace of the Highest Wisdom are opened by means of it. By means of His difficult riddles He has given them an arduous task, but He also gives them their wages withal.

But what about that first people? What about the unbelieving people? Alas, although it has ever so luminous a light, it prefers the darkness. It is the enemy of light. The unregenerated personality chooses against Christ and against His truth and in that way disowns everything which it did understand in His instruction.

These people are also affected by the maschil. In the last analysis, everyone in the world gets what he wants. We know that the much tormented Old Testament preacher wanted to reach out above the circle of human science and of human investigation to the absolute, indubitable truth. Now if this hunger, which the Preacher knew, is not satisfied by the Christ, we can say that Christ is vain. That is one side of the truth about Jesus Christ. But this truth has another side. When the people who listen to Him would rather hunger with the Preacher than be satisfied with the bread of Christ, their choice for hunger instead of bread and for the vicious circle instead of the straight line of revealed truth is a gruesome sin which carries condemnation within itself, which calls God's judgment down upon it.

In this way, then, Christ bears his maschil into the world. He is the great proposer of riddles. He is that now also and it is as such a presenter of riddles that He makes His appearance as the great sifter, and as the divine judgment. For the maschil is also an instrument of judgment.

As often as Christ speaks in parables, He compels men to present themselves as they are. The maschil is essentially a sifter; it reveals what is in man. The reaction to the maschil can be one of two possibilities. To everyone who hears it, it is, until further explanation ensues, a riddle. That the two have in common. But this is the difference. One person will hunger for the truth; together with the Preacher of the Old Testament he will honestly long for the light. In the depths of his solitary life he will look to the divine Word which answers all his questions and puts his soul at rest. Now this person will say to himself: I have in my hands a lock which I cannot open; it is a secret lock. But I know one thing: Christ has the key. I shall go to Him at once and ask Him what He wishes of me; I shall ask Him what preaching He has hidden in the maschil for me. Such is the course of a disciple who comes, asking, "Tell me the meaning of the parable."

But there are others who take the opposite course in their thinking and secret pondering. They also experience that they cannot satisfactorily explain Jesus' word. And secretly they are glad of that, for they do not really want to face Him honestly. At least not as He is in His person and doctrine. And these use the fact that He speaks in parables as an argument for stopping the attempt at finding their solution. They turn the maschil against the Christ who gave it, for they regard it as a precious privilege to say: "He spoke so obscurely that I am compelled to advise myself." They think they have made a very delightful discovery when they say: "He gave me a riddle; He let me walk about in a maze from which there was no escape. Hence it is no fault of my own that I have stayed inside my vicious circle." They are so glad that the riddle gives them a kind of excuse that they forget His willingness and ability to put into their hands the thread by which they can escape from their vicious thought-cycle. They have a lock; it is a secret lock, and as far as He is concerned, He has not given them the key. Consequently they take the liberty to putter with the strange lock after their own fashion in order that in that way they may cling to their own wisdom and their own mistaken science.

Thereupon—just notice it—you will find that a new prayer is being composed. It is the prayer of the ignorant. No,—I am not mentioning Annas by name, nor Multatuli, for how could I dare not to name myself? This only I know—that every maschil spoken by Jesus elicits prayers from people: the prayers of publicans and the grim prayers of the "ignorant" who are terribly happy about being able to blame God for having darkened His sun and who just then break their leg upon the rock of offence.

Surely, if these people were honest with themselves in relation to Christ they would want to ask Him what He meant, and would want to ask Him for a further explanation. Even the person who eagerly wants to condemn Jesus as the great proclaimer of vanities in the world must do that. But if one is unwilling to let Christ be the explainer of His own proverbs, he uses the riddle which God puts to him as an argument for staying in the night of darkness. All so-called "prayers of the ignorant" complain about the maschil, but secretly rejoice in it; they jot it down in their memorandum book, supposing that it will come in handy in the last judgment. Let God wait; they have their reply.

We can say then that it is God's zeal for the crisis, for the sifting, which hurls the maschil into the world. It reveals the heart. After this, friendship and enmity will have to give a further account of themselves.

What is the conclusion of the whole matter? Who are you, son of man, who are you, you who compose the prayers of the ignorant? How dare you take the maschil into the condemnation of Christ? Who are you, daring as you do, to deny the prophecy of Christ because of the maschil? May that maschil teach you to forget to tremble, and to shudder? No, it is just when the maschil is pronounced by Christ Himself that it is a thing to inspire trembling, a mystery in which revelation is not hidden, as though it never wanted to be made manifest. Instead, it is a mystery in which revelation is proclaiming aloud that it has been very well known. The maschil does not deny the manifest character of Jesus' instruction, but assumes precisely that, and it forces you back into the aisle out of which you have departed so quickly. It was the aisle in which the clear prophet spoke a word to your soul as the Good Shepherd. Surely, if Christ spoke in parables only, He would not be the bread of heaven. Then the hungering soul of the Preacher would not have found satisfaction with Him. But the fact is that He presents His maschil only in the place where He has first made His word and deed clearly manifest, and where He always stands ready to answer everyone who asks an honest question about it. Because that is the fact, this maschil is an awful thing. Christ takes you out of the full light of the midday sun, places you in a dark room, and asks: Now you have seen that there is light; which do you want, light or darkness? By means of the maschil Christ provokes the sense of hunger, and a conscious sense of uncertainty. Just that—a conscious sense of uncertainty. Therefore we say that the maschil, yes, even the maschil, is a last instrument of grace, just as a rude awakening of a man who lies in danger of freezing because he is about to go to sleep in the cold also is grace. If this man loses consciousness, he will fall asleep—forever. The maschil is light. Everything which reveals, and everything which reveals inner truths, is light. The one will return from the maschil complacently to the labor of his own soul, in order to pay out money for that which is not bread, and to devote effort to that which cannot satisfy. The other will be just so much more desirous for the true bread which God extends to them. He eats the roll. Has it the label "maschil"? No matter, he takes it and eats. It may be bitter, or sweet, or both together. No matter, God will teach him. . . .

Therefore we can say that all the treasures of wisdom and knowledge lie concealed in the maschil. These lure us, and invite. In His maschil Christ makes us sense that all of His plainly spoken answers contain so many wonderful truths in their mysterious depths that He has only to turn His prophet's cloak inside out and we will see that this cloak is lined with the stuff of riddles. On the garment which as a prophet He wears among us, the names of God and of God's virtues are embroidered in human characters; even the foolish cannot go astray. But the inside of His sublime cloak is embroidered with figures of cherubim, or is it of demons? In any case they are figures which I cannot understand and which lure me either to leave Him or otherwise to trust Him entirely, and to seize Him by His garments, the very thing by which He would be seized. Christ's prophetic instruction (to which He appealed first in the presence of Annas, in the beginning of His trial) is very manifest; it makes the hidden things obvious. But Christ's maschil which He now hears brought into the trial against Him again makes the obvious hidden.

Accordingly the person who has heard Christ speaking in riddles, is in a position to make only one practical application. He must bring the riddle to Christ Himself, he must bring the letter in which the conundrum is written to Jesus, asking: Do Thou break the seals, read me the words, explain to me the hidden sense, for blessed is he who is not offended by a riddle-speaking Jesus.

The maschil keeps me from making God's word the word of man. It keeps me from saying of the sun of righteousness: I have found the formula of its light. The maschil reminds me in the most painful if most effective manner that I may not separate the Word from its sublime Speaker. That is the great admonishment contained in the maschil of Jesus.

And it was this admonishment which also lay contained in, and was brought to the foreground in the maschil which Jesus spoke when He purged the temple. If one separates the enigmatic word which He spoke at that time from the speaker, and if one refuses to relate Jesus' external action and audibly spoken word to His inner essence and to His continuous revelation at all times and places, one can make of Jesus precisely what one pleases. Then He can become a destroyer of the temple or a builder of the temple, a rebel or a reformer, a destroyer or a fulfiller, a magician or a prophet, an ironical proposer of riddles or a physician, one who presents divine answers or a relative of the Egyptian and Greek oracles—who also spoke in riddles in an effort to conceal the fact that they had nothing to reveal. Then Jesus can become the great prophet of Israel, one who tempts God by a display of stupid, haughty boldness, which is a blasphemy of the tenor of the holy temple, or one who trembles before God and fears Him, who honors God's temple as being God's house, because God dwells in it Himself.

Unless the historical manifestation is not explained in terms of God's eternal concept of Christ, then Jesus and His maschil is included in the same classification as circumscribes other world powers and world peoples; then He is passively taken into the vicious circle of which the Preacher complained, together with us all. But Jesus is the Christ and it is as the Christ, that is as He is in His office, in His messianic office, that He pronounces His maschil. The maschil of Jesus irks people intensely precisely because it makes everything subservient to Christ. All who hunger for God out of the depths cry aloud to the maschil of Jesus for the answer of Christ. But the person who knows not this hungering for God, rubs his hands as he deals with the devil, and as the devil teaches him the statement he is requested to repeat to God later on: If I am lost it is Thy fault; Thou dost speak in riddles, at least the prophet *whom Thou gavest me* does. The italicized phrase was used before. Adam used it. And some of Adam's children learn it by heart even though Adam himself quickly revoked it.

But Thou, my Saviour . . . Thou, who art the second Adam . . . now Thou art caught in Thine own snares; Thou art being entangled in Thine own skeins. Incomparable necessity: the Son of man is caught in His own crisis. At the beginning of His public ministry He casts the maschil into the life of His people. Now, having arrived at the end of this ministry, He is reaping—is He not the Surety?—His own bitter fruit.

If Christ had not introduced the maschil among the self-satisfied guardians of the temple, His sentence would not have been pronounced against Him so quickly. Then the Sanhedrin, which had struggled so long in vain in order to find some kind of charge against Him, would have found nothing. But now these members of the Sanhedrin discover the maschil which Christ Himself originally laid down.

No, we do not mean this in a sense which would make Christ responsible for their distortion of His word. The atrocity of this distortion remains the responsibility of the false witnesses. When they distort Christ's words, "Break down the temple," into the other statement, "I shall break down the temple," they are guilty of falsification which is entirely the sin of the false witnesses.

But for the rest, we maintain that Christ Himself has done this. It is apparent that Christ's riddle was remembered for a long time in Israel. He has been teaching for three years; and not a single point of the whole store of His discourses is brought to the fore, save this riddle, spoken at the very beginning. In this way, by pronouncing the maschil, Christ at the very *beginning* of His official ministration, Himself brought the *end* nearer.

By means of that maschil Christ began to *sift*. Sifting always implies that sinners are being irked. A Christ who wants to sift, looses His own murderers against Him. Christ sifted. He intensified the hunger of the hungering souls, and then gathered them under the shadow of His wings, to comfort their trembling hearts with certainties. Hearing, these heard, and seeing, they saw, and observing, they did indeed discover. But at the same time, and by the same means, Christ also hardened the others, inasmuch as they were hardened already. He made hard the heart of fat, and hearing, these did not hear, seeing, they did not see, and observing, they did not discover.

This, too, was the will of Jesus. Therefore the fact that the maschil now turns against Him may be said to be His own work. The crisis spoken of in Revelation 20:11 was loosed against Him by His own riddle and all His days are but a single day of passive and of active obedience to His God.

Therefore the beginning of the session of the Sanhedrin, as told in the gospel, is a beautifully artistic conclusion to the end of the preliminary session before Annas. You can see that for yourself. In the presence of Annas, Christ concluded by laying bare the vicious circle in the argumentation of the world, the circle, that is, which would explain life in terms of life, and the historical manifestation, the external side, of Jesus, without reference to Christ. The same thing happens now in the presence of the Sanhedrin. The riddle which Jesus proposed has not been solved by anyone present here. Nevertheless, they force the enigmatic out of the enigma and proceed to "explain" the unknown in terms of the way they wish to understand Him. They proceed to explain Jesus' riddles with the aid of commentaries which the flesh has written. They do not understand Jesus; but in spite of that they hurl Him into the maelstrom, into the vacillations of life, able as these are to give birth to rebels and to reformers, to those who would destroy as well as to those who build the temple. In short, they proceed—they are forced to it!—to look upon Jesus as though He were but a subordinate part of the world. They explain and interpret Him in terms of the world itself—as though they understood that. The overbearing character, the brutality of the blow to the cheek administered by the servant of Annas, returns daily, in the Sanhedrin first, and later in the conflict of the spirits. Every instance of applause with which the Sanhedrin greeted the false witnesses, every excited pulse among these old gentlemen who turned the maschil against Jesus is but another blow against Jesus, an attack on the heart of the Chief Prophet, a mockery of the Bearer of the sovereign authority, an overlooking of the messianic issue, even though that issue made itself obvious in the maschil to a painful extent.

Accordingly, the episode which introduces the maschil of Christ into the debate occupies its own unique position in the account of Christ's passion. Annas in his preliminary session and Caiaphas' Sanhedrin and its official hearing are perfect complements to each other. When Jesus had to give His account to Annas, they began to assume that His discourse was not clear but enigmatic. They overlooked the obviousness of His instruction in an attempt to blame Him for speaking obscurely. Here, in the presence of Caiaphas, they turned the tables around. To the extent that Christ actually spoke in riddles, they treated those riddles as though everyone understood perfectly what was meant, as though even the simplest could easily appreciate their meaning. Now they tell Christ: You are not preaching under the full light of the sun, but in a dark room. Tomorrow—no, even today—they tell Him: The roof of your dark chamber leaks; we understood and appreciated everything you said. On one and the same day the mystery which is in Christ is confirmed and denied, according to the whims of the flesh. Therefore the one who is always responsible is Jesus Christ.

In this way, then, the maschil of Jesus becomes the predominant element in the trial. The high priest not only demands an answer from Jesus in reference to the maschil at once (Matthew 26:61; Mark 14:60), but at the cross of Golgotha the theme of the maschil returns for consideration (Matthew 27:40; Mark 15:29). In fact, even after Christ's death and resurrection the maschil was turned against Jesus' disciples, for Stephen too seems to have been sentenced because the Sanhedrin, too old to learn,[1] had no objections to using the maschil of Christ against him also (Acts 6:11-14).

Now let us bow before the sovereign authority of Christ. He has loosed the storms over His own head, but He also places us in the whirlwind of that world-process of sifting between good and evil, between the obedient and the disobedient. Therefore we enter into the same judgment with Him. The riddle He spoke lies on the table; it is embroidered on His garments; it is involved in doctrines. Hence our heart, too, is made manifest. Some day it will become apparent whether we are willing to ask Him for the

---

1. And this happened, mark you, after the prophecy stated in Verse 64 had been fulfilled (see Chapter 7).

answer to His own riddles or whether we condemn Jesus in the light of our self-vaunted wisdom. Not to appreciate Christ and nevertheless to act as though we knew Him—that is the peculiar evil of the Sanhedrin. So the servant, so the judge; so the preliminary hearing, so the official session.

But who is not like the Sanhedrin according to the flesh? Alas, our heart also would rather hunger in the company of the Preacher, than be satisfied with the bread of Christ. By nature we, too, choose the vicious circle, "explain" time in terms of time and Jesus' external deeds in the temple in terms of the externalities of Jesus and of the temple. Now this our sin also is unmasked in each and every maschil of Christ which is too great and wonderful for us. In the last analysis, every riddle from which we have forcibly turned ourselves aside, every doubt with which we did not flee to Christ's authority, is just so much applause for the false witnesses of the Sanhedrin; it is to be on the wrong side of the condemnation released by the maschil.

We must fear that at this time there are many of these doubters. They mumble the prayer of the ignorant, and write it on the fan with which they cool themselves in the overheated room which is burning with the fire of judgment. With this beautifully embroidered fan they flatter themselves even in the presence of the chair of their judge. But their doubt is not a real doubt and the Judge knows it. It is but the effect of their unbelief. They overlook Jesus' revelation and do not know that the dignity of His own revelation has hurled the maschil towards them to do His work in them.

In this matter we can only choose for or against. We can but believe or reject. If we acknowledge that Christ by His maschil governed and intensified His trial, we will catch a glimpse of His suffering, He has unloosed the crisis, and now He Himself becomes involved in it. He has made the filthy more filthy still, and the unrighteous more unrighteous, and now all that filth is flung into His face and all that unrighteousness beats against His soul. Oh terrible necessity! Here is a Christ who can say nothing, who must be mute over against His God. A Christ who is buried under the chaff which He has Himself separated from the wheat.

We catch a glimpse of His *majesty* also. One who enters upon His suffering in this way, one who has already fixed the terms of

His sentence at the beginning of His public appearance, that is, after the purging of the temple, may be beaten down a thousand times, but if so He will rise again ten thousand times. Break down this temple, and He will arise at once. Yes, just now the filth which Christ has loosened still beats against His face, against His gentle face, His cloak, His soul. But so great a majesty is contained in this passion, that faith is already assured that He, when the crisis which breaks through at this time has been entirely completed (Revelation 22:11), will sit upon the seat of judgment, lifted up, so high and so safe that all the filth and all the unrighteousness of the world cannot soil Him throughout eternity. This will be the day of judgment. That day was never so simple as it is now, as it is in the plain logic of the events of the present.

Finally, we get a glimpse of the Suretyship of Christ. Behold, He is bearing our guilt today. *We* were the ones who loved nature, and wanted to redeem the time in terms of the time. We, each one of us individually, are the ones who have rejected the "why" of revelation and of its manifest character. We are the ones who cry our false "whys" aloud before God simply in an attempt to escape from his "therefores." Of the pincushion of His maschil we make a pillow; we pull all the pins out of it. And *for this great guilt Christ bears the penalty.* He who once pronounced the maschil not because He lacked certainty but precisely because *it wanted its reward from men* now hears all the members of the Sanhedrin. He also hears you and me as we boldly proclaim that we knew the truth long ago, that we know enough about Him, that we have "placed" Him. Thus we avow that man can conquer the problem of God incarnate. For this false glorying in the *therefore* of our pride Christ later must pay a price so high as to induce Him to conclude His profoundest utterance from the cross with a "Why, why, why hast Thou forsaken me."

Here is the fully assured person who can propose His maschil on the top of the mountain of highest wisdom, when He Himself has sunk beneath the foot of His own mountain of truth. The Speaker of the maschil later becomes His own sacrifice on the cross. God puts Him to death with His own maschil. Meanwhile men jeer at Him: Ha, breaker of the temple, when will the building start? Thereupon Jesus sobbed: God, Why ? He sobbed; His own maschil had cut off His breath. And this is called Suretyship. The Surety who first called out His *therefore* now sobs out His *why*.

But God be praised. In His *why* also the Surety did not turn from God to Himself. He wanted to solve His own riddles only at the gate of God's palace, with His ear close to God's infinite heart. Thus Christ suffered, leaving an example for us. He left an example of how to respond genuinely to the maschil. Take all your riddles to Him who proposes them. The "why?" must be immediately referred to "My God."

Speak for yourself now. Does the maschil hurt anyone—except Jesus? No, indeed, the pain of the maschil is not a pain of death unto death for him who *believes*. On the contrary it is to be aroused to love and to life. For everyone who has found his Prophet as Surety, the maschil is the great appetizer for the daily recurring banquet of Christ's prophecy, which leads the meek in their way, and satisfies the hungry with bread, and never satiates. Whoever has once eaten out of His hands will always return to His table, even though He spices His foods with the galls of the maschil. *Even though?* . . . No, but *because.* . . .

Christ Standing Mute Before the Sanhedrin

CHAPTER FIVE

Christ Standing Mute Before the Sanhedrin

● *And the high priest arose and said unto him,
Answerest thou nothing? What is it which
these witness against thee?
But Jesus held His peace.*
MATTHEW 26:62,63a.

THE *chief* Prophet maintained the *profoundest* silence in the presence of the highest court there ever was in the world.

Those are three striking adjectives: the "chief" Prophet, the "profoundest" silence, the "highest" court. As for the last one, we have previously pointed to the fact that the Sanhedrin by virtue of the direction of God, the great Lawgiver of the theocracy, was the highest juridical body in the sphere of spiritual law in the world.[1] Athens is the foster-mother of beauty, Rome is the center of world empire, and Jerusalem, in a similar category, is the city of religion, of revelation, of spiritual authority. Accordingly, the Sanhedrin, up to the moment of Christ's apology, bears the heavy responsibility and the high honor of being the first and highest court of justice in religious matters. Spiritual authority as it is found in the world finds its points of culmination there. As for such irregular and "wild" pretenders to authority in spiritual things as Melchizedek represented, no one need fear being troubled by them any more. Who had ever seen Melchizedek come to life in the world? Melchizedek is a person about whom one can only preach sermons and write commentaries. No, for spiritual regulations and critiques one must go to the Sanhedrin.

In very truth, therefore, the highest Counsel is here in session. In that Council our chief Prophet and Teacher is present. The

---

1. *Christ in His Suffering*, p. 58f.

conjunction of these two, of Council and Teacher, would lead us
to suspect that the discussion would go on incessantly. Surely the
highest college of law is duty bound to speak, and the chief Prophet is similarly bound. The chief Prophet, the highest council,—
that at least guarantees a religious discussion, one would think.

But instead of vigorous speech the profoundest possible silence
characterizes this place. *Jesus held His peace.*

Various explanations for Christ's silence in the session of the
Sanhedrin have been given. One commentator argues that Christ,
our High Priest, stood mute because of resignation, just as Aaron
was once silent before God when God struck him. These suppose
that Christ saw in the Sanhedrin nothing but the chastisement of
God, and therefore overlooking the Sanhedrin, He said nothing
to God, without paying any attention to the Sanhedrin at all. Another commentator will say that Jesus maintained His silence by
way of protest, first of all, against the injustice which had been
done Him when the Sanhedrin began its official procedures by riding roughshod over all kinds of rules of law. Then there is a
third group who are inclined to believe that Christ held His peace
because defending Himself would not "do any good anyhow."
Now it is self-evident that there is an element of truth in these
and similar explanations.

Nevertheless, these cannot constitute the full explanation. If
one limits oneself to these reasons, one would have to marvel later
on when Jesus does not persist in His silence but begins to speak.
If it were actually true that Christ could respond to the injustice
done Him and to the plagues which God inflicted upon Him in
a genuine way only if He stood mute, His later speaking would
virtually be condemned.

Or, on the other hand, if Jesus had kept His silence only because He did not want to "cast His pearls before the swine," He
would have been playing extravagantly with God's pearls. Now
there is a tendency sometimes to give our attention solely to
Christ's silence, to use it as a beautiful theme for a sermon about
"the silent Prophet, the silent Priest, and the silent King." But if
we should at any time accentuate His silence too emphatically, or
should name it the only means by which He could assert His official obedience, then the prophecy of Christ would be nullified by
His later speaking, just as His priestship and kingship would then

also suffer shipwreck on the rock of His spoken word. There is no more dangerous application of what is a rather foolish proverb anyhow: namely, that speech is silver but silence is golden.

No, we must leave things in *their context*. Naturally we recognize the Christ, also in His silence, as Prophet, as Priest, as King. He is always fulfilling all His offices; whether He speaks or holds His peace, He does it all to the glory of God. But if we want to understand Christ's silence correctly, we must pay attention to the *relationship* in which it stands to the whole gospel narrative. Then we must beforehand be convinced—after all, faith is simply full of presuppositions—that Christ's silence at a given moment must have a specific purpose in the whole of this wonderful and strange trial.

Now whoever sets himself to the task of reading the gospel of the passion patiently and believingly with this presupposition clearly in mind, will gradually be able to see that Christ is silent at one time and that He speaks at another time for a *definite* reason. Moreover, the meaning of Christ's silence in the presence of the Sanhedrin as well as in the presence of Pilate and of Herod will also become clear to him to a certain extent. Such a person tells himself beforehand that three instances of silence must necessarily have three different meanings, that each instance of speech and silence has its own specific meaning whether it take place before the Sanhedrin, or before Pilate, or before Herod. It is only by a complete recognition of the justness of this general exegetical rule that a believing student of the Scriptures can cling to the truth that every new and different thing which the Christ of God does *is* new, and different, and pure in its reaction to the particular afflictions of the moment.

That is also the reason for which we may not be satisfied with the contention that Christ by His silence was simply resigning Himself to the will of God. An exegesis which is satisfied with such an explanation is but another revelation of that same, unfortunate one-sidedness which so frequently has profaned and contaminated our thinking about the Man of sorrows. We mean the one-sidedness which pays attention chiefly, or solely, to Christ's *passive* obedience at the expense of his *active* obedience. Naturally if we pay attention solely to Christ's suffering in obedience, to His patience and meekness, we have said enough if we interpret Christ's silence to be an expression of a calm resignation, an acquiescence in the will of God, even though that sublime will is leading Him to His death. But Christ manifested more than a passive obedience. He *remains active* to the very end.

And that is the case here also. To the extent, first of all, that Christ does not give a wrong answer to the Sanhedrin, His silence is indeed a "speaking" revelation of the *Lamb of God* which willingly allows itself to be led to the slaughter. But, on the other hand, the silence of Christ in this connection is also a *deed*. It is an expression of His lordship. His own strong will is on this occasion regulating the course of the trial, and intervening in the critical moments of it.

It may be true that by His *resignation* to what God is inflicting upon Him, Christ is manifesting obedience. But that does not take away the fact that He may abuse the law of resignation towards God by resigning at the expense of men. In this connection, this means that Christ may do no injustice to the Sanhedrin. The chief Prophet may, as a man, withhold nothing from the Highest Council which is necessary to that council at this time for its salvation. Even if the Son is compelled of God not to take His place in the judge's seat, but in the open circle in which the Sanhedrin regularly places its accused, Christ, nevertheless, may not passively let that come upon Him which does come. For He still has a task over against this assembly which is seated to do justice. If His silence had merely been an expression of resignation and not a deed also, a redirection of the trial to its genuine purpose, Christ would have become a debtor to those who accused Him. Then the second Adam would Himself have been unjust in the exercise of His office.

By virtue, then, of the presupposition of faith previously named, we shall now look for the *deed* in Christ's inactivity. We shall seek out the *speaking* in His silence. We shall try to find the *active* obedience in the passive.

In this connection we remember how, in the preceding chapter, mention was made of the so-called maschil of which Christ had made use in His speech next to the temple. This maschil, this riddle, had been brought into the discussion by the false witnesses

who were contaminating the atmosphere around Jesus. Now Caiaphas himself comes to demand both text and exegesis of Jesus.
Or—to be very accurate, even that is not quite true. In fact, we
might wish that he had asked for both text and explanation. Then
Jesus would have answered him by once more citing to him at the
behest of the government which he honors the genuine text of His
maschil. But the terrible fact is that Caiaphas, although he is
the judge, does not ask for the "text." He asks only, and he does
that very formally, for the explanation. Whether or not the text
which they were quoting to him on this occasion was accurately
presented or not does not affect him at all. At least in the presence
of the Sanhedrin the witnesses did not agree with each other
about that "text." The one cited the maschil of Jesus in one way,
the other in a different way. No, the text was by no means certain.
Plainly, a faithful judge would, before he did anything else, want
to determine the precise phrasing of the text; not until he had
done that would he demand a further explanation. But what does
this judge do? He loses his poise, and without any kind of dignity, demands whether the Nazarene will care to explain what He
meant by that strange statement He had made. And without giving any further attention to the uncertainty of the text of Jesus'
speech, he hopes to hear an explanation at once out of which he
can forge a chain of condemnation for this proposer of riddles.

It is this explanation which Jesus refuses to give.

He refuses because in His prophetic work Christ moves along
His own ways. If he chooses to pronounce the maschil without
giving its explanation, that is His own privilege. The distinguishing characteristic of the maschil is precisely the fact that it is a
text without an explanation; that, and also the fact that by means
of it people who listen honestly, and are willing to investigate, are
compelled to preserve the literal text in its exact form, or else the
explanation will be hopelessly impossible. Can Caiaphas actually
suppose that Christ is going to bury His own texts by way of a
premature exegesis of them? By no means. True, Christ will
presently give the one great explanation of Himself which will at
bottom explain all of His discourses, and disclose their secret.
That will take place when He says with an oath that He is truly
the Messiah. But His maschil—that He will leave alone. The
maschil is His privilege because it belongs to His office and no

government will ever succeed in compelling Him to deny anything which is a part of the work of His office.

Therefore we can say that this is the element of Christ's active obedience: He maintains His maschil: He holds His peace.

Just what this means in reference to His trial we can perhaps appreciate best if we ask ourselves for a moment just what would have happened if Jesus had not stood mute, if in place of His silence, He had carefully exposed the meaning of what He meant by His maschil. That maschil, we remember, was to the effect that His body was the temple which men would break down and which He Himself would rebuild in three days. Now if Christ at this moment had given this complete explanation to these people, He would not have spoken a word at the right time. But the Just One of Israel knows the time and the way in which He must do things. In the first place, riddles and parables are explained only to those whose hearts are open to them. After all, only such people are in a position to hear what is being said. Here, however, in the assembly of the Sanhedrin, there are only insusceptible hearts. These are the birds which never pick up any seeds on the threshing floor of righteousness; they are, on the contrary, birds of prey which feed on rotten spoils.

Moreover, what would have been the results if Jesus had expressed Himself completely on the issue of this particular part of His prophetic speech? If Christ in this conclusive hour, and in the presence of all the witnesses, had pointed to His body, and had said, "This is the true temple; just break it down, and within three days I will restore it," Jesus would have been doing irretrievable damage to the Sanhedrin as well as to Himself.

Let us note each of those considerations for a moment.

We said that Christ by a premature disclosure of the maschil would have done damage to the Sanhedrin. In that case, He would have prophesied that the Sanhedrin would certainly break His blessed body, that the Sanhedrin would certainly put Him to death. He would have indicated that so much had been clear to Him for years, that the iron will of God, who is seated above the clouds, had so directed it, and that the sublime decree of election and reprobation, that the predestination of that exalted God, had in His sovereign good pleasure appointed Him for this very purpose from all eternity. Plainly, at this place and in this hour, that would have been an untimely preaching.

No one, surely, has anything to do with the hidden things. Only revealed things are the yardstick by which we should measure what we do and do not do. The hidden things are of the Lord, and the revealed things for us and our children. Now the revealed things, the holy books, all the prophets taken as a unit, had indicated definitely enough the standard according to which we should act, and had indicated it to the Sanhedrin also. The revelation of the Messiah had, in fact, been so adequate that if it had been obeyed, Jesus would not have been crucified by the rulers of the world. Therefore Christ is silent about the hidden things. Could He want to be wiser and more compassionate than God, who chooses to instruct by means of the Word? And would it have been compassionate in Him if Christ said: "Ye are predestined with me even in this same hour"? No, that may not be said; it would be the greatest brutality to say that, to say that Jerusalem is being made the equivalent of Egypt today (Revelation 11:8). Christ knows that. Just what did God say to Egypt? Listen, Scripture does indeed say to Pharaoh, "And in very deed for this cause have I raised thee up, for to show in thee my power; and that my name may be declared throughout all the earth" (Exodus 9:16; Romans 9:17). But every Pharaoh in the world can take this word in either of two ways. God can make His power manifest in the world by Pharaoh's triumph as well as by Pharaoh's decay; by his repentance as well as by his hardening of heart. And God's name can be declared throughout all the earth not only over a grave of Pharaoh, but also at the moment of his being received into the Father's house. God never gives a human being a prophecy about his future perdition. Predestination is God's great warfare against fatalism, and the preaching of it is that also. For he has also predestined the fact of responsibility. No one is ever told that his perdition is absolutely certain, and that he lies under the irrevocable judgment of a hardening of heart. Such an announcement, certainly, would dull the predestined awareness of responsibility. In fact, it would break down predestination. Besides, it would do injustice to the majesty of God, calling aloud as it does in the Word with a "most earnest cry," and by means of that cry making everyone responsible for what he does and does not do. Moreover, it would be doing injustice to the love of God which is proclaimed aloud in the announcement of the possibility of repentance. Did you think, perhaps, that the prophecy of Christ was a kind of forecasting, a kind of fortune-telling? Not that, surely, but it is a sending out of God's light. And this light God indeed did send out. In His maschil His light even lured the curious, just as a strange star lured the Magi to the solid Word. The prophecy of Christ is never a kind of divination. Accordingly, it never puts one under the accursed ban of an absolute, eternal, predestined unproductiveness. It does not do that as long as the God of Christ has not announced: Let him bring forth no more fruit in all eternity. It does not do that as long as this saying of God is not taken up into the sublime announcements of the Kingdom, which take place there in that Public Court. The prophesying Christ makes everyone face himself; He asks everyone what he wants to do with the Word of his God.

Therefore Christ does not tell the Sanhedrin that the Counsel of God has chosen this hour to break down the body of the Son of Man, the temple of the Spirit. The Good Shepherd does not take the opportunity for repentance away from the bad shepherds, by assuring them beforehand of the impossibility of it. True, Christ does know that the Sanhedrin will be to Him, who is the fulfillment of the true Israel, what Assyria was once in the eyes of Isaiah. Assyria and the Sanhedrin will be a rod, with which God inflicts the penalty; these will be the saw with which God cuts down the trees of Israel. But the fact that the Sanhedrin will realize the Assyrian-service in the true, great, and only Israelite is a fact which is not preached to the Sanhedrin as a *fatum* to which it is inescapably subservient, for then the High Council of Assyria, seated on the chair of David and of Moses, would say: Are we predestined to be *Assyrians*? Come, let us then prove that we are Assyrians. Could it be God's fault that the saw will rebel presently against him who draws it? Will it be reckoned against Christ, if in the judgment day "the rod should shake itself against them that lift it up" (Isaiah 10:15)? No, no, this glory Christ will not grant the Sanhedrin; the theodicy of the last day may not be allowed to break upon the Christ. Accordingly He wraps His cloak about Him, covers His maschil, does not explain His riddles to those who would abuse them anyhow, and—O incomparable grace—He keeps even this degenerated college to its own legal name. He does not say to the Sanhedrin, "You are predestined to the great, to the acute destruction of the temple." He says simply: "I demand that you do your duty: it is your calling to be the guardians of the temple." And He does not say to the select elders of Israel: "After all, you are Assyrians, drawn up in battle array against the Son in God's great universe." No, He lets them be what they are, and simply says: "Ye are Israel. Therefore I want to tell you that I am the Messiah. Know now what ye would do with Him." Thus Christ lets the responsibility rest squarely upon the shoulders of the highest Council. By His absolute silence He is obeying the predestining God. For this is to tremble before the God who is in election: namely, to let Him do what it is God's work to do. Thus Christ compels His judges to leave the hidden things to the Lord and to busy themselves with the revealed things.

We can say, then, that Christ's silence over against the Sanhedrin is a perfect revelation of justice. He is by no means eager to become the rock of offence over which they are to fall. A "careless" omission—how ridiculous our poor language in these things proves to be—, a bold and hasty exegesis of a text that has not even been critically ascertained, and Jesus, outside of His office, would have announced their condemnation to the Sanhedrin. But that would have meant that He, independently of His office, would have been a stumbling-block upon their way. For there is no one in the world who will ever circumvent the absolute assurance of his own predestined condemnation and this assurance, accordingly, God never gives to any man.

Now it was the majesty of Christ that He laid not a single stumbling-block in the way of anyone on that road which all men and all devils literally bestrew with stumbling-blocks and with rocks of offence.

O exalted majesty; O great Christ, eternal light, Thy way is strewn with stones. Eager human hands throw them before Thy feet. Ardent passion of devils arranges them for your difficult going. Laws of eternity forbid all the angels together to keep Thy foot lest it should stumble upon a rock. Nevertheless, Thou, O Christ, didst not play with a single stumbling-block; Thou didst not lay a single one in the road. Thy incomprehensible office was more than enough for Thee: to be set as a fall and a rising again for many in Israel was more than enough for Thee. Thy office satisfied Thee so completely that Thou didst not play a single indifferent game with it in the days of Thy sunshine, nor unleash a whirlwind in it, when bulls and goats, the "wild beasts" of Jerusalem were baying Thee. Thou didst suffer under the responsibility of this office, this being set as a fall and a rising again of many. And never in Thy office didst Thou act arbitrarily. That simply was no part of Thee. Hence Thou didst hold Thy peace, in order that Thou mightest speak at the proper time. Neither by Thy speaking, nor by Thy silence, neither by a false exegesis, nor by an untimely explanation, neither by placing text and exegesis over against each other, nor by wrenching text and exegesis apart, didst Thou, my Saviour, place the rock of offence in the way. Thou *wast* the rock; that was enough for Thee to endure.

In this, O Saviour, Thou didst find grace with God and the angels. They may not praise Thee to Thy face, but, surely, God keeps a memorandum book. Canst Thou suppose that it would not be written there above that Thou, although surrounded with stumbling-blocks on every hand, didst not once inadvertently kick one with Thy foot in the direction of the president's chair of Caiaphas, or of any of the seventy chairs standing in the court? Thou didst do justice to Thy judges.

And by doing justice to them, Thou didst also condemn them. For, now, the maschil tells them: If you wish to explain time in terms of time, and if you wish to analyze Jesus' words without any reference to Him who spoke them, you must walk in the flames of fire which you yourselves have kindled.

The maschil is an expression of the great art of the prophet of heaven. He lets us feel the impotence of all speech which is cut loose from revelation. And he who would not enjoy the benefit of this thing by going with his unwholesome life to the Physician of his life, will be left to shift for himself. Every maschil ever pronounced announces to the meek who cannot escape from its entanglement: "Who is among you that feareth the Lord, that obeyeth the voice of His servant, that walketh in darkness, and hath no light? Let him trust in the name of the Lord, and stay upon his God." Thus also every maschil that was ever spoken proclaims to those who prefer to assert themselves, even when they are caught in the coils of the maschil: "Behold, all ye that kindle a fire, that compass yourselves about with sparks: walk in the light of your fire, and in the sparks that ye have kindled. This shall ye have of mine hand; ye shall lie down in sorrow." Today it is the second of these judgments by the silent Christ which accrues to the Sanhedrin. He lets the maschil lie just where men would have it be: that is, in the vicious circle of a "worldly" speech, which refuses healing from above. Salvation will wipe away all tears that are wept for the sake of the maschil, and will answer all questions. But an unsolved maschil is the beginning of the judgment.

And this was the judgment which the silent Christ pronounced upon the Jews.

If we retrace our steps now, we will see that Jesus' silence at this particular moment is an act of justice to Himself also. Accept for a moment that Christ without any further ado had stated exactly what He meant about His maschil, about his temple which they could break down and see restored again within three days. Then He Himself would have lured[1] the people to overrun the place where He is to be buried later, in order to see what would become of this fortune-teller. If Jesus Himself, standing before the Sanhedrin, had emphatically said: "Ye must bury me, and within three days I will arise again," then . . .

Yes, what then?

Then the Prophet Christ would have identified Himself with the fakir who also lets the wonder run amuck in the slough of his self-ostentation. He would have identified Himself with the oriental figure, who plays with his body and with himself not by way of causing the wonders to contribute to salvation, but by way of garnering praise for Himself. If Christ had lifted the heavy burden of complete responsibility from the shoulders of the Sanhedrin, and if He had placed the advent of His resurrection-life,

---

1. The issue here is the deed of Christ Himself, for the Jewish leaders were not ignorant of Christ's own announcement of the resurrection. Compare Matthew 27:63. In this connection, many observers also think of such other passages as are found in Matthew 12:39f.; 16:4; 21:42; 26:61; and 27:40 (Compare Zahn). And still others think, but that with a "'perhaps," of John 2:19 (Grosheide, *Kommentaar*).

coming as it did through a predestined death, in a sphere in which
it is possible to look at the miracle without being involved in it,
Christ would have profaned the majesty of prophecy, and would
have exchanged it for the empty ostentation of a clever magician.
And He would have made Himself intolerable in the eyes of God.
For He must accept death from God's hand, He must accept the
personal breaking down of the temple from God's hand, but He
emphatically may not accept it from the hands of men. By virtue
of the secret will, we must say to God: Feel free to break down
the temple of my flesh. But it is the revealed will which He must
minister to His people: never, not in all eternity, break down the
temple of my flesh; it will be your condemnation, if you do so.
That is why He may not by an untimely disclosure of the meaning
of the maschil lead the rulers of His people astray, invite them to
a *sacrificium obedientiae,* to a joyous sacrificial feast, at which the
heavy burdens of complete and infinite responsibility are cast into
the fire—inasmuch as He would have given permission to His
strange funeral feast. No, no, He cannot do that. The "burden
of the Lord" has a place here. If Christ had lightened that burden
by calling attention away from the revealed will and to the hidden
will, He, who had to be the greater than Moses, would have fostered fellowship and would have mingled with the Egyptian sor-
cerers who opposed Moses. Then Christ would have been the
third, or really the great first, in that unholy coalition of Jannes
and Jambres, who opposed Moses and the truth (II Timothy 3:8).
Then it would have been by His fault that Jerusalem became an
"Egypt" (Revelation 11:8). Then Golgotha, that holy place of
judgment and necessity, would have been degraded to a fine occasion for a game, to an invitation to an interesting experiment
in the laboratory of Satan and of God. Then the resurrection of
Christ would not have represented the breaking of the New Testament Sabbath through the shadows of Israel. But then, at about
the time when God would cause the clock of His New Testament
Sabbath to strike, a multitude of curiosity-seekers would have
poured in the direction of Jesus' grave in order to see whether the
fakir could actually arise from the dead. Then God's holy Sabbath joy would immediately have become contaminated by the
profanum vulgus, which, in that case, would have been invited by
Jesus' own word. Cross and resurrection would then have consti-

tuted an examination, instead of a judgment. These would then
have been presented in Christ's own announcement as a fencing
bout between Spirit and Beast, between death and life. But we
may not climb the hill of death to feast on a spectacle; we may
climb it only to place ourselves under the judgment. Had Christ
explained the maschil without demanding faith, the scornful cry,
"Let us see whether Elias will come down," would have issued in
that other cry, "Let us see whether the angels will come in their
fiery chariot to get Him." And such mockery would then to a
small extent have become Christ's own responsibility. Also for
Him—an untimely exegesis of the maschil can harm Him for all
eternity. If He Himself takes judgment, if He takes the tension
of the sermon on the mount out of His trial, then He will Himself rob His work of its strength, and will perish with us. One
does not play with God's lightnings; Christ may not forget that.

God be praised: He could not forget that. Consequently we see
Christ busy in the struggle for the maintenance of the sacredness
of God's house. He leaves the maschil as it is, unexplained. By
doing that He convinces the children of darkness of an obligation
to go to no one else with all their honest questions save to Jesus
Himself. But that is not all He does. He also sees to it that the
redemptive facts which God is now making ready, remain holy
and undefiled. For Christ is at this time striding through all the
world in order to release the forces of law and gospel. The great
redemptive event is about to be born of an accursed death and of
a blessed resurrection of Christ from the dead. Now it is a great
joy to us to know that Christ's silence before Caiaphas and before
the Sanhedrin left the maschil just what it was—a maschil. No
recklessly spoken, untimely word relieved the tension of the events
of the day of the Lord. The praise of folly is never sung in Christ's
discourses. The gospel never offers itself as an experiment. Jesus
Christ maintains to the extent that is possible for Him the character of the great mystery of godliness: God was manifest in the
flesh, justified in the Spirit, seen of angels, and believed on in the
world (I Timothy 3:16). In virtue of the essense of this *mystery*,
His resurrection, the restoration of the temple of His body, will
have to remain a mystery, to be revealed only by the intransigent
Word. It will never prostitute its chaste holiness before the eyes
of a people which would like to see the last great stunt of the ma-

gician of Nazareth. Even though that resurrection will be a wonder of world-perturbing might, still—no, *therefore*—it will not be prostituted before the eyes of those who have gone out to see a magician. The miracle comes to the world with authority: it asks acknowledgment solely through the preached word. The miracle is never a piece of evidence which God is giving man as an "argument" in a peace conference between God and worldly unbelief.

Again, therefore, we see the great gulf which is fixed between canonical and apocryphal gospel. We have repeatedly pointed to the fact that the Apocryphal Gospel lets an avid Jesus perform His miracles simply for the sake of ostentation.[1] In it the miracle is but a sensational something to which every redemptive purpose is alien; it is a miracle without holiness, and without necessity, a miracle which is sheer play and in no sense represents awful seriousness. Indeed, if Christ had presented the wonder of His most astounding restoration of the temple as a piece of sensationalism, He would have been quite in line with the apocryphal emphasis.

But Jesus held His peace. This is a transporting moment, for in it Christ's sublime silence draws the absolute line of demarcation between a canonical and an apocryphal narration of the Gospel. It may be that the miracle of resurrection exists in His mind in a perfect state; His knowledge of it may be pure, strong, and very great. Nevertheless, this Christ lures no one to Himself by means of worldly publicity.[2] The Passover will never be a dazzling display, an ostentatious spectacle, but it will be the great advent of justice to Himself and to the world. The Passover is not an end in itself, but simply a fact of redemption and of judgment. O sublime majesty; O silent Christ. Thou dost refuse to "explain" Thy maschil by means of an untimely discourse to carnal men, but dost explain it by means of the events in which a speaking and a judging God comes to the world.

O sublime trust, O goal-conscious Christ. At the beginning of Thy ministration of office Thou didst turn Satan back when He suggested that Thou perform a breath-taking miracle in front of the temple.[3] And again at this time thou dost regard the temple

---

1. *Christ in His Suffering*, p. 108 f.
2. See *Christ in His Suffering*, p. 108 ff.
3. Leaping from the pinnacle of the temple.

court as being altogether too holy for a miracle which would astonish externally but convert no one.

The silence of Christ is as reasonable as the canonical Gospel. It is as serene as the dew on a clear morning. It vindicates the canon of absolute authority over against apocryphal Jewish presumptions, first of all, presumptions which regarded the Messiah as a breath-taking wonder-worker, and over against those piteous fireworks, next, which an unbelieving world is eager to set off when it proceeds to explain the Messiah in its own way. And it also vindicates the absolute authority of the canonical Gospel over against my sins, O my Lord and my God.

Feel free to break the temple down now. For a temple it is indeed. Yes, and more than a temple is here, for God is dwelling in this Christ. God and the Spirit are dwelling in Him, and entirely without restraint. This is the Holy of Holies; this is the temple in its fulfillment. And, just as the ancient temple had once been built without the distracting sounds of hammer and saw—inasmuch as it was to be God's house—so Christ will presently restore the temple of the body without the profane accompanying noises of the mob, and without inviting the *profanum vulgus* to come and defile His holiness. In other words, the conclusion of the matter is that Christ by maintaining His maschil rescued the redemptive event as such and kept the holiness of God from becoming profane. This was the great demonstration of His active obedience; this He did by a silence greatly and highly to be prized.

That is the first conclusion: active obedience. This obedience exercises its authority. By maintaining silence, Christ kept His judges from deriving an official phrasing of their sentence from His maschil. It is remarkable that Christ's words about breaking down the temple and restoring it again do occasionally occur in the haranguing of the crowd, and in the mockery which periodically came to the fore during the course of the trial, but are not used in the official sentence of the Sanhedrin. This is Christ's own achievement. He compelled His judges to return to the main issue, and to return to the main message which, quite uncamouflaged, and with no hint at all of the veil of the maschil, would soon be repeated in the form of the testimony that He was indeed the Messiah, the Son of the living God.

Now that we have seen the active obedience of Christ at work in His silence, we may speak of the passive side of His obedience. Again we look upon the Man of sorrows who stands mute and dumb as He gives Himself up to death. Alas, it had been determined that He should make the riddle about the destruction and restoration of the temple true in actual experience. He had to explain the statement not by an untimely, ostentatious word, but by a bloody event coming at just the right time.

Thus He is to be punished for that which is not His own sin. Now He must actualize His confident utterance about the destruction and restoration of the temple by letting His body be broken and by building it up again from death itself. In this we worship Christ's passive obedience.

Silence, silence . . . in this we bow before the will of the Father. Silence, silence . . . He scorned to speak when speaking could have hindered His death or made it prosaic. And He scorned to hold His peace when it was a matter of confessing His Messiahship. In speaking and in silence, therefore, He is obedient to His death.

Such silence is a resignation to God. He stands, as a sheep dumb before his shearers. Now He is the greater than Aaron who, although afflicted for no sin of His own, acquiesces in the will of God, and lets Himself be led where justice must lead Him. Now He is the silent prophet who proclaims aloud the atrocity of sin, the holiness of justice, and the adequacy of the messianic self-revelation: I am He. Now He is the silent King who calmly announces, "He who does not understand me even now, He who has not appreciated the sense of the maschil even now, need not reach out His hand to me." And now He is also the silent Priest who obediently goes upon the way of the cross.

In the presence of the Sanhedrin Christ was tempted. His own riddle was being used against Him; and great was the temptation to free Himself from the terrible death by a single word. One untimely word, and the very concept of His death would be transformed into the dazzling glory of a miracle, of a miracle so splendid that there would be nothing of humiliation in it. This was a temptation just as severe and exacting as the proof to which He was put on the mount of transfiguration. On that mountain also the great question had arisen whether Christ by a premature speaking or an untimely silence would depart from the way of the perfect ministration of office.

In this temptation Christ triumphed completely. Moreover, this triumph adds a new terror to the cross. No, this does not mean that Christ could prove terrible only in His silence, for His silence is precisely the way by which He arrives at the important utterance later: I adjure thee that I am the Messiah. No, that which adds a new terror to the cross is not solely that the maschil is still unsolved, but is owing also to a clarity, to an eloquent and convincing potency of a Messiah who reveals Himself. Jesus held His peace because He had said enough. Presently a superscription will be hung over His martyred head bearing the words I.N.R.I., Jesus the Nazarene, the king of the Jews. That is the "title" which Pilate will give Him. The Jews will petition for a different "title," for another superscription. As a matter of fact, everyone will conceive of his own personal title for the crucified Christ. But above any title which the fiendish hatred of our flesh will conceive for the cross, the calmly accusing finger of the unexplained maschil will always arise.

Jesus leaves the judgment hall. They let Him go, and every one knows that in reference to this man they still have an unexplained riddle. The maschil has not been satisfactorily accounted for yet. The test has not been ascertained, and the explanation has not been given. If only there were a grain of truth in the teaching of the person who says that a man can keep from revealing himself in his public utterances, we could safely say that Caiaphas' statement, "What need have we of further witnesses?" is virtually a betrayal of the secret sense he has that the Nazarene is not being dealt with justly, and that the unexplained maschil is detracting perceptibly from the judge's self-confidence.

But do not condemn Caiaphas. Confess instead that Christ's death in the cloud of an unexplained maschil places a huge question mark over the cross on which you and I, by which you and I because of our sin hanged Him. Every sentence which the flesh pronounces upon Jesus contains within itself an unsolved riddle, and the consciousness of that. Let us watch, therefore, and fear, now that Christ has taken His secret with Him to the grave, obstinate from the viewpoint of men, patient from the viewpoint of

God. He takes His maschil with Him to the grave now. Now
the riddle of Christ becomes a command:

> *If you His saving voice have heard,*
> *In faith accept His precious word —*
> *Dare not rebel, but follow where He leads.*

For Christ Jesus is the temple of God. Every temple has its
mysteries. The maschil is His mystery. But the temple of God
does not live by the grace of its own dark corner. Light falls upon
it from above, light issues from the sides, light comes from within,
and there is such abundance of light that even the foolish need not
go astray. And as the light falls upon Him, a voice can be heard,
saying: This is He, this is the Messiah, the Son of the living God.

For in this great temple of God, which is broken down now,
and will quickly be built up again, the question (which remains
after the maschil) is not the obstacle which stands in the way of
the answer, but the preliminary and recurring divine answer is the
incitement of a thousand new questions on the part of those
blessed souls who throughout eternity will call: Thou art He;
Thou art the Messiah, the Son of the living God; and because
Thou art that, Thou must become that more and more manifestly;
and because we know that, we want to investigate it eternally.
Thou hast explained Thyself, and hast explained God. Explain
Thyself further, therefore, and explain God further. Explain
Thyself and Thy God throughout all eternity.

Thereupon my Jesus will never again hold His peace. His silence was the way by which He earned the right to speak eternally. His silence moved His Father's pen; the Father wrote and
wrote again as silent angels watched.

He wrote of Jesus saying that He would give Him all speech
in heaven and on earth, now that He had learned obedience from
that which He had suffered, and speech from the silence He had
kept.

Christ Taking an Oath
Before the Sanhedrin

CHAPTER SIX

Christ Taking an Oath Before the Sanhedrin

● *And the high priest answered and said unto him, I adjure thee by the living God, that thou tell us whether thou be the Christ, the Son of the living God.*
Jesus saith unto him, Thou hast said.
                                        MATTHEW 26:63b, 64a.

CHRIST passes from a state of silence to that of expression. Up to this time He has manifested His obedience by His silence; now He will give expression to that obedience by His speaking. In fact He will make use of the oath.

He takes this oath at the last meeting of the Sanhedrin which that body may regard as officially warranted by God. For as soon as the veil of the temple shall have been rent, the Sanhedrin, too, will be dismissed.

That is why this particular meeting represents a high point in the life of Israel. Israel has almost reached the very top of the high mountain of all her prophets, priests, and kings taken together.

In the form, then, of this last session of Israel's high council, the proudest monument of the marvelous nation which has now completed its journey through the world confronts Jesus. And the question it asks Him is, "Who art Thou?" In this question all of the centuries meet at a point, all the long centuries from Abraham to the present. Many are the epochs that looking down upon this session, await its decision. In this session the life of Israel may for the last time assert itself in an official-spiritual capacity and may once more take its stand at the zenith of the nation. And at this session, in which the ends of preparatory ages meet, Christ *swears* with a precious oath that He is *the Messiah, the Son of the living God.*

The curtains of this session hall have never hung so tensely suspended as they do now. Never was a spoken word so becoming to the place in which it was spoken as was this final word. The oath which was sworn here was the unfolding of a drama, a drama which had gone on for many years. This oath was the great theme of the fugue of world history, and was now developed to its loftiest height. Men felt that this could not go on; that the organ must cease playing now. The oath which was a last chord sounding in the oratorio which God had been conducting from the time of Abraham's prologues to this present action, to this last act in the final meeting of God's elect people, represented by its Highest Council, and placed at the head of the peoples. It is upon *that* gathering, then, that the oath of God suddenly impinges.

No, indeed, never was spoken word so appropriately fitted to the place and occasion.

But the Sanhedrin itself did not understand this. It did not know just how oppressive the atmosphere in its session hall really was. It did not sense just how depressingly the burden of the centuries weighed down upon its meeting. There seemed to be room to spare in the book of its minutes.

Hence from Caiaphas' point of view the way which led him to go with Christ into the hall of oaths was a purely human way. It was simply the ordinary work of an ordinary human being.

Caiaphas made up his mind that this man *had to* be put out of the world. Now that the summoning of the false witnesses has gained him nothing, now that the desired unanimity is still lacking, now that both text and exposition of a reason for condemning Christ are wanting, Caiaphas is compelled to make use of the last resort: the oath. And, as he does so, He faces the problem of the Messiah squarely. He touches on the messianic issue in its extreme complication and in its austerest meaning. Note that he does not ask Christ whether He is "a" Messiah, or whether He is a harbinger of "the" Messiah, or whether in some respects He sees Himself as the equivalent of the Messiah in His life, speech and thought. No, he asks Jesus whether in His whole person and in the totality of His thought and conduct, He is the Messiah, *the only, the great, the predestined One,* the meeting place of *all* the world's ways, and the bearer of the *great* mission.

That Caiaphas now reaches the point of swearing an oath, and of putting this question as he does, can from his point of view be understood easily. As for that oath, he simply had to demand it. Nothing seemed to be ascertainable on the basis of human testimony. Besides, Jesus' deliberate silence has prevented Caiaphas from extracting a poison from Jesus' last words out of which to concoct a new charge. Hence he makes use of his official status as a high priest, as a legal authority, and demands that Jesus take an oath. Now this oath was an acknowledgment of the fact that up to this time uncertainty had prevailed. It places the Nazarene in the *presence of God.* Yes, we can say that this was an ironic happening. The Son of God was placed in the presence of the majesty of God. However, this is not surprising. It is but another instance of that common, tragic irony characteristic of all unbelieving life which is always appealing to God in an attempt to escape from an appeal to self and in an effort to deny God's right to appeal by simply ignoring it.

Moreover, it can also be appreciated easily that Caiaphas and the Sanhedrin now immediately take up the *messianic* problem. There had been some provocation for asking Jesus — we say this humanly speaking — about the conclusion at which He arrived in His self-appraisal and self-evaluation. Caiaphas had a good reason for wanting to know whether Jesus did or did not regard Himself as the Messiah. That provocation Caiaphas could find in the immediately preceding controversy which had been carried on by the false witnesses. These "witnesses" differed among themselves about Christ's statement in the matter of that marvelous reconstruction of the temple to which after its eventual destruction He would dare to commit Himself. Building, reconstructing the temple, yes — that was important. Had not prophecy named just such rebuilding of the temple the *characteristic work* of the Messiah? Had it not been said: "Behold the man whose name is Branch: and he shall grow up out of his place and he shall build the temple of the Lord: even he shall build the temple of the Lord, and he shall bear the glory, and shall sit and rule upon his throne" (Zechariah 6:12, 13)? Surely, the tone of this prophetic utterance was sufficiently penetrating to give the fact that Jesus had called Himself a temple-builder a meaning of which Caiaphas now must make use. Is Christ, the Messiah, the official temple-builder, the fulfillment of prophecy, or is He not that?

It is possible that the passage just cited from Zechariah's prophecy was in Caiaphas' mind. True, these words are not a part of the text, but it is unreasonable to believe that no more words were exchanged between Jesus and the Sanhedrin than are included in our Scriptural passage. The account of the Gospel, naturally, gives us only the high spots in the sequence of events; the stress regularly falls on the conclusive and not on the subsidiary factors. It is quite possible, therefore, that Caiaphas remembered the text just cited from Zechariah. This is especially true because the passage just quoted speaks of the *glory* of the Messiah. This glory it regards from two points of view. It tells us that building the temple is the Messiah's peculiar work. In building it, He lets the glory of all of life ascend *to God*. By means of the "precious things" which the world offers, He proceeds from the *natural* world to the God of all *grace*. Just such reference is the essence of the sabbath-task of temple-building. But, in the second place, Zechariah also indicates that the Messiah "shall bear the glory" *Himself*. God will beautify Him, will adorn Him with every beautiful thing. God will prepare a throne for Him; He shall be great and shall reign.

If we keep that background in mind, it will not be difficult for us to follow the pattern of Caiaphas' thoughts and to trace the scheme of his thinking. The true Messiah is to accomplish the building of the temple in glory. But what, pray, is this Nazarene going to do? Look: chains are dangling from His wrists. He has neither form nor comeliness. The Messiah of Zechariah's prophecy is to mount a throne. But up to this time all thrones have thrust the Messiah aside. According to Zechariah 6:13 the true Messiah is to succeed in uniting the priesthood and the kingship. He will succeed in merging the offices of priest and king. But this Nazarene has incurred the animosity of every priest. Is it not true, gentlemen, that the priesthood will have nothing to do with this Nazarene? Let Him say, then, if He dare in our presence whether the divine oracles named in Zechariah 6:12 and 13 are applicable to Him?

Again — we do not know whether this statement from Zechariah was directly quoted by Caiaphas or not. It is not unlikely that he did quote it. Especially not when we recall that this circumstance would explain Christ's later statement to the effect that hereafter He *shall be seen, seated upon a throne, and shall actually receive the power of God, actually receive the glory of His kingship from the hand of the God of all "priests."*

Whatever these particulars may have been, certain it is that Christ's public ministry itself sufficed to raise the question whether or not He were the Messiah. True, we remember that at times Christ charged His audience and those favored ones whose garments still had in them the perfumes of love, that "they tell no man." But later Christ called Himself the Messiah outright, and in no ambiguous terms. In more than one public discourse which Christ spoke to the Jews the theme of the false and true Messiah was sharply emphasized. And on these occasions Christ plainly declared Himself to be the true one. The circumstances themselves, therefore, prepared the way for Caiaphas to arise from his chair and to adjure Christ by the living God, that He unmistakably assert whether He was the Christ, the Son of the living God.

Then Christ broke the silence and answered Caiaphas. He *had* to speak now; under the circumstances that was the only appropriate manifestation of obedience. However, we may not forget that His speaking in no sense indicated a relief from suffering. The heaviness of soul continued, the suffering and the labor continued during the expressed reply as well as during the silence.

Caiaphas' question and the demand that He take an oath represented severe humiliation for the Christ. As a matter of fact, those few words, "I adjure thee," are the most excruciating form of Christ-denial conceivable. The oath, surely, is demanded only in exceptional instances. And the peculiar characteristic of Jesus Christ is that all of His words are spoken in the binding medium of the oath.

We have several times had occasion to recall Christ's sermon on the mount. We did so for a good reason. The sermon on the mount is a declaration of the law of the kingdom of heaven. It was because of His relentless insistence upon the absolute imperatives of the sermon on the mount that Christ was crucified. Now this sermon has always presented something of a problem to those who have pondered upon it. Somehow it did not seem to fit the actual world. No conceivable or actual form of human social organization seemed to leave room for a personal, individual life which answered adequately the principles laid down upon the mount. And that says nothing of any social organization actually embodying those principles. The sermon on the mount seems to be the most utopian scheme ever proclaimed; it appears to be the great *oratio obliqua*. It suggests much ado about nothing.

But the sermon is very clear in telling us that it describes the true life as that life is lived in the atmosphere of heaven. It shows us that Christ does not regard things as they actually are as the standards for building the kingdom of peace and virtue, but that He has the kingdom of heaven make and maintain its own laws. Besides, the sermon shows us just as unmistakably that this heavenly kingdom with its lofty idealism makes all things temporal and actual subject to the absolute demands of the exalted Lawgiver in heaven.

Accordingly, in such a context of ideas, the oath also had to be included in the sermon on the mount. We know that the Jews of Jesus' time were used to swearing oaths on the most trivial of occasions. The oath was invoked for every little thing in the daily routine; boldly and unblushingly they swore the most precious of oaths in connection with all the little exigencies of the home, the kitchen, and the shop. As a result, of course, the potency of the oath was diminished, and its edge blunted. In short, these Jews incorporated God's name into the name of things which were not God's; they took the awesome and miraculous out of God's name, and the consuming fire out of God's house. This they did by sinfully "taking for granted" the tremendous realities of the kingdom of heaven.

The Christ preached the sermon on the mount. He said that things should be approached from the other side. Men must not draw eternal things — God's name, God's being, God's temple, God's residence, God's work — down to the level of the actual in order to accommodate these to finite human life. Eternity makes its own demands and these, consequently, are immutable, absolute and inescapable. The principle of wisdom is not to suit the heavenly to the earthly, but to refer all actual and temporal things to the perfect seriousness and authenticity of the heavenly and eternal. It is the part of wisdom to become used to the atmosphere of God, to breathe and live freely in the climate of absolute seriousness and truth. In pursuance of that principle, Christ during the course of His sermon says: Let your yea be yea, and your nay, nay. This is His reply to frivolous exchange of oaths customary now among the Jews. When they take the oath upon their lips in connection with the meanest and most trivial things — meanest and most trivial in their own estimation — they are but manifesting that their lives have at no time learned to tremble in God's august presence, that they do not appreciate the great Presence of the power, the immanence and the puissance of God and of the kingdom of heaven. Just why do these Jews resort to the oath so facilely in the market place, in the cattle trade, and at every little occasion? Simply because they are used to making their utterances while standing outside of the bourne of God's presence. He who on occasion states that God must be witness to a thing simply is stating, is he not, that in making his other speeches on other occasions he leaves God out of consideration? Now that too is wrong. But such conduct, at least, acknowledges the greatness of God and the awful terror of His judgment. But the man who calls upon God's name in connection with every little this and that, and who does so without feeling the awesome sense of being in the presence of God, sins continuously. The first person sins because he reserves God for special occasions; the second sins because, although he includes God in the routine of his daily business, he does so without fear and trembling. But in the kingdom of heaven — such is Christ's emphasis — a man must try to combine the good in each of the two positions. In God's kingdom every single thing should experience the tension of the presence of God. So much is to be learned from the second man. But in that case everything which refers us to God's presence ought to fill us with a sense of respect, inasmuch as God is in it, sees it, hears it, and judges it. And that the first man to whom we alluded can teach us.

Now the practical world of the Jews condemned this kind of teaching as making for a topsy-turvy universe. The Jews, you see, are departing from all the fundamental ideas of divine law. And this process of segregating actual life from the kingdom of heaven is, alas, so common that everyone is taking it for granted.

As a matter of fact the whole of Jewish life is quite independent of the legislative God, and of the kingdom which lays down its own fundamental laws, and makes them binding.

Over against this distorted life, then, Christ has manifested Himself in the sermon on the mount as the struggling Messiah, as the One who must make the crooked straight. By means of His sermon Christ again wants to raise the life of His people which has disappeared under the floor on which the very feet of the lawgiver are resting back to the high plane of the awful mystery of His silent but sublime majesty. To all those people who, because they are not living in the atmosphere of law are actually living carefree lives, Christ says: Let your yea be yea, and your nay, nay, for whatsoever is more than these is of the devil.

Whatsoever is *more!* Not, whatsoever is *against* these. All "respectable" Jews and all "good" people and all "conventional" citizens like to say: Whatsoever is opposed to yea and nay is of the evil one. Only when it should be yes and it is no, do such people become aware that something is amiss. Outright agnosticism, outspoken heresy, revolt against established authority — in these only can such people recognize sin.

But Christ sees matters differently. For Him evil begins the moment one abstracts one's yes and no from the sphere of the infinite, the eternal, the absolute. Our yea and nay, He says, must be fully informed by eternity. In fact, they must be so surcharged with the atmosphere of eternity that there is no room for *more.* The true version is not something artificially created. He whose yes and no come as the product of the soul's struggles with God need not raise his voice or have recourse to oaths, for such a man professes to live under the pressure of the absolute command, and therefore imparts to his affirmation and denial the force of an oath. After all, the greatest sin is not, in the first place, that a vow is broken, but it is that a person regards the making and fulfilling of vows as something which can be done apart from the living presence of God. There the sin begins. Consider in this sense, for instance, the vows which men exchange with each other in reference to traffic regulations set up for the common good. The rules governing such traffic are conceived and fixed solely in terms of the commercial needs of a metropolis. Man always regulates his legislation in terms of man; he acts autonomously; in his legislating he leaves God out of consideration. However, in the city of the earth, the traffic must be directed by the raised arm of God, the chief Lawgiver. In the city of God, traffic cannot be conducted on one level, for the communication is going on between the people and God. The first table of the law cannot be separated from the second for one moment. Christ wants to tell us that sin does not begin where heresy has actually interfered with right thinking, but has already come in as a chronic malady the moment the problems of orthodoxy and heterodoxy, of yes and no, are cut loose from the absolute demands of the eternal truth of God. Not only does the heretic sin, but also the so-called orthodox man who does not feel the burden of a binding pressure in the presence of God. In fact, the latter is, by and large, the first of transgressions in the house of God, or, to put it better, the sin of the former begins in the shape of the transgression of the latter. The Pharisees maintain a sharp lookout for heretics and they do well. But when they fail to ask in the center of God's forum about what is truth and what falsehood, they have already contaminated the atmosphere, both for their favorites and for those whom they dislike. Such is the first great heresy. Such is the heresy of the heart out of which are the issues of life.

Now by disseminating these ideas among the people Christ dismissed the oath completely in as far as the free communion of the citizens in that kingdom of heaven is concerned. Such was the painful labor of the Messiah to raise His people back to the level of the theocracy. Thus He heated the floor on which the feet of these people were dancing.

To this, His own rule, Christ always remains entirely faithful. *He* spoke all of *His* words in the light of the full day. He took them straight to the heart of God. He compiled no dictionary of formal and dignified phrases for use on certain occasions, retaining the jargon of the vernacular the while for all ordinary purposes. No, into all of His words He poured a content which was authentic and serious, freighted with the burden of eternity. As He senses it, the usual weighs as heavily as the unusual.

Therefore we can say that *all of the words which He spoke were oaths.* Christ never had to place His hand upon the Bible at the occasion of an inaugural, for the Word of truth is in His heart and ever issues from His mouth. In thought He adjures

Himself each moment. He does not need the ritual. He is ever
in an atmosphere of oath-taking, for He is always living in the
kingdom of heaven, in Paradise, even though He is in the desert
of the passion throughout these years.

Now if you cling to the fact that Christ was continually adjuring Himself, without making any use of a formal ritual for the
purpose, you can begin to sense how grievously Caiaphas *humiliated* Him. We repeat: this request which Caiaphas put to Him
was the most gruesome form of Christ-denial conceivable. Im-
plicit in it is the denial of the fact Christ has never spoken,
thought, or prayed, except as standing in the presence of the eternal and living God. The suffering of this was for Christ as bitter as death. The man who denied Him in this way was His
judge. It is evident now that the judge cannot but condemn Him.
He faltered in his best moment, the moment he exacted the oath.
All the words of hatred and scorn, all the spitting, and beating,
and buffeting were not quite as serious as this demand: "I adjure
thee by the living God." Christ had as the Messiah given His people the sermon on the mount as the fundamental ministration of
the Word. In that sermon He placed His people under the spacious vault of truth. But in the Sanhedrin, where God puts Him
over against His legal judge, the full arc of the justice and truth
of God has disappeared behind a painted screeen on which little
stars have been embroidered. Stars and attractive little cherubs,
embroidered perhaps by some respectable Jewish ladies' aid society at which one feels himself to be at home "chez soi," and not at
home with God, "coram deo." In the place of judgment godless-
ness entered first; thereafter, and consequently, ungodliness came
in.[1] It was therefore a heavy burden which the Author of the
sermon on the mount had to bear when God subjected His Son
to authorities such as these. He who needed no adjuring is now
adjured, just as is every heckling Jew in the market place.

We do well to appreciate fully that Christ's suffering because
of the Sanhedrin reached its zenith here. Suppose for a moment
that Caiaphas had calmly listened to Christ's defence, that the

---

1. For that reason the Sanhedrin, by first explaining the burden of special
revelation (their "exceeding great weight of glory") on the basis of the life of the
people and of the social and political life of the nation, had to yield to the vicious
circle even though the special history of revelation had in principle overcome it
(the relationship between general and special revelation in history).

Sanhedrin because of the oaths which they themselves had exacted, had acknowledged that He was the Messiah, that all the buffetings to come later had been spared Him, that these men had now come to make the confession: Well then, we believe Thee; because of the oath which Thou hast sworn, we believe that Thou art the Messiah. Come now, let us talk together about the future of Israel. Even then, surely, Jesus would have been abused, mocked, blasphemed, and terribly afflicted. For then also, by simply demanding the oath, they would have been denying blasphemously that He was always living in an atmosphere of oath-binding seriousness. Any agreement which such a group might enter into with the Christ of God upon such a basis would at bottom have been and remained denial, disobedience, and unbelief.[1]

Nevertheless, even though Christ is suffering greatly when the demand that He take an oath is put to Him, He obediently takes the oath. He was moved to this not solely by the respect for the authorities designated by God, but also by His direct messianic duty.

Christ must still acknowledge the authority represented by the Sanhedrin. He must still acknowledge this spiritual court. Hence He takes the oath. The oath does not conflict with the justice of God. The ritual harmonizes with the idea. The transgression is that of the judges; it is not His. Just a moment ago when the judges together here had trampled on justice, Christ refused to subject Himself to them. His silence was a complete condemnation of their travesty on justice. He refused to allow the authorities to break up the avenues of revelation which He Himself had paved — recall, for instance, what He said of the maschil. On the other hand, however, when the authorities demand that He take an oath which enables Him, together with them, to stand in the presence of God in order that He may confirm the "good confession," He stands ready to comply with their request. This represents several advantages. It puts Him in the one place where He wants to be. It puts Him in the atmosphere, in the medium,

---

1. The sin of unbelief, in the preparatory sermon, for example, can be very severely reprimanded if one takes the text of Caiaphas: *I adjure thee.* In line with the argument above part of the discussion could treat of the difference between the oaths God swears to Himself and the oaths which we demand of Him (He that believeth not God hath made Him a liar.) In this way such issues as asking for signs and insisting upon certainty are also seen from a proper perspective.

of God's omniscience, omnipotence, omnipresence, and holiness. There is another advantage. By arranging His speaking and His silence as He does, He can teach the Sanhedrin a true knowledge of itself. In the Sanhedrin, too, He can be the "falling and rising again of many." For there are sheep in this stable also. An accused who can be made to express Himself only when the oath intervenes between Himself and His judges is taking that means to say that the rest of the judges' conduct, be it the presentation of the charge or the answer to it, is acting apart from God. For the accused to employ such a method is for Him to aggravate the guilt, the condemnation, of the judge.

But Christ is also willing to take the oath now for the sake of His messianic office. Remember, Caiaphas has just raised the one important question in the world. He has asked whether Jesus is the Christ, the Son of the living God.

By this question all discussion of peripheral matters not related to the central issue is barred. Only the main issue will be discussed now. The question is not whether Jesus is a harbinger in the messianic cycle, nor whether He can make a rather formidable showing of Himself, can fearlessly hold His own in that corner of the temple where the gallery of the messianic types can be seen. No, no. The all-important issue now is whether He is or is not *the* Messiah. Is it true, Nazarene, that you are going to let the issues of the world converge upon us? Are you consummating the ages? Is it true that God "who at sundry times and in divers manners spoke to us through the prophets has in these last days" spoken to us through you? Art Thou the Son?

Had Christ been mute over against these questions, He would, as the Author of the sermon on the mount, have been a traitor to Himself, a traitor to the world given to Him for redemption, and a traitor to a universe which He must deliver from perdition, or at least from the tedium of the vicious circle, by virtue of the power of eternity. Above all, He would then have been a traitor to God who sent Him.

Christ must break the vicious circle now. If He is the Messiah, the last, the chief, the predestined One, then the very cycle of time has its consummation in Him. Then the world through Him will rise straight to the plane of heavenly, sovereign, transcendent, and positive redemption. If He is the Messiah, then from this moment on, this moment in which the Messiah puts Himself in the center of the movement of the world, the crisis of the world will be brought about. Then the vacillations, the terribly fatiguing vacillations of blessing and curse, of faith and unbelief will be frustrated by His equilibrium; then the present world, the world of common grace, will rise vertically to the plane of heaven, of perfect special grace, or it will, on the contrary, descend straight to the hell of perfect bereavement, also of the smallest measure of grace.

Come, Christ, and make the reply. Now doth Thy soul bear the responsibility for the whole world. Now everything is conditioned by Thy answer, and Thy expressed reply is as important and as ordinary now, as unimportant and as unusual as being born and dying are, as the resurrection from the dead and the return to judgment are. Ah, speak now, O Christ, and take the oath. Say but a word; be very simple, very common, Christ, my God. Be very simple, my Saviour, and the windows will tremble and crash. All the windows will break, and all the hearts, and all the thermometers by which they would measure Thee. Swear, O Christ; for Thee to do so is as natural and as ordinary as the caress which brushes a child's forehead, as a breath of Thy sublime sleep. O Saviour, speak, Thy purpose and attention fastened on God. God is standing behind the president there. He has ever heard Thy voice; He hearkens every day. Speak now, Thou Christ Jesus, and say: "I swear that Jesus of Nazareth, bound or free, is the predestined Messiah and that this hour is conclusive for eternal weal or woe." So wilt Thou bring time to its consummation. The world will never again be able to rid itself of Thee. Thy speaking will inoculate the world with the serum of eternal judgment, and thus be the loosing of every bond in which it lies ensnared. The world lies bound in the web of a relentless, vicious circle. Death and life, grave and cradle, failure and success, justice and injustice, the yearning for the Messiah and the blasphemy of Him — these balance each other. But if Jesus of Nazareth will, under the pressure of the oath, put Christ in the center of the world's activity, that world will fill out its measure of sin, and thus loose the bonds by which the last judgment is still held back. Then — and this is the second result — the surrender of souls to God, the worship and the faith of the called of God, will cause the work of God's true church to flourish until the last day. Swear now, O Christ, for the iniquity of the Amorites is not yet full (Genesis 15:16). And, is it not true that a great birth, the birth of a church, is due according to the programme of the great Creator of all things? Swear — time hurries on, say the Jews; Thy oath is due, saith Thy God.

Thereupon Jesus opened His mouth and said just two words: Thou sayest, or, Thou hast said.

Two short words, as simple as yes and no. But those two words had the force of an oath even for the Jews at this time. By pronouncing them in reply to a demand for an oath, Christ assumed the burden of the demand, and *swore* that He was the Son of God.

This was the last and the perfect fulfillment of Christ's prophetic office in the state of humiliation which He performed over against His people. In the final hour He reaches into the highest council and confesses Himself. Now He has sworn this good confession in the presence of the Sanhedrin and of Caiaphas. Now His official obedience has attained perfect faithfulness to itself. And this was done in the very hour in which the demand of Caiaphas was, as we saw, a denial of Christ, just as Peter's extravagant oaths, as we shall see later, also denied Him. Over against this denial of His work and of the essence of His being, then, Christ places the good confession.

For Israel this trial has now reached its deepest depth. Israel began by asking about His disciples and His doctrine, about His temporal, His external, His mundane manifestations. Now it is asking about the essence of His being. This question brings about the decision, for the essence explains the work; the peripheral manifestation does not explain the central significance.

Then Jesus swore by God; He swore by Himself. He is God and man in one person. That also proved to be the great concealment. That which the incarnation began and death consummated became one reality when the Son of God swore by Himself. Hence the oath can benefit only Him who takes the oath, and God, and Christ at His word. The God who swears by God is merely saying yes. He cannot transcend His own word. His yea is yea. His nay, nay. Whatever man would have which is more than this is of the evil one. God, swearing by Himself, is simply God, saying yes and no. But this is of as tremendous import as is everything which God does. Hear, Israel, God is swearing by God. The futile attempt of worldly wisdom to appraise Jesus in terms of His own disciples and doctrine has been frustrated. This vicious circle has been supplanted by a luminous arc, a circle again, it is true, but now it is a wonderful one: God appealing to God. What else could He possibly do? The simplest thing is the mightiest, and all of His mighty deeds are as simple as is the morning light. But what else could Jesus do except to have God swear by God? As far as heaven is exalted higher than the earth, so much higher is the circle of God exalted higher than the circle of men. God swears by God; why any further argument about this on our part? What is more reasonable than authority?

The ground under the feet of Jesus was not on fire; there was no burning bush in the vicinity — only the chair of the priest. Someone sat in it, a man preening himself; and all of his adornment was but a maligning of the stars and of God. Irrespective, however, of the fact that the Sanhedrin remained essentially unperturbed and that no burning bushes were seen, this hour is of greater importance than the other one in which Moses met Jaweh.

Then also God pronounced His name. The mightiest name has the simplest shape. I am that I am, He said. Could any name be simpler? Any more humiliating? What in the world could God possibly say besides this? He is who He is — and that ends it.

Now just as Moses learned to know God as one who called Himself Himself and as One who turns man away from all inquiries about Him with a holy smile and a reference to Himself, so God now swears by God.

That ends the matter. God dismisses the session. O God, He has gone already. No more may be said. He will not allow another word to be spoken in all eternity.

Take the shoes from your feet, for the ground on which you are standing is holy ground. God swore by God. In all questions put by professional theologians God refers us to Himself. He is what He is. That is His terrible name. Now that it has been uttered, the plagues begin to take effect in Egypt, the exodus of Israel begins, and we all take our position in front of a Red Sea. To the one it will be a grave, to the other a way across. No, I made a mistake. I mean *the* Red Sea.

Thou hast said. Thereupon the earth quaked, the heavens shook. The angels fell back, and the blessed took respite from sighing.

For He said it. An oath binds Him to me. The crisis has come. And all of the thermometers are bursting because of the heat of the atmosphere here. He is the Lord. Did He not come to bring fire upon the earth?

Religion is terribly simple. That is why no man can appropriate it in his own strength. And the cause of this is an oath-swearing Jesus.

Christ Vanquishing the Vicious Circle as the Son of Man

CHAPTER SEVEN

Christ Vanquishing the Vicious Circle as the Son of Man

> ● *Jesus saith unto him, Thou hast said: never-theless I say unto you, Hereafter shall ye see the Son of man sitting on the right hand of power, and coming in the clouds of heaven.*
> MATTHEW 26:64.

CHRIST'S speaking and silence, Christ's teaching and ac-tions, Christ's instruction at the pulpit of His passion and His maschil, Christ's self-revelation and His self-conceal-ment, in short, everything which Christ Jesus is, was bandied to and fro by those who had to judge Him, within the circumference of that circle which is exceedingly vicious, the circle of earthly, of mundane scope. It all took place within that circle which God had never touched upon, the circle of carnival, and of the knowl-edge of vanity.

As the Messiah He pointed out that circle;[1] thereupon He con-demned it;[2] and finally we observed that He patiently bore the wrath which came to Him when He wished to break it,[3] when He wanted to vanquish the wrath which the unregenerated life fostered against Him because of its extreme love for the vicious-ness of the circle.

It was a beautiful sight to see Christ maintaining His maschil over against the fatigued but self-sufficient drifters, who are stretching their snares from one to the other wall of their vicious circle of life. A very beautiful sight, indeed. Surrounding Jesus

---

1. If I have spoken evil, bear witness of the evil, but if well why smitest thou me?
2. Why smitest thou me? An allusion to the messianic problem.
3. Insistence upon the maschil as a riddle, which has no solution yet; silence over against the distortion of the maschil by the false witnesses.

were all those reliable lights of Israel, and underneath them was the Christ who has not the formulae either for His bright sunshine nor for what they call His Nazarene lamps of heresy. There stands the Christ, a poised and a calm judgment. He stands there with His riddle, but He holds the Book of Solutions in His hand. Why the riddle? In order that all those who can no longer sustain their lives within themselves might flee to Him from the narrowness of the vicious circle; and also in order that those who prefer the tedious movement of the vicious cycle of natural life to the vertical ascent of the Son of man, and who will be offended by the "folly" of the straight descent of the Son of God, might be made to appear what they are — betrayers of God, and asserters of themselves.

That, and that first, was the silent Christ. Thereupon Christ spoke. He spoke plainly and emphatically. He swore with a precious oath. He swore by God that He is the Messiah, the true intervention coming from above, and the One who at the right time will again ascend from below. Now when Christ confessed Himself to be the Messiah, He placed the whole problem which was being treated in the judgment hall of the Sanhedrin in its proper position. The oath of Christ discloses their Messiah to His judges. That Messiah is the revelation of God, the most special revelation of God, impinging upon and entering into the earth from heaven; and He is also the one who hereafter will again ascend from these depths of annihilation to heaven.

Both in the descent and the ascent He will move vertically, without meandering, without once tracing a "crooked line." Thus does Christ, standing within the vicious circle, draw the straight line. He draws it from heaven to earth. The reaction will either be that of faith or that of unbelief.

Unbelief will say that this man must be reckoned with the malefactors. He is drawing a straight line, they maintain, which bisects our own. That is an atrocity of devastation, and it is done in the holy place where it should not be done. Take it away, remove it; whoever reads this, mark it: *lectori salutem*. But faith will rejoice. Now that Christ permits the straight line of His revelation coming from above and reaching down below, and rising from below and extending up to heaven, to bisect the accursed plane of the vicious circle, He is healing the world and redeeming

mankind. Now He stands in the Sanhedrin, a living condemnation of all those who, prompted by the will of the flesh, choose to
return to the vicious circle and to their condemnation; but He is
also a living wonder of grace for every Nicodemus who would
flee from the vicious circle which is luring Israel to its death, and
who would flee from his own sombre narrowness to the Christ,
even though in doing that he must endure the sight of the dead
Jesus.

The fact that Christ by preaching the Messiahship does indeed
conquer the distress of the captives of the vicious circle becomes
plain to us from the words which He spoke. Mark what He
says: Hereafter ye shall see the Son of man sitting on the right
hand of the power of God and coming on the clouds of heaven.
Surely, these are words which do not harmonize with the dominant tone and prevailing style of the Sanhedrin. They fall like so
many stones, so many unassimilable bits, into the meeting. But
when Christ pronounces these words, He is as the highest Prophet and Interpreter of the words of God grasping the prophecy of
the Old Testament and explaining it in terms of heaven.

This is the word of the New Testament — in His blood.

The first thing to strike our attention here is the fact that
Christ prophesies. And it is but another evidence of the majesty
of this most exalted Speaker of God that He pronounces a word
pertaining to His kingship in the form of the ancient prophecies.
We may not forget this element of prophecy in this speech which
Christ makes before the Sanhedrin: to do so would be to make
ourselves less worthy than that body. For when the Sanhedrin
proceeds to mock and defy Jesus later on, their activity differs
from that defiance which is heaped upon Christ in the presence of
Pilate. Here, before the Sanhedrin, it is precisely the *prophetic*
office which is being mocked. In Pilate's presence Jesus is being
mocked as a *king*: think of the reed, of the crown of thorns, and
of the gorgeous robe. True, this same kingship is now being defied by the members of the Sanhedrin as they spit in His face and
buffet Him, by way of asking: "Is this, perhaps, your 'hereafter,'
your ascent to God and ascent with God, and can this, perhaps, be
your share in His exalted glory?" Nevertheless the profoundest
implication of their grim defiance does not consist of this. What
they are doing especially is that they are mocking His prophetic

office. Jeering and grinning the while they say: "Prophesy unto us O Christ, who is he that struck thee?" Very diabolical, this
mockery. However, it has one thing in its favor. It proves that
Israel's leaders have understood that Christ was standing in the
council of the Sanhedrin in a prophetic capacity. When He announces that He will come in His glory after a while as the Son
of man, He is interpreting prophecy, a prophecy handed down in
old time, and He is interpreting that by virtue of His authority
as the first and best interpreter of the Scriptures.

We can find the prophecy which Christ is entertaining in His
heart and explaining by His words in Daniel 7:13. If we read the
verses at the head of our chapter in connection with their context, we see that the same line of approach characterizes it which
has characterized our previous chapters again and again. In other
words, we hear the paean of victory which the history of redemption will sing because it has vanquished the fatal movement of the
vicious circle of common grace as manifested in general history.
We hear Daniel telling of the breaking through of the messianic
kingdom. That kingdom, He tells us, will break right through the
circle of natural, mundane life. Accordingly, we do well to pause
as we watch the prophet Daniel delineating for us the lines of the
future by means of a few deft strokes.

The seventh chapter of the prophecy of Daniel contains a
vision, a dream, which the prophet received in the first year of
Belshazzar, the king of Babylon. When his kingly father had
gone into exile, Belshazzar had received jurisdiction over the
Babylonian empire. Now in the first year of the epoch of the
rising sun of Belshazzar of Babylon, God takes the spirit of Daniel and shows him how the confusion, the action and reaction,
the swinging pendulum of forces active in the world are nevertheless always subservient to the steadfast law of God. Daniel
himself was greatly comforted by this sublime vision, for he had
suffered much because of this fatiguing vacillation of human life.
The theme of Ecclesiastes was sung into his ears every day and
was there developed in the manner of a fugue. Vanity of vanities, all that is here below! Vanity of vanities, that is the char-
acterization the spirit of Solomon must assert as its plaint over
the ruins of the ages. For what has remained of Solomon? His
powerful realm has been destroyed. The pagan who in the days

of Solomon had respectfully looked up to Israel's great king had now moved against the kingdom of Solomon, broken its power, and destroyed its beauty.

Nevertheless, there is no distress now. The living prophet of today cannot weep eternally with the dead Solomon of yesterday. The prophet sees the morrow dawning. He sees how this process of perpetual vacillation, of needless action and futile reaction will some day be broken in two. True, this process of change and further change, this shuttlecock movement of events was going on in his day also. Hardly has the ruler who put Israel in bonds returned from his devastating work before he himself is sent into exile. Accordingly, the first year of the reign of Belshazzar had most conspicuously demonstrated the vanity of the vicious circle of life.

Another time is coming, however. The future belongs to the Messiah, and the prophet receives a vision in which everything on earth is placed in a higher light. He sees four animals arising out of the sea. Mark that word: the sea. Why the sea?

> The sea, the sea rolls on in endless undulation,
> The waves divide and then unite again,
> They shift and move, returning to their source
> In myriad and changing formulation,
> Singing a glad and plaintive song along their course.[1]

We can say therefore that the sea is especially typical of the vicious circle of our captive lives: they shift and move, returning to their source; the sea, the sea rolls on in endless undulation.

Thus the sea with its endless undulation, with its movement and counter-movement, with its ebb and flow, was a suitable figure expressive of the world of men. In Daniel's prophecy, also, accordingly, the sea is the symbol of the forces which churn the world of nations into a tumult, and which whip the movements of culture into an endless ebb and flow.

Now Daniel sees four beasts arising out of this sea of nations. The four beasts are symbols of the four great powers, of the four great empires of the world. These four are: first, the Babylonian empire; second, the Medo-Persian empire; third, the Macedonian empire; fourth, the Roman empire. These four empires — the Lord tells him — are to follow each other in succession.

---

1. William Kloos.

The message is a tragic one. It is tragic because it reveals that not one of the four powers will be able to accomplish the government of the world, or bring to rest the tumult of that sea of nations, that great expanse of restlessness. The one great power will but build its kingdom upon the ruins of the other.

There is the first beast. The first beast is a lion with the wings of a bird. However, the bird must lose its wings, and be transformed a little later from a four-footed creature into a biped. This is a striking image of the decay of the Babylonian power which began with a portentous strength but later perceptibly lost ground. This is but a repetition of the endless ebb and flow. Then there is the second beast, "like to a bear." Three of the half-broken ribs of the opponent which he has made his prey still are caught between his carnivorous teeth. This violent beast, although ready to spring, will also lose his power after a while, and see that his passion for preying will come to nothing. The endless ebb and flow, again the endless ebb and flow. Then comes the third beast, a leopard with four heads and four wings. This beast also represents life's tedious circle. For the Greco-Macedonian empire represented by the leopard is divided later on, and made into four parts, into four empires. This too represents the ebb and flow. Finally the fourth beast comes, representing the Roman empire. It cannot be compared with any other animal. This beast has huge iron teeth, massive legs, and ten horns. Nevertheless, dangerous as it may be, it does not escape any more than do the others from the fatal vacillation of the vicious circle of all mundane life. The sea, the sea rolls on in endless undulation. Into this each of these animals is thrown. This fourth animal is also bandied to and fro by the cyclical turn and return of natural life. In the midst of the ten horns a new and small horn arises, a horn ever growing. In order to make room for this horn, three of the others must be removed. This is also the endless ebb and flow.

Restlessness everywhere. The whole world is involved in a game of position and transposition, of planting and supplanting. We would almost feel like referring to an eternal recurrence, but . . . but? But God intervenes and lets another force enter into this world of the vicious circle, another influence impinges upon the sea of the nations, upon this graveyard of reciprocally carnivorous animals. This new influence, this new element, puts an end to the mutable and the ever-changing in the world, and substitutes for it an immutable, an unchangeable, and steadfast rule.

Who will teach us the songs of this immutable Kingdom? Praise be to God, for He teaches us those songs of praise. Praise be to God who, caught as our lives are in our vicious circles, permits His Christ to interfere with them. God lives, and in the Messiah He manifests Himself with a dazzling glory dawning over the sea, the sea. The prophet saw that everything in the sea of nations was in a state of endless undulation. Was there only one statement which could truthfully be said on earth: We are given a moving kingdom? But prophets look up. Daniel, too, being seized upon of God, learns to lift his tired eyes to the hills. And behold, over yonder, away up yonder he can see it. Whoever looks to the hills, whoever fastens his eyes upon heaven will come to the great discovery: We are given a kingdom which cannot be moved. The eternal God now makes His appearance upon the clouds. He presents Himself this time in the form of an old man, a venerable graybeard, who very calmly and far exalted above the restless ebb and flow of the world of nations, is seated upon His throne of fire steeped in the clouds of heaven.

But this God is not a *Deus otiosus,* who, highly exalted upon His throne, is unaffected by the world. Even less is this God a "being" who lives only in the hearts of men. No, this God of Daniel is united with the world and with the sea of men in an abiding covenant. He has entered into this covenant by means of one who is "like unto the son of man," though a genuine human being. No, heaven is not exclusively a banquet and it is not exclusively a place of rest. The walls of heaven have not been set up as a partition shutting out the kingdom of heaven, circumscribing a luminous wall of festivity and revelry in which salvation antiphonally responds to salvation, and in which one chorus of angels antiphonally responds to another chorus. No, that circle of salvation seeks contact with the circle of perdition here below, in order to vanquish it and heal. Between the Ancient of days in heaven and the ferment of human beings here stands one who is called the Son of man. He may approach His God freely and frankly; for He knows that He is like God. But as the Son of man, He is also like men. Hence He is the Mediator, He is the

Messiah. He effects the living relationship between the circle of
salvation there above and the circle of condemnation here below.
No, no, that circle of salvation in heaven is not vicious for us
children here on earth.

> God is no king resplendent on a throne,
> Surrounded by a far-flung angel host
> Who endlessly repeat a single boast,
> While clarion notes in golden horns are blown;
> Long bell-like chords from ringing cymbals roll;
> Through all the sky the echoing sound is known;
> While God directs the dance, and God alone
> Conducts it unto heaven's fartherest pole.

No, God is not such. Nor is His heavenly circle such. He presents the Son of man to us. The circle of His seventy-times-
seven blessednesses enters into the circle of our misery, the vicious circle; it enters into our circle unto salvation, and vanquishes
it. Hence God takes the Son of man, crowns Him with honor,
pours blessing upon His head, lays His hand upon His heart, and
places Him not in the midst of those angel choruses in order that
He might be the center of . . . yes, of what? of a sublime festival
in heaven, a festival in which the angels constantly "repeat a
single boast," antiphonally sing their praise in the endless cycle
and ever-recurring vacillations of heaven's imminent blessednesses? No, no. This Son of man is placed in the center of the earth.
He relates the clouds which are God's fiery chariots to the restless sea of the dull, dead life here below. In His own time He
enters into the empires of the world, walks on the blood-soaked
ground still shaking with the noise of war and of the four envy-
fed beasts, establishes a kingdom for Himself and us whose authority indeed comes from above and whose florescence will indeed
be for the praise of the Ancient of days. But it will be a kingdom,
nevertheless, which will maintain itself here on earth, among men,
and within the pale of the vicious circle. Thus will He establish
contact, and a living and powerful contact lasting forever, between
the Eternal one there above and those who are the captives of
time here below. Thus He will establish the contact between the
self-sufficiencies of heavenly blessednesses, and the futile and vain
movements and counter-movements of the world empires here
below. He will reveal an immovable and steadfast kingdom here
on earth by virtue of the power of heaven. To that end He is now
being authorized by the Ancient of days, by God Himself. With

this authorization in His hand He steps down to the earth and receives the honor of all people whom the new man shall have to bring forth for His new kingdom.

Have you observed all these particulars very carefully from the Scriptures of Daniel? If you have noted his writing very painstakingly, you will discover in Daniel 7-13 a powerful prophecy of the Messiah, who steps into the presence of God *iure suo,* who comes to the world with heavenly authority, and who consequently will break the vicious circle by putting an end to the perpetual transpositions of the empires of the world, by putting an end to the four beasts who prey on each other, and by substituting for it the steadfast, immutable, eternal, and vertically ascending messianic fellowship. This will be a fellowship in which the Messiah will also include those who in Daniel's prophecy are given a glorious name: "But the saints of the Most High shall take the kingdom, and possess the kingdom forever, even forever and forever" (Verse 18).

If you are still able to do so, turn back from Daniel's prophetic chair to Christ who is standing before the chair of the judge. Lord my God, is the Son of man here? Is He here so far removed from the chariots of Israel, so far beyond the sight of all their horsemen? Yes, the Son of man is here, and everything is against Him, everything is opposed to Him. Nevertheless, He knows Himself. He is singing a song in His soul, a very old song. It is the song of Daniel, the fugue of the Son of man. Mark, He is beginning the recitative, He is announcing the theme. Today, He tells the Sanhedrin, this prophecy is being fulfilled in your ears. When Christ preached in Nazareth for the first time He applied the prophecy of Isaiah to those who heard Him. Thus He now applies the prophecy of Daniel to Himself.

That first time when Christ said that prophecy was fulfilled in Him He placed the whole emphasis upon the fact that His messianic mission was amiable and comforting, that He came to comfort the meek and establish the miserable ones. But now, as He applies the prophecy of Israel to Himself for the last time, and points out how He is fulfilling it, He stresses the violence and the vehemence of His messianic office. He tells them that the power of a king is His. He tells them that this power of the king will become manifest very soon. Hereafter, He says, they shall see the Son of man. Hereafter. Christ does not leave the word of prophecy stranded in the future, where so many people would safely put it, in order very piously and with due anxiousness to leave its implications to their posterity. No, He applies the prophecy to this very moment. *Hereafter,* from now on, they shall see it; for the Son of man is here. He is now achieving His deepest depth, and in doing this He will prove to be very man. Together with all the other sons of men He will be bandied to and fro between the forces of death and life; He will be dashed to pieces against the hard wall of the vicious circle of all mundane activity. Consequently, in His death He will first prove to be the Son of man. However, when He enters into the deepest depth of His distress and passion, He will occupy a central place in it. He will be the Representative, and the Head, and the Bearer of all those oppressed people, who have arisen with Him out of the sea of the seasons and the times.

This is His first and His great fate; and this will begin at once. But, when He has entered into His deepest depths He will afterwards again feel free to walk into the presence of the Ancient of days as the Son of man. He will arise by virtue of His intrinsic qualifications. He will speak to God as the Son of man, in communion with men and unto their salvation; He will feel free to place His hand upon the throne and to desire that the crown be given to Him by the Ancient of days, the crown for His own human head.

This will take place at once. *Hereafter,* from now on. As Christ takes His own word into His mouth, He is placing His hand upon a milestone which He has reached on His way. Hereafter. Once He put it this way: Hereafter ye shall see the angels of God ascending and descending upon the Son of man. When Christ said that, He manifested Himself as the Son of man situated in the depths of His passion. The angels, the subordinates, had to come to Him and watch for Him. Now that the deepest depth has almost been achieved, He — such is His authority — reverses the rôle, and points to the fact that He will transcend all angels, and feel free as the Bearer of the crown to make His appearance before God, ahead of all angels.

Hereafter ye shall see it. When Christ said that the first time He was subject to the law of heaven which permits the angels above to remain in contact with the earth below. God's angels came to earth from heaven; they watched and paid attention to the Son of man, left Him and returned to heaven, and there told God everything about this exceeding great Child of God. The Child could not appear before the Father. Men bound the Son of man, even though they did not acknowledge Him at any time. Now everything will change. Now the Son of man will maintain contact with heaven in virtue of His own authority. He will make His appearance before His God, and the power of God will not consume Him. He can withstand the power of God, because that power of God is with Him. Thus, having the earth as His vantage point, and constantly maintaining communion with His people, He will communicate with the Father's heaven. And in like manner He shall return to the earth in order to give His kingdom a place there, to give peace to the world of nations which now can find no peace, to put an end to its fatiguing vacillations by means of the steadfast character of His immutable kingdom, and in order to arrive at the day of days.

Consequently Christ does not prophesy the coming of the last day of judgment in a way which might suggest that He had an interest only in that last moment, when He shall return upon the clouds. For there is a continuous process of government and of the exercise of justice going on from the moment of the resurrection to the time of His return. And everything in this continuous process will culminate in that translucent final day.

This, then, is what Christ said. His word, His sublime word becomes a trumpet call, penetrating the world. They shall see it. The Sanhedrin also shall see it. They shall see it hereafter, from now on. No, not that the Sanhedrin will see it in faith. They will not see it as spiritual people in the right way, discerning aright. For they will overlook the real essence of the immovable kingdom to come.

Yes, they will not know whence the wind cometh, but they will hear the sound thereof. The source of the four winds of the earth they will be able to name. These are the winds which blow in the circumference of the vicious circle of nature. These are the winds which Daniel knew by name when he explained the storms of the great sea of nations in terms of the four winds of heaven (Daniel 7:2-3). Yes, indeed, the people will know whence the wind comes on this day, the wind which blows over the great sea of the world; tomorrow they will know as much about the wind of the morrow; and each day will be sufficient unto itself, and will have enough of worldly wisdom within itself to predict the weather and the wind.

But the wind which is to blow *hereafter* will have its origin in the deep treasure-room of heaven. This will be the messianic wind. Of that wind they will hear the sound, but they will not know the origin.

They will hear its sound; the storms of Pentecost will be heard; the spiritual evolutions of the church will not pass over the world imperceptibly. Hereafter they will see it. Even *they* will see it.

Plainly, these were sublime words on the part of the Son of man. They were hurled into the face of the Sanhedrin as a judgment. This prophecy of Christ manifests its majesty by the very fact that it does not support itself by any kind of evidence. The self-testimony of Christ is even more sober on this occasion than when He once explained Himself for John, His harbinger. When Christ assures the Baptist who loves Him that He is indeed the Messiah, He points him, by way of supporting the wavering man, to the signs which He has done to the blind, the deaf, the poor, and the dead. But now that He manifests Himself to this Sanhedrin as the Messiah, He does not refer to His past. He does not authenticate Himself by any signs. For a sign is a sign only to the man who believes. In His sovereign way, Christ points only to His future. He tells the judges of His people that He will exercise His might.

That must suffice for them.

Accordingly, Christ speaks differently about His future now than the people have been speaking of it during this week when they drew Him into the city of the fathers. We have previously pointed out[1] that the crowds then honored the Christ because of the many mighty deeds which He had done. Especially the powers which they had "seen" became the substance of the hosannas which they sang to the Son of David. Now it is true that Christ Himself again emphasizes the element of might, of power, in His prophecies. They shall see Him, He says, at the right hand of

---

1. *Christ in His Suffering*, p. 123.

the power of God. However, by relating His Messiahship with a cross ("hereafter"), He also introduces the element of offense into His messianic preaching, and makes this element tangible: *hereafter* . . . Thus He Himself appropriates that which His people did not know of Him and could not confess about Him. He appropriates, He assumes, the humiliation as the way to exaltation; He undertakes the course of the depths as a condition for achieving the way of the heights. He accepts for Himself all the viciousness of our world-circles by way of pressing upwards out of and above the crooked line of the circle of our captive lives the straight line of ascent to God. "I ascend to my Father and your Father, brethren; hereafter I shall ascend. The way is a straight way, it is the shortest way which God could mark out."

We can say, then, that the statement of Christ is a sublime turning aside from vain hosanna-shouters. He invites all those who sing hosannas under the vine of His blood, first of all, and under the fig tree of His cross, next. The vine is a burning bush, the fig tree is a thorn. By thus confessing His kingship as one which must be achieved by means of death He sets Himself against the whole of the Messiah-expectation of His day. Surely, the Jews will laugh about His statement: *hereafter*. As far as they are concerned, they would not use that word until a strong man should come who could throw down the gates of Rome and raise his flying banners above the restless sea of the world, and that *at once,* understand.

However, Christ pays no attention to the gate of Rome. In fact, He allows the guardians of that gate to cast Him out. He gives the same privilege to the watchmen upon the gates of Jerusalem. His kingship definitely awaits the sentence of the Sanhedrin and of Pilate. After all, His vindication lies behind the clouds. This malicious Sanhedrin may say that He is a false Messiah, and that His death will be well pleasing in the eyes of the judge of heaven. Over against that judgment, however, Christ puts His own: I am the true Messiah; My death is the fulfillment of My messianic calling.

We do not say that Christ did not in another sense pay attention to "the gate of Rome." On the contrary, Daniel himself had already said that the unchangeable kingdom of the Son of man would put an end to the reciprocal animosity of the four

beasts. Hence, this is the hour for the fourth beast for Rome,
and for the Son of man. Christ's kingship spells the decay of the
Roman empire. But that fourth empire will not decay because
of the fact that the kingdom of the Son of man will conform itself to the manner of war employed by the "beasts," but because
of the fact that He, as the Son of man, will release a spiritual
and eschatological power on earth, which will raise His kingdom
above all that is "flesh" and all that is bound by the limitations
of time. This fleshly, mundane life is busy at Rome adorning itself with gold. In this respect, Rome becomes a type of the
dazzling Antichrist. But the judgment of Christ comes upon
Rome from above; it does not come from below; it does not issue from the restless sea of the world. The sea of the world will
wash up the figure of the Antichrist later; he is the small horn
of Daniel's prophecy. But he will be thrust down by a judgment
which comes from above, because the Son of man who has come
up out of the sea of the world with us could not be held captive
by it. The "little horn" and the "branch" (Daniel 7:8; Isaiah
11:1), the "little horn" and the "rod," these will ever remain
two things. The first is the Antichrist; he can only grow among
the other horns, and on an undecapitated head, the head of the
fourth beast of Daniel. But the Branch and the Rod is the Christ
of God. He is born by a wonder; for He can flourish out of the
stem, and out of the *dry* ground. His growth is not a phenomenon of nature, or a manifestation of history; it does not spring
from the vicious circle. Hence the origin of the Branch already
guarantees the destruction of the "little horn," the late florescence
of the realm of Rome. "Wherefore we receiving a kingdom
which cannot be moved, let us have grace." "Yet once more I
shake not the earth only, but also heaven." "For our God is a
consuming fire" — in His Son of man (Hebrews 12:26-29).

Thus Christ spoke to the Sanhedrin. He made foolishness perfect and offense infinite. For just as Christ was talking of His
kingdom, which should descend to the earth upon the clouds of
God's power, hereafter, the cock crowed. The curse of Peter
shattered the air. "I know not the man." That was the answer
to the mighty *hereafter.*

Nevertheless, *hereafter* this will take place. By passing through
denial and humiliation Christ will achieve the glory of the Son of

man which makes itself the subject and the object of all Christian prophecy and which makes the cursing Peter a witness on the feast of Pentecost, testifying to the great powers of the world to come.

Let us not, however, abandon this discussion, until we have given some attention to the completeness, to the adequacy, of Christ's confession spoken to the Sanhedrin. By this spoken word He broke the vicious circle. And He will vanquish the vicious circle again by His accomplished deed. This much for His spoken word. He took His precious oath and said: I am the Messiah. This He did by way of proclaiming that He was the Messiah, "the Father of eternity," amidst those witnessings and inquiries, amidst those fantasies and critiques and humanly fabricated comparisons which bandied Him to and fro between the powers of the earth. Thus He introduced His word, and the high service of the Word into the vicious circle to which you and I are captive, and thus He vanquished that vicious circle. Next to the word, however, is the necessity of the deed. For He is to assume the power of God, and by the power of God to triumph over the confusion of the world. By means of His word and deed, then, Christ vanquishes the vicious circle of the world, the crooked cycle of our uncertain lives. Thus was the judgment and the blessing set free in the world.

For that crooked line about which the Ecclesiast spoke so often and persistently has a double function. On the one hand, it is a hindrance to the curse which came upon the world for the sake of sin, a hindrance to keep it from conducting the life of the world straight down to eternal death. In this sense, therefore, the crooked line is a postponement and a moratorium of the death sentence which would have thrust a cursed world into the depth of hell by the straight route of death itself. In this sense, too, we can accordingly speak of the circle of common grace, regarding it negatively as restraining the full power of curse and death.

On the other hand, however, that crooked line is also a postponement of the true and boundless life which would soar straight up to God and to full and unrestrained blessedness. For the cycles of our temporal life have by God's redemptive will been inserted between the first sin and the final penalty. These consequently are a moratorium; they represent a postponement of the punishment, in order that by means of it He might cancel the penalty and prepare the way for a breaking through of grace in Christ. These cycles will therefore continue until the process of redemption, of the most special activity of the special revelation of history, the continuous Christological work of the "day of the Lord,"[1] shall be complete. Thereafter that "great day of the Lord" will see the new life, which cannot yet fully unfold its capacity for blessedness and glory, nor triumph or soar directly to perfect blessedness. Accordingly the vicious circle which we have been called upon to deplore so often will always remain vicious, for it would never have existed if it had not been for sin. If evil had not entered the world, the world of the *alpha* described in the first chapter of Genesis would gradually but certainly have developed until it had reached the *omega* of completed things. Hence the circle which fatigued the Ecclesiast is vicious; it is vicious because it is the effect of sin.

On the other hand, however, the compassion of God proclaims aloud against the judgment. There are struggles of grace in the fatigue and weariness of the world's vacillation. The cycle to which our lives are captive represents a postponement of heaven but also a postponement of hell. It represents a delay (by virtue of the "common grace" and the "common judgment") for eternal death as well as for eternal life.

Hence Christ is very terrible and mighty when He presents Himself before the Sanhedrin as the conqueror of this vicious circle. Standing in His own place, in the place where He belongs,[2] He releases both judgment and blessing. He opens the doors of hell and the doors of His own festive chambers. True, Christ is here suffering the judgment of men; but He who for our sake allowed Himself to be sacrificed together with the other captives of the vicious circle is at the same time the Judge of heaven and of earth. Jesus' "hereafter" is a striking revelation of His perfect self-awareness. From this time on this shall take place. The moratorium has been recalled. Hereafter every man is duty bound to conform himself not to common but to special revelation. Hereafter any prophecy derived from common grace unattended by a sincere desire for special grace is but a rejection of

---

1. For the concept "day of the Lord" see *Christ in His Suffering*, Chapter 18.
2. See Mark 13:44.

the Christ into the vicious circle of this hopeless life. It is to take one's place in the electric chair in which Caiaphas today has tied himself. All moratoria have been recalled: *hereafter,* from now on.

Yes, indeed, from now on they shall see that Jesus is the Christ. To me, too, the world must disclose the fact that Christ is not only an angel, being wafted up and down in the skies, occasionally casting a glance upon the earth, proud and important but cold and without redemption. To me, too, the world must disclose the fact that Christ is the Son of man who has emancipated the original qualities of humanity in the life of His kingdom and of His free, sovereign self-existence by means of fellowship with the living God.

Hereafter the circle of this wearisome life will be broken. Hereafter nature will be vanquished by grace. Hereafter the dead will rest from their restless work, because of the fact that the Sabbath has come and the vacillation of the world has been put at rest by the Son of man. The great labor is accompanied by the great rest, *hereafter.*

Hereafter I shall take up the cup of salvation and preach His name. His name is not God only but Lord also. The question was once asked and the voice of the questioner was the voice of the tired Ecclesiast: "Behold the work of God: for who can make straight that which He hath made crooked?"

No one could do that. God Himself cannot do that. For God Himself has in His great compassion made the crooked lines. He — to summarize the whole matter — drew a crooked line between Adam's first sin and Adam's straight descent into the realm of death, in order that He might cause that history to be born which brings about the interchange of day and night, of death and life. In this history, which interposes itself between the breaking of the line of Paradise represented by the first world, and the straight line of the development of the curse, on the other side, God makes room for Christ and for the history of redemption. The crooked ways — alas, from our point of view they are very vicious, for they do not suffice to bring heaven or hell near. They cannot be bent straight, and they keep hell and heaven back from breaking through. But, observed from God's point of view, these crooked lines are luminous. God's will to grace projected them in order to save the world through the peace of Christ.

Therefore, behold the work of the Lord, the work of Jaweh, the covenant God, the God of special revelation. For who can make that straight which He hath made crooked? I can, Christ Himself says, in this sublime moment of the might of the Son of man. I alone can do that. I am doing it already; hereafter ye shall see it; ye shall see your vicious circles broken. Behold the work of Jehovah again, for who can ever make that crooked which He just now has bent straight?

Hide yourself now, and flee, for the time of the breaking through has come. This ministration of the word of Jesus Christ in the presence of Caiaphas has a more than volcanic power. It casts every human being in front of the gate of hell, or portentously hurls him before the gate of heaven.

O Man of sorrows, O Lord of sorrows. These are overwhelming joys. I see abysses and hear the sound of a volcano. Presently the veils must be rent, for all moratoria, all postponements of blessing and of curse, have been recalled today.

Christ Sentenced to Death by His People

CHAPTER EIGHT

Christ Sentenced to Death by His People

● *Then the high priest rent his clothes, saying,*
He hath spoken blasphemy; what further need
have we of witnesses? Behold, now ye have
heard his blasphemy. What think ye? They
answered and said, He is guilty of death.
MATTHEW 26:65,66.

C HRIST first held His peace in the presence of the Sanhedrin; thereupon He spoke, and in speaking expressed Himself completely. Therefore death now overtakes Him.

Now it is inevitable that death come. His word, to which He gave full and free expression, releases the storm of reckless elemental forces. The storm breaks over His own head first of all, For He is the Son of man. It strikes Him down. Every member of the Sanhedrin rises from his seat to join in shouting: He must die. Their shouting is freighted with the burden of God's tempests in this hour of Christ's ministration of the Word.

The clock overhead was about to strike twelve. Tensely hung the weights.

The narrative at this point is short but eloquent. After a long investigation the Sanhedrin have as yet unearthed nothing to justly warrant a death sentence against Jesus. But Christ Himself has enabled them to discover what they want. His own declaration to the effect that He is the Messiah and that from now on His messianic inaugural will set in, gives the Sanhedrin the evidence they seek: namely, a clear and nicely circumscribed statement coming directly from the Nazarene, witnessed by many, and quite sufficient, they supposed, for the sentence they wished to pronounce. Accordingly, the high priest gets up from his chair. He asks his fellow members what their opinion is. Do they wish

157

more witnesses? Certainly not. This one statement suffices. The conclusion is easily reached: the Nazarene has blasphemed God. Blasphemy—that is their charge; that is His guilt.

Just what, we wonder, was this blasphemy? According to the Jewish books of law many offences were subsumed under the head of that charge. An exhaustive list of transgressions headed by the caption "blasphemy" would prove too long to insert here. In general we can say that that person was regarded as a blasphemer who made arrogant statements against the law, or who "stretched out his hands against God." Blasphemy was held to be a more serious transgression than idolatry; the blasphemer, it was maintained, sinned not only against the commands of God but also directly against God Himself and against His honor.

Now this charge of blasphemy was being leveled against the Son of God. True, this is not the first time. Jesus had also been charged with blasphemy the time He had forgiven the sins of the people and the time when He had dared to say: I and the Father are one. By making that assertion, the incriminating judgment of Jewish authority had maintained, Jesus was arrogating the privileges of God to Himself. The right to forgive sins was solely God's prerogative, they held; and they went on to say that the Nazarene, by naming Himself the equal of God, was robbing God of His honor.

It was in line with that same tendency that the high priest now declared Christ to be a blasphemer of God. For Jesus had just unmistakably asserted that He would enter into His glory and would take His place, presently, at the right hand of the Father. Moreover, He had said that this would take place *hereafter*.

We must remember that this last word hereafter should be emphasized here. By using it Christ emphatically states that His suffering and death are to serve as the way to His enthronement, to His glorification high up beyond the clouds.

Now the fact that the Messiah, when He should appear, should mount the throne and sit next to God was a conviction among the Jews also. But these supposed that this stately coronation would take place in public. All of God's excellent people and all the world, too, would be present, they thought, to witness the wonder of that inauguration. God would give expression to a clear call addressed to the Messiah: My Friend and my Favored One, take the higher place of honor.

But that which Jesus lays claim to here in the presence of this Sanhedrin does not correspond to the features of that other picture at all. This Jesus would be known as the Messiah and would experience His coronation hereafter. In other words, He makes the coronation independent of the world of visible things. Very facilely He ties up that sublime, heavenly event with His own actual suffering and with His death. It is this feature of the presentation which the logic of His Majesty the high priest must call blasphemy. For, according to the priest's well substantiated attitude, this means that the filth of the world is being recklessly strewn over the throne of God. According to this, the arrogant bearing of the rebel-rabbi of Nazareth is unblushingly mingling the pollution of actual life with the immaculate glory of God's throne. The scum of this world is, without any transitional modification whatever, deemed worthy to decorate the throne of God. Repulsive, such Nazarene pride! Precisely that which the broom of the Sanhedrin quickly sweeps away from its holy door and out of its precious corner is being identified with the beatific panorama of the heavenly Paradise.

This is blasphemy. If Christ really is what these say of Jesus, then His coronation, taking place without perceptible transition, is indeed blasphemy against heaven, an obliteration of the lines of distinction between the ugly and the beautiful, between the profane and the holy.[1]

This, then, becomes the most important—or better, the only— count in the formulation of the charge against Jesus as drawn up by the Sanhedrin: blasphemy.

Now it occurs to us at once that Caiaphas is sounding a very *different* note at this time from that which he struck when he first advised the Sanhedrin to lead Christ to His death. We have observed before[2] that Caiaphas, as the president of the Sanhedrin, pleaded for the necessity of Jesus' death. Then his argument had been a different one. This one man, he had said then, must die for all, in order that the disturbance He causes may not induce the Roman authorities to completely rob us of all our authority.

1. Compare Strack-Billerbeck, *Kommentaar zum N.T.*, Volume 1, p. 1017.
2. *Christ in His Suffering*, p. 51, ff.

You see that in terms of such logic the death of Jesus was being defended upon a utilitarian basis. Now Caiaphas and the Sanhedrin take a different lead. Now the reason named in the charge is not being grounded upon a utilitarian basis which would necessarily be a human one, but upon a legal basis which is divine. First it had been argued that Jesus' death was desirable in order to keep the body of the Jewish people wholesome and well: the social unity of God's people required His death. At this time, on the contrary, His death is deemed necessary in order to preserve the spiritual unity existing between God and His people. The argument now goes that if this man who has blasphemed God does not die, His sin will not merely call out the *Roman* sword but also arouse the wrath of *God* against the guilty people. When they had first considered the case of the Nazarene, they had concluded not so much that the intolerance of the Sanhedrin simply had to cast Him out as that the intolerance of Roman authority, which simply would brook no mass revolt, could not be ignored. At the basis of this argument, you see, had lain the assumption that they themselves might, if necessary, still have been able to endure the Nazarene. But here, in this last session, the members of the Sanhedrin make an appeal to the Holy intolerance of God. It is *heaven* that cannot tolerate the blasphemer. Again, you see, the Sanhedrin divest themselves of the responsibility for intolerance by appealing to the law of God, a law which, as it happens, makes it binding upon office-bearers to put the blasphemer out of the midst of the people. Just as in the ancient Paradise, man had placed the responsibility for his conduct upon his neighbor, upon the outside world represented by the woman and the serpent, first, and upon God Himself, who after all had "given" the woman, then, just so the responsibility is now first transferred to the outside world represented by Rome, and then to God Himself. "Here we stand: we can do nothing else." Necessity demands that we act as we do.

We do well to note this attempt on the part of the Sanhedrin to divest themselves of responsibility. It shows us how gruesome is the blasphemy—we reverse the charge—which is given expression in the pathetic symbol resorted to by Caiaphas when he rends his clothes. We read that the high priest did indeed rend his garments. The action was a symbol of grief. It is a symbol which recurs often both in the Bible and in other books as the appropriate token for giving expression to a sense of abject misery.

Now we shall not ask, as so many have had a way of doing, just what clothes Caiaphas rent at this time. The text gives us no assurance at all on this point. There is no basis for thinking in this connection, of the official priestly cloak, and even less of the robes worn by the high priest, for they were not in the temple, and the official temple-dress was consequently unnecessary. But to ferret one's way into such particulars can hardly be justified. True, it is worth remarking that to a certain extent and under certain circumstances the practice of rending his clothes was forbidden to the priest. In general it can be said that he was not allowed to give expression in this way to mourning. The priest does not keep his eyes bent to the earth, but raises them up to God. According to the stipulations of the law, therefore, he was not allowed to mourn the death of a private person. The death of members of the family might perturb and excite others, and these might be allowed a glance at the grave and a day of weeping, but the high priest, and in general even the priest, always had to uphold the dignity of his office. Isaiah, the moment children were born to him, immediately acted as a prophet, and—as is evident from the name given the children—he related this happy domestic event organically to his official calling. Just so the priest, one whose soul had been excited to zeal by official fire, might not allow himself to be detained by taking a glance at the grave, and might not, together with profane people, rend his garments because of a death in the family. In Israel every office proclaims aloud the great ultimatum: let the dead bury the dead, but do thou, O bearer of the office, come quickly! Profane people take a day off for the funeral; they rend their garments; they weep at the gates of the cemetery. But priests are office bearers; they keep their attention unswervingly fixed upon the living God. He is their destination; en route to Him, they must keep their face raised to the sun. The priest is on his way to the eternal East; consequently no death may detain him. God's servant may "greet no one on the way." That means that he may not be distracted by the living. And might he then let himself be held back by the dead? No, those who appreciate the priesthood as a full consecration of their persons, of their strength, and of their gifts to God, as a turning to

God which can brook no turning back once the hand has been set to the plough—these will understand that the priesthood may not rend its garments in the presence of the dead. That which lies at the periphery of actual, mundane life, may not deflect the priest. He must ever turn and return to the center of things. No mere incident may move a priest to mourning, for his laughing and weeping, his putting on and rending of clothes represent ministration, approach to God, persistent concern about the central truth of God and communion with God.

Observed from this point of view,[1] the rent garment of Caiaphas the high priest is nothing but the result of his "big" words about Jesus' "big" words. Jesus had said: "I am the Messiah; my enthronement will soon take place; and he who does not believe this blasphemes God." That was *Jesus'* significant statement. Caiaphas follows in turn with his and says: "To say that is to speak blasphemy." Thereupon he rends his clothes by way of saying that this Nazarene and his spoken declaration were not merely an incident, an externality, a tiny speck on the periphery of Israel's life, but that it involves the *nervus rerum,* the quintessence of life and death, of truth and falsehood. As Caiaphas would have it, that which Jesus the Nazarene says here is not a passing incident which the high priest may ignore inasmuch as this man of Nazareth will himself see to it that He and His work are interred in the graveyard. No, Caiaphas maintains, He is the greatest obstacle to the work of God in Israel. The Nazarene is worth going to the trouble of rending his clothes for, inasmuch as he attacks the essence of Israel's religion; God has His bow in His hand, and will send the shaft straight to the heart of the Sanhedrin unless that body puts this transgressor out of the way together with all the ungodly. By making use of this token, Caia-

---

1. We agree with the interpretation defended by P. G. Groenen, *op. cit.,* p. 261, who says that the prohibition of the practice of rending one's clothes does not apply to priests in general. Compare also Grosheide, *op. cit.,* pp. 332, 333. True, some think that we may infer from Leviticus 10:6 and 21:10 that the priest may on no occasion resort to rending his garment. "But in Leviticus 10:6 some mention is made of a special occasion. In other words, the priests were not allowed to manifest tokens of mourning for Nadab and Abihu who were killed by the fire of the Lord; and in Leviticus 21:10 allusion is made to a manifestation of sorrow on the occasion of the death of a private person. However, the prohibition did not hold for other circumstances as is apparent from I Mach. 11:71. And was it not required of the priest that he be more sensitive to blasphemy than any other person on this occasion?" (Groenen, p. 261).

phas presents the problem of the day as being one of unusual importance. The priest who ordinarily may permit himself to be detained by nothing is now being withheld on his route to the Father's heart by this Nazarene. By the act of rending his clothes Caiaphas ascribes to the event of the day a singular importance. According to Jewish rabbis, blasphemy deserved the practice of rending one's clothes. Eliakim, Shebna, and Joah came to Hezekiah in rent clothes because Rabshakeh, the commander in chief of the army of Sennacherib, had blasphemed the God of Israel (see II Kings 18:37). We can say, then, that when the high priest rends his clothes because of this day's blasphemy, he is taking upon himself the rôle of Hezekiah and his ministers. And this superscription is being written over the Nazarene: Fellow of Rabshakeh, blasphemer of Israel, one who profanes the holy God at the sacred wall of the city of God. Caiaphas grieves at the thought that so false a member could have become incorporated into the body of the people. Alas, alas, to think that Abraham should have given birth to such a son. Brethren, let us mourn in God's presence, for God's sake and for God's benefit. May our rent garments prove to heaven that the ointment of Israel's divine apothecaries knew how at the proper time to rid itself of this obnoxious fly.

You see that Caiaphas is appearing in the rôle of a procurator of heaven and of the great Name. He takes the burden of the people upon his own shoulders. That which the death of Annas his father-in-law—the old man is sitting beside him—that which the death of his own wife, of his children, of his brethren could not elicit from him, that the word of this Nazarene achieves. For the Nazarene has blasphemed God. Thus Caiaphas shares in Israel's grief because it has given birth to this abomination of the Nazarene. Thus he at the same time evades the great question whether or not Jesus does the *essential mourning* in God's distorted universe. Caiaphas rends his clothes, for he shares the guilt of Israel which has been unable to prevent this blot from disfiguring the immaculate garments of the bride of heaven. By means of his torn clothing, Caiaphas covers the broken heart of Jesus lest it ask Him the great question about the share which *God* Himself through Jesus Christ took in *our* sin.

That, then, was the guilt of Caiaphas. He completely eliminated the high-priestly concept of satisfaction and reconciliation from his theology. Really it is astonishing to think that in the trial of Jesus Christ His priesthood was persistently and completely ignored by the people. We have pointed out already that Christ's prophetic office was subjected to mockery: Declare unto us, who hath struck thee. His kingly office is similarly made the butt of jest and the object of disdain on the part of Jewish and Roman authorities and non-authorities: blows, the crown of thorns, the reed, and the purple robe. But the priesthood? Alas, who has taken note of that? At no time did Caiaphas penetrate through to the core of things. The man who as a priest allows himself to become perturbed about the "phenomenon" of Jesus Christ never once as he pleaded against Him saw by his mind's eye the great law of the priesthood. Had he understood the hidden meaning of Israel's priestly office, Christ's death, Christ's being bound could have appeared to him as the way to resurrection and to life. Instead, he remains unaffected by his own problem as a priest, and he pronounces the charge of blasphemy upon Him who wants to pursue the line of priestly ministration to its deepest depth in order that thus He may draw its highest heights out of Himself also. And this, surely, was the offer, this was the personally achieved power, the personally accomplished privilege —that significant threefold theme of Israel's liturgical music. Caiaphas, couldst thou not listen to thy own voice one hour? Was is so great a sin in the Nazarene that He took seriously thine own themes: those familiar themes, personally achieved power, personally wrought privilege? This ignoring by the high priest of precisely that which should have charmed the priest's attention keeps us from thanking him for what, in other respects, was a trenchant formulation of the problem. We are almost inclined to praise him for putting the issue so clearly. For it is quite true that what Christ says of Himself now does indeed detain all priests who otherwise can be held back by nothing.[1] Christ's one word, *I am the Messiah,* suffices to stop all timepieces, even those of priests who are wont to go steadily to their destination even in the presence of death. Hence the fact that Caiaphas granted our

---

1. Compare the unison passage in Bach's Passion of St. Matthew: (*Er hat gesagt*) *ich bin Gottes Sohn.*

Lord the great honor of tearing his clothes in His presence, and of replacing the opportunistic arguments which he had used before by a basic legal argument, would have been a great merit in him if only Caiaphas had related the problem of the Nazarene to the fundamental issue of the priestly office (reconciliation through satisfaction, suffering and death) and if, furthermore, his rent clothes had been but the symbol of a broken heart. As for the first, however, Caiaphas did not even give Christ time to express Himself completely. He had no ear to listen to the word that Christ by His death had to pay retribution to God's justice, that His decrease had to be the increase of His people. Accordingly, in reference to the second point, the rending of Caiaphas' clothes was not really an expression of his profound grief. It could be described better as a concealment of his great joy, of the greatest gladness that can move human flesh: the joy of self-vindication over against the priest of another order. When Caiaphas rent his clothes he did not rend his heart. He was merely acting. In his own heart, surely he was glad that he had a count on which he could condemn Jesus.

The unimpaired majesty of Jesus Christ becomes apparent from Caiaphas' conduct. That conduct tells us that we cannot even put the problem—to use a mundane phrase for a moment— we cannot even put the problem of Jesus of Nazareth correctly without reference to Christ Himself. Caiaphas' formulation of that issue is as acute as "flesh" can possibly make it. He speaks of blasphemy, he tears his clothes, and he says that this is no idle detention on his way to God. To this extent his is a true testimony. But the full significance of the problem of Jesus Christ is apparent to and experienced by that man only who has learned to see and live and think in Christ Himself. Such a man will see above the rent garments of Caiaphas the broken heart of Jesus, and will know that this was the great detention of the priest of our confession, and at the same time His great stride forward on the way to our redemption and reconciliation. The full bearing of the significance of Jesus Christ is appreciated only by those who are themselves included in Christ. He who is the priest is also the prophet. Yes, it is possible to speak of titanic pride (it is so easy to detect pride in others) in Caiaphas when he dares to call that blasphemy which is nothing less than the self-revelation of

God in the flesh. Gross arrogance it is, but this arrogance does not inhere in what he expressed nor in stating the charge so truly, but in his *wanting* to put it as he did, and in his *not wanting* to listen to God and to His Christ. Caiaphas' sin did not consist of expressing himself at the time when Christ was making His self-declaration; but the fact that he deliberately wanted to conclude what he did conclude, constitutes his haughtiness. Not his caustic speech, but his indifference to God's speaking, proclaims his pride. As for the rest, all that is alive must say with Caiaphas that here, at Christ's self-confession, the issue of tolerance is quite out of the question. Only when this problem has been ruled out by you and me can it *a parte Dei* again be linked up with your destiny and mine. One or the other, the death sentence or worship is in order here, nothing else. One or the other: Christ is deserving of no tolerance, or He alone is the means of our still finding tolerance with God. Either Christ is the object of God's intolerance for His own loss, or of God's edict of tolerance for our good.

Caiaphas did not understand that. To understand it one must be living in the Christ. When he rent his clothes he was groping for just such life. But in his groping, in his feeling for it, he was prompted by a perverse will. That is his condemnation.

We have said that it was God who rent the clothes of Caiaphas. Ah, the heavenly mockery, the exalted irony of that! In the last session in which the Sanhedrin might officially meet, the high priest rent his clothes. He said: *quis non fleret*?[1] The man who may never express sorrow, never manifest mourning, who may let himself be detained by nothing, now mourns officially, for he can go no further. The Nazarene stands in his way. Caiaphas, you have spoken truth and said the right thing. Such is the answering voice of God. You have spoken truth, but unto your own death, God thunders. The priest rends his garments: for the moment, mourning keeps him out of the service. God accepts this formulation of the problem by tearing the clothes later behind which He Himself was concealed in Israel; that is, by tearing the veil in the temple, the veil of the sanctuary of the Old Testament dwelling place of God. By that token God will eternally dismiss the Sanhedrin, remove the office of the priest forever and choose

---

1. Who would not weep?

crepe as the uniform decoration for a temple which is now dedicated to death.

Christ the high priest withholds the hands of every priest:
quis non fleret? Praise, praise the Lord, my soul, with all thy
strength.

God, we said, comes forward a second time and rends the heart
of Jesus. For the fact that His people now point Him to His
death grieves the heart of Jesus most acutely. He had come to
His own, and His own receive Him not. It is true, of course,
that the Sanhedrin could not harm Jesus, for the Sanhedrin could
not put Jesus to death without the authorization of the Roman
government. The sentence of the Sanhedrin had to be confirmed
by that of Pilate.

But it is just that which aggravates the suffering of Jesus. Imagine for a moment that the Jews had been able to send Jesus
into death without the authorization of the Roman empire, and
of Pilate the procurator. That judgment of the Sanhedrin, then,
would not have declared that it regarded Jesus as being accursed
by the whole world. A father sometimes punishes his child within the boundaries and regulations of family life when he would
by no means like to make that child subject to the chastisement of
the outside world. The church sometimes punishes someone according to the regulations of the church, but does not by that act
accede to a motion of striking his name from the books of the
world. Just so it is conceivable that Israel had wanted to sentence the Nazarene within the pale, within the limits and laws, of
the Jewish nation, and at the same time by no means have wished
to see Him be accursed by the outside world in general. But when
as now the Sanhedrin pronounces the death sentence upon Jesus
because it maintains that Jewish laws and legal interpretation demand it, and then goes on to ask Roman authority to confirm
the action, this act means nothing less than disowning a child
of Abraham, not only in Abraham's presence but also in that of
the pagan world.

We can say, then, that the sentence of the Sanhedrin having
been made in full cognizance of the fact that it required Pilate's
confirmation, was the severest possible condemnation of Christ.
For Christ as a child of Abraham this sentence is conclusive. As
a legal pronouncement this decision of the Sanhedrin weighed

more heavily upon Him than did the sentence of Pilate. Pilate gives Jesus up with a shrug of the shoulders; Caiaphas does so with rent garments. Pilate gives Him up while washing his hands in innocence; Caiaphas says: If I may not surrender this man to Satan, all my official work will be fruitless, and I have sacrificed to God in vain. Pilate says: Perhaps He is a threat to the state —perhaps, perhaps; and Caiaphas: Most certainly He is a threat to the universe—there is no doubt about it. Pilate says: His death is one way out of a difficult situation; at least I hope it is; I could wish very much that it were. Caiaphas concludes: His death is an act of justice; it is a restoration of justice; the world cannot go on except over His dead body; I swear that this is so. Pilate argues: The peace of my divine Cæsar will be preserved by His death. And Caiaphas: Remove this offence, for my God cannot keep His holy Sabbath this way; and my orthodox faith has a great respect for the Sabbaths of God. Pilate gives Jesus up while he asks the conundrum, what is truth? Pilate gives Jesus up because of excessive pressure being put upon him; Caiaphas because his office compels him to. Pilate surrenders Jesus in the name of human law (*ius*), a law which must seek out and work out that which is best for the well-being of society. But Caiaphas surrenders Jesus on the authority of spiritual, divine law (*fas*), a law which has no concern about how it can be of service to the people but only in making all things work together for the glory of the most blessed God. Pilate sentences Jesus alogically (Why ask what truth is, when expedience can be our only norm?); Caiaphas sentences Him swearing that the Logos, the eternal Word, by whom all things were made, demands the death of the Nazarene.

Then God rent the *heart* of Jesus. God had introduced Him into the loins of Abraham, had sent Him into the world, into the fellowship of Abraham's flesh and blood. Jesus' heart did beat and had to beat in harmony with the heart of Abraham. But the blood of Abraham and of his degenerate offspring refuses to accept the blood of Jesus. His own receive Him not. He is driven out by His own blood; and this is called the purging of Israel, of an Israel which knows how to rid itself of infectious matter. Thus God wrenches the heart of Jesus out of the body of Israel. That means excruciating pain. It is true that while *God* was tearing this heart out of Israel's physical body, He was also destroying His people. But that was *no comfort to Jesus.* If He had consoled Himself with the thought that His destruction as a child of Abraham also involved the destruction of all that was carnal in Abraham, this would have constituted His first sin. Then He would have been guilty of death, guilty not for our sakes, but because of His own transgression.

Therefore suffering is His only portion. God steps up to Him and tears His heart out. *Quis non fleret?* Father Abraham is saying, praise the Lord, my soul, with all thy strength. His flesh has been torn from His body; both His heart and His head have this day been lost to Him. But His *Te Deum* never ceases. Jesus, Jesus of Nazareth, Thy Father Abraham joyfully longed to see this Thy day; and he saw it and was glad . . . Jesus, Jesus, darest Thou assume the burden of Thy own word? For Thou Thyself hast said it.

But now God arises, and, raising His voice above that of the Sanhedrin, He cries: He is guilty of death. We have noted before that Caiaphas' utterance, "One must die for all," was a statement made by God as well as by the high priest.[1] That applies also to Caiaphas' conclusion, which pronounced Jesus guilty of death. This statement, too, is in this unique hour being sounded in the world from hell below and from heaven above. Both of these make use of the tongue of Caiaphas to pronounce the sentence in human language. Jesus is guilty of death. According to the one, because He has blasphemed God (that is the first explanation); according to the other, because He has taken the blasphemy of others upon Him (that is the second commentary). The conclusion is the same: He is guilty of death. The one, in commenting upon the sentence says: He almost caused the world to vanish in the fervent heat of the wrath of God called out upon it by His unbearable blasphemy; but we at the opportune time rescued the world by casting before Satan the sacrifice of this least worthy of men in order that the wrath of God might be stilled over the ship of state. The other explanation says: God rescued the world by having all the guilt of blasphemy converge upon Him, by putting Him in the place of all those who by their sins have mocked and blasphemed God.

---

1. *Christ in His Suffering,* p. 61 ff.

Never was it as plain as in this awful hour that the question of sin and of virtue is not a question of taste but of necessity, not one of utility but one of justice. Not one conditioned by the needs of felicitous social life among men but one which has bearing on the relationship existing between God and creature. Since this sublime hour the language of man is no longer a mere children's prattle but has become a psalm sung in condemnation of the curse, a doxology condemning blasphemy.

For the Word became flesh and this Word *is inescapably relevant to all things.* All human words are measured by the standards of this one Word. Either Christ blasphemes God or all those not included in Christ blaspheme Him. However that may be, no human speech after this last session of the Sanhedrin can declare its independence of the Word which was in the beginning. No longer are there idle words.

Rend your clothes; mourning befits the universe. Rend your garments, for He who has never wept will meet His crisis here. But in your weeping remember that the grief must spring from the heart. Rend your *heart,* therefore, and not your garments. In the last analysis doxologies and blasphemies are not little things. They issue from the inner life. In the beginning was the Word and it tabernacled among us; and it wants to tabernacle within us also, and remain with us into eternity. The *end* of Caiaphas and the flesh is the torn garment. But the *beginning* of all those included in Jesus is a broken heart.

That broken heart God will not despise. He yearned for it greatly when He broke the heart of Jesus as He stood behind the chair of Caiaphas. So highly did God esteem our broken hearts that He gave the torn heart of Jesus for them. They were worth that much to Him. Alas, alas, if He had despised the broken and the contrite heart . . . then had He despised the broken heart of His Son precious as it was! And then Caiaphas would have deserved that a monument be planted for him at this crossroads of the world.

Christ Being Mocked Upon the Prophetic Mountain

CHAPTER NINE

Christ Being Mocked Upon the Prophetic Mountain

> ● *Then did they spit in his face, and buffeted him, and others smote him with the palms of their hands saying, Prophesy unto us, thou Christ, Who is he that smote thee?*
> MATTHEW 26:67-68.

CHRIST has been given the death sentence. Now He is made the butt of mockery. From this is evident the decay of a period which luxuriates in the fruitlessness of its vicious circle. And from this is evident also the complete and awful character of sinfulness of any life that is lived outside of God.

Surely, to send Christ to His death is to do a very big thing. Only one response is becoming to a so formidable event: profound reverence, and a complete crushing of the judges who were condemned, yes, elected and constrained, to take the place of God for the day. For that, after all, is the rôle of Israel's judges. They have their appointment from above. It was the will of the living God that placed them in the seat of the judge, and issued to them the mandate: go out and do God's work; let God's voice move over Israel's threshing floor through your mouths. That is the first condition which limits them. They carry the keys of God. The are still office-bearers and, accordingly, they work under the pressure of the word: Whatsoever you shall bind on earth shall be bound in heaven and whatever you loose on earth shall be loosed in heaven—provided that your binding and your loosing is a genuine response to the command of God from whom you have your commission.

But there is also a second reason for active mourning and for an attitude expressive of the high and awful seriousness of life. They have just sent someone to his death. That is always a ter-

rible thing. It means surrendering a man from a life of "becoming" to a state of eternal, immutable "being." It means the letting go of a man who still moves in a world of opportunity for
improvement into a state which assures his stumbling into another world of certain evil. It means taking a man out of the
range of human sight, which is still able to see in him a possible
elect person of God. To put a man to death is to give expression
to the certainty that this man can be none but a reprobate.

Now this sublime seriousness of the event of the day should
have impressed the Sanhedrin with all the solemnity of its significance. Looking up, the members of the Sanhedrin preach a life
which is forever immutable; looking down they portion out unchangeable death. They give Jesus into Satan's hands, but before
they do so they claim that their hands while delivering Him up
have been tremulously placed in the hand of God. It is God, therefore, who through their agency, is delivering Him into Satan's
hands. They themselves are servants, mere servants, who, like the
rest of mankind, can live by grace alone.

If Israel's judges had appreciated the burden of their office they
would have pulled down the curtains of their session hall as a token
of mourning because of the sentence which God had exacted from
them. But the truth reveals itself in all of its naked actuality; they
literally laugh the seriousness of the occasion out of court. They
make fools of themselves. Hardly had Caiaphas pronounced the
sentence before the tension which the Sanhedrin has felt recedes
and a gruesome drama of mockery and defiance takes the floor.

Such is their sentence . . . Had the Sanhedrin sensed the burden
of the high responsibility of its office and the tenseness caused by
the relationship existing between God and it, that sense of responsibility and awesome pressure would have remained after it had
reached a conclusion also. For God is ever placing man in an atmosphere freighted with significance and responsibility.

But that which had made the Sanhedrin feel depressed was not,
of course, the presence of God. No finger had written a sinister
script upon their wall, as it had once in the house of Belshazzar.
But God's finger had once written the law on tables of stone —
yes, such a story was told in the history books. However, that
was long ago. Come, get up now, and have your fun at the expense of the fate of Joshua of Nazareth.

The old gentlemen do get up from their places. They have their fun, and at the expense of the Nazarene. Look: they spit in His face. A symbol of defiance, a token which spoke a language very well known to the Jews.[1] Besides, they strike Jesus with their fists. For, according to the meaning of the original text of these various reports, this beating was not merely a slapping with the open hand but nothing less than brutal fisticuffing. Now to beat a man with one's fists was in the estimation of the Jews to give expression to a token of utter scorn.[2] To these methods for giving vent to their mockery, furthermore, they add the spoken word by way of lashing His spirit and His soul. First they blindfold Jesus. Then the worthy gentlemen make their approach, accompanied after a while by the house-servants and slaves who are gradually growing less reticent and shy. They step up to Jesus, strike Him on the face, and then, grinning maliciously, say: Come now, prophesy unto us: who was it that just gave you the lusty blow? They dance around Jesus, mocking His prophet's name and His prophet's calling. They have at times observed that the Nazarene was referred to as a "great prophet arisen among us, with whom God has visited His people." One of the titles given Him by popular usage was that of "the Prophet." Besides, He Himself had just prophesied about His future. To all this now, to the people and to the people's prophet, they take exception by resorting to the device of caricature. Let this latest pretender to prophecy say, if He can, who it was that just struck Him. What, you say He cannot see the fellow? But prophets are supposed to see what ordinary mortals cannot see.

You see that prophecy is being identified here with a kind of knack for making predictions. The illuminating function of God's prophets is identified with something which amounts to little more than fortune telling. According to this pitiable notion of it, to prophesy means simply to light flickering little flames in those places which the sun never reaches. But of that misinterpretation of the rôle of prophecy these mockers take no note. They are not susceptible to suggestions such as these.

But there, in that other world, Christ Himself is watchful and alert. Accordingly, all this constituted appalling suffering for

1. Numbers 12:14; Deuteronomy 25:9; Isaiah 50:6; Job 30:10.
2. See Matthew 5:39.

Him. Again the physical and the spiritual suffering go hand in hand. Yes, He is wounded in the body; the slapping, the fisticuffing hurt Him. But He suffered especially in His soul, for Christ is being mocked while He stands upon the mountain of prophecy.

What is meant by this prophetic mountain, you ask? That can be indicated. Its contour is very clearly outlined. God, who is the Father of all illumination, had established a high mountain of prophecy in Israel. Today Christ is standing upon it. He is standing upon its peak. All other prophets by whom God spoke to the fathers stood on levels below that which He now occupies. None of these spoke the whole truth. None had succeeded in pushing the heavy load of prophecy to the very top of the hill of the prophets. True, they climbed high, very high, but none scaled the peak. They were born on the mountain's declivity, and on its slope they were buried.

Now Christ stands in the presence of the Sanhedrin. Christ is the chief Prophet. In Him God's speaking is fulfilled. In Christ, His prophet, God reaches the peak of prophecy. In His Son who is fully and completely man, God scaled the top.

Now as Christ stands there at the apex of that prophetic mountain, just after He has been pronouncing that full-bodied prophecy which succeeded in placing Himself and His judges under the full illumination of God's sun, and which related the place where He stood to the Ancient of Days, and to the immovable kingdom of Daniel 7—now that highly prophetic mountain in Israel is cut down to the level of the plain of Moab. Remember, this is done not by the Romans nor by the pagans but by the chief officers among His own people. They take the tension out of the atmosphere, they release a smoke-screen to hide the sun. After all, the sun can be very annoying at times. They reduce the prophecy of the mountain top to the fortune telling in the valley of superstitious folk. They set up their establishment on the peak towards which many centuries have made wearisome progress. That establishment is nothing but a fortune-telling grotto. In it they demand that Christ prove that He is master of the trick of saying who struck Him last. Such conduct indicates that they identified the pure atmosphere surrounding the peak of God's prophetic mountain with the dank,

disgusting stench pervading the grottos of the fortune tellers and
magicians of the plain.

It is for this reason that this particular piece of mockery is to be
differentiated from that which overtook the Saviour later in the
palace of Pilate, and also from that with which He was afflicted on
the hill of the cross. True, after Pilate's sentence also, Jesus was
mocked. Simply recall to mind the crown of thorns. And He was
made the butt of mockery again in Herod's presence. You remember the gorgeous robe. Moreover, He was mocked even as He
hung on the cross itself. Remember the jest-prompted summoning
of Elijah, and the way in which the people abused Jesus' maschil
—His breaking down and His rebuilding of the temple.

Each time that mockery recurs, it occupies a different, a unique
position in the gospel of the passion. First it is *Israel* that mocks
Him; next the world of *heathendom;* then the *false brother;* and
finally it is the company of *all these together.* Israel first: the Sanhedrin, judges and servants both. Heathendom next: the soldiers of Pilate, prompted to do so by Pilate himself; in other
words, the servants and their patrons. After that the false brother:
Herod, who traces his lineage to Edom, that is, to Esau, Jacob's
pursuer from long ago even to the present time. And finally, these
all acting as a unit mocked Him, when all those who stood around
the cross joined in defying the Christ.

Therefore we say that the mockery which Jesus has to endure in
the presence of the Sanhedrin occupies a unique place in the account of the passion. He is standing upon the mountain of prophecy. While there He is being degraded by His own people. He was
humiliated by this mockery because the prophecy which in Him
reached the highest possible point of knowledge was identified with
the drab caricatures which fortune tellers used in trifling with
God's name, with God's pellucid truth, and with God's messianic,
prophetic mission. Need we ask whether Christ suffered because
of this humiliation? Hardly. We have already observed that
Christ Himself, even in the presence of the Sanhedrin, left His
maschil unexplained precisely in order that it might never be His
fault if the world should convert His most sacred mysteries into
an idle game, a curiosity,[1] an *entr'acte* in its carnival of vanity.

---

1. See chapter 5, p. 104 ff.

However, in spite of the fact that Christ, to the extent that He could, purposely kept the holy mysteries of messianic dignity from becoming the idle games of false caricaturists, He was not spared this suffering. They mocked the most awesome and most profound function of His life; they converted His office into a joke. Therefore we can say that the stinging mockery contained in the "Prophesy, prophesy . . ." is grievously painful to the spirit of this Son of man; as painful, indeed, as the nails will be presently when they penetrate His palms.

The fact that in this same hour a lost cock once crowed, and that it had to crow because God wrenched the creature's beak wide open in order that what Christ as a prophet had foretold to Simon Peter might be demonstrated — that fact no one understood, and that cock no one heard. Nevertheless such crowing would have been a fitting answer to the brutal question-and-answer game which the Sanhedrin was conducting, for it would have become apparent from this that Christ could prophesy about heaven and about a cock under heaven. Had He not beforehand governed the crowing of that cock and had He not pronounced this prophecy concerning the cock while He was in a condition of unmistakable communion with the Almighty God? Which is the easier: to say Judah ben Zadok is the man who just struck me, or to say that in this exact hour, after this particular statement of this specific person, the cock will crow? Which is the easier: to know who was laughing just now or to control the omnipotent and omnipresent power of God which can open a cock's beak at precisely the pre-appointed time? For to do this last thing is to perform a miracle greater than to cause a comet to come, or to stop the sun in its course at Joshua's behest.

However, you need ask no questions today, O Nazarene. The time has passed in which you can put those disarming questions: Which is the easier? Pray, who would take note of a cock now, crowing somewhere in the distance? The Word is within you, and is hidden there.

Things are still thus in the world. Men ask for proof of the fact that Christ is the Prophet, the preacher of truth, the great light. And indeed the proof is there; we are next to it; there is nothing between us and it — but there is none to see the evidence.

By nature there is not one who can see it. Who, indeed, would look for the will of God in the phenomenon of a crowing cock?

The one thing needful for us, therefore, in view of this, is to find the Surety for our soul. What will it profit us to condemn the world by saying that it is the equivalent of the Sanhedrin if we do not find Him who is able to consume our condemnation? What good does it do us to condemn the Sanhedrin, to exhaust our imaginations in an effort to find words fit to curse the folly of this High Council? Can scathing attack save us? Would we not be the more guilty the more we should, while scurrilously maligning the Sanhedrin, think ourselves superior to those mockers? As though, indeed, our flesh would have acted differently under the circumstances than theirs!

No, their work is ours. Hence it is unbecoming to us to throw the penetrating rays of caustic censorship upon the Sanhedrin. For we ourselves must sense and experience the criticism which God exercises upon all flesh when He issues His summons from the top of the prophetic mountain. Whoever has been made sensitive to the truth of that will begin to ask: Show me my Surety; point Him out to me, even as He is in the mockery which He must suffer on His prohetic mountain. He, then, who finds His Surety will discover Him precisely in those most excruciating of afflictions. Attend once more to the Form for the Lord's Supper: ".... where He was bound that we might be freed from our sins; that He afterwards suffered innumerable reproaches, that we might never be confounded."

This points us to the essence of the matter. For Christ, having been mocked on the peak of the mount of all prophecy, in the place, that is, of perfect relevance, of perfect seriousness, of the awful tension of God and of the angels, is now to be defied. In other words, He is treated as though He stood outside of the atmosphere of high seriousness. He is dressed in the motley garb of a harlequin, the garb in which the world in its odd sense of humor puts its friends and especially its foes.

By mocking Jesus in this manner the Sanhedrin is putting Jesus outside of the pale of law. Christ against Christ the outlaw. He is placed outside of the sphere, outside of the domain, outside of the wall and of the gate of that province of law whose boundaries have been fixed by God's covenant choice. Men may treat Him as they please. He is no longer acknowledged as having any rights in Israel.

We know that He had been thus rejected from the circumference of law before. This took place when the *servant,* in the presence of Annas, struck Him. Now His *judges* do the same thing. When the servant struck Him, he was, from an official point of view, doing so against the law, for he did it before a charge had been lodged against Jesus. But *now the judges themselves* attack Jesus. The charge has been filed, and now they say: Thou blasphemer of God and of the highest authorities, thou who permittest the storm of blasphemy to beat against the mountain of prophecy, we thrust thee out of the domain of law. As far as we are concerned, people may do with thee as they please. Philistine, the Samsons are upon thee.

Note that this time it is a *legal act* which puts Jesus outside of the sphere of ethical law. The game of mockery which ensues upon that act is its logical sequel. For what is mockery, downright mockery at bottom but the act of putting the subject of its jest outside of the domain of law? What is it but to say by word of mouth and to confirm by the act that the object of the mockery is irrelevant to righteousness, and that truth cannot assume a serious demeanor over against it?

There is an awful harmony here: on the one hand, the spitting, the buffeting, the blows; on the other, the mockery of the statement: Prophesy, and tell us who gave you that stinging blow. Observe that two elements are active here, the *act* and the *word*. The *act* of the jeering crowd greets Christ as the outlaw, as the man unaffected by law. And the *word* of that same crowd proclaims that He is the outlaw — one gasping for air, and finally dying, outside of the sphere of law. For mockery, simon-pure mockery when it is unmixed with tears, is simply a denial of seriousness.

In the whole world there is but one power which can give things the character of a high seriousness. That power is God's Word of *law, the* law according to which God and the world are differentiated from eternity, but according to which God and the world are also placed in relationship to each other in conformity with His will and according to His sovereign good pleasure. In the final analysis, it is according to that law that each thing in His eternal good pleasure takes its place and has its unique *meaning*.

In terms of this law everything has its own meaning, yes. Strictly taken, there is no such thing as vanity. Fiction and the idol only are vain. Even idolatry is not vanity. For all that exists in reality has either preserved its harmony with the law, is kicking against the pricks of the law, or is included in the struggle of the great "Yea" and "Nay" which is going on before God, the law, and the Word. Hence, when someone begins to mock, his mockery, if it is pure, becomes an act of brutality. Mockery then becomes a cruel defiance, for it denies someone his *rights* over against God and the universe. Virtually one regards the person who runs the gauntlet of mockery as one who belongs to the vanities of life. One classifies him with the idols and we all know that an idol amounts to nothing.

Inevitable, logical mockery numbers its victim among the ex-gods — the figurative language is taken from the Bible itself. All mockery which is unmingled with ingredients of wrath and love, and which has not sprung from the source of truth, calls its victim Belial, Belial![1] And that means: good-for-nothing, idler, one to whom God even pays no attention, taugenichts.

Now that is the way the Sanhedrin addresses Christ Jesus. On the mountain of prophecy it cries aloud: What, thou a Messiah? Thou! Nay, but thou art Belial, an empty vessel, a worthless one.

We are the ones who do the mocking. We do it; and they call us the most respectable in Israel. Know this, that our mocking is a luxury reserved for judges. It is an exaggerated but a significant mockery. We refuse to say, Hail, Messiah! We say only, Belial, good-for-nothing, unhappy caprice of the Will which for the rest created the world. We call you Belial and ask, What fellowship hath Christ (Messiah) with Belial?

Thus the Sanhedrin. And, really, what fellowship is there between Christ and Belial? Paul can ask that question everywhere and at every time. Gamaliel can. Caiaphas can. And Nicodemus. And we all.

We said a moment ago that simon-pure mockery, as soon as it places someone outside of the domain of law, becomes defiant.

---

1. Compare my *Tusschen "Ja" en "Neen,"* Kampen, J. H. Kok, p. 32 ff.

Mockery and defiance are not identical. Between the two lies the dimension of law. As long as mockery is mixed with seriousness and as long as it seeks a relation to truth, consciously or unconsciously, it still acknowledges that a person resides within the circle of divine law. But defiance drives its victims outside of that circle and does this fully conscious of the fact that it is doing so.

Hence we must discriminate carefully if we are to determine whether mockery in a given instance is still compatible with God's holiness, love and justice, or whether by approximating defiance it breaks the bond which relates it to God's justice and law.

We can say in general that mockery as such does not necessarily represent a defiance of God or even of man. Mockery which sets itself up on the basis of reality has the merit of calling things by their real names. That frequently gives it a comic effect; this comic effect may not issue from the mockery itself, but, in part at least, from the persons who listen to or observe the mocker. Then, too, the tendency towards the comical can sometimes arise from the fact that it calls those people by their real names who have never wanted to be known by them. Mockery can present a man who is a giant in his own eyes as the puny dwarf which he actually is. A prophet presuming unctuously holy endeavor can be presented by the caricaturists in all the meagerness of his spirit and the lethargy of his intelligence within which he activistically and officiously bobs back and forth; his confines are limited, he never undertakes competition in the great arena of the spirit. Again, a man who gets up on the high pedestal of philanthropy can be revealed by the mocker as one who makes himself obtrusive as a stickler for his own precious prophet. Such people immediately become the objects of mockery. Hence, if the mocker does not distort the truth, or wrench the ratio of overstatement and understatement out of proportion, he can be of service and his mockery can remain compatible with the holiness of God. His caricaturing is then a demonstration of truth; it is a rent torn straight through the mask of hypocrisy. It is the water which seeps through the bottom of the dyke, the firm dyke which was to protect the lowland of our smug self-satisfaction or of our unpardonable arrogance against the high tide of common sense, honesty, and integrity.

On the other hand, however, mockery can just as easily become a weapon in the hands of an undeserving one. If in such cases, this weapon causes wounds which cannot be healed because the poison of the mocker has introduced gangrene into them; the fault lies not in the weapon of mockery, but in the soul of him who manipulates it. Therefore, we can still say that in spiritual struggles mockery need not necessarily be evil. We know that God is Himself presented in the Bible as a Mocker. We read that He *laughs* because of the folly of men. Now when heaven laughs, when God mocks, because of the feverish and activistic folly of men, His mockery always represents a holy revelation of that concealed truth which the world simply would not countenance. We shall say nothing further about these considerations because they have been discussed incidentally before this. Hence if we were to pass judgment upon this or that instance of mockery, we should not be governed by whether or not it gives expression to the truth. It is not enough for the mocker to call things by their true names. The only important question is whether the mocking arises from a heart which is itself in direct relationship to truth. In this consideration, surely lies the difference between the mockery of God and the defiance of men. Among men the difference between mockery and defiance can never be exactly designated. Neither is found in a pure condition in the human heart. Human mockery is always mixed with other ingredients. Hence it will always be fraught with danger — especially with danger to the mocker himself. Yes, he will often, while mocking, be speaking the truth. But if the sin which dwells in his own heart has not yet been consumed he is, to the extent that such sin in his bosom still contributes to the mockery arising there, in principle like the devil. The devil also tells truths about others. But he himself is not in the truth. We know that he does not desire it but despises it. He is that devil who refers the standards of law to others but not to himself. Hence he does not always maintain the whole of the relationship of all power and of all created beings to the law of God. He uses the law arbitrarily. He plays off the idea of the lawless one against the word of the lawgiver, and vice versa, and he does this in whatever way pleases him most. Accordingly, his diabolical mockery may be a sneering declaration of "a" truth, but it can never be a complete maintenance of "the" truth. He never draws up his position together with the victim of his mockery under the arc of the holy justice of the Lord.

Not so the living God. In Him, to mock is always more than to tell the truth; it is also a full maintenance of the truth. God's mockery in every respect acknowledges the law which He has laid down for man and for every creature. The arc of that law is never bent in such a way as to put anyone, even though he be the devil, outside of its circumference. We can say, therefore, that God never recognizes such an entity as the "outlaw." That is the great, the infinite, the fundamental difference between divine mockery and human defiance. Why do the heavens laugh, and why does God mock? Because He places over against the false front of sin the truth of reality, and this He never does without simultaneously proclaiming and maintaining alongside of the contrast between appearance and reality that other and abiding antithesis between good and evil. God's mockery never sees its object as being independent of law. Hence it is never satisfied by merely pointing out the pigmy stature of a man who had counted himself among the giants on the earth. At that point human mockery generally stops. It delineates the contours of folly in its victim, but it does not raise the issue of guilt either in itself or in him. Such human mockery is conceived and born independent of a clear vision of the great lawgiver and outside of the circumference of the revealed law. Very often the person mocked escapes in the eyes of the mocker, and very often the mocker in the eyes of God escapes from the absolute demands of God.

Now you can see our purpose in raising these considerations. We want to point to the fact that the mockery carried on by Israel degraded itself to the diabolical level when it placed Christ, who is the lawgiver, and who Himself bears the law in His bowels, outside the sphere of law. Ecce homo, behold the man. Thus said Pilate. Ecce exlex, behold the man for whom God would not trouble Himself to place a finger upon a stone tablet, or to write down one memorandum in His journal. Thus say the Jews.

In this way, then, their defiance becomes diabolical. They change the boundaries of the domain of law in order that they may escape from the terror of the thought that to do so is utterly impossible. They manipulate the law as they please; for he who plays with law makes himself the target of its arrows. He who thrusts another outside of the domain of law, places himself above it. As if he could . . . This is the last resort of a man who is defending himself against the Chief Lawgiver, but who is unwilling to admit even to himself that he is merely toying in his effort to escape from his dread.

In this, accordingly, inheres the difference between the mockery of the Jews and that of God. God too knows what it is to laugh, to laugh a holy laughter, but God in His laughing never recognizes such a thing as an outlaw. He does the opposite. He makes the law binding upon every object of His sublime mocking. Even though all heaven seems to rock with raillery because of our derailment, still that very same sublime laughter of God (Psalm 2) points us to the fact that the signals of the two tables of law which God gave could have kept the coach of our life from meeting with this disaster. God's mockery always brings the law to bear upon the matter, is ever reaching out for the law, never intervenes unless accompanied by the law. He is, to the extent that He reveals Himself to us, the last remedy: He seizes upon the emasculator of law for his life's sake: He brings the law to bear upon him. Yes, God's mockery may be a prediction, sent by way of warning, of that macabre accompaniment with which the heavens will greet the vaunted arrogance of sin, and of the sinister prophecy presently, of the destruction and of the catastrophe-ridden guests at the banquet of unrighteousness. But God maintains His law withal. He does so now and He will do so eternally. He does it here and everywhere. Even in the regions of hell, He lets the echo of the law resound against the wide walls of every human soul, and of the entire community of hell. God's laughter is His deliberate maintenance of the law, just as the intercession of Christ is the maintenance of the Gospel.

Human mockery is not satisfied simply to take a position below the exalted laughter of God. By moving in the direction of the satanic, it puts itself in opposition to God's mockery.

To such mockery, to such defiance, the taint of sin necessarily clings. Hence it in turn immediately becomes the object of God's sublime laughing. The defiance of the people who beat, and spit upon, the Christ, and who degrade His prophetic office to the level of the meanest fortune telling, strikes truth full in the face, refuses to call Christ by His right name, and if it can, tries by ignoring it to put Christ's work to death. But the chief thing is that their mockery, which turns into defiance at last, places Christ outside of the sphere of law. The soldiers of Pilate at least threw a mock-garment around Jesus, but Their Eminences, the Sanhedrin, let the outlaw stand outside of the sphere of justice altogether. They let Jesus wander around through the universe naked. They do not bring the law to bear upon Him. Even though He is called the arch-liar, they do not call Him to repentance. They do not call upon God. In fact, they do not even surrender Him into Satan's hands.

If only they had done that much: if only they had given Christ up to Satan, for — this may seem strange to some — delivering Christ up to Satan is quite different from defying Him. Had Christ, in a formal session, after God's name had been called upon and full cognizance had been taken of all the incisive words of the law, been delivered up to Satan by the Jewish authorities, He would at least have been subjected to a process which recognized the magnitude of the event. Then His sentence and everything which followed it would have remained a part of that great synthesis of binding seriousness and of the eternal, infinite, and weighty dispensation of the law. Then the soul and spirit of the judges would have been moved equally by and their attention concentrated on death and life, hell and heaven, Satan and God, world and church, falsehood and truth, eternal woe and eternal weal, absolute yea and absolute nay — just as the soul and spirit of Paul were moved when in an hour of prayer he and the church at Corinth were united in spirit and purpose, even though he was absent from them in body. Yea, just as Paul and the church at Corinth were when, together with the church, he sent out the energies of prayer to God and delivered into Satan's hands the hardened sinner of that church (I Corinthians 5). Had the Sanhedrin, after struggling with God in just this way, delivered Christ up into Satan's hand, their sin would have been less severe. Their act, then, would at least have been taking cognizance of law. They would have been able to say with trembling lips: O God, here we stand; we cannot do otherwise. God help us. Amen.

But no trace of such spiritual trouble is perceptible in the Sanhedrin. They do not surrender Christ to Satan. They go farther: they thrust Him outside of the domain of law: they buffet Him, beat Him, spit upon Him, they laugh, they grin, and they do it in unison, master and servants together.

In doing this they become guilty of what can no longer be called mockery. This is not mockery but defiance, poisonous and demonic. This is not giving a condemned man to Satan, the giving accompanied by a broken heart, and the whole done in the name of God. There is no summoning of the law here, no asking the law to set up its walls on all sides of this meeting of judges and of accused. No, Christ is being surrendered into the hands of any or all. Satan may have Him, the angels may have Him; even timid angels if they wish to, may still hurl a wilted flower at His feet, some little vestige of their heavenly banquet. Nothing matters in reference to Him any more. Law does not affect Him. Never will evangelical grace summon this evil one to repentance, or any teacher of the law speak pleadingly with Him by way of inspiring Him to prayer before He gives up the ghost. No father in Israel will ever plead with the Nazarene and say: My son, give honor to God.

Plainly, then, their mockery becomes the opposite, the very opposite, of God's mockery. Even as God's wrath is the other side of His love, and is always the highest conceivable form which the maintenance of His justice, of the justice of His love in all of its tendencies and decrees takes, just so the mockery of God is simply the other side of His infinite passion for truth, and is a maintenance of truth in all of its holinesses and sublime tendencies.

But that which men are allowing to come upon Jesus here is not love, and consequently is not genuine wrath either. Truth is no part of it, and consequently this mockery has nothing in common with the mockery of God.

Therefore Jesus suffered terribly. Mockery runs up the side of the mountains of prophecy and, having arrived there, becomes defiance.

These are unattractive because they are diabolical contrasts. If there is one place near which defiance should never come that place is the mountain of prophecy. For such mockery dares to develop the theme of an outlaw, is indifferent to right relationships, and never measures with an accurate rule. How different this from what God, the Father of the spirits of all flesh, does on His mountain of prophecy. There He puts everything under the most

searching of beacons and teaches us to discern very discriminatingly. Prophets can feed upon those discriminations and flourish
only because of them.

But Israel's judges, standing upon the very top of the mountain, distort the truth and make it obscure. This according to the
laws of a simple and inexorable logic must lead to the direct degradation of their official rights as prophets. The defiance hurled
against Christ, the chief Prophet, by Israel's mentors in the concluding act of their last official session deserved God's rending of
the veil of the temple later, God's destroying their credentials, and
His letting the spirit of discrimination and prophecy move into
Jerusalem. Into Jerusalem, but past them. For it comes with a
quivering echo into the hearts and heads of Galilean fishermen.
The mountain of prophecy was eternally defamed by its own last
sons. Then God called the unanointed to His mountain — unanointed, yes, but bearers of His own pure spirit. His doing so
was an act of *justice* as well as an act of grace.

Meanwhile we must not forget that this mockery constituted
awful suffering for the Christ. When defiance thrust Him *outside
of the domain of law,* His true, His mysterious being as it *is* basically and essentially, was being ignored. The secret meaning, the
hidden logic, the logos in the life of the incarnate Logos — all
these were brutally negated. One hesitates to touch on these things,
for these hands tremble only when the lightning visibly strikes
here and there with a thundering report. But it was most excruciating suffering to Christ, when He who bore the law in His
bowels, was ejected from the pale of law.

Nevertheless — to this point was He come. Necessity demanded it. Had Christ been condemned for anything which was peculiar or characteristic of Himself as such, He would not have been
in His person what He had to become: namely, the falling and
rising of many in Israel. Christ as a living person can never be
separated from His work. Either the whole Christ is condemned
by the "flesh" or the whole Christ is appropriated and embraced
by the "spirit." Therefore we can say that the defiance hurled
against Him on the mountain of prophecy was not an accident.
It is precisely in this defiance that the denial of Christ reaches its
bottom. It placed the Lawgiver outside of the law; it removed
the Preacher of Truth from all problems of truth; it removed the

Bearer of judgment far from all serious and whimsical issues.

The world must necessarily arrive at an outlawed Christ at last. This diabolical invention is but the continuation of the old folly of sin which once worked in the dark at the door of God's house and took the lie for granted in the God of truth.

This was the keenest edge of Christ's acute pain. In the very moment in which heaven must laugh because of the folly of men, of men, that is, who name their lawgiver an outlaw, Christ Himself *may not laugh.* The clear, uninhibited vision with which God is able to see the mountain of all prophecy, and the high vantage point which God enjoys, are not possible to the *man* Christ at this time. This time afflictions engulf Him *from below.* In Gethsemane there was a resting point; in the garden His irony discovered the equilibrium; there His groping soul could find itself again in order that, after being reinforced by God, He might continue on the way. But now He is again being driven away from that resting place. The drama of His passion has reached the second act and it moves on without interruption. There is no respite here; instead a perturbation continues the battle in His soul. The same Jesus who in Gethsemane could triumph and express His triumph in the confident utterance, *Sleep on now, and rest,* cannot at this time say: *Have at me, buffet me to your heart's content.* For feverish restlessness drives Him on. Judgment strikes him. Besides, they whom He sees around Him here, and whose foul breath is blown into his blindfolded face are not disciples, but enemies.

However, Christ may not allow Himself to succumb to this passion in a passive way. His suffering must ever be a *laboring,* and He must persevere in the labor. We should like to characterize the labor of Christ's soul which is prompted by the defiance which is hurled against Him as the labor of prophetic discrimination and also the labor of a mediator's love.

In the first place He must suffer the labor which is caused by trying to keep things clearly discriminated. Yes, the eyes of His body have been blindfolded, but those of his Spirit have not. Who, indeed, could blindfold the eyes of Christ's spirit? No, He sees, He discriminates, He remains the spiritual man, and thus He preserves Himself and us. "Prophesy, prophesy," they tell Him. And to themselves they say, "He cannot, He will not succeed to-day." But they do not know that it is precisely as a prophet that

He is laboring heavily. For prophecy is much more than a knack
for guessing the names of the people who happen to be blessing
or cursing one. To prophesy is to see God's name, to hear God's
name, to preach God's name, and to clearly discern God's being.

And in this sense, Christ prophesied. His prophecy in this particular hour inheres in the concrete ability to "distinguish the body
of the Lord" even in the face of the man Jesus who is being spat
upon at this time.

Prophesy, O Christ: who is he that struck thee? Now note
this. He knows very well who it is that struck Him. Repeatedly
He answers: It is God. And again the reply comes: It is God
who smites me. Thus does Christ distinguish the great God who
is doing this buffeting in the presence of these milling Jews. Christ
has continued in the maintenance of His Holy Supper. He dis-
tinguishes the body of the Lord though it be covered with spittle.
Praised be He who stood at the table of the communion of the
New Testament, distinguishing the body of the Lord. Besides, in
His incomparable forsakenness He does not drink judgment unto
Himself nor does He eat judgment unto Himself. "For he who
knew no sin, him hath God made sin for us." And God asks Him:
"Canst Thou not see me?" Yes, Father who art in heaven, He sees
Thee; the bandage which is blinding His eyes proves to be a favor;
to the extent that He is not distracted from the outside, He is bet-
ter able to look inside and to set His soul in search of God.

To see God means to see distinctions, to see discriminatingly.
To see God means to discover differences, to have perspective, to
see distance, to stand and to remain standing erect on the mountain of the prophets. Thus does Christ discriminate sharply and
lucidly. He labors and labors. His struggle is carried on while
He is mute, but it works profoundly and intensely, ever distinguishing. These by their scurrilous attacks upon Him are trying to
drive Him from the prophetic mountain; but He climbs it and
scales the peak.

Lord, art Thou seeing clearly, art Thou making sharp distinctions? Ah, see on now, for Thy own sake; see on, lest we perish
with Thee. Discern the fact that the judge is there seeking Thee
because He is seeking us.

Yes, I know that now. He tells us gently — I know that too:
Do you be still. I hear Him saying that He has distinguished be-

tween the second and first cause. Because He has He is my Saviour, my Surety, He who paid my debt. Let no one tell me that His bearing the defiance, that His absorbing the spittle and the slime suffices to pay that debt. That is but the passive obedience. The active obedience must also be satisfied. By it the second Adam kept His prophetic spirit awake and alert over against God. Adam hears God and sees Him in the soughing of the winds through the trees of Paradise; the second Adam hears and sees God even in the coiling and hissing of snakes.

Yes, He is great and He is obedient in discriminating between the "ultimate" and "approximate" cause. He knows that these members of the Sanhedrin are doing the distinguishing in their way and with evil intent. But God has determined that it should take place in His way, and He does it and intends it all for the good.

He makes distinctions: Blessed, therefore, is He who mutely prophesies within the house of His own sublime soul, and who does it in the name of the Lord. Very lucidly He distinguishes between the second and the first cause, between human defiance and the sublime mockery of God.

Men say: Aha, that good-for-nothing! They are wrong. God says: Aha, that worthless one! And He is right. For Christ stands in our stead, "He who knew no 'worthlessness', Him hath God made 'worthlessness' for us."

Praise be to God: the Prophet and Teacher He has sent to me has made careful distinctions. No bandage put on Him at the impulse of impetuous wrath could detract from His holy mind. Sharply He discriminates; and then He meditates. To His own soul He says, "Wait on the Lord, Thou pious soul. Take courage, for God is rejecting me from the domain of law, hallelujah. Through me, therefore, God is maintaining His whole law, hallelujah amen." To Himself He says: "True, these defy me with evil intent; but God mocks me for good. It is good, it is a benefit of grace; grand, consuming seriousness of God . . ."

He admonishes His soul saying: "These are they, indeed, who hurl me from the top of the mountain of prophecy without asking where I will come down. These give me up as one cut loose from every norm; they surrender me to any who is willing to put me to death. But God delivers me only into Satan's hand, and God is right in all His doings. God's Spirit, drawn up against their polluted spirits, has already decided to give me directly into Satan's hand. What He does He does with justice. He it is who does this. The heavens laugh, but in their laughing, they mourn. O great necessity — all the heavens exercising their irony for the sake of the grief with which I am afflicted because of my Suretyship. But I can believe still, Father, for I know that irrespective of Thy sublime mockery all Thy counsel 'treasures up wrath'. Lord, my God, I praise Thee, and I believe in the justice of that mockery which preserves the wrath and the law unimpaired. I have seen my judge; I do not stand outside of the domain of Law. I move in a medium of seriousness. This great, fearful heart is not beating in vain. Thou art not hanging me between time and eternity as a curse, as those who mock and defy me. But Thou dost suspend me as a curse in time, completely in time. Completely, because driven by the pressure of eternity. Accept my thanks, Father: there is still seriousness for Thee and me. Father, I thank Thee for not thrusting me outside of legal relationships, for now I can redeem my people and can tell Thy name to these men who are drunk with blood now and will be drunk with wine later . . ."

A Christ who could labor as hard as this and discriminate as keenly as this never failed of being the Surety and Mediator. He finds reconciliation for us with God. He suffers the mockery in our stead. It is in our place that He endures the mockery of God and the defiance of Satan.

The mockery of God and the defiance of Satan, yes. For we have deserved God's grand mocking. We are the dwarfs who kicked against the throne of God. We ordered our expensive seven-league boots for our violent attack against God's throne — but the throne does not budge. We call our names great; and we are incomparably small. We call our sin virtue, though it represents folly and enmity without. We present our wiles and our lies as though they were serious and indicated a passion for the truth. However they are but the generation of vipers. Then comes God's mockery; then comes His sublime laughter. He humiliates us even though as He does so He brings salvation to us. The mockery of God may be very terrible, but it makes no man an outlaw. It cuts the soul in two, but it does so in order that the divided soul can be united in the fear of God's name. Only if in this earthly life we remain God's enemies essentially will God put that deplorable condition on display in the cracks and crevices of the perfect house of sorrow. And even then He will not cut us loose from the law, but will keep it binding for us eternally.

We have earned the mockery of God, for we have earned the punishment of hell. But Christ wanted to take our place. The fact that in the Mediator's progress to the stage of God's mocking He never once lost the proper distinctions, spells our salvation. A Saviour who can keep His eyes upon God can also discover His people among those who spit and scoff; He can include us in His strong will, in the plan of His redemption, and in the deed which, at any moment now, will fulfill that plan.

We must say more, however. The defiance of Satan was also deserved. By our sin we have subjected ourselves to the master of our own choice. The master is Satan. We who thought we could remove God from His own litigation by sinfully opening a case against Him, have as our punishment been given to Satan by the justice of God. Then — it had been our will — God's mockery delivered us up to Satan's defense. In Satan, mockery is demoniacal. True, he caustically calls things by their right names. And to that extent He differs from the people who in their mocking distort that truth, in part at least, and who cannot, therefore, name the victim by His full, real name. But Satan never keeps his spirit pure. Although he is himself subjected to the mockery of God, nevertheless he carries on his own defiance over against others who share his condemnation. Although he is himself related to sin, he demonstrates its ludicrousness and never ceases doing so. On this banner hell continues to embroider all its maxims. Just as a Satan hurls his defiance at those in hell, so every person there who is steeped in sin hates every other person. The one curses the other and mocks his afflictions. Hell is so perfectly sustained by the principle of dissolution, of separation, that it is comforted by the fall of those who arrive there. Thus hell becomes the comfortless world of defiance, as well as the deep abyss of God's dismissed prophets. Dismissed prophets, indeed. For seeing distinctions clearly is a gift which returns to everyone as soon as the vain banquet of his revelry in sin has ended. Hence the defiance of every man in hell, of every other man there is but its sinister business. It is the continuous laughing out of court of seriousness, of infinite things, by the grim byplay of desperate defiance. And yet it is at the same time a vain pretense at seriousness, inasmuch as it tried to measure every small norm by the great standard of God.

It is a comfort to us to know that Christ was defied in our stead. He was tried on the mountain of the prophets. There, back of the curtain of death, He tasted of the hellish terror which exists in the deep abyss of all dismissed prophets. The Sanhedrin has a world-wide significance. The judgment of God makes its last members top-heavy. Then they fall against Jesus Christ. As soon as their mouths opened Satan's laughter rent the air. But Christ Jesus continued to stand erect.

He had noticed the mockery and He sang a song in God's honor. He had borne the defiance, and He sang a hymn of love for His people. Because and since this took place in the world, no one can ever be an outlaw again. Now everything has significance. None will ever escape from the extended arms of God, of the God who carries a table of stone in each hand.

Lord, preserve me, or I shall perish.

A voice replies: Ecce homo, go out to meet Him. Look up to the prophetic mountain. There is great seriousness of life, evangelical and gracious in the insult which wounded Christ even unto death. By His stripes we are healed, and by the insult heaped upon Him we have our reward.

Christ Being Isolated a Second Time

CHAPTER TEN

Christ Being Isolated a Second Time

● *And Simon Peter followed Jesus, and so did another disciple: that disciple was known unto the high priest, and went in with Jesus unto the palace of the high priest. But Peter stood at the door without. Then went out that other disciple, which was known unto the high priest, and spake unto her that kept the door, and brought in Peter. Then saith the damsel that kept the door unto Peter, Art not thou also one of this man's disciples? He saith, I am not. And the servants and officers stood there, who had made a fire of coals; for it was cold; and they warmed themselves: and Peter stood with them, and warmed himself.*

And Simon Peter stood and warmed himself. They said therefore unto him, Art not thou also one of his disciples? He denied it, and said, I am not. One of the servants of the high priest, being his kinsman whose ear Peter cut off, saith, Did not I see thee in the garden with him? Peter then denied again: and immediately the cock crew.

And again he denied with an oath, I do not know the man. And after a while came unto him they that stood by, and said to Peter, Surely thou also art one of them; for thy speech bewrayeth thee. Then he began to curse and swear, saying, I know not the man. And immediately the cock crew.

JOHN 18:15-18; 25-27; MATTHEW 26:72-74.

B EFORE touching on the subject of Peter's denial of Christ it will be worth our while to ask ourselves just what we expect to discuss. Perhaps it is not putting it too boldly to say that in many of our sermons about Peter's denial we introduce a break into the passion story, a kind of pause which recurs annually during the seven-week season of Lent. Not that we sever the text we choose from the gospel of the passion, for no one would think of doing that. But the moment many of us begin to ponder

this "episode," we all too frequently follow in the rut of an ap-
plicatory sermon about Peter's *soul,* or otherwise set ourselves
the task of presenting a study "zur Psychologie des Petri." Then
we speak, either with sympathy or disgust, about Peter's act of
denial, add an application in which the audience is compared with
Peter, and, depending upon our personal attitude at the time, draw
certain conclusions from these parallelisms. Much reference, of
course, is made to Peter's remorse and to his fears. This is generally done in a poetical form; at least the treatment is always
a lyrical one. Perhaps Jesus does come in for some consideration;
perhaps He is alluded to once or twice—say, when He looks upon
Peter and when His glance causes Peter to burst into tears. In
other words, two favorite themes generally arise from this connection: the "glance" which Jesus casts upon Peter, and the tears
which he wept bitterly. Now we will admit that much significance
can be attached to the effect of the eyes of Jesus upon those of
Peter. For we, too, believe that the mastery which Jesus exerted
with His eyes when He looked upon Peter was a far-reaching and
salutary one.[1]

We ask leave to remark, however, that a sermon which limits
itself to these considerations is something quite different from a
preaching of the suffering Christ. All times are fit occasions to
talk about the tears which Peter wept, about the potency inhering
in Jesus' eyes, and about the conflict in the soul of Jesus' impetuous pupil, Simon Peter. All times are fit occasions for that; it
makes no difference whether the day be included in the passion
weeks indicated on the calendar of the church. But he who would
preach the suffering Christ must not present psychological sketches
"based on" Peter's denial, for to do that is not to preach the suffering Christ. That is to preach about some subdivision or other of
the doctrine of redemption, about the course which the life of grace
takes in the human soul, and which is illustrated then in the dramatic story of Peter's denial of Christ, but that is not a preaching
of the suffering Messiah. He who would preach Him may not
even be satisfied when he has pictured the irresistible appeal of Je-

---

1. At this point the author inserts a sonnet of Heiman Dullaart which serves
to illustrate and typify this preoccupation with the "subjective" influence of the
eyes of "Jesus" upon the "soul" of Peter, a preoccupation to which the author is
here taking exception. The poem is omitted because in the translator's opinion
it is too authentically artistic to be faithfully reproduced.—Translator.

sus' eyes simply by way of getting a kind of messianic flavor into the sermon. Instead, he must begin and end with Christ, and must feel bound, from the beginning, to the underlying principle that Christ's passion is at this time entering upon a new phase of suffering. Proceeding from this idea he must try to discover the route by which Christ now moves towards deeper abysses of affliction in the moment of Peter's cursing and swearing.

Unless the event is treated in that way, the "passion" sermons are not worth that very serious title. At best they are but the treatment of a subject (that of repentance, for instance, or of remorse, or of the power of God as manifested in Christ, or of the first cause of repentance) which can be considered just as well on any Sunday of the year.

Accordingly, we commit ourselves consciously now to the theme of the history of revelation in the passion as we make our starting point and constant emphasis the fact that Christ because of Peter's denial becomes more deeply intrenched in His isolation.

We have referred before to the isolation, to the forsakenness of Christ. We did so in connection with the flight of the disciples in Gethsemane, and with that of the anonymous youth who while fleeing left his loin cloth behind him. Perhaps the question arises with you whether it is good sense to raise the motif of Christ as He is in His isolation again at this time.

We reply at once that it is reasonable to do so. For the process by which the Son of man is left absolutely alone comes to Him in varying tempos. The theme will return again later on. That will be when the sun hides its light from Jesus and when God in the darkness which lasts three hours, hours as long as three eternities, forsakes Him and makes Him the victim of a death caused by bleeding and being utterly forsaken.

That point Christ has not now reached. Yes, He is approaching it. The course of Christ's suffering moves on at its tragic pace. The first time we saw Christ in His isolation was in the first part of the gospel of the passion. It overtook Christ as He entered upon His suffering. Now He has arrived at its second stage. He is passing through His passion. In this stage also He tastes the bitterness of absolute isolation. This drives Him to the third stage, to be treated in our third volume, in which we see Him suspended in darkness. The isolation which began in Gethsemane was intensified as He stood before the Sanhedrin, and will become infinite in that concluding movement which may be called: Christ emerging from His passion.

We cannot ignore the climax any longer. It becomes an obsession. For that which accrues to Him now must be a heavier burden of suffering than that which was His when the disciples fled, and when the bashful boy, that candidate for the threefold Christian office of prophet, priest, and king, was taken from Him.

The roaring of the water rushes on; the awful quiet grows more oppressive; the solitude ever increases.

In this connection we think of the statement in the psalm where we read: God hath spoken once; twice have I heard this. Note the pronounced emphasis of that statement. It tells us that our hearing is not the equivalent of God's speaking. We human beings must listen twice to a statement which God has spoken once, and we must do so for two reasons.

The first reason is that our sinful life by nature is opposed to God's speaking. Hence we must listen to His voice twice in order to learn the meaning of what it says, in order to be captivated by it, in order to thoroughly appreciate its significance. This is a reason which does not hold for Jesus Christ inasmuch as He is without sin. But there is a second reason. We human beings must grow in attention, must develop in the capacity for and the act of hearing. The river bed along which the stream of revelation is slowly driven must be worn deeper and deeper in our inner life; we must be prepared more and more for becoming receptive to God's utterances. Now this development, this deepening of the stream of revelation in our lives, this becoming more and more receptive to God's speaking, characterizes Christ also. He is sinless, yes; but He is also true man. Think, for example, of His significant statement about having learned obedience from that which He had suffered.

To return now to our starting point. God addressed Himself to the soul of Christ once, saying: Be forsaken. Twice Christ heard it. And He will hear it once again. The second time that Christ noticed the threat of His being forsaken, of His being completely isolated, is this moment in which Peter denies Him by his oaths and curses.

Naturally, we must not think that this denial was an expression of something new in Peter, of something which had not been characteristic of him before, something which up to this time had gone quite unnoticed by the Master. The polluted springs welling up out of the dark recesses of Peter's heart had long been active in their subterranean abodes. Peter's sin of denying the Christ had been conceived in his soul long before this moment in which it was born. Who, then, would dare to say that, as Jesus was aware of it, a new thing was taking place when Peter denied Him? Had He not Himself predicted beforehand that this very denial would occur? Had He not said: Before the cock shall crow twice, thou shalt deny me thrice?

No, this moment adds nothing to what existed already, to what was already impregnating the atmosphere and the polluted hearts of men. Jesus Himself knew "what was in man." And He also knew what was in Simon Peter.

Jesus knew it, knew it precisely, and knew it well. But the experience of it—ah, the experience of it, and the suffering of it in actuality—that was new. The actual experiencing and suffering always contribute a new element to the passion of Christ. Once God had pronounced the fact of isolation; but in this moment of Peter's denial Christ is feeling it a second time. The first experience of isolation (the flight of the disciples) and this second experience of it (Peter's denial) differ greatly from each other. The first time the theme is being specifically realized. The details, the particulars, of that grievous affliction begin to become actualized in Him.

Can you personally appreciate this new experience of Christ? His first isolation was terrible, but the disciples at least, when they fled, did not choose to oppose Him. They simply chose in favor of themselves, in favor of their lives. They lack the strength to make the full affirmation, but not one among them stoops to positive negation. But now, as Christ is being thrown back into abject forsakenness a second time, the last disciple whose soul's ebb and flow courses through that of Jesus, positively chooses against Him. Peter's answer is full of enmity: I do not know the man. Can it be that Simon Barjona is not quite sure of the name of Joshua of Nazareth?

We can say that when Christ experienced what was meant by isolation that first time, the fatal thrust of the affliction reached His *flesh* only. But now that Peter thrusts Him into profound isolation, the thrust reaches His *bones*. The figure is a Biblical one, and lucid enough. It is precisely that which the faithful disciple, the positive confessor, the confidant of Jesus does. This he does who was twice forgiven for speaking a satanic word. Indeed, he was forgiven much. And can he really love so little now?

That first time the disciples fled. But at least they said nothing. Theirs was a dumb flight. But Peter, as he immerses Christ in awful solitude this second time, curses and swears; his oaths and his profanity shatter the night.

In fact, those fleeing disciples a little while ago—or is it a long time ago?—cry out as they flee: I know Him; yes, one and all, we know Him; we know Him, therefore we flee. But Peter, denying Him, segregating Him now, asserts: I know Him not, good people, I know Him not. Hence, I can keep on comfortably warming myself at the fire. When the disciples fled from Christ, they, by the act of their embarrassed fleeing, proclaimed aloud: We are abandoning Him for the future, although we confess to having had dealings with Him in the past. But Simon Peter says: I knew Him not, and His future does not affect me; His problem is no concern of mine; all this commotion about the Nazarene leaves me cold.

The disciples isolate the Master according to the soul. But Simon Peter delivers the Master up to the pain of solitude as He is in His office and in the ministration of that office. In short, Peter abandons the Christ according to the spirit.

We shall return to that last consideration again. But is it not true that in the short space of time that intervenes between the capture and the nightly session of the Sanhedrin, God is greatly and quickly aggravating Christ's suffering? When Christ must plunge into a deeper recess of the abyss of curse and death—and this is intentional on heaven's part—Peter is brought into His way, and made to swear in Jesus' hearing: Who is that stranger? I do not know the man.

If anyone should think our phraseology somewhat irreverent, we would remind him of the duty of appreciating what a blow on the cheek and what a fatal thrust to the loins mean for Jesus, and how actual is the realism of an event in which a disciple can declare himself independent of a host whose intimacy he has enjoyed at His first communion, at His last passover, and in Gethsemane.

We shall say very little about the chronological order in which the particulars of the day took place. In putting together the several episodes we shall not be doing any guesswork if we form the following pictures in our minds.

First of all we must know that Simon Peter had fled with the others when the Master was taken captive. Then, when the band had gone on, he, prompted not by curiosity but by love and by the inner conflict raging within him—these made his flight seem unpardonable—felt constrained to follow the Master again. In this endeavor he was accompanied by another person. We are not told who this other man was. Some think that it was John; but others raise objections to this supposition. These say that there is not a single reason to justify the assumption that John accompanied Peter. And they suggest that we must think of this second person, who had access to the inner court of the high-priestly palace, as one of high descent, one who must have belonged to the followers of Jesus in a more general sense. Be that as it may, the right of access enjoyed by this second person—he was known to the people at the palace—was used by him as a means of getting Peter into the court also. Now it may be that this court should be thought of as the part which connected the two wings of Caiaphas' palace with each other. However, it may also be that the court lay between the dwelling place of Annas and the house of Caiaphas.

That is enough to throw the necessary light on what follows. As Peter enters, the servant sees him and asks whether he perhaps also belongs to the company of "that man." Peter disavows it; but when she talks to him again later as he is warming himself at the fire, she persists in making the suggestion. Peter can only deny it anew. The ground at his feet may be aflame—that makes no difference; he holds his position. A little later another of the maid-servants reiterates the suggestion that he too was with Jesus, the Nazarene. Naturally, this interests the onlookers. Here and there a group of people begin to congregate. One can detect a whispering among them. Peter may enter a second disclaimer, may shift from foot to foot in his effort to keep his poise and to deflect this embarrassing attention which is being paid to him, but the fact is that he has now twice lost his game. The cock may crow: Peter clings to his place. What is more, he swears an oath to confirm his disavowal.

Even that does not mark the conclusion of Simon's temptation. After about an hour, another person approaches him, and this person touches a vulnerable spot. For this fellow is a relative of Malchus, the man whose ear Peter struck off in Gethsemane. This man, moved by curiosity perhaps, steps up to Peter, notes his manner of speaking, detects that he has not yet overcome the inflection peculiar to a typical Galilean, recalls further that he has seen this very man in the glare of the torches and candles in Gethsemane, and, consequently, announces: That man also belongs to his crowd; he is one of the Nazarene's friends.

That was placing Peter "on the spot." If he were to acknowledge now that these had told the truth, the eventual condemnation of Christ would also spell his doom. Accordingly he denies having had any association with Him. He uses strong words in his denial. He curses and swears, swears many heavy oaths.

The curses and the oaths reach the ears of Jesus. This is the moment in which they are leading Christ across the inner court, whether by way of conducting Him from Annas to Caiaphas or from Caiaphas, that is, from the session of the Sanhedrin, to the waiting room which will detain Him until the events of the morning.

Just as Jesus passes Peter, the cock crows. God opens the beak of the fowl, because He needs it to call Peter's attention to the word which Christ had spoken beforehand. That is the first demonstration of might in the schedule of heaven. Priests and asses, Levites and serpents, Sanhedrins and cocks, each and all have their place in the programme of the kingdom of heaven, and each speaks at its appointed time. But there is a second manifestation of power now in the kingdom of heaven; Christ fastens His eyes fixedly upon those of Peter. This irresistible glance of Christ whose mouth is mute but whose eyes are just so much more eloquent combines with the sign of the cock's crow to break the chains to which Peter's soul and spirit have been captive. It breaks his heart. All his curses turn in upon himself. A sob—and Peter stumbles out of doors to weep very bitterly. He has rejected the faithful heart, smudged his uniform, trampled upon his banner, and all this in a moment.

Why say more than that about Simon Peter? We would seek not him, but Jesus. What did the denial of Simon Peter mean to the Saviour? That is the only question deserving an answer here. There is no gain in talking further about Peter. Simon, too, must go back to Jesus; and we all must learn to take our eyes off Simon's soul and to attend exclusively to the Christ. The truth is such as Heiman Dullaart once had Peter himself say:

> O Christian sinner, fallen in the way, come see
> A guilt incomparable in me,
> And see the love in the Redeemer's face
> For every penitent who trusts His grace;
> I feel the former fevers burn,
> The ancient fires now return;
> Defying envy, might, and sword
> Danger and death, I seek my Lord
> That He, though bound, may set me free.

What has the spirit of prophecy to say to me as I see Christ standing there forsaken and denied. But one thing: namely, Behold the Man of sorrows. He is the Man of sorrows but the penetrating glance which He fastened upon Peter tells us also that He is the Man of highest wisdom. He knew when Peter spoke His "big" words; even though He stood at a distance, He knew all. Then He experienced the pain, more keenly, more bitterly than in Gethsemane, of the fact that henceforh communion would be impossible to him. That was part of it, but not all. When certain things are withheld from a person, that person merely suffers the poverty and meagerness of a negative something. But Christ in His suffering also senses the positive side of isolation. The sin of His people cuts His soul with its acute right angle of death and curse, wounding Him positively. He must know that the seed of the woman, the spiritual seed of Abel and of Seth, is disintegrating and falling away from Him who is the crown of that woman's seed, the Saviour of Abel, the afflicted man of innocence, the end and glory of the generation of Seth.

Alas, Christ is being forsaken, abandoned, at each of His own zeniths, thrown down from each of His own mountain peaks. He stood on the prophetic mountain and there He was humiliated. The place was His own—it was peculiarly His own. Now again

He is standing on his own heights, on a peak which is peculiarly His, for God has placed His foot on the hill of the Seed of the woman. But the one of that most holy seed who was nearest of kin to Him forsook Him. And did more: he denied Him. In the hour of the crisis, Christ Jesus must observe that the seed of the woman is disintegrating. He may not, He can not, and He does not want to comfort Himself with the thought that even He is the very one who will bind together that disintegration. He feels that He is one with all the rest of that seed. The enigma of Gethsemane comes back, and in an even more serious guise his time. We observed then that Christ could not comfort Himself with the thought of the coming life as He stood over against the impending death. Now we must observe again that He cannot solace Himself with the thought of the assurance of His coming power of reunification (drawing all people unto Him) as He stands here, surrounded by this awful abandonment, and filled with a realistic sense of complete isolation. For He must desire His own even as they are in the very act of rejecting Him. Christ knows that He is one with them all. He must confess before the Father that all are conjoining with Him. Should He fail to do so, He could no longer be a Mediator in this unique hour. Completely rejected though He is, He must now, with the full force of His love, draw these all unto Himself. He must confess them with all of His strength, not before men, but before the Father. He may not act as though this were already the day of judgment—that great day in which He will some day refuse to confess those who have not confessed Him.

Certainly, the sorrow of this true seed of the woman is an incomparable grief. He sees a great rent being torn in the mystical body in which, as the Head of us all, He knows Himself to be incorporated with us. Yes, this is incomparable abandonment: to be the point at which disintegration sets in—the nucleus of the process of dissolution. Ecce homo: Behold the man: the great seed of the woman. His soul is being driven into solitude. By whom? you ask. By Cain and his ilk? Yes, indeed, by the friends of Cain. But by the friends of Abel too. The great Abel, that is, the greater than Abel, can achieve salvation for the children of His spiritual generation only through absolute abandonment. All who have eaten bread with Him, who have greatly desired to eat bread with

Him in the kingdom of heaven, have rebelled against Him. There is no friendship to support its own Author; no food to feed its own Root.

Accordingly, Jesus' soul no longer has a tribune from which to express itself in the world. Nor did anyone approach the place of intercession used by His love. Or if any came, it was but to chase Jesus away, to chase Him away in order that the wicked Absalom (for so they called him) might no longer lure the subjects of the great David of the future, the coming Messiah, whom the Jews await, away from Him. He may no longer talk with anyone. Pray, Peter, do not talk too loud; not too loud; for He might hear the voice, and the priest in Him, it may be, might yearn to comfort you in the place of communion which is His love. Then He would feel even more painfully that His hands and feet are bound, that He may exercise His right to comfort no longer. Be very still, Simon: He may want to draw Himself up by the help of your extended arms, and experience that these too are denied Him. What echo is there to throw His voice back? What resonator responds to His calling? Ah, my God, is it His lot to have to be the rock of offence against which Peter must stumble in his impetuosity? Lord God, hast Thou Thyself made the heart of this people fat, and dost Thou "send" Him "leanness of the soul," who would find pasture with Thee?

But even this is not the end? Simon isolated Christ, the solitary One, as He is *in the conflict of His office also.* Simon swore against Him by the use of oaths and it is the oath which has done this to Him. That preciously sworn oath is what thrust Him, as the bearer of God's office, farther into the abyss than anything else in Peter and in Peter's denial.

Caiaphas swore with an oath.

Christ swore with an oath.

And Peter also swears.

All these are paying in the same coin—but they are paying the enemy. They are robbing Christ. It is precisely the oath-swearing of Peter which aggravated His suffering, and which most severely tested the strength of His messianic will to redemption.

We must step nearer now to listen to that oath.

There are two kinds of denials: a denial with, and a denial without, the oath. The two are not equally severe. When Simon Peter denies Jesus by means of an outright disclaimer, he has loosened his hold of Jesus' soul. But when the oath is added, and the self-condemnation, then the basic concept of Christ's *office* is also being rejected. The denial taken simply as a denial separates Peter from Jesus' existence. But the denial accompanied by the oath is a repudiation of the purpose of Christ's existence, and a disavowal of the *raison d'etre* of the Christ. Peter takes an oath.

We shall say no more about the swearing of oaths as such, for we have spoken of that before in this volume.[1] It is enough to recall here that from Christ's point of view a casual act of swearing an oath means a complete self-withdrawal from the possibility of meeting God, and from the sphere of communion with God. The man who lightly takes an oath upon his lips has wrung himself loose from the sense of dread which he should feel at the mention of the name of God. When Simon is swearing his perfervid oaths, he is wounding Christ's spirit a thousand times worse than he would be doing if he were simply to deny the Master without the act of swearing. Peter is not merely laughing away the sublimity of Jesus' soul, but also the substructure of Jesus' maintenance of His office, the great assumption underlying all His words and thoughts, the basic principle governing all He does and does not do. By taking the oath, Peter not only disclaims all share in the joys and sorrows of Jesus' soul, but he also disavows any participation in the background and underground, in the life principle of Christ's official life.

Peter's oath, therefore, had to reach Christ's ears in order that He might be absolutely isolated, not only as He is in His life-functions but also as He is in terms of His most basic and official being. The disciple who disowns Jesus Christ by means of his facile laughter, his resounding oaths, and his positive curses, is withdrawing from the very atmosphere of which Christ says, "Only in this medium is it possible for me to live." Simon Peter, who lightly swears his oaths, completely sets his Master apart on the mountain of Israel's perfected existence. He puts Him on exhibit on the mountain of prophecy also. There the wind of God's justice beats against the innocent Jesus, draws out the tornado of

1. P. 124 ff.

Satan's wrath, and blows the poison of Israel's flesh into Jesus' face. And thus even the last disciple to follow Him sets Him apart, alone. This means not only that Peter leaves Jesus to what in the future may chance to happen to Him; no, it means that he positively sets Jesus outside of the pale of friendship. Simon rises up to oppose Christ's quintessential life movement; by his facile oath-taking, he mocks the simplicity of Jesus' service of God, a service which calls yes, yes, and no, no, and which regards, irrespective of its further content, whatever is more than these as coming from evil. Do not forget the modification, irrespective of its further content. Even if Peter had confessed his association with Jesus, had admitted that he had sworn his oaths unnecessarily, that he was spiritually warming himself at a fire of his own lighting, that he was maintaining and honoring the degree of absolute zero, the absolute zero of God's law-laden presence—even then he would have caused the Saviour uncommon suffering. Simon denies, and that is something. He denies with an oath—and that is everything. Simon swears. He wounds the Rabbi not only in terms of the externalities of His Work, he mocks not only this or that manifestation of "Jesus," but he mocks the climate in which Christ must live, the atmosphere which Christ must breathe. He laughs at the thought that Christ has lungs which can inhale with impunity only the air that is found on God's mountain peak.

Simon's swearing, then, was severer suffering for Christ's soul than the blow of a hammer was for His body later. Simon's false oath laughs in haughty and derisive laughter about that which for Christ is simply and absolutely primary. A person can be grieved by nothing quite as much as by a maligning and negation of his basic life-theme, of his basic life-motivation, of the *raison d'etre* of his being. If on occasion one acts out of character, and people mock one's conduct, then the mockery is actually a kind of vindication of one's dominant and prevailing character. But when a person's character itself is being mocked, when the scheme of his life, its basic and unifying principle, when that which for him is self-evident is being blatantly mocked and defied, then such a person feels that he is being subjected to the crucifixion of his spiritual self. And thus Simon Peter crucified his Lord, Jesus Christ. He crucified Him spiritually, crucified and buried Him as God's office-bearer, as the Author of the naive yet very consciously ut-

tered statement: Wist ye not that I must be about my Father's
business? Surely that simple statement made self-evident the fact
that He was filled with God. No need, certainly, to swear an oath
when God's own sun shines full on one's face!

Therefore we may not underestimate the significance of the
oath which Simon swore; we may not limit our consideration to
the fact that he swore it.

In the same hour in which Christ is struggling to preserve the
purity of the oaths, and the possibility of persevering in the kingdom of continuous oath-taking, in the very moment, that is, in
which He officially, as the Servant of the Lord and of the authority, swears the oath in the presence of God and of the court, Satan
by means of Simon's lips had the oath falsified. In one and the
same moment, then, two oath-swearers are standing in the judgment hall of Israel. The one swears his oath in obedience and thus
emphatically dedicates His life-seriousness to God; the other
takes the oath in the strength of the old man of sin and thus demonstrates how troubled the atmosphere of the world is, how the
heart of man has been withdrawn from the law of the dwelling
place of God, and how natural man must deny Christ not only as
he manifests Himself in His ordinary life functions but also as
He is in His essential being. Simon, Simon, Do you see what you
have done? You have presented three incidents of falsehood by
swearing, and by swearing just as positively as did the decadent
personnel of the lost priests of a decaying people; and you have
related those three incidents to a state of being, have related the
acute transgression to a *state of chronic decay.*

The people must see this and hear it. Just as Mary's act of
anointing must be remembered by the whole world, so the Spirit
has directed that these ill-savoring oaths of Simon be remembered.

You ask why the Spirit perpetuates the memory of these un-
edifying things? Ah, do not put it that way. He wants you to see
the Christ and to remember Him. The Spirit would present the
Christ as He, entirely alone, went through all the stages of suffering inherent in the word, that is, in the Word of the sermon on
the mount.

Alone, entirely alone. Such was His appointed task. For Christ
gave expression to that which He had *seen and heard* (John 3:32).

No one in all the world had ever spoken thus. In the sermon on the mount He also gave expression to that which He had seen and heard. Quite naturally, therefore, He touched on the subject of the oaths.

But He who gave expression to a statement which in conception and intent can only proceed from Himself and from God must bear His own ordeal. In the last analysis it is the task of the solitary to be alone unless they can succeed in becoming a life-giving spirit.

Today this miracle is being achieved in the Christ (I Corinthians 15:45). However, the miracle cannot take place without suffering. Hence He must be alone in His fundamental, basic motivation. He must be alone over against the via dolorosa of the word, over against the whole sermon which He pronounced on the mount about the kingdom of heaven. Some interpreters have a way of thinking which suggests that Simon sinned against this or that text which might be cited from the sermon on the mount. Against this or that text denied by the flesh, contradicted by the unsanctified mind, yes. But the situation is worse than that: the background of the sermon, the substructure, the scheme, the fundamental purpose and tendency of the sermon, it is this which sin and flesh are here denying.

That is why Simon uses oaths to deny; that is why Christ heard those oaths, and why He had to go on in spite of them, to go alone and along a way which was hardly paved with texts and figures borrowed from the sermon on the mount. He says: swear not at all. Simon, you are as ill as you are because you cannot be ordinary. The angels are very ordinary, very common in the presence of God, and I am. We swear no oaths. Alas, how thou dost grieve me.

Have you seen the Man of sorrows in His isolation? Then you may go on to say: In His isolation lies His strength; in His bondage He performs His task. Look, they are leading Him from one corridor to another. He is bound; He cannot speak; He can do nothing. The usual avenues of contact between Jesus' soul and the soul of Simon are barred by those people who are passing judgment on Jesus. Accordingly, Jesus appropriates this fact; He does not approach Peter and He says nothing to him. But there

is still one language left to Christ with which He can speak. It is
the language of the eye. Christ, turning around, looked at Peter.
And immediately the cock crew.

Those were two quakes in the kingdom of heaven. Christ
opened His eyes; and the cock opened its mouth. The last point
first. We do not agree with those who prefer to ignore the cock's
crowing. These say that the expression "the cock crew" was nothing more than the usual, daily phrase for indicating time; and
they sometimes add the unproved contention to support their position that there were no cocks in the city. According to this, the
phrase "immediately the cock crew" means only that a certain
hour had arrived. This interpretation is wrong. The text says,
"Immediately the cock crew." Obviously, the "immediately"
would not make sense if no cock had actually crowed. Besides,
Jesus had predicted beforehand that it would take place just as it
did actually occur.

Hence we must say that the crowing of the cock is a separate
moment, a unique step on the way which God traverses, and on
which He works miracles from beginning to end. The fact that
the cock crew at exactly this time, and that the dispute in which
Peter was involved reached its climax just now and that Christ,
by being led from one place to another, was given a chance to fix
His eyes upon Peter's soul, represents a confluence of circumstances possible only to divine providence. The cock's crowing at
just this time was a *wonder*. God wanted the miracle to take place
and He arranged it so that Peter's soul might by this means be
led back to its Lord and God. The conjunction of these three
events in a single moment is surely not less miraculous than—to
select a comparison at random—the rising of the star which
pointed the Magi to God and to the manger. One cannot speak
of degrees of the miraculous in speaking of miracles. The
forces which caused the waters of the Red Sea to wall up and be
released again are the very same which at God's appointed time
governed a cock's crowing, the chatter of a conglomeration of
people, and a conflict between an old and a new man.

The confluence of these three moments proves to be an even
more striking evidence of God's *providence* if we remember that
the cock had crowed before, but without arousing Peter to introspection. Now the familiar sound of the fowl recurs and now

Peter's consciousness is shocked. Suddenly the meaning of Christ's own words spoken before Gethsemane leap from the subconscious margin to the crest of Peter's attention. Whence that contrast between the first and second crowing of the cock? Why should the cock-crow mean nothing to Peter the first time, and everything the second?

There can be but one answer. The reason is the *overwhelming effect of Jesus' eyes.* Christ *desired* the cock's crowing with fear and trembling. He fastened His eyes upon heaven and at the same time upon Peter, His weak disciple. Most miraculously do the ways and avenues of the providence of God and of the fore-vision of the Son of man coincide here. Now that Christ can turn His eyes upon Peter He, very human the while, cooperates with the high God who is exalted above the clouds but who is also very present, and who is present in Jesus' words and heart. God's government and maintenance together form the mystery of His providence. And God's providence is an almighty and omnipresent power. Accordingly, it is God's providence which, according to the will of God, opens and closes the eyes of men, and which opens and closes the door of their normal and of their subconscious life according to His genuine counsel. It is that providence which permits the complications of the discussion between Christ and the Sanhedrin and the discussion between Peter and the soldiers and servants to issue in a climax in its own way and in its own time. This providence it is which in its sublime purposiveness opens and closes the mouth of a fowl in order that everything may at exactly the right time perform its right function in the universe. Everything—servants, soldiers, asses, slaves, and the jealousies of slaves, these and the soul of my Lord Jesus who is being subjected to murder,—all combine to perform their function at precisely the right time.

This is the one thing—this is the providence of God, the almighty and omnipresent power of God which is present also in a cock's mouth; this, and the *concursus* of Jesus who as the servant of servants carefully seeks out His route in His striving to reach God's providence.

And the second thing is the potent humanity of Jesus Christ. As a *servant* He worked in the direction of the providence of God; now He will be clothed upon with power from above. God puts an overwhelming potency into His tired eyes. Now those eyes can lure with a potency as irresistible as the cords of love. God has a commission for His Jesus. Just for the moment, God wants to lead Christ past Simon. Just for a moment God will give Christ the chance to do something, to do everything for Simon. For just one moment God will create the possibility of human fellowship between Simon and Jesus. Only the language of the eyes will be possible there, however; and eyes are always restricted to a narrow focus. Nevertheless, on that very narrow path, in that split second in which God's speeding judgment leads Him past the restless soul of Peter, Christ must fasten all the energies of His genuine humanity on Simon's soul in order that the crest of Peter's conscious attention may again recognize the symbol of the crowing cock, and in order that the power of Satan may now be broken in him. As genuine man, Christ must by means of His eyes exert an energy so strong and puissant that our meagre, human words, which mutter something about telepathy, auto-suggestion, hypnotism, and the like, are by comparison hardly an approximation to this great human reality which inhered in Prince Messiah and resided in the Son of man.

Jesus looked upon His disciples in just that way. Now that He was become a man, He consciously joined Himself with that God who, when Jesus was still a child, directed a star in the sky so that it would lure Magi to a King in the manger and who now opens a cock's mouth so that it may lure Simon back to his King on the cross. This was incomparable obedience and awful passion. For Christ is like us in all things, sin excepted. Because He is like us in all things, because He is true man, His soul is inclined to concentrate on its own passion. To be condemned to death, to have to go on the way of the cross, robbed of the common favors of God, mocked and defied by the first citizens of the state, is for one who is true man so severe a trial that he could wish to say: Let me alone; I have enough to do to bear my own burdens.

But this day God directs the soul of Simon Peter to the tired heart of Jesus. That God knows that this is an assignment of responsibility, that this is to muzzle the ox that treads out the corn lest he should eat before he does his work. The Son bears all the burdens, and must nevertheless fasten His eyes on Simon and lavish all His energies upon him. Never was a telepathist or hypnotist as mortally tired as was the case when Jesus fixed His will upon Simon, concentrated His full attention upon Peter, lest the Father should let a cock crow in vain. Yes, God describes a circle around Jesus' attention, a circle in which angels and devils are included—angels and devils, and cocks, and the spirit, the old man and the new, the spirit that is willing and the flesh that is weak. Within this circle, which is spacious enough for the attention of the suffering Christ, the Christ of God must accomplish genuine obedience.

Oh, incomparable passion—to bear death and the death sentence, and in spite of that to have to work creatively and in life-giving fashion with the soul of Simon. To be beaten by all the watchmen of this world (Song of Solomon 5:7), and in his own city and nevertheless to have to excite love where it no longer cares for itself any more. A bitter affliction—to be placed at the crossroads of the world, to confront the most painful enigmas which God's providence can put, and yet to have to accommodate Himself to that providence of God in each moment. To be ready as soon as the cock crows, to be ready in order that He may immediately send out all the energy of His love for the preservation of Peter's soul in that brief moment in which His eyes can focus on him. This He must do in order that those whom God has given Him may not be lost. O grievous commandment—to have a God who has blown all those given Him by the Father away from Him, and who nevertheless forbids Him to lose as many as one of those given of the Father—even when that one disowns the Son by his act of cursing and of swearing. O inexorable law of God—to have to work in cooperation with God, to give cocks and souls and spirits safely into His hand in the very moment in which He knows He has been forsaken of God. This is incomparable suffering.

But in the course of this passion the obedience of Jesus' soul exerts itself beyond measure to stay inside of the limit of the commandment. Heaven and earth cooperate in this moment. True, heaven may work mechanically through a cock's mouth, but it lets Jesus act on the basis of His own resources, and move at His own prompting. And He has understood the Father perfectly. By virtue of His own energies and forces He works organically in the direction of heaven so that His eye may at the right time release the energies of eternal life in Simon's soul, and so that this disciple may again pay attention to cocks, devils, and God.

God's servant was never more obedient than when He, prompted by His own sense of responsibility, conformed Himself to God—to the God who in the crowing of the cock laid all His obligations bare before Jesus. Never was Jesus greater in His acknowledgment of God. Never did He respond more sensitively to the times and circumstances of the Father. We will never see Him more beautiful in His love than He is here—isolated, all His attention fixed upon this given disciple of the Father, and upon the Father Himself.

Ah, how can we praise God enough for the vision of the absolutely isolated Christ, and for the fact that in His office He was quite alone? Only that one is faithful to official obligation who greatly desires the office even when everything attractive, when all that is congenial (the word has a sublime connotation here) has been taken from it. Has the office of Christ nothing to give Him except cold solitude; does the service rob Him of everything; does God come to insist on all His claims on love, and will He as He does so not even give Him the favor of a pair of faithful eyes with which to appreciate? Must the keeper of the sheep fasten His heart upon the lord of the flock, even when the sheep by their conduct seem to be goats; and can He still remain faithful at all? If so, that man has made it plain that His desires are purely for the sake of God.

That means that He is Christ—ordained with God the Father, anointed with the Holy Spirit. Thus did Jesus take the task of the shepherd upon Himself. The office gives Him a responsibility from which all appeal and congeniality have externally been removed. There is not so much as a prayer of Simon to maintain spiritual fellowship with the Master.

Nevertheless the Master fulfilled the office. He kept giving Simon the paternal gifts of God. He kept adding His spirit to Simon. Simon, Simon, gold and silver have I not, and words and gestures have I not, but what I have I give you: look closely upon me. Spirit of God, Spirit of the Son of David, *veni creator spiritus*, there lies one who is wholly naked. O God, the office calls me, and I come, and I have greeted no friend upon the way. Father, I have no friend any more. The *friends* are gone; henceforth I

shall have to call *brothers*. Henceforth God's *seed* will have to
spring from my blood. No, I have not avidly joined myself with
Peter in order to be rid of Caiaphas, not even for a moment, O
Father who art in heaven. The servant of the Lord has not paused
to greet anyone while en route; He had gone right on. He had no
friend; at least, He felt the companionship of none. Nor did the
servant curse the one who swore. The Lord said to Him: Curse
David and his son. The Lord pronounced the curse, the curse of
the great abandonment. Father, I did not greet my friends when
Thou didst call, and I did not curse the man who swore against
me when Thou wast teaching me how to extend the blessing. I
only sought out Thy child, Father; I did so in passing, and did so
intentionally and naturally. I have administered the office, and
have found the comfort of luxury nowhere under heaven. That
luxury is with Thee, where communion is, and where I cannot
come except I drink of Thy cup. Father, in Thy thoughts I have
not broken faith with the company when I suffered grievously
because of an individual. I looked at Simon, but was not slack in
finishing the course for the great congregation. Caiaphas, I am
here. I did not fail to respond when the powers that were bade
me go.

No, indeed, He paused nowhere; He greeted no one on the
way. Therefore He would weep—could weep the tears of Simon,
but He had to do so in faith. For He may not yet see the tears of
Simon, and seeing, enjoy them. The hour for such comfort is not
yet His.

And Peter, going without, wept bitterly.

True, God put his tears into His own bottle (Psalm 56), but He
advisedly saw to it that they were not gathered up into Jesus'
flask. Jesus may do but one thing: He may labor for Simon. And
rest also? Yes, later, not until later. The storm raged past Him,
the moment sped by, and Peter went outside. He went outside because he himself wished to, of course; but he went also because
God desired that it should be so. God conducted him out of doors,
in order that Simon's tears might not serve as a premature comfort to the Man of sorrows.

We know that Simon found Jesus again in these tears, but
know also that Jesus may not yet rejoice in that. Not until later
may He ask: Simon, lovest thou me; Simon, lovest thou me?

Yes, He may ask that later, but not now. The dew which now lingers over Simon's soul as a blessing to him and a comfort does not rest upon Jesus. He knows all things, yes, but He must experience all the suffering which inheres in the things He knows.

And Peter, standing without, wept bitterly.

O bitter necessity. Time was when Jesus could say: Get thee behind me, Satan. He *had* to say it. It was a part of His passion. Now He would like to cry out: Step out before me, thou angel of God. But He *may not* say it. Sorrow is His only portion. His voice can find no place. He moves rapidly now in the direction of His comfortless death. And Peter may not do his weeping inside.

My Jesus passes by again. Jesus of Nazareth passes by. Someone shouts as He goes: Who will follow? But as He goes Jesus fastens His heart upon God. He cleanses the atmosphere which has been contaminated by Peter's weeping. He pronounces His yea over the eternal election of Simon Barjona, and He softly sings the new song: I come, O God, to do Thy will. I will compensate for the false oaths which Simon swore. Father, Thou knowest all things; Thou knowest that I love him.

Christ Led Back to the House of Bondage

CHAPTER ELEVEN

Christ Led Back to the House of Bondage

> ● *When the morning was come, all the chief*
> *priests and elders of the people took counsel*
> *against Jesus to put Him to death: and when*
> *they had bound him, they led him to Pontius*
> *Pilate the governor.*
> MATTHEW 27:1-2.

THUS Christ was condemned to death. While seated in official session, the Sanhedrin declared the Saviour of the world to be guilty of death. Now they go on to the next act: they deliver him up to the secular judge. It is true that the "church" thirsts for His blood (in the original of verse 1 the word translated *people* is one which points to Israel as a spiritual nation, as a covenant or "church" people), but only the secular authority is able to pour out Jesus' blood.

Hence they are to go to Pilate today and are to say to him: lord, this man has sinned against heaven, and especially against thee. He does not deserve to be called a son of Abraham. Make Him one of Rome's hirelings. The hirelings, too, are not registered in official census. Just so, this man is no longer counted among men in our books; He has become an outlaw to us. Come, join us, and strike His name from the books.

Our text tells us exactly what happened. Early in the morning —the exact time has not yet been determined definitely—the Sanhedrin came together officially to pass judgment upon Jesus for the last time, and to determine what ought to be done next.

We must pause to say that there is a great difference of meaning among expositors about the purpose for which this early morning session of the Sanhedrin was held. Some think that the death sentence still had to be confirmed officially, inasmuch as, strictly taken, this body was not allowed to pronounce the death sentence on the same day the witnesses were heard. Others surmise that they simply wanted to deliberate further upon how their plans might best be carried out. For it was plain that they would have to reckon not only with the difficulties presented by a mass of people who were in a state of excitement, but that they would also have to hit upon those means and methods which would most effectively and quickly elicit the Roman's approbation of their wicked plan. They had to determine how the charge might be phrased best, to consider what ought and ought not to be said.

In other words, the exact purpose for which this morning session was called will perhaps never be clear to us, but it is not necessary that it should be. That which we should know is clear enough. The Sanhedrin is determined to be rid of the Nazarene; and they act upon that resolution by immediately going from their own hall to that of Pilate. They are intent upon getting official approval from him for carrying out the death sentence against Christ.

Just who and what Pilate proved to be upon this occasion affects the important issue very little. Much has been written about Pilate, about his work and public career, about his character and about his governmental policies. The several interpretations of each of these subjects differ greatly among each other. For our purpose we need to know only that Pilate is acting here as the representative of Roman authority. The empire of the world has placed him here, that empire which goes by the name of Rome. Now Rome had governed Israel precisely as it has pleased for some time. It had sent Pilate to this particular province of Syria, that is, to Judea. Under the direction of God, Rome gave him legal jurisdiction over the people of Israel, and thus over the mundane, historical manifestation of Jesus Christ. Pilate's authority was both civil and military. In other words, the whole of the Roman empire stands back of Pontius Pilate and acts through him.

The moment, therefore, in which Jesus is sent to Pilate does begin a new phase of Christ's suffering. That which is to take place now is not a matter-of-fact rubber-stamping of the sentence which Israel has already pronounced upon Him. The vehicle of death in which Israel had placed its Messiah did not move to the place of curse and destruction as automatically as that. Instead,

Pilate had to judge Christ independently. The spiritual people of Israel is one thing; Rome's empire is another. And both have to pass sentence upon the Christ.

This, therefore, is the piteous state of things. Israel turns to the world for assistance in destroying its own Redeemer. In short, Israel returns to the house of bondage; Israel goes back to Egypt.

The journey from the palace of Caiaphas to the house of Pilate represents the return to the abandoned house of bondage. Israel while en route to the old Egypt takes its own yoke upon itself again, and takes it with Him who said, "My yoke is easy, and my burden is light." The people who would have nothing to do with Him now conduct their own Messiah, that is, their own Yoke-bearer, to the house of Rome. The yoke of Rome is not easy, and the burden of Rome is by no means light, but Israel will gladly bend its neck under the burden of that weight if only the neck of the Messiah of Nazareth is broken at the same time. It prefers this to listening to Him who invited them to an easy burden and a light yoke.

Thus Israel goes on its way to the house of bondage. Behind the clouds the angels raise their voices in that hymn of the redeemed: Thou art the Lord who didst lead Thy people out of the house of bondage, out of the land of Egypt. But as they sang, God turned a page of His holy book, and pointed to the passage which said that His people had again sought out the place of bondage, and that, accordingly, in the future another and a different communion would flourish for Him, a renewed church which in the essence of its being would hate the house of bondage and would convert the mourning of Egypt's and Rome's enslavement into a bitter lamentation about that other house of bondage which is the house of sin. This other fellowship of the new covenant would from now on be called blessed of the Father and would share in a grace and glory capable of leading them eternally from a state of bondage into a state of freedom. These contrasts, although they may not have been clear to the Jews, are in faithful accordance with the trend of the biblical history of revelation.

We want to indicate that this is the case by pointing out briefly: first, the relationship between Israel and Rome; second, the relationship between the priesthood and Rome; and, third, the relationship between Christ and Rome.

This much we can say about the *first* consideration. When the Sanhedrin as the representatives of the people of God conduct Christ from Caiaphas to Pilate in order to beg him to allow them the terrible favor of Jesus' death, that which is revealed is the relationship between the people of God and the Roman empire. Whoever has followed the lines of development characteristic of the history of special revelation, whoever, that is, has followed these guided by the light of Scripture, knows that the Bible time and again preaches and maintains the contrast between the sphere of special revelation and grace and that other sphere in which general revelation and grace make themselves felt. Since the days in which Abel stood over against Cain, the seed of the woman over against the seed of the serpent, Isaac over against Israel, Jacob over against Esau, Babel and now Rome, the Bible has ever maintained that these contrasts do not spring from the vicious circle of purely natural life, that they cannot find their explanation in the ever-recurring movement of action and reaction. Instead, the Bible insists that these contrasts spring from a basis as fundamental as the seed of the woman and the seed of the serpent, of election and reprobation, of freedom and slavery, of eternal life and eternal death. It may be that to the research student in history who has an eye only for that which is included in the circumference of life's vicious circle, these contrasts are little more than the normal vacillations of natural forces. Such a student may see in them no more than the ever-returning undulation of thesis and antithesis, an illustration of that ironical and inevitable logic according to which Israel pounces on the neck of its enemy one day and must itself bow before the foreign yoke. But the Bible tells a different story. It introduces into this age-old conflict between the world empire and the people of revelation the *messianic element,* and sees the great crisis of reprobation and election realized in it. A line of demarcation drawn by a handwriting as old as eternity bisects the contra-polar movement and counter-movement of the history of men. And we all stand either on the one side or on the other side of this line of demarcation. Hence it was not employing a false logic of inferences or a mere delight in spiritualization, which inspired Christian exegesis to a deeper and ampler New Testament interpretation of the caption standing at the head of the law.

We remember that this caption says: I am the Lord Thy God which have brought Thee out of the land of Egypt, out of the house of bondage. Now those who explain this statement according to the methods usually employed by "general" historical research, discover in it simply the contrast between Israel as one cultural influence and Egypt as another. As for the house of bondage, such students see in the flight from the slavery of Egypt nothing more than a general, historical, daily recurring phenomenon or change in cultural influence—a very common occurrence, indeed, in which the oppressed everywhere break their bonds and in which the tyrant everywhere feels the thongs of his own whip returning eventually to bruise his own back.

But He who reads the Bible, and *believes*, knows that when God led Israel out, He was leading out the people of special revelation. When God removed Israel from Egypt, He was removing Christ from Egypt. This is so essentially true, and the deeper meaning of Israel's own departure from the house of bondage so plainly inheres in this, that we may not call Israel's exodus a mere analogy to Christ's victory over the slavery of death, or to the redemption of the Christian church, which is the body of Christ, from the sin of that house of bondage later. The great exodus of Christ and of the body of Christ from the bondage of sin and Satan was the real purpose for which God Himself rescued Israel from Satan's grasp. As a matter of fact, we can say that God began rescuing Christ and the body of Christ from the bondage of sin and Satan in that historical moment when, under Moses' conduct, He led Israel out of Egypt.

Therefore we can also say that Israel's redemption from the house of bondage which was Egypt was essentially Christological. Take the Messiah out of the picture and the whole event loses significance. Then everything becomes as vain as the vanity described by the tired Ecclesiast of the Old Testament as he looked upon the things circumscribed by the vicious circle and saw only action and reaction, thesis and antithesis, movement and counter-movement, *and nothing else*.

We should tremble, therefore, in the presence of a God who gives everyone what he wants, what in the deepest recesses of his being he really desires. We should tremble and beware.

At this time Israel, by means of the Sanhedrin, comes to ask a favor; it asks that the bones of David be broken. For the name of the Messiah is David. Thus Israel confessed that it wished to profit from the great accident, from the circular movement of the great cycle of cultural and political history. It refused to acknowledge that its national history could be interpreted only as being essentially Christological in character. In an axiomatic as well as in a theological sense, Israel profaned its own eschatology by considering and "solving" the problem of David, the problem of his kingdom, and of his eternal lamp. This it did with the aid of a light other than that of the history of special revelation.

And since it has done that Israel has voluntarily been taken captive by the cycle of its own natural life. Grace no longer redeems it. The people who had once been rescued from the bondage of the world now return thither. They ask the judge of the world's house of bondage to permit Israel's best blood to be shed. Egypt is one with Babel and with Rome as an enemy empire of the world. These all arise from the same source just as the "four beasts" of Daniel do. The Pharaoh of days gone by lives on now in the Cæsar of the Babylon which is now called Rome. Israel is giving up its own First-born—He is also its great Only-Begotten —to the latest Pharaoh. It presents itself with a polite bow, and asks that he throw the Child into the river.

Such conduct represents the return of an entire people to an abandoned house of bondage. By means of it, this people is acknowledging that the vicious circle has a lasting and a legal status. Accordingly its fate can be delineated ironically by the figure of a dog returning to its own vomit. They are a people who in the play of world forces and world powers automatically go back to their unproductive source.

But even though Israel chooses to shut itself up within the narrow confines of natural life, not as Jaweh's covenant people now but as just one more cultural influence among the many nations, God will countenance no interference in causing His covenant grace to triumph, and the straight lines of His evangelical grace to reach their fulfillment. When Israel delivered Christ into Pilate's hands it forfeited absolutely the freedom which God had given it. This people no longer understood that the war of liberty which God had won for it in the day of Moses had been an essentially spiritual conflict. It had been a spiritual warfare, an emancipation from the bondage of worldly tyranny, but it had been an emancipation from the bondage of sin also. And now that this erring people does injustice to its own exodus and denies the privilege of its own freedom, now its surrender of Christ to Egypt must necessarily be called a retracing of its steps through the wilderness.

This people of God is forfeiting its rights to the ancient privileges. While on its way to the house of bondage Israel presents its petition to the autocracy of the world, and does so in the presence of Him who is greater than Moses. It asks for the privilege of eating out of Pharaoh's hand again. It asks the death sentence for the very One who is the fulfillment of Moses.

Therefore Israel made room for another, and prepared the way for us who are the communion of the New Testament. In this perturbing hour Israel cleared the way for the emancipation of the new, the mature, church which is gathered together out of all nations, and which as it bows before Jesus Christ recognizes in Him the greater than Moses who delivers us from the bondage of sin, and thus prepares a place for us in the eternal kingdom.

When Israel on that last, the dying day of Jesus, went up to Pilate early in the morning, it was reckoned as a spiritual people, to be valued above all other peoples (*laos,* verse 1). But when at the end of the journey it had reached Pilate's palace, it called itself one nation among others, and wished to be appraised by the same standard by which other peoples were evaluated (*ethnos,* Luke 23:2). A people that can sell its beautiful and honorable name at such a price is traveling the road of death. By changing from *laos* to *ethnos* Israel degraded itself to the plane of the other peoples of the world (*ethnos*) and so paved the way for the New Testament church, the inclusive *laos* of God's prophets, priests, and kings in Christ Jesus. God buries no one. Men dig their own graves, and do so by their own choice.

In the *second* place we must consider the relationship which exists between the *priests* and Rome. For those who saw the chief of their ranks sitting in the presiding officer's chair were the priests of Israel. This high priest delivers that other High Priest into the hands of the world's representatives and adds the request that He be forever removed from their midst. As he does so we hear in his voice the polemical arguments of the old priesthood, arguing at the very gates of Rome. He argues, so that Cæsar may hear, against that better Official who is a priest not according to Aaron's order but according to the order of Melchizedek.

Now this, for all who read the Bible in the light which it sheds upon itself, represents the decay of the priesthood. The priesthood had ever been involved in argument and wrangling. Without discipline and dispute, without break and schism, without zeal and rejection a priesthood cannot exist in this world. However, the argumentation of the priesthood must be governed by the spirit and not by the flesh. And if we listen to the record of the disputations of the priesthood in Israel as it is recorded in history, we will notice that two subjects come into the foreground prominently. The first is the deathbed of Jacob. The second is the farewell address of Moses.

When Jacob died he said something about Levi (Genesis 49). While dying he shook his head in disapprobation, for Levi had carried on a quarrel; he had been a wrangler. He had quarreled about the problem of Father Jacob, but not about the problem of Prince Israel. When Shechem had seduced Dinah, Levi had undertaken to punish him. He had taken steps which avenged father Jacob's family pride and the family loyalty of Levi's brothers, but which had done so in a purely carnal way. The quarrel which Levi conducted then was a quarrel of the flesh, for the flesh, and by the flesh. No one had asked how it might be possible for messianic light to pass from Jacob's house to that of Shechem. Not a moment of thought was given to the spiritual, messianic element which should hallow every war in which Jacob is a participant. In fact, Levi went to the other extreme. The false zeal of his flesh went so far that he mocked a sacrament which was a sign and seal of messianic, spiritual grace. He asked Shechem and the inhabitants of the city to circumcise themselves. Levi falsely promised Shechem that after the circumcision, the ritual of transfer to the spiritual communion of Israel, he and his people would also be accepted by the family of Jacob as determined by ties of blood. And when this seemingly pious requirement was satisfied, Levi proved that he meant none of all his pious words. Instead of accepting Shechem into the fellowship of Jacob's blood and Israel's spirit, he faithlessly breaks the vow, institutes a massacre among the citizens of Shechem and thus becomes guilty of gruesomely mocking the sacrament of the Lord's holiness. He proves that his quarrel has its origin in, is conducted by, and is being carried on for, the flesh.

That is the first phase of Levi's violent wrath as it expresses itself in the world. Levi "knows" his brothers as brothers according to the flesh, and he "knows" his father and mother as being his parents according to the flesh. In the quarrel which Levi conducted the spiritual blessing of grace is actually being prostituted into a merely external protection of family pride and carnal arrogance. Hence Jacob dies with a sigh of disapproval upon his lips. He was sad because of the quarrel which Levi had carried on.

Later in the Scriptures—Deuteronomy 3—there is a more specific discussion of Levi's quarrel. The discussion is carried on by one of Levi's own family. Moses speaks of it. As Moses prepares to die, he refers to Levi again, and looks upon him as a wrangler, as a man insisting upon sharply defined antitheses.

However, in the place where father Jacob curses, there Moses rises up to bless. Jacob and Moses both make the wrath of Levi the subject of their farewell address. However, over against Jacob who condemns and curses the quarrel of Levi stands Moses who puts that quarrel into a hymn of rejoicing. The hymn of praise which he sings over Levi's head rises up to God who, because of Levi's violence, exalted and accepted him. Moses' hymn rises to God who because and together with the brutality of Levi accepted him as a special favorite.

Does it seem strange to you that Moses should praise what Jacob chooses to curse? Nevertheless, that is what actually happened. Besides, we should not suppose that in the course of years Levi's quarrel subsided, or that the fires of his zeal were extinguished. Moses is quite willing to acknowledge that Levi continues to be filled with the spirit of quarrel. He alludes to the fact that Levi long ago, at the side of Sinai, painted his sword red in his effort to punish those who worshipped the golden calf; and he also refers to the fact that not long since Levi had again taken up violent quarrel with those who had celebrated a feast of immorality and idolatry in the camp of the covenant people. This had taken place in that dark hour in which Israel had given itself up to sin at Baal-Peor. At that time Phinehas, the priest of the tribe of Levi, had raised the hands which were wont to minister the sacrifice of atonement, against his unspiritual brethren.

Yes, Levi was still very much the wrangler. But there was this difference, and it gave Moses cause for rejoicing. Levi's quarrels were now springing from a different source. Jacob's objection had been that Levi's quarrels had been carnal in character. Levi "knew" his brothers and his father only according to the flesh. As he saw it, the generation of his father Jacob was included only in the vicious circle of natural life. Levi's quarrel at the time had nothing of the messianic in it.

But as Moses looks back upon this most recent instance of Levi's rebuke, he acknowledges in him a different motivation. Levi no longer "knows" his father and his brothers and his sons. Levi, regarded now as a tribe, naturally, has transferred the quarreling from a carnal to a spiritual plane. Now he does not even think his own family too good for the penalty of purging which the quarrel of the Spirit of the Lord comes to carry on against the flesh of Jacob and of Esau. Levi, working through Phinehas now, does not look for family ties but for the fellowship which comes through the Holy Spirit. He is no longer storming against Shechem but against sin, also against the sin which dwells in his own house. "For this was the time in which the judgment against the house of Levi should begin." Thus did Levi repent of his past. He subjected the things of nature and of the flesh to the far greater consideration of the Spirit of God. He subordinated birth to rebirth and the tie of the blood to the bond of the covenant. Thus he quarreled against his brothers in order to make room among them for the holiness of the Lord, and for the rights of the covenant — that is, for the Messiah.

You ask how it happened that the zeal of Levi succeeded in escaping from Jacob's curse and in arriving at the blessing of Moses? This is the explanation. God Himself quarreled against Levi. God had tested him, and had stormed against him by the waters of Massah and Meribah. Moses' voice catches in his throat as he thinks it, for there God had quarreled with Moses and Aaron, the two greatest of the tribe of Levi.

That had been when they *struck* water out of the rock. They had been told to do something else. When the people had called for water, and God had wanted to give it, they had been told to speak to the rock. God wanted the water of the miracle to be accompanied by the hearing of the preached word. Moses' speaking was to be a part of the wonder of the day, for what good is it to a thirsting covenant people for God to give it water, if the word is not given at the same time? For Moses and Aaron this was the most significant matter; for the rock which poured out water really was an image of Christ (1 Corinthians 10). Therefore the wonder which calls forth water out of the rock must be accompanied by the preached Word in order that God's name may be hallowed. Thanks to the word which hallows that name, the miracle would not fade away as did the running water, but would be recalled as an instance of sacramental grace which could open men's eyes to the perfect messianic gift of the future, and thus bring the people to an acknowledgment of the wondrous ways of God becoming manifest in Israel in the person of the Messiah.

But Moses had not spoken. Neither he nor Aaron had at that time hallowed the name of the Lord. Levi had quarreled again in these his two greatest representatives. And this time he had quarreled not against Shechem, but against his own brothers. This quarrel was again carried on in such a way that the flesh polluted the channels of the spirit, even though the fountains of the spirit had been reached. Levi had stormed and quarreled again; Moses and Aaron had inveighed vehemently against Levi's own "murmuring" brothers. Again he had done so according to carnal and not according to spiritual laws. His sharp wrath had been poured upon the children of Israel, but because of their caustic speech, he had neglected the word of the Lord. The service of the word was replaced by a quarrel inspired by self. Then the Lord Himself quarreled against Levi in Moses and Aaron. In the presence of the whole people God denied these two giants the privilege of admission to the land of promise. Thus Moses and Aaron learned that God is willing to accept those who quarrel, that He even gives them a definite place in His kingdom, but that every quarrel must give full and free expression to the messianic idea, and in that way subject the flesh to the spirit of God. This judgment of God Levi had acknowledged in fear and trembling as a holy and a good one. Levi, who had always wrangled at the prompting of the flesh, now becomes humble as God conducts His quarrel against him. And when Levi turned the rudder around, God also reversed his fate. The Levi who heard his wrath being cursed at Jacob's deathbed is now being acknowledged by the way of purgation as a quarreler by the grace of God, and as such is given the blessing of the priest. He asserts that the spirit of God is inspiring this hymn of war and peace, this farewell hymn of Moses in which Moses sings of the rights and grace-given privileges of Levi.

What Moses said is that God's urim and thummim were to be entrusted to Levi. These two stones which the priests were to wear in their robes, and with aid of which they were to ask what was the Lord's will, were now given to Levi. Hereafter Levi might as a judge and a priest pronounce the word of curse and of blessing, of rejection and acceptance, of quarrel and of peace, of yea and nay, and of approbation and reprobation.

Since that time the priesthood has been endowed with the urim and the thummim. This privilege carries with it the heavy responsibility of declaring war and peace, of saying yea and nay, of binding and loosing on the earth, and of carrying out the super-quarrel, the dia-crisis of the Lord among the people.

Levi knows that he owes the privilege of the urim and the thummim, the privilege of declaring judgment, to the miracle of grace. He knows that as he himself is subject to the quarrel which God is conducting against him and which purges his own sin, he may himself execute God's quarrel in the world and thus recognize and carry out the conclusive decision of the urim and the thummim of the Lord in the whole of life.

Now to return to the hour in which Christ is being led to the house of bondage. Caiaphas leads and behind him follow the whole of the priesthood. In other words, this is none other than Levi. These are the old priests, the priests of the generation of the glorified past. As always they quarrel, they wrangle. At present they are carrying on their argument with the Nazarene. They have read the urim and the thummim and have said: These stones of Jaweh pronounce a curse against Jesus of Nazareth. Sheer curse — that is the message they have. The curse is an unmixed one. God is saying nay to Jesus, and the "nay" has no modifying overtone. Hence Jesus must die. Together they go to Pilate, the company of the tribe of Levi. And they say: "Yes, we know that you also must judge Him, but it is according to our law, according to the Levi-law of the quarrel that He must die." That the urim and the thummim[1] have infallibly said.

O Levi, Levi, wrangler between the Spirit and the flesh! When in the ears of the world and in those of Rome and of Egypt he conducts his quarrel against the Nazarene, he identifies himself with the dog returning to his own vomit. Levi quarrels, and he strikes the rock, "and the rock was Christ." Levi no longer ministers the word of God. He simply asserts his own flesh. He no longer recognizes his brother except as he is according to the flesh. Rejecting his brother-Nazarene he comes to beg that the heathen give him a writ of capital punishment for a fleshly brother. Why? Because he has this fault to find with a son of Abraham: namely, that He wants to subject the flesh to the spirit, and that He, regarding Levi's blood as impure the while, wants to subordinate the flesh to the Word and to the ancient covenant. Levi does not recognize his brother. But to say that is not to praise him, as Moses once did when he used the same words to call Levi a brother. Levi's failure to recognize Jesus of Nazareth, his brother according to the flesh, is not due to his maintenance of the will of the Lord but to his assertion of his own flesh. It is an expression of Levi's quarrel of the flesh and of nature against the preaching of the Nazarene. Levi would save himself. Therefore when he led his own brother according to the flesh to Pilate, Levi signed his own death warrant. Cursed be his wrath for it is violent. When Levi throws out the bearer of the office according to the order of Melchizedek, he forfeits his own office forever. Levi quarrels against his Messiah, waives the redeeming Spirit of Christ, does indeed desire the glamor of Moses but not his messianic mystery. Hence the march of Levi's priests to the house of Pilate is another profanation of the holy war.

Henceforth Levi is dismissed. Begging, and bristling with wrath, he stumbles up Pilate's porch to ask a death warrant for Abraham's best son. In doing so he is prostituting the Saviour, he is honoring over against the citizens of the Shechem of his day, the family pride of Jacob's flesh at the complete expense of Israel's messianic spirit. He is trampling on the sacrament, reject-

---

1. It is unnecessary to say that this is naturally figurative speech, in these times.

ing the Lamb of the Passover, and is administering death. Cursed be his wrath for it is evil.

Thereupon God's own hand took the urim and thummim out of the priestly robe and gave them to the Son. Now He has been given all rights to curse and to contradict in heaven and on earth. But on this important condition, of course, that He will bear the quarrel of the Lord against Him without murmuring, that He will die outside of His Canaan, in order that He may suffer the curse in His own flesh.

Melchizedek will dismiss Levi, but not until Levi himself has reported at the house of bondage. And Melchizedek will bless the lost sheep of Levi no further with his lavish pentecostal blessing, until Levi himself has acknowledged that he is empty-handed. Or can we say that a beggar knocking at the door of the house of bondage for a favor is able to fill the arms of God to overflowing?

In the *third* place, we pause to note the relationship which, as is plainly outlined here, exists between Christ and Rome. Jesus goes to Pilate as the Son of man. We have observed before[1] that Christ Himself had the prophecy of Daniel 7:13 in mind as He walked on the way of death. He knew that He was the Son of man, empowered from above to put an end to the empires of the world, and to make room for His own immovable kingdom.

Now that luminous, prophetic picture of the future, described in Daniel 7:13 is overshadowed; now the scroll of prophecy of the old Daniel is thrown as so much rubbish on the heap of "evangelical folly" and of "messianic offence." What? Is this the Son of man who is to destroy the world empire which Daniel saw? Surely, that cannot be. He comes to Pilate in fetters; He comes to Rome bound. What can this man achieve against the kingdom of iron and clay which Daniel saw? Plainly, Christ as well as Levi is subservient to Rome and Rome will soon, will very soon, tread upon Him.

Thereupon they led the Son of man from Caiaphas to the throne of the Beast. They led the Son of man from Caiaphas to a place beneath the feet of iron and of clay, that is, beneath the

---

1. Chapter 7, p. 140 ff.

feet of the image which bodied forth all the empires of the world taken together.[1]

This too is foolishness and offense. It is as foolish as the cross; as offensive as any and all of the great concealments of God in this world. The Word disappears from sight in the stream of paradoxical phenomena. Prophecy is being laughed at here; the kingdom, reputed to be immovable, finds that its king is being trodden upon en route from Caiaphas to Pilate.

This is the way of the house of bondage. This is the way of death. This is the course of the lie. From the viewpoint of faith, this is the way of thorns, of foolishness and offense. May God be very gracious here. But that He cannot be on this occasion. He cannot be that here. May He be gracious to my soul; for from this time on it will be possible for Him to be gracious again.

Thereupon they led Jesus from Caiaphas to the house of judgment. Strange reversal: the dead are about to bury the Living. The judges are about to deliver Him up who is the very one from whom they have their commission. These wranglers, whose duty it is to build for peace, quarrel with the Prince of their peace and I am one of them. I belong to their accursed company.

Do not restrain me now. I would go to Jesus. I would fall at His feet, and kiss Him again and again. Because I am walking the path of the dead anyhow, there is but one escape for me. He is the life and the way, and He is also the truth. He conducts Himself from the hall of judgment to the house of the Father, from the place of bondage to the throne of freedom, and from the quarreling which is solely Spirit-motivated to the immovable kingdom which, uncontested now, proceeds to draw its spacious circle on the new earth.

From now on I shall see the Son of man sitting on the right hand of the power of God in heaven. And from now on I shall be better able to read and to understand the law of the Lord. Hereafter I shall take the tables of the law into my hands, read the familar words, "I am the Lord thy God who hast led thee out of the house of bondage," and I shall interpret this faithful statement of the Old Testament in the light shed upon it by the New. I shall say to my soul: Look upon this Jesus. He is the

---

1. Pp. 141-142.

Lord thy God who for your sake was led back to the house of bondage. And to that Lord Himself I shall say: Thou art my Surety, O Lord; this hast Thou done for me.

Thereupon He will speak to me again, but now in the fulness of the revelation of the new day. He will say: I am the Lord thy God who have led myself into my, and thee out of thy, house of bondage. As for thee, do thou learn gratitude, and the first principle of it: *the law,* the law, seen in the light of the Gospel.

For we know that Moses went up out of the house of bondage in order to make room for the Lamb and for His fulfilled service.

Christ Confronted By the Dead Judas

CHAPTER TWELVE

Christ Confronted By the Dead Judas

● *Then Judas, which had betrayed him, when he saw that he was condemned, repented himself, and brought again the thirty pieces of silver to the chief priests and elders, Saying I have sinned in that I have betrayed the innocent blood. And they said, What is that to us? see thou to that. And he cast down the pieces of silver in the temple, and departed, and went and hanged himself.*

MATTHEW 27:3-5.

ISRAEL led its own Redeemer back to the great house of bondage; it delivered Him who was the head and crown of Moses into Pharaoh's hands. You ask why Israel did this? Because it hated freedom? No, but because it wanted a different freedom than that which Jesus chose to give. And therefore it wanted a different prophesying of that freedom. Well, they could very easily have confronted Christ, the prophet of true freedom, by many of the prophets of that other freedom which they wished. If it is true that the people failed to place the two kinds of prophets over against each other, it is also true that the angels did not hesitate to do so. They set the one over against the other, and God did this also.

Two prophets of that other freedom were brought into judgment together with Jesus on one and the same day, and were cited before the throne of God and men simultaneously. One of these was Barabbas to whom we shall refer later. The other was Judas Iscariot, of whom we have spoken before.[1] This was a striking contrast. Jesus Christ wants to give Israel its freedom,

---

1. *Christ in His Suffering*, various chapters.

239

but His people give Him up to the house of bondage. And here are those "other" heroes of liberty who on Christ's own day have seen their ideal of freedom called into judgment. On the night when Jesus' soul departed, Barabbas celebrated a great feast and the body of Judas Iscariot lay shattered on the ground. We can say that both of these were dead; but the angel said of both of them that they were not buried.

The banquet of Barabbas is not complete, therefore, without the death of Judas. For God shows us in both of these that false freedom may indeed be able to announce its festivities, but that the end of these is despair. Barabbas' happy frame of mind and Judas' bitter despair are seldom compared with each other, but from God's point of view they are but two phases of a single process. And above these contrasts, which in another sense are not contrasts at all, God has put His Son on display. He takes the life of His Son in the same moment His death purchases the true freedom, a freedom born not of the flesh, but of the Spirit.

This struggle of the Spirit of prophecy to demonstrate in the events of this darkest of all days of freedom the issue of two crusades, the one for the true and the other for the false freedom, has its origin in the death of Judas Iscariot. Everything becomes awful now. There were but two of these crusades, not three. The person who thinks that there were three, one by Barabbas, one by Judas, and one by Jesus, minimizes the seriousness of matters. Tragedy loses its tragic force the moment it increases the number of its conflicts. Two conflicts cause a stricter tension than three, three than four.

But in this drama of death's day of freedom the tragic conflict arises from the antithesis between two crusades. The Barabbas who laughs and the Judas who commits suicide are not opposed to each other as well as to Jesus Christ. The one may laugh and the other weep, but both are a single phenomenon. In the struggle for the false freedom, both laughed and both wept.

However, the Son's struggle for freedom is the antithesis God places over against both of these. Hence it is a part of the calling of Jesus Christ to endure this suffering in which God confronts Him with Barabbas' frothing cup not only but with Judas' ebbing blood also.

At this point, we must follow the narrative for a moment. After his sinister betrayal, Judas could find no peace again. He saw Jesus given up into the hands of murderers and, restless and tortured in his conscience, he followed Him in his thoughts. Now, as ever before — such was his nature — he did not join the others, but locked up all of his fears within himself, taking counsel with his own soul and his own spirit only. He kept back his anxieties with his own hands. He erased the question marks which his own fingers had written upon his conscience; he personally obliterated the exclamation points of his tortured sense of self-sufficiency. Now, with a bitter despair, he wars against the logic of the facts which he himself has unloosed. In the last analysis, Judas also was in his own fashion an "idealist." Hence he could not feel at ease now. Once he had passed the crisis which had its climax in the act of betrayal, it became clear to him again that if it were true that the Judean, the idealist, the nationalist, the chauvinist had in part prompted him to the act of betrayal, it was also true that his love of money had been one of his motivations.

It is not always possible to keep back introspection, to keep from seeing oneself as one really is. It was not possible for Judas. He saw himself as he was, at least in part. Thereupon he began to make discriminations. He said to himself that he must go to heaven or hell. He feels that he is very near his death. The veil of sin disappears after a time. The hand which keeps turning the mirror aside tires at last; then there is nothing to hinder us from seeing the motives which have prompted our soul to the act of sin, and from discerning precisely the several causes. Then self-revelation comes with a pang. We wake to find that while we were in our sinful drunkenness, that while we were steeped in the sleep of sin, we have tossed ourselves naked. And we discover besides that our son, Ham, has invaded the privacy of our room. Judas now also arrives at the moment of reflection. He detects the differences between one motive and another. He sees at once that it was something more than the orthodox yearning of his Judaistic soul for Israel's national freedom which drove him to the act of betrayal. Yes, that obstinately held idea of freedom may have induced him to take exception to Jesus Christ — for Jesus certainly was not living up to that ideal. Still, he cannot deny that his greed has also played a part. That fact he can no longer hide from himself. The knowledge one learns from Satan is very clear. But it comes too late, and it does not convert the heart to and by means of a father's love.

At this point, then, Judas falls into Satan's sieve. That evil spirit convicts him of sin, righteousness, and judgment, but the Holy Spirit does not simultaneously unite him with the righteousness of Christ, with Christ's merits, and with Christ's satisfaction for guilt. Now that he has confessed to himself that his avarice was one motive prompting the betrayal, all those other rationalizations derived from his Judean orthodoxy disappear. He discovers suddenly that although Jesus did not come to establish an earthly realm of freedom, He never thwarted a single cry for liberty. He becomes fully convinced that in the persistent contest of war and peace such as Judas had wanted to conduct, Jesus had borne himself as one whose "character" was unimpeachable, even according to Judaistic ethics. Accordingly, Judas now faces the atrocity and the "immorality" of Jesus' death. All patriots who have "character" must say, "But this is not the royal way of doing things." They must say that even though the place is seething with priests. Judas confesses it to himself: he has tainted the banner of his Judean order with innocent blood. He confesses to himself that those who shed that blood were tyrants.

When he sees Jesus being driven from the judgment hall of the Sanhedrin to the praetorium of Pilate, he understands that nothing can be done about it any more. The blot of blood can never be cleansed from his knightly banner. Judas is no longer an honest man, he knows, not even in the eyes of men.

Therefore the thirty pieces of silver burn in his hand. Mark the plea of this man who has often passed by Jesus, but has never entered into Christ. He goes to the chief priests, throws the money at their feet, fully confesses that the blood of Jesus was innocent blood, and says, "I have sinned, betraying innocent blood." This is the cry of despair uttered by a broken man, who comes back to his father confessor because he has no other to whom he can go. Nevertheless he knows that he has lost respect for the chief priests. And these have nothing to say other than that he may see for himself what course things will take with them and with his former Master, and that they cannot worry about his scruples and regrets. Hence the confessor stands alone in the darkness. Piteous and despairing, he stands alone in the night.

The night is cold and frosty, and there is no one to cover him. God does not — He has not been asked to help. The people do not, the father-confessors do not help him, and Judas' own soul, too, cannot comfort him any more. He leaves these fathers who have no good word to say to him, and goes out into the night. No, he does not weep bitterly there; he swallows his tears. This was ever his manner. He has changed, and yet he is the same. He stops to talk with no one. He soon finds himself a secluded spot and there he hangs himself.

A comparison of Matthew's account with what is written in the Acts of the Apostles reveals further that Judas, who hanged himself on a tree, could not be supported by the branch after a time, that he fell forward to the ground, and lay there disemboweled.

At this point our thoughts can take various directions. We can study the figure of Judas; we can tediously and patiently try to plumb the depths of his soul. We can attempt to point out the wide divergence between his sorrow, between his manifestation of grief, on the one hand, and the spiritual remorse which is in conformity with God and which leads to genuine conversion unto salvation. We can consider the difference between Peter's denial and the remorse which followed upon it and which was fruitful unto salvation, and Judas' fruitless coiling about on the same human plane. We can even stop to point out that the words which Judas spoke were not the expression of a heart which is truly penitent and converted to God.

Those are possibilities and each might be pursued with profit. For it is true that Judas does not by his manner of speaking and confessing appear to be a true penitent. "I have sinned," he says. But what the passage really states is this: "I have made a mistake." And this confession is nothing more than a condemnation of a particular thing; it is not a condemnation of the evil root of which that thing is the product, nor of the whole condition of his lost life. It is true, besides, that Judas condemns his act only as measured by human standards and not as evaluated in comparison with the eternal righteousness of God. Moreover, although

Judas admits that Jesus' blood is innocent, he does not take a refuge in this blood as having in it the power to make others innocent before God. In addition, we can say that although Judas comes to make his confession before men, he does not come to God; he does go to the confessional of his former paymasters, but he makes no admission to the one Paymaster of all human guilt. Him he should have seized upon in order to implore Him to give him that which could have ministered to his peace. Yes, he no longer condemns the man Jesus as He is over against human law, but he does not seek the shelter of Christ over against the divine judgment. Then, too, by determining his own penalty he does what is the prerogative of judges and thus manifests an arrogance which would certainly not be his if he had been converted to God in Christ.

All this is true, is very true. But it is not appropriate for us to emphasize such issues now. Our purpose here is not to discuss true and false repentance, true and false remorse, human as compared with divine law, or anything of that kind. Our subject is Christ. Christ as He is in His suffering. Our theme is the redemptive event as it impinges upon the chaos of natural history — that redemptive event which by means of special revelation reveals the naked essence of things, and brings them to bear upon the conscience.

Because that is our subject, we cannot take time to present a psychological treatise on Judas and his remorse, nor even a theological study of the same theme. The important question is what significance the death of Judas has for the holy event of the day, that is, for the death of Jesus Christ, for heaven, for sacred history. As we lead our thoughts in that direction, we see that Jesus is compelled to face the corpse of Judas. Here again Jesus Christ must prove to be the Elect of God, savouring sweetly because of the anointing of the Holy Ghost; He must prove to be the living, the strong, the son of David as he is in his immovable kingdom.

Now who, in this connection, can keep from thinking first of all of the invisible world? There is a way on which only spirit-sent souls travel; it takes its course straight through the meandering paths of the world. If we really had eyes to see that invisible world in all of its movement and life, it would have our undivided attention. Then we should want to see to what surprising extent these invisible forces busy themselves with the world that we can touch and see. He, especially, who lets the holy Scriptures have their say in this matter will direct the attention of his soul to these spiritual forces in the air. He will think immediately of the activity of angels, and of the activity of the souls of men.

As for these angels, we have seen them make their appearance more than once in the history of the passion of Christ. But may we ignore the work done by the souls of men? Certainly not, for this would mean that we were being unfaithful to the God of revelation. God Himself in His gospel has given us a glimpse of that seething activity and life which arose in the world of departed souls because of and for the sake of the death of Christ. Those who doubt this should look ahead for a moment to what we hope to discuss more fully later[1] when we shall listen to what the Bible has to say about those souls of the redeemed who have died before, and who become alive at the moment of Jesus' death, in order to make their appearance in Jerusalem (Matthew 27:51-53).

We shall give separate attention to this activity of the souls of departed saints later, but here, in connection with the death of Judas, a part of the concealing veil is removed for us. On the morning of the same day in which God sent out the souls of the redeemed who had to go from heaven to earth at the moment of Christ's death, God calls the soul of Judas before Him in judgment. There is a disturbance on the way of the souls. It is a mighty disturbance, and no wonder. The stone which God is throwing into the sea of all the worlds today sends its generous wave out everywhere.

That is evident here also. There are souls who must go down to earth. They stand ready to carry out their mission faithfully. That mission is to present the testimony of the saintly dead. They will come. Presently they will go out upon their mission. The moment the King of glory enters heaven, they will leave it. The great "loss" of the moment — not to be present at the welcome given the soul of Jesus when it enters heaven — is something they gladly endure for God's sake when obedience to Him demands that they go on an errand for Christ. But what folly is

---

1. In the next volume of this work.

such language. The word "loss" is in no sense compatible with that other phrase which characterizes heaven, "perfect blessedness." But heaven and the redeemed souls regard obedience as being blessedness. When the will of God sends them on a mission, it is their great delight to carry out the errand. At this time, however, while these souls hold themselves in readiness to descend to the earth as soon as the soul of Jesus has entered heaven, the soul of Judas makes its appearance in the world of spirits, in that world of invisible things.

Judas' soul had enjoyed the company of Jesus' soul throughout the three years of Jesus' official career. The earth quaked, the deep was moved, a shudder disturbed the world of spirits. Judas' soul stepped ahead of that of Jesus and confronted the judgment. This event represents the transplanting of the offense and foolishness of the cross to the supersensuous world. The same heaven and the same God who must forsake Jesus, and are beginning to forsake Him now, and the same angels whom God withholds from giving any service to Jesus' human soul, must all join in judging the soul of Judas, for he has betrayed Jesus. Those who together forsake Jesus must arise in judgment against him who also forsook and abandoned Him. Judas forsook the soul of Jesus, and that will be his condemnation. Moreover, the condemnation must come from heaven itself, from God, from all the angels who pronounce their amens upon it and who, nevertheless, basically and absolutely forsake and abandon the Son also.

In this the offense of the cross became tangible in heaven and in this the folly of the Friday of the great death became concrete. Christ is regarded as an offense on earth, and heaven itself punishes Him for being such. But in the soul of Judas the offense of the cross is simultaneously punished with the bitter and grievous cup of death. A wave of restlessness moves through the company of the angels and the heavenly souls. But when Judas enters into judgment, heaven can only judge this last great representative of the Old Testament who helped build the gates of the new. Heaven has no choice but to judge him according to all that is written in the books about the justice and truth of God. That, if we wish to use the word, is a paradox. Heaven holds vials of wrath in each of its hands, and will pour them upon the head of Jesus Christ very shortly. Nevertheless the same heaven confirms and seals with an oath in the hearing of the ravaged soul of Judas, the question: He who does not love the Lord Jesus, let him be accursed: maranatha . . . .

It took great faith on the part of the redeemed souls and on the part of God's bravely faithful angels not to be offended by the condemned Judas. By faith in this connection we of course mean simply that in heaven, too, one must cleave to God perfectly and not to the self; one must cling not to what one experiences in each particular moment, but to God's single inclusive plan for the future. In heaven also one may not let oneself be governed by anything but the will of the Eternal which has been revealed. Heaven, too, although it has of course attained the full measure of the luxury of manifest revelation, must live by faith. It must live by the Word, the same Word which curses the very Jesus whom Judas had to bless from Zion. Judas' soul appears before God, and all God's servants must pronounce their amen upon the sentence of that God who rejects Judas because he has rejected the one whom God also has cast out. A strange judgment of heaven! Never in the invisible world was there a moment in which the divine judgment passed upon a son of man was as strange, as "foolish," as much of an "offense" to the flesh as it was now that Judas entered into the radiance of manifest revelation above.

Yes, if you wish to use the word, all this is *paradoxical*. But that after all is little more than a word. Rightly considered the speech and the utterance of heaven in this moment of Judas' entrance upon the spiritual world is quite in accord with its usual tenor. Just what, after all, is it for which heaven is blaming Judas? Not for the fact that he has forsaken Jesus whom heaven also has forsaken. Heaven's charge against him is that he has not accepted this forsaken Jesus as the Surety for his own soul. For that and for the fact that Judas did not seek his own blessing in the curse of Jesus Christ. When heaven condemns and forsakes the One whom Judas has also condemned and forsaken, heaven is condemning Jesus as the Mediator, is condemning sin, the sin of Judas and of all men. But Judas denied and betrayed and despised Jesus because he never acknowledged the Mediator in Him. Hence it is safe to say that heaven never affirmed the mediatorship of Jesus Christ as being the content of faith more strongly than when it rejected Jesus and Judas on one and the same day. This tension which was caused by the darkest of Fridays was not limited to the earth; heaven which judges the world and angels and men and all things in the shadow of the Almighty, fully shared in this tension. Heaven was involved in all of our problems. Father Abraham, rejecting his own child, Judas in the hour in which God is forsaking the holy child Jesus, greatly desired to see the end of this day. He saw it and rejoiced. The end of the day brought the soul of Jesus into heaven. But Abraham never proved to be a father of faith more than when he, before the end of this day came, cast off that idler of Abraham's fleshly generation, although he knew that Judas' destruction was the beginning of the destruction of Abraham's fleshly race. In rejecting Judas, Abraham disowned his own fleshly children, and greatly desired the spiritual children who are by faith in Abraham. Hence he could sing now of the sacrifice of the Great Isaac from whom a knife was not averted, and could at the same time reject Judas who thought the sacrifice of the Great Isaac was folly, and who would have averted the knife from him, had he still been able.

Abraham was the father of the faithful, and he was that after his death also. In this hour of Judas he is also the father of the church of the New Testament. He is Abraham, the father, who leaves the eldest Son, the great Doer and Meriter outside, and who celebrates the festival with the youngest son, he who would be freed from sin. That is the redemptive event which is celebrated in heaven as it is on earth. That is *faith*.

So great is not found on earth. Nor was so absolute a preaching of the *Mediator* ever heard on earth as took place now in this court of judgment.

We must add, however, that thick veils hide very much from our view here. We do not know whether Judas, as he opens his eyes on the other side, wishes that one of the dead may descend to the earth in order to tell his brethren that Jesus is truly the Christ. We do not know whether that profound longing of the rich man which Jesus pointed out in the well-known parable also stirred in the heart of Judas at this time. But if that prayer of the rich man was also the prayer of Judas' heart, we can say that his prayer was heard. For when Judas appears in the presence of God, the souls of many departed saints stand ready (Matthew

27:52) to descend to the earth to enter the holy city and to preach to the "brethren" of Judas among others that Jesus is indeed the Christ.

Nevertheless, the holy city will not turn to God because of the preaching. This was the great confirmation of the judgment. Judas enters the invisible world to find that an unimpaired view of Jesus Christ is possible only to him who looks upon the Mediator from the vantage point of the Word.

It was very quiet in heaven that day. *Two* souls entered into judgment beside Christ: the soul of Judas and that of the converted murderer. Two entered into judgment: the one had much in his favor, the other had much against him. God pronounced judgment upon them, declaring that Jesus Christ cannot be discovered in human experience neither above nor below the clouds, but that even in heaven He explains Himself only in terms of Himself and always with divine authority.

When Abraham added his amen to the verdict which decided against Judas and in favor of the murderer, he desired to find his own seed only among the generation of his great Son, the Greater than Isaac. Thus He again by faith put Isaac to death, relying in spite of the judgment against Judas on the assurance that God would raise Him from the dead, and confident that He should see the seed which Judas had refused to look for in Him.

The report of the suicide of Judas on the day of Christ's sacrifice opens up another perspective for our thoughts when we take note of the *history of special revelation* as it has been realized thus far. We have spoken more than once of the place which Christ occupies in the house of David. It was His glory, we said repeatedly, to be the great Son of David and to be his crown. Again and again, we observed, this royal lineage of the Christ was pointed out in prophecy. Hence we are not looking for more or less coincidental analogies and parallelisms, but are simply touching on the significance of sacred history when we compare the story of the man who betrayed the Son of David with the text of that other Biblical record of the suicide of the man who betrayed David himself.

In other words, we are to compare Jesus and Ahithophel. You remember the story. When David had to flee from Absalom, his own son, it was Ahithophel who betrayed him. This treachery on the part of Ahithophel was, doubtless, the bitterest cup which David had to drink. For Ahithophel was certainly the man who had lived intimately and in close contact with David; he had counseled David on many matters; as David's close friend and cabinet member his advice to David was like the voice of an oracle. Now this Ahithophel with whom David had eaten bread at one time rises to take exception to his king. As long as Ahithophel hoped that he could cause David's destruction, he, together with Amasa, had been the very soul of the revolution against David. However, when the tables were turned eventually, when it became evident that God had not given David into the hands of his enemies, Ahithophel, hearing that David was returning to his capitol at Jerusalem victoriously, left the city, went to his home, arranged such matters as needed arranging, and then hanged himself.

Therefore we can say that two gallows hang suspended over the row of graves belonging to the house of David. One stands at the head of the row, and one at the end. At the head, raising its sinister beams into the sky over David's grave, stands the gallows of Ahithophel; and at the end, suspended over the grave of David's great Son, we see the gallows of Judas. Between these two suicides all the princes of David's house lie buried. When the first of the royal funeral processions comes into the house of David, the celebrities present rub against the corpse of Ahithophel, who committed suicide because of David. And when the last grave opens to receive a king of the house of David, that is, when it opens to receive Jesus, the dead body of Judas is put on display next to that grave. This is the body of Judas, who committed suicide because of Jesus, because Jesus was not what in Judas' opinion He ought to have been. The first father of the king, and the founder of the house of David had to die with his face turned towards a traitor who had hanged himself in protest against David's life. And now the last to bear the crown in the house of David must die with his eyes turned towards a traitor who hanged himself because of Him.

These comparisons are sombre enough. The circumstances are analogous in many respects. Just notice them. Ahithophel was one of David's confidants and Judas was one of the inner circle of David's Son. Ahithophel had a place in David's advisory cabinet, and Judas was one of the advisory group of the apostolic circle surrounding David's Son. Ahithophel had conspired with David's enemies against him; Judas had done the same over against the Son of David. And finally Ahithophel hanged himself when it appeared that his plans had run aground on the will of God and on the logic of the events in the life of David himself. And Judas similarly commits suicide when it appears that his conduct is incompatible with the will of God and with the logic of the evangelical events in the life of David's Son.

There are similarities enough, as we see. But there are also tremendous differences. The most important, the most essential difference is that Ahithophel can reproach David for good reason, but that Judas can find nothing blameworthy in Jesus Christ inasmuch as the great Son of David is guiltless over against Judas of Kerioth.

Yes, David was not guiltless in his relations with Ahithophel, and, for the matter of that, with the whole people. He had not continued to be the ministering, theocratic king, but he had become like the oriental despots of his time. He was beginning to resemble a sultan. That becomes apparent especially from his shocking transgression with Bathsheba. Bathsheba herself may have been ever so culpable, but David scandalously abused his power when he had her come to him, and when he craftily, and under the guise of justice, sent Uriah to his death. Ahithophel's relation to all this, you ask? He was involved in it in two ways. In the first place it must have grieved Ahithophel, as an earnest counselor in shaping kingdom policies, to see David trifling with the blood of his best and most faithful officer (for Uriah had not only been a good soldier for David, but he was also a member of David's bodyguard). It must have offended Ahithophel that the king who certainly had not supplanted Saul purposelessly, now falls into Saul's sins and dares to tread upon the marital happiness of a son and daughter of his people. A king who conducted himself and publicly forgot himself as David did was setting a bad example, and was abusing the kingship for personal gain.

To this another consideration must be added. If we may be allowed to share the opinions of various authentic expositors of the Bible and students of history in the combining of certain Biblical data, we will say that as a person, too, Ahithophel was most intimately concerned in David's transgression with Uriah and Bathsheba. Ahithophel was Bathsheba's grandfather. She was the daughter of Eliam, and Eliam was the son of Ahithophel. Now it certainly was a painful discovery to this punctiliously refined, this able, this highly honored grandfather, to find that the king with whom he was on such friendly footing, had played with the life and the honor of his granddaughter, and in such a way that it would soon become a public scandal. Could it really be that the king was interfering as audaciously as this with the family relations of his own courtiers? Were Ahithophel's rank and intellectual competence not sufficient to protect a young granddaughter?

For another reason, too, David's sin with Bathsheba had deeply wounded Ahithophel's soul. The name of Bathsheba's husband was Uriah and when Uriah had refused to degrade himself before the king by covering up the king's scandal with his own name, David had hit upon the diabolical idea of putting Uriah out of the way, and of using the sword of the enemy for the purpose. He decided that he would have the man put on the "firing line," on the "front," we would say today. Meanwhile the king lived on in his luxurious palace . . . In comparison with such a tyrant, Saul seemed a paragon. But — to return to Uriah — this man was a colleague of Eliam, Ahithophel's son; the two together were strong men who belonged to David's bodyguard. And when David put his own bodyguard to death, solely in an attempt to cover up his personal shame, and to be able to marry Bathsheba, the "war-widow," — well, then it was as clear as day that the blood and even the honor of David's best defenders counted for little with him.

Ahithophel, accordingly, was seriously wounded in his deepest soul. Moreover, who could blame him? A family scandal had completely spoiled his old age. David had demonstrated with a shocking frankness that the life and honor of his most intimate confidants and aides were not sacred to him when it pleased his despotism to dally with them. This is the tyrant who is no longer serving theocratically, but thinks only of being served himself. Whoever pauses to think how deeply this must have grieved an aristocrat like Ahithophel — and, remember, he had to keep it all to himself for David's sake — must be inclined to agree with

Ahithophel and to feel an aversion to David's psalms. If only we had experienced what this old man had felt . . . .

Indeed, Ahithophel could reproach his king for good reasons. Hence, when David presently returns to his capitol from his exile, and everyone knows that God is not going to make this tyrannical hedonist an object of public disgrace, but is to return him to the throne, Ahithophel cannot stand it any longer. He does not want to live in the same world with this David any more. His repressed ire, his thwarted sense of justice, and his scandalized family pride — all these had cried aloud for justice when David had gone into exile — all had prayed God that He who had dethroned Saul, depose David also. Tyrants and despots, Ahithophel felt, had no right to parade in God's country, or in God's city. But the fact proved to be that God did not dethrone David; Jaweh returned him to the throne. Therefore Ahithophel complains against God, and curses the government which lets such people live. Finally he hangs himself by way of protest against heaven and against David. His act is a protest against the throne in heaven and the throne on earth. And we can say that this protest contains several truths. It is an expression of astute if impotent objection to an attack on his personal integrity; there is something in it of the "die-hard" aristocrat who would rather make a public break with David than ignore his sins for the sake of the meagre comfort of the thought that his great-grandchildren will be of the royal blood.

So much for Ahithophel.

Now we must return to Judas, and to the Son of David, to Christ. What faults can Judas find in Jesus? He has betrayed the Son of David. He has said, just as Ahithophel said of David, "The title of king is not safely His; He does not deserve a king's office." But after the betrayal the pendulum swings to the other side for Judas. Jesus is to be sent to His death. You see that what happens is the exact opposite of what happened to David himself. David is betrayed by Ahithophel, but before long Ahithophel sees David returning to the throne. Judas betrays Jesus, and before long sees him entering into inevitable death. That is the first difference. There is another. Although Ahithophel obstinately insists that he has betrayed guilty blood, Judas must confess that he has betrayed innocent blood. God forces Judas to this confession; He does so in order to vindicate the history of the house of David in Christ Jesus. When Ahithophel surrenders David, he has much to complain of, many charges to make. But when God finally yields His son into death's hands, after Judas has betrayed Him, this same Judas, the second Ahithophel, cannot substantiate a single charge which he directs against Jesus, the Son of David.

Frankly now, was this comparison of Judas and Ahithophel a too far-fetched inquiry or an analogy which simply "happens" to be coincidental? Not for the person who is looking for the perspective of prophecy, not for those who know that God, to whom a thousand years are as one day, sees the grave of Ahithophel standing next to that of Judas, and the grave of David beside that of Jesus. No, this is no place to speak of coincidences. God draws the line of David through the centuries, and He makes manifest the essence of the struggle which all flesh again and again conducts against the sovereign good pleasure which comes to place David and his Son upon the throne. He comes to all those who have the patience to think through to the deepest implications of the Ahithophel-David relationship in its bearing on the Judas-Jesus relationship, to demonstrate that the opposition which the enmity of the flesh opposes to the bearers of the Sovereign will and to the seed of the woman does indeed have its origin in what that seed of the woman did amiss, but that the essence of the enmity is the sin, is the perverse will, is unbelief, is enmity itself. Take all the sin which David did out of David's house, and give David a perfect son, and you will find that the generation of Ahithophel will nevertheless refuse to live in the same world with David and his Son.

The death of Ahithophel was occasioned by David's sin, but the most fundamental cause of the suicide arose in Ahithophel himself. It was inherent in his bitter anger which refused to acknowledge God's government as it proceeded to vindicate David solely in terms of God's sovereign pleasure. Ahithophel refuses to live with David any longer, because he is warring against God's will, because he cannot endure the Gospel of free grace, as it returns David — mark how the penitent weeps — to the throne, and accompanies the return with a message that God justifies the ungodly — freely.

And this is also true of Judas. God has taken all guiltlessness away from him. The blood of Jesus was innocent, perfectly innocent; Jesus had done Judas no wrong. To Jesus all semblance of oriental despotism was entirely alien. That became abundantly clear in the room of the Passover, where Jesus, knowing full well that Judas would prove to be His Ahithophel, nevertheless breaks bread with him, and raises not as much as a finger against him. And that is saying nothing of the incident of Malchus, even though Judas was present on the occasion when Jesus refused to countenance any form of despotism in His relation to that slave. *Moreover, Jesus had called Himself the Son of David.*

Now, you ask, does Judas hang himself, nevertheless? Yes, he went out and hanged himself. Why? By way of self-accusation, self-condemnation? But a genuine self-accusation, surely, can proceed only from *the Spirit of Christ;* therefore, at bottom, the suicide of Judas also represents a rebellion against God's sovereign good pleasure which Christ is revealing *in His own way.* It is this which goes against Judas' fabrications, which causes him neither to laugh nor to gnash his teeth as he sees the ruins of the Messiah of God's sovereign will. Those ruins Jesus Himself had predicted. But Judas refuses to believe. He does not want to accept a Gospel which justifies the ungodly — *freely.*

We can say, therefore, that the house of David and the seed of the woman are always a rock of offense in the world. Take all of the sin out of the picture, if you will, and demonstrate that at bottom no other conflict exists between David and Ahithophel, between Judas and Jesus, than that of an acceptance or a rejection of the law of election and reprobation. Even then — no, then especially — the children of the flesh will set themselves grimly against the house of David of both father and Son, and will go to their death as they gnash their teeth. Ahithophel reproaches David, saying: You are too much of a despot, and are guilty of great sins. And Judas blames the Son of David while asserting: You are not despot enough, although you are sinless. But both commit suicide because they do not want to breathe the same air that is breathed by God's elect, the companions of David, the invited ones of David's Son. Apparently the death of these traitors is a protest against the house of David, but actually it is an expression of their grim opposition to the election of God — an election which

causes fruit to spring forth out of dry ground — and to a Good
Pleasure which establishes the kingdom according to the counsel
of God and not according to any human philosophy. Ahithophel
lies next to Judas in the grave, and on the countenance of each of
them a grim, malicious expression of protest against the *Gospel
of free grace* may be seen. Theirs is a protest to a free grace that
placed an unworthy David back on his throne, and that causes
Jesus to say he is a king, but of a kind which Judas does not want
to see. He is a king of cripples and of blind men, of the poor and
the maimed; a king not according to outward appearance but according to the spirit of meekness, crowned with a mediator's
honor.

God lives — hence the death of Judas becomes a new suffering
to the Christ. Satan throws the dead Judas at the foot of the
throne of God, just as once before he laid the body of Ahithophel
at the foot of David's throne. The world of spirits — do not fail
to reckon with that. Just notice: Satan has done the impossible.
He desired greatly to contaminate the fragrance of God's love
with the stench of a corpse, and he desired to do it in heaven. He
quarreled against Jesus, appealing to Judas' arid death. In one and
the same day the death of the apostle Judas is called into judgment
with the death of Jesus, the Great Apostle of God. In the presence
of God, Christ Himself is being confronted by the dead Judas.

Do not Thou be perturbed by it, O Saviour, Son of David. Thou
didst not murder Judas, didst not even incite him to murder; Thou
hast done him no wrong and this truth, too, is being written into
God's book today.

Jesus, Jesus, theodicy of God, apology of the house of David.
The angels know it; the great book contains a record of it: Thou
needest not to blame thyself for anything over against this dead
body of Judas. Thou hast purged the house of David. Thou hast
atoned for everything that flesh could reproach in David and then
Thou didst stand before the world, asking all Ahithophels: Have
you any other objections to raise?

In answer, I hear them all testify against Thee. Yes, we have
this against Thee: Thou art the bearer of God's good pleasure.
That is the foolishness, that is the offense in Thy life. Because of
it, we refuse to sleep with Thee under the same roof of stars. We
would rather die than do that.

Thus the "foolishness" and "offense" of the cross of Christ has not only, as we have observed already, been tranferred to the heights of heaven today but also to the depths of hell. The soul of Judas has made its appearance while on the way to judgment in the world of spirits. The man who has souls in heaven, who can thank God for what Judas has done for them — that man is destroyed, and Christ is his rock of offense. This makes the foolishness of the cross and its offense more patently apparent in the spiritual world of heaven and hell than it ever was before. When Judas is swallowed up in darkness because of the judgment, his downfall proclaims the offense and foolishness to all the souls in heaven above, and to all the recesses of hell below.

The wonder, in the last analysis, is that Jesus' soul was able to remain entirely poised when God confronted Him with the corpse of Judas. We may believe that Jesus, who saw a Nathanael sitting under a fig tree, and who always sees clearly the fatal issue of sin, knew that Judas committed suicide. Can it be that He knew everything about Simon when that disciple denied his master, and nothing at all about Judas? Surely, that is untenable. But, in His unfathomable grief, He maintains His own unimpeachable integrity as He and His conscience face the dead Judas. He can look straight into God's eyes, and straight into the future of His long way of suffering without blinking.

There are people who find it very easy to pray for strangers the petition, "Father, forgive them." But to their immediate neighbors these people frequently are an offense. But when Jesus, a little later, prays the same prayer for strangers, His prayer does not curse what He has done for Judas, His neighbor. For He did Judas no wrong. Yes, there are those — in fact, we are all such — who must immediately smother all their fine prayers and all their philanthropical intercessions when one calls their attention to the misery of their wives, of their children, of their next-door neighbors. But when Jesus, in the very moment perhaps in which Judas falls to the ground becomes the intercessor for those strangers who are His murderers, and knocks at the gate of Paradise to ask admittance for the man crucified next to Him, the Father cannot dismiss Him by pointing at the body of the dead Judas. For Jesus did Judas no wrong.

This precisely is His justification before God. Jesus was the Mediator, and as Mediator He vindicated Himself over against Judas.

Now broad perspectives open up before us. Judas and Ahithophel are not two exceptional cases about whom decent people must shake their heads. God buried them and He placed no special marker over their graves. They are buried quite ordinarily next to all those others who ruin themselves by taking offense at the mediatorship of God's *good pleasure*. God did not compel Jesus to face the dead Judas by way of *testing* whether it would cause a flush of shame to cover His face, as though He were one suspected of murder. God was summoning you and me into court. We, *we* must make our appearance in judgment, we must learn to see those two next to each other before the throne of God. We must learn to see the broken Jesus and the broken Judas, must learn to see the house of David that has been destroyed and the bodyguard of Saul, an Ahithophel who simply cannot live with the poet of God's psalm. *We* must be present at this confrontation. All the angels must give us their undivided attention, must see how we conduct ourselves there. For the angels want to know whom we choose, and in whom we believe. It is fortunate if we can still blush in shame because we have so often raised objections to David and to Jesus, even though we reach the conclusion: innocent blood, innocent blood! Then we will know that the only escape left us after this most painful experience of soul is the avenue of humble prayer. As we face the dead body of Judas, our one escape will be a prayer asking to be confronted by the broken body and shed blood of the Son of David. *Except for that* we should be lost eternally; *because of that* we can confess our faith in the Mediator of God and man.

The death of Judas is the beginning of Christ's Passover feast. We should remember that the first cantos of the Hymn of the Passover are full of references to *justice*. And one learns to scan God's verses of justice and grace only in the school of sovereign good pleasure. Such scansion is the great stumbling-block. But what else would one do on the Friday which puts Judas to death in the morning and Christ in the evening? I believe in Jesus Christ, God's Only-Begotten, David's high-born Son. I believe that He was cast into hell, but also that He Himself descended into hell. No, Judas, you did not want Him, but the feast of the Passover could not wait for you. The serpent on your grave argued in vain against the second Adam, and confessed that she was more effective in paradises than on graves.

Christ's Blood Accepting a Memorial in Jerusalem

CHAPTER THIRTEEN

Christ's Blood Accepting a Memorial in Jerusalem

> ● *And the chief priests took the silver pieces, and said, It is not lawful for to put them into the treasury, because it is the price of blood. And they took counsel, and bought with them the potter's field, to bury strangers in. Wherefore that field was called, The field of blood, unto this day. Then was fulfilled that which was spoken by Jeremy the prophet, saying, And they took the thirty pieces of silver, the price of him that was valued, whom they of the children of Israel did value; And gave them for the potter's field, as the Lord appointed me.*
>
> MATTHEW 27:6-10.

THE history of Abraham's rights of inheritance begins and ends at a graveyard.

It begins at a grave. Abraham for a considerable sum of money bought a garden which might be used to bury Sarah's body and which his family even in their death might regard as a place of their own. This was the first struggle in which Abraham, who was a stranger among the heathen, engaged, in order to command a piece of the promised land. Thus he possessed in his death that which he did not actually own in his lifetime.

Now the seed of Abraham has almost reached its end. This is a significant moment. When Abraham bought his field, he was still roaming about, but he was on his way to the inheritance which had been assured him, to the promised Canaan. Now, many centuries later, the seed of Abraham still peacefully occupies that promised land. Abraham is still living in the ancient Canaan, but he is about to begin his roaming about again over the whole earth.

A few more minutes will speed away, and the fleshly seed of Abraham will have lost its right to a place in the world. Only a few more moments, and he will have become unfaithful to the divine calling by means of which God's sovereign will gave him a graveyard first, and a fertile country then. The Jews will have become unfaithful, yes, because they refuse an honorable grave to Abraham's great Son. Because of that they will have forfeited their right to their beautiful country. A few more moments, and the seed of Abraham will begin its sad, age-long vagabondage: the nomadic life of *the wandering Jew*.

Now that seed of Abraham has reached another crisis, and now the history of his inheritance again culminates in a graveyard. This takes place when Judas throws the thirty pieces of silver back into the temple. The priests are compelled to say of the very wages which they themselves have weighed out: "This is a scandal to the holy place; this money lies where it does not belong." And then they take those coins which deserve no place in the temple and use them to buy a graveyard for strangers. This is the moment of the purchase of Akeldama. In this moment Israel's rights to its inheritance are forfeited.

We must recall for a moment the events which lead to this purchase. When Judas noticed that nothing could be done for Jesus or himself any more, he rushed into the temple and threw the money he had earned by treachery at the feet of the priests. Judas wanted to be rid of those coins. Hence he upsets the tables of the money-changers, even the tables standing outside of the temple wall. Life has nothing to offer Judas now and the wages which enabled him to live for four months[1] at the expense of the Sanhedrin, and thus gave him an opportunity, if he wished it, to look around for a more suitable vocation[2] than that which had been his during these years with Jesus, mean nothing to him. He has no use for this money now, because he sees nothing in life worth living for.

Thereupon Judas went his own way. We shall say nothing further about that. We give our attention to the priests, to the

---

1. *Christ in His Suffering*, p. 70.
2. This gives us a glimpse at Judas' soul, which we must be honest enough to take: perhaps he had wanted to use the thirty pieces for his current expenses while he calmly looked about for another position.

scribes and to the Sanhedrin. They were embarrassed to know what to do with their own money. They felt that it was tainted money. It was tainted with the blood of Jesus. Intuitively they sensed that this money was not clean. It was not consecrated money, for it had been used to traffic in blood. Accordingly, they do not dare to add these coins to those in the temple. The temple is a hallowed place, and this money has served in war.

Could one wish to use money, tainted with human blood, to cover the expenses incurred in the temple-service? Could the guardians of the temple permit the tables of money-changers to stand right-side-up within the sanctuary? By no means. The Nazarene had merely imagined that they had made a house of merchandise of the house of God. Even David, whose hands were tainted with the blood of other men, was, because of that blood, not allowed to build a temple. Hence they do not want the blood which clings to these coins to be in their presence. Holy, holy, holy is the Lord Sabaoth. He who dwells with His Levites, who lives with His clean priests in a clean temple.

So much is certain, then: this money must be kept outside of the house of God. Not that a separate commandment dictates it in so many words. But various commentators point to such places as Numbers 35:33-34 where reference is made to blood which defiles the sanctuary, irrespective of how it has been shed. And they allude also to Deuteronomy 23:18 where we are told that the hire of a harlot or the wages of a dog may not be brought into the house of the Lord for any vow. In short, say these priests, all that has been earned by foul means may never be dedicated to the perfect temple service. Hence this blood money also must be kept out of the sanctuary.

But what can be done with it? Can it be equally divided among those present? No, it might be harmful, and, besides, it originally came from the treasury of the temple. Hence it would be better to assign it to some public use, to some good cause.

As yes — the solution finally comes. After careful deliberation they decide — at exactly what time we do not know — that they will use these pieces for buying a plot of ground which can be used as a cemetery for strangers.

From this decision we get a glimpse of the worth of the wages which had been paid Judas. The amount was enough to support the traitor for so many weeks, and was enough to pay for a piece of ground, large enough for a graveyard.

However that may be, it is remarkable that *prophecy* again insists upon being most strikingly fulfilled among the people of revelation. These Jewish leaders when they proceed to buy the field naturally take great pains in the selection and purchase. But it is also true that God has directed everything pertaining to this crooked business according to his most special providence. We read that they bought a field which had belonged to a potter. This means that the piece of ground had very likely been used by a well-known member[1] of the potter's guild for carrying on his business. The field very likely lay on the southeast slope of the so-called valley of Hinnom, a place which prophecy had pointed out as a striking symbol of hell, that great house of the dead. The purchase of this particular piece of ground was, as we have mentioned before,[2] a fulfillment of prophecy. We observed then that the prophet Zechariah had once predicted that the thirty pieces of silver, with which Israel had sent the Good Shepherd to His death, had to be thrown at the feet of the potter, and we indicated also that the thirty pieces were an unjust price in the eyes of God. Being a foul and filthy price, it had to be brought to a foul and filthy place.

Now it may be true that the text at the head of our chapter does not quote Zechariah himself, but refers to the quotation from Jeremiah. Irrespective of what we may think of that, we can at least be sure that the Evangelist was thinking of Zechariah's words.[3] Hence this is more than a "striking detail" and more than an allegory (which, because it is subjective, must at bottom always be a profanation). God intentionally governed events in such a way that prophecy was even literally fulfilled according to demonstrable, officially registered data. There is a potter here; he is here literally. Filth and impurities are here, and are literally here; for what could be more foul than a cemetery, especially a

---

1   A. Nede, *Die Leidensgeschichte unsers Herrn Jesu Christi nach den vier Evangelien*, II, p. 15.
2. *Christ in His Suffering*, p. 76.
3. Many different attitudes are taken towards this problem. The marginal notations of the "Statenbijbel" have suggested that the solution could be reached by means of textual criticism. Others believe that Matthew was in several places thinking of Jeremiah, but that he found the summary of all these references in Zechariah. Compare Grosheide, *Kommentaar Mattheus*, p. 339, and Groenen, *op. cit.*, pp. 306-308; and the standard commentaries.

cemetery for "strangers"? And God's holy mockery is here. The prophecy of Zechariah had already mocked the price at which God's faithful shepherds were "evaluated" by calling the sum a "goodly price." That same irony is active now.

This establishes beyond a doubt that Israel does not know what to do with its own blood-money. The treasury of the temple was used in order to take the great Builder of the temple captive. But, for the rest, this people which is treading upon its Shepherd does not know what to do with the thirty pieces. It bandies its own stipend to and fro between its spiritual leaders, until finally the coins come to rest between unwhitened graves (Matthew 23:27).

Yes, the money which Judas returned to the temple is used to buy a cemetery, a cemetery designed for strangers. Now we may not "spiritualize" these things. Unfortunately this has been done more than once.

"In reference to Matthew 13:13, where Jesus by way of explaining a parable says, 'The field is the world,' commentators, after the fashion of certain church fathers, point to what the blood of Christ has achieved for the world. For the price of His blood, they explain, the field of this world was purchased as a place of rest for us who are strangers on the earth."[1] Hilarius takes the fact that this field was designed for strangers to mean that the price of Jesus' blood would not benefit the Jews but the heathen, to the extent, of course, that they learned to believe in Christ. And Chrysostom and Augustine also thought that the field of the potter represented the church.[2]

Those who would "spiritualize" the material in this way miss the core of the significance of the whole event. Akeldama is not a divine prophecy about the church of the New Testament which never speaks of the heathen at the expense of the Jews, but lets them both together grow up out of the truths of Abraham. It is not a prophecy of God about the church but a protest on the part of the Jews against the church of the New Testament.

Even in Akeldama — for that is what the place is called later (because it had been bought for the price of blood) — even in Akeldama we can see a protest against the Spirit of Pentecost.

---

1. Groenen, *op. cit.*, pp. 304-305.
2. *Ibid*, 304-305.

For the Spirit of Pentecost will come after a while in order to bring the heathen and the Jews together by means of Christ's death, and in order to break down "the middle wall of partition." But the Jews strongly reinforced that middle wall of partition. It almost seems as if they purposely wanted to disown the prophecy and the judgment which God had proclaimed when, on the Friday of Jesus' death, He rent the veil of the temple. By means of that rent veil, we know, God is preaching that there is no holy place left in the world for the representatives of carnal Jewry. But those who turn the thirty pieces over and over, at the same time pretend to cling tenaciously to the inviolability of their age-old rights. They set apart a graveyard for *strangers*. In other words, they once more declare emphatically that a distinct line of demarcation separates Israel from the heathen. Here Israel's dead are to be interred; there those of the stranger. Here a child of Abraham must be buried; there the child of the stranger. The difference between a Jew and a non-Jew is the greatest conceivable difference. The middle wall of partition, they insist, is not to be broken down in all eternity.

In fact, it may even be that their passion for insisting on distinction is carried even farther. It is quite certain that the word "stranger" does not refer to the "heathen" but to those people in general who could not be counted among the holy people and could not be regarded as citizens of the holy city in a restricted sense. Perhaps the term refers to alien Jews, those who were born outside of the country, and who frequently visited the city on feast days. Moreover, it is also possible that the term "stranger" refers to proselytes.[1] But when we think of this meaning of the term, it is even more evident than when we think of it as referring generally to the "heathen" that the passion for distinction and separation was exerting itself to the limit among these Jews. To set apart a special cemetery for strangers is to insist on the distinction between what is Israel and what, strictly taken, is not Israel, on the difference between the natives of the country, or even of the city, and those outside of it.

Therefore we say that Akeldama is a protest issued beforehand against the flourishing communion which God for the sake of Christ will presently build up on the feast of Pentecost — when

---

1. Nebe, *op. cit.*, p. 15; Grosheide, *Kommentaar*.

God, for Christ's sake, will wipe out all distinctions between Jew and non-Jew, native and alien, initiate and proselyte, and when He will call Jew and heathen together to repentance in Jesus Christ.

Seen under the proper light, the purchase of Akeldama appears to be the most vivid illustration of the carnal thinking on the part of Abraham's lost sons with which we have met thus far. They array against the God who rent the veil, who moved their landmarks, and who mocked their passion for distinctiveness from on high. Akeldama was purchased with Judas' blood-money; it represents the wrath of Rachel who weeps for her children and will not be comforted because they are not. Just as weeping Rachel will not dry her tears because she blames Jesus and will never forgive Him for doing an injustice to Abraham's flesh, and for not accepting the nation as a special nation, just so Rachel's dirge is sung now as the Sanhedrin proceeds to dedicate Akeldama. Hoping against hope, they insist even to the point of appealing to the cemetery that the children of the home are different from the children of strangers. They refuse to accept the teaching of the Crucified One who said that those of all nations who fear God and deal justly are acceptable to God. Akeldama is a protest against Jesus and His open-hearted precursor who once preached this message to them: "Say not among yourselves, We are Abraham's children. For God is able of these stones to raise up children unto Abraham."

No, they are and will remain the children of Abraham, and the whole face of the world must, they insist, continue to be divided into nooks and corners. This part for the citizen, that for the strangers, Barbarian and Israelite must be kept separate in the world. After all, an alien scent lingers even in a death shroud. Akeldama, field of blood: newest and most obsolete of cemeteries.

We know, of course, that the Jews who hit upon the idea of setting Akeldama apart as a way of disposing of the thirty pieces did not look upon the matter in this way. Just as they were quite unconscious of the fact that the particulars given by Zechariah— the potter, the thirty pieces and the like—were being literally fulfilled in their odd transaction, so they were quite unaware that they, by keeping Judas' blood-money out of the temple, were making themselves subject to the threat of the ancient prophecy. The consideration that money tainted with blood had no place in the temple was, naturally, an outgrowth of the Levitical character of the laws of purification but it was not in itself a proof of the fact that such money was *ethically* tainted. Levitical cleanness or uncleanness is not the same as ethical cleanness. Hence when the authorities in Jerusalem refuse to receive this blood-money into the temple, they by no means want to have it supposed that the shedding of blood made possible by this money was not well-pleasing to God. They mean only that the temple will not be served by such anti-pacific contributions. The temple is irenical; consequently it wishes to have nothing to do with the price of blood. The business of war is not suitable to temples.

And although these leaders appeal to David who was also kept from building a temple with "bloody hands," they are nevertheless a long way from David. David's hands never manipulated the stones of a temple, but David's heart and mouth sang psalms for the temple, and the psalms were messianic in character. These curators of the temple share David's bloody hands, but not his messianic heart. So thoroughly have the psalms of David become lost to their spirit that they oppose them diametrically. They sell the real Author of those psalms, the great Son of David, for the price of blood, and their thirty pieces of silver can find rest only on a cemetery designed for strangers. Yes, their hands are tainted with blood, but not with the blood which soiled the hands of David, for David's had been dipped in the blood of Israel's enemies, whereas theirs are soiled with that of David's own Son.

The taint of this blood Akeldama cannot wipe out in all eternity. In vain do the Jews write the betrayal of their kingdom in the soil of a graveyard. Now that they betray their Kingdom, that Kingdom knows of no stranger other than themselves and their life.

But was not the fact that in Jerusalem itself the blood of Christ accepted a memorial for itself a triumph for God? A place for the blood of Jesus was reserved in the vocabulary of the Aramaic vernacular when the official language of the temple refused to put the blood of God's sacrificial Lamb into the hymns of the temple. God established a memorial for the blood of Jesus in the language of the tiny, of the unitiated. Akeldama, Akeldama, field of blood, field of the great blood, field of the unique blood, the blood of Jesus.

Thus God prepares for His Pentecostal blessing. Though the holy Hebrew language of the temple was mute about the blood of God's sacrificial Lamb, the vernacular, the Aramaic dialect (as is really the sense of the word) preaches the blood of Jesus aloud for all times, carries it into the market-place, and creates a memorial for it in the daily conversation of the masses: Akeldama, Akeldama.

Now this is not the defeat of revelation but its forward march. When the great and the eminent refuse, the meek and the humble may come. When the lords of the temple say that they will be silent about this blood, the vernacular carries the memory of it farther. As the natives of the house enter the temple gates they hear a voice saying: be silent about that blood; ignore it, cover it. But the strangers, who are brought to Akeldama by their family or by a few poor acquaintances, will pass under an arch which has the superscription "Jesus' blood" written in the popular tongue.

This, if we wish it, is material for a beautiful allegory, for the nomenclature of the speech-making congregation in the case of Akeldama corresponds to the facts of the feast of Pentecost. In Akeldama, as a matter of fact, the feast of Pentecost is already coming. God has already transferred the blood of Christ, the great subject of the conversations of the whole world, from the Hebrew to the Aramaic, from the language of the temple to the vernacular of the common people, from the tongue of priests to the jargon of street-cleaners, from official academic learning to officious popular mood, from Israel's legal bearers of glory to those who speak an alien tongue, the offspring of a mixed race. God has preserved the sound and the voice of Jesus' unique blood, and He has crystalized it in the unwritten superscription over the graveyard of Akeldama. The blood of Jesus is remembered by the dead and the living, by Akeldama and by the Holy Supper.

Therefore Akeldama is a condemnation of carnal Jewry. We have observed before that the people of Israel by rejecting the Messiah were following the course of "the dead who buried the dead." But this is even worse. Here the dead bury those who are called unto life. Now that Israel proceeds to crucify its own Mes-

siah, the offer of salvation comes to the "strangers." As God
grants the privileges of Zion to these "strangers," the Jews say:
we must see to it that these strangers remain very small, very
humble, even in their death: Akeldama, Akeldama.

And then the voice of God pronounced a clear and ringing
prophecy. The history of Israel — and now we return to our point
of departure — the history of Israel and of its inheritance-rights
began at a graveyard and ends at a graveyard. Remember Abraham who for a high price bought a field from the "sons of Heth."
But a great and a tragic difference separates that Abraham, who
bought a small piece of ground for his dead, from the Sanhedrin.

Abraham bought a place for his own who were among "strangers" but the Sanhedrin buys a place for the strangers who are
among their own. Abraham buys a grave because, although Canaan is his according to the promise, he does not actually possess
it. The Sanhedrin buys a graveyard on the assumption, doubtless,
that it has a right to the land of the fathers and actually possesses
it. But God has declared that Israel's right to Canaan and even to
Akeldama — those few square feet in an obscure corner — are no
longer the property of the people now that they crucify the Christ.

At Akeldama the great robbery begins. From this point on
Jewry is dismissed; from now on the Jews will have to roam over
the wide world. When Abraham bought his cemetery he bought
and paid for it honestly. But when the Sanhedrin buys a field, it
pays for it with the price of blood. The money which Abraham
set aside for the first piece of the promised land he was to occupy
had been given him by God Himself. But the money the Sanhedrin paid for a graveyard for strangers was robbed from the
temple, and was used to sell God Himself in the person of His
Son. When Abraham bought his grave, that which separated him,
his dead Sarah and his coming generation from the strangers until the days of Christ was his faith, and God's promise, and the
messianic spirit. Today the Sanhedrin buys a field for strangers;
again it emphatically draws a line of demarcation between itself
and the stranger. The day of Abraham has been fulfilled but they
do not see it, and do not want to see it. Hence it is not faith this
time but unbelief, not the promise but a falsely interpreted law,
not the spirit of Christ but the flesh which puts its seal on this
deed, a deed signed in the year of Christ's death. Abraham hoped

against hope that he who for the present had to buy a parcel of ground for his dead, would sometime through blessing become the owner of the whole of that rich land. But the Sanhedrin hopes against hope that it can still escape from the judgment, the very judgment which guarantees the strangers the rights of Israel itself.

Thus we can say that Sarah, the princess, was buried among strangers by faith, hope and love. But the princely Son of the queenly Sarah, the emancipating Son of the emancipated mother is being buried today by unbelief, self-deterioration, and terrible hatred. Had Akeldama existed when Jesus died, the Jews would not even have deigned to bury this Son of Sarah there. He belonged to those who are wholly accursed, to those who must be given a place with the wicked in death. Akeldama is far too good for Him. Therefore Akeldama, which is an expression of God's judgment against Israel's essential death, has come to us. We are strangers. Akeldama tells us, Except you repent, you shall similarly perish. You will also belong to those who as candidates for life point out the place of interment for others beneath your rank, when, as a matter of fact, you have yourself eternally lost your rank. The price of the blood of Jesus Christ — thirty pieces — was set aside to buy Akeldama. But let us not proceed to build the graves of the prophets, for the other side of this peculiarly Pharisaical piece of work is to purchase an Akeldama. Jerusalem, Jerusalem, thou that stonest the prophets, that buildest the grave for the prophets away out beyond Akeldama, but in the same city of Sodom and Egypt where our Lord was also crucified, Jerusalem, Jerusalem — no, we refuse to look at your graves any longer. We would look at the cross; we would follow Jesus who is on His way to Pilate, and who will give His blood in order that it may accomplish miracles of life in the dry field of the world for all those who are strangers by nature, but would be heirs by grace.

We would tremble in the presence of the judgment of Akeldama. It is not for nothing that to the right and to the left of the cities of men there are cemeteries, cemeteries for strangers. These are the Akeldamas in which Jews are buried. Those who were not Jews designated the place and said: "That corner; use that for a Jew."

Father of Abraham, grave of Sarah, chariots of Israel and the horsemen thereof! Akeldama in Jerusalem — the end of Sarah's grave, the beginning of those wanderings of the wandering Jew. The curses of the Arab, the psalms of the pentecostal congregation, and the steady gale of the day of Pentecost have driven the outcast Jew from his unwhitened graves.

For Christ is everywhere. He walks among the graves of strangers also. His relatives are there; Sarah looks to Akeldama for her many children, before long, in the last day. She knows very well that her great Son has achieved this, her Wonder-Child whom she bore and nursed with such great difficulty.

Christ Being Thrust Outside of the Sphere of Mosaic Law

CHAPTER FOURTEEN

Christ Being Thrust Outside of the Sphere of Mosaic Law

> ● *And they themselves went not into the judg-*
> *ment hall, lest they should be defiled; but that*
> *they might eat the passover.*
>
> JOHN 18:28b.

THOSE who would appreciate the suffering of Christ and the curse that accrued to Him, those who would taste of the dregs of that passion, must return again and again to the thought that Christ is being thrust outside of the sphere of law.

The concept of *Christ* as outlaw has appeared several times in this second volume. We noticed that in the presence of Annas Christ was placed outside of the sphere of canonical law. The servant who struck the Master on the cheek did so in violation of law. We can say that at this time Christ was put outside of the circle of civil law. Thereupon, we observed that Christ was defied on the mountain of prophecy. They beat and they buffeted Him. In other words, the leaders of the people cast Him out of the domain of ethical law. Anything was good enough for Jesus. They could do as they chose with Him. Laws had not been written with Him in mind. Therefore we say that Christ was set outside of the sphere of ethical law, that is, of the decalogue. On this occasion that which happened to Him before Annas was confirmed. He was treated as one having no civil rights. Thus they were not only, in that first preliminary session of the Sanhedrin before Annas, reaching back to the defiance heaped upon Christ after the sentence of the Sanhedrin, but they were also reaching ahead to what is to come now as they thrust Him out of the sphere of the ceremonial and symbolical law.

277

Not until this last thing has also been done is the work complete. Not until then is the profanation of Christ as outlaw, at least in so far as His people are concerned, entirely exhausted. Now the whole of the sacrosanct law which God gave Israel can be subsumed under these three classifications: the civil, the ethical, and the ceremonial. These three together constitute the law according to which God led His people along the messianic way; through these He realized His will and His counsel in effecting the history of redemption. Now if Christ, because of the curse resting upon Him for our sin, must be made Christ the outlaw, He must be completely thrust outside of the law. Otherwise His suffering and His curse are not yet complete. It is not enough that they take away from Him the protection of civil and ethical law. This process of removing Him from the domain of right had to reach a sharper crisis: they had to cast Him out of the sphere of the Mosaic, the ceremonial, the symbolical law also. Only then, as far as Israel was concerned, would the task be completed. Only then would Moses and the Prophets, the law and the prescriptions, in short, the whole legislative activity of the Old Testament, the whole inspiration of the Holy Spirit as it had been poured out in the Old Testament up to this time — only then would these all arise in judgment against Christ who was made sin because He was accursed for our sake. Only after Jesus had been plunged into an externally perceptible judgment also would He who was called the Nazarene be completely excommunicated by the Old Testament. Only then would they, in the name of the messianic image, have rejected Him whom the image bodied forth. Only then would Moses who gave the symbolical law, and Elias, who had again intensified the force of that law for the indolent priests, the ignorant prophets, and the indifferent kings, be officially summoned into judgment by the people of Israel to testify against the Nazarene. Then only would the Jewish nation in its ignorance, of course, but also while being fully responsible, hang up the picture which is diametrically opposed to the one of Christ on the mount of transfiguration.

At the beginning of the gospel of the passion, Moses and Elias had come to the mountain as messengers of God to tell Jesus that He must die in Jerusalem, but also that He would in that fulfill the lifework of Elias and Moses. They emphatically call Jesus *into* the sphere of law. Christ who is the origin, the mediator, the purpose, and the sublime, evangelical mystery of their legal work —*He* is expressly called *into* the domain of that law.

But could the Christ on His way to His suffering have tasted of heaven's luxury unmolested? That would have been too much for Him. No, He will have to compensate for all His joy: God will convert all His feasting into mourning.

Now God must convert into mourning the festival of His meeting with Moses and Elias, who drew their circle around Him, saying: Thou belongest inside it. However, Moses and Elias must now emphatically keep Him out of it, saying: Our laws reject Thee; they do not pertain to Thee; they have no bearing on Thee. Naturally, Moses and Elias will not do this themselves. The San-hedrin will do it; but by means of the Sanhedrin, God Himself will be doing this work, the God of Moses and Elias. Just as God Himself later delivers up Christ to the cross by means of Pilate, so God Himself now makes Christ an outlaw by means of the Sanhedrin. God Himself now has become Christ's enemy, ex-cluding Him from the area of relevance of all of Israel's laws. Judas has betrayed Him, has he, and Simon denied Him? Yes, and to this end: Moses will not deny Jesus; through Moses God will excommunicate Him. For is He not the Surety?

Now note this. Christ can be harassed perfectly by the sombre counter-design of the dazzling brilliance on the mount of transfig-uration only when the people of Israel and the Sanhedrin summon Moses and Elias into judgment against the Nazarene. Now these two, and this time according to the inevitable logic of the flesh to which the Judge on high affixes His seal, will again have to tell Jesus that He will die in Jerusalem. They have given Him this message before; now they must repeat it.

But it is not they who fill in the details of the message. He must die in Jerusalem, yes, and outside of the city gates. They must tell Him that their sphere of law can contain Him no longer. That like a pariah He is being cast out of the communion of Is-rael's ritual, that He apparently is not the comforting, mysterious secret of the law, that He has been made sin, and, accordingly, that He is reckoned with those unholy ones whose life is a contin-ual warfare against the law. Moses and Elias must regard Him as the great stumbling-block which stands in the way of a breaking through of evangelical grace, the grace for which Moses as well as Elias was reaching.

Only when this has happened, only when the sphere of ceremonial law, too, has driven Jesus of Nazareth out, crying "unclean, unclean" against Him, will everything written in the Old Testament and in the whole law of revelation — by unbelief of course, but through these by God the Judge also — be summoned into judgment against Jesus of Nazareth.

Just that much happened to Him today. Unclean, unclean! God sends Moses in pursuit of Satan, who comes to mobilize all of Jaweh's laws against Christ, and to excommunicate Him. We know that excommunication means to deliver the rejected one up into Satan's hand. The Jews do not have that in mind, it is true (p. 186), but God does. It is just that which God achieves through them.

Such is the awful significance of what is told us in our narrative by the finely discriminating evangelist, John. What we have in our text is not a little particular which at best has only a chronological significance. It is just this chronological significance, however, which has occupied at least ten writers. We read that the whole Sanhedrin arose but took great pains not to go into the judgment hall lest they be defied for eating the Passover. No, this is no insignificant detail. It is a real, historical complement to everything that has gone before. It is a dogmatic amplification of the sombre fact of the curse which God by means of the unspiritual, Jewish exegesis of the Old Testament opposes to the Saviour of the New. We, accordingly, shall not delay long in considering the matter of chronology which has set so many pens in motion. The nature of this book keeps us from doing that. Suffice it to indicate the argument of some to the effect that the chronological facts which John puts into our text are in contradiction to the accounts of the other evangelists. They believe, on the basis of what the other evangelists say, that the Passover meal had been eaten on the morning of the day on which Christ was delivered up to Pilate. John, according to them, is referring to that part of the progam of the feast which is still to take place. Now John says that the Jews refuse to go into the judgment hall. Why did they refuse? The answer is that for them to enter the hall of a heathen in this way would, according to the ritual, be to defile themselves for the

Passover. This they would circumvent, lest they should have to eat the Passover with an uneasy conscience.

Now if it is true that the phrase "to eat the Passover" refers only to actually partaking of the Passover lamb, we would have to agree that John's presentation of the chronology of events conflicts with that of the other evangelists. Others have, however, satisfactorily explained the apparent difficulty. These maintain that the phrase "to eat the Passover" may be used in a narrower and a broader sense. Even though the phrase originally referred to the actual partaking of the feast, the center of which, naturally, was the eating of the lamb, it is still possible to deduce from several sources that the same phrase was used for such activities of the feast as followed upon the actual Passover meal. The celebration was by no means completed after the lamb had been eaten. Moreover, the regulations governing Levitical cleanness were binding for these later activities also. Hence the person who wanted to celebrate the feast, and who wanted to take part in each of its activities and to conclude it with the others, had to preserve the ritualistic regulations of cleanliness punctiliously throughout the day in the manner designated by the law and custom regulating feast days.

There is, therefore, no conflict at all between the several accounts of the evangelists; no one need dispute the unity of the narratives. Accordingly, our thoughts take a different direction as we read of the scruples which caused the Jews to halt at the steps of the court house. This event gives us a glimpse of the tragic conflict that exists between the Jewish *externalization* (formalization) of the law and the revelation, and the true, messianic, *spiritual* fulfillment of it. How meagre and yet how human the Jews prove themselves to be here. They fear that they will not be able to partake of the Passover because of a defilement which might be theirs if they should enter a heathen house. They do conduct Jesus to Pilate, but they do not enter the prætorium themselves lest it hamper them in carrying out their share in the remaining schedule of the celebration. A superficial treatment could very easily work out various contrasts here between the extravagant sin which the Jews are willing to undertake, on the one hand, and the punctiliousness with which they keep their days "clean," on the other. Here is reason indeed for recalling Jesus' utterance about those who strain at a gnat and swallow a camel. Yes, we will even go farther and say that at no time was the pronounced contrast between the gnat and the camel as conspicuous as it is at this moment. While being mocked and defied, Christ is delivered up to death by a most atrocious injustice, and at the same time the letter of the law, amplified by human customs, is being fastidiously observed.

However, it would not be appropriate for us to work out these pronounced contrasts in a superficial and cynical fashion: it would not do for us to shake our heads superciliously at the stupidity of those who are responsible for them. Jesus never follows that method. There is something more than mere "pettiness" at work here. In this also Pharisaism is but following the course of its own intrinsic logic.

What we have here first of all is an "externalization" of religion. Christ was the *form,* the purpose of all the laws that God gave to Israel. No one ever had the key that would disclose the meaning of law, save Him who saw it as a particular moment, as a unique phase, of that history of redemption in which God throughout all the preceding centuries had searched out and pointed to the Christ. But the Jews have thrown away the key which God gave them to the law. They externalized the law; they made it a purely formal thing by explaining it in terms of itself, by not allowing the evangelical light to throw upon the screen the image of the meek, the lowly, the gentle Messiah which was contained in the law. Once they had explained the law without reference to Christ Jesus who was to come by grace, they proceeded to cut the "symbols" loose from the "body," the types from Him they typified, the ceremonies from the Spirit, the lamb of the Passover from the Christ, ritualistic cleanness from regeneration, the priests from the Chief Priest, the covenant fellowship of Israel from the covenant fellowship of the new dispensation, the flesh of Abraham (his natural fatherhood) from his faith (his spiritual fatherhood). It is this distorted logic of an erroneous apperception of the Scriptures which expresses itself in a rejection of the Christ at the same time that a painfully fastidious insistence on the letter of the law is maintained. Such conduct lets the children of sin go on cherishing the illusion that they are doing God a service by staying outside of a pagan court, a court in which leavened loaves are served on the day of unleavened bread.

In the second place, we have here the tragedy of self-assertion, a self-assertion which, once it had misunderstood God's laws, proceeded to add to them by means of human regulations. Once a person has lost his hold on the spiritual content of the law, and has no further need of penetrating what was at first the transparent wall of external ceremony with an eye enlightened by the spirit, it must necessarily follow that a misdirected zeal will make that wall firmer, denser, and sturdier, so that it may not be broken down in all eternity.

Thus did the Jews add their stipulations to the law of God. In other words, they emasculated God's law by means of their human regulations. After all, the stipulation that a pagan house could be entered only at the cost of ritualistic defilement was one which could be found nowhere in the laws.[1] True, the law indicated in Deuteronomy 16:4 prescribed that during seven days of the Passover season the Jews might have no leaven in their house. But that prohibition says nothing about shunning a pagan palace because of the fact that there is leaven in it. The stipulation which the Jews feared so anxiously is one which the Rabbis and Scribes have added to the regulations found in the canonical books. Similar additions were those humanly contrived ones which Christ expressly opposed in His conflict with the Pharisees and the Scribes. These all were the interpretations of the Scribes, as we know them from the *mishna*, for example, in which a law such as the one involved here is given. Not the Author of the law but the false interpreters, the Rabbis, were responsible for such legal interpretation. In this matter also "the great God proves to be more merciful than the churchistic Jew. The rabbis had unnecessarily accentuated the separation which God had intended to be temporary. Never had the law absolutely prohibited the Jews from making contacts with a heathen, or with a heathen house. What God had forbidden was the fellowship or the making of covenants with pagans. When the Jews refused to enter Pilate's judgment hall 'lest they be defiled' (John 18:28) they simply proved to be the pitiable slaves of a tyrannical formalism."[2] Who now would dare to dismiss these Jews as people who strain at gnats; who would dare

---

1. Strack-Billerbeck, *Kommentaar zun N.T. aus Talmud und Midrasch*, Volume 2, Excurs zum Todenstag Jesu, D. 11, p. 838.
2. Dr. B. Wielenga, *Van Jerusalem naar Rome*, Volume 1, p. 456, Kampen, J. H. Kok.

to think that by dismissing them in that way he had completely characterized the whole of their sinful attitude? Throughout the centuries the tragic tale has been the same: the moment the liturgical man no longer sees *through* the wall of symbols and of visible things in the city of God, he inevitably falls into the habit of merrily spinning out human laws and regulations. And in this respect also the Jew who shuns the prætorium will experience precisely what everyone experiences who has not seen the Christological significance of the Scriptures.

A third significance may be seen in this tragic event also. Not only do the Jews assert themselves *externally* as a Hebrew nation over against heathendom when they shun the prætorium of the procurators, but they also assert themselves *internally,* that is, within the sphere of the Jewish congregation itself. There, too, the priests and the members of the Sanhedrin want to maintain their dignity as a privileged caste on this beautiful feast day. For, even if they had entered the house of the pagan, they would have had a chance for active participation in such activity of the celebration as still remained on the schedule. All that they would have lost is the dignity of their position. Now we know that throughout the Passover great caution in the matter of Levitical cleanness was emphatically enjoined upon everyone as an important requisite. Each day, for instance, the streets were swept. And when they were actually sitting at the festal meal the liturgically clean had to be kept carefully separated from the liturgically unclean. If they were walking on the carefully swept street, the ritualistically clean persons enjoyed the middle of the road; the unclean had to stay on the side. Moreover, there was a separate, high-flung arch through which those passed who in a legal sense were clean. Those who were not had to take the humbler side-route.[1]

Naturally, the Jewish authorities remembered that as they were at present they could take that middle course, and in passing through the gate could take the high route of clean people. In this we see the delight in preeminence, that characteristic of the Jewish caste-spirit, asserting itself to the limit on the day of Christ's death. The Jewish leaders will not forfeit at any price the privilege of that dignified procession along the middle of the thoroughfare

---

1. Gustaf Dalman, *Orte und Wege Jesu*, 3rd edition, *Gütersloh*, 1924, p. 299.

and through the gate which must be raised for them as they pass
through it. They want to appear as though they especially are
crowned of God. This, then, is the bitter irony in terms of which
the Bible outlines a conflict between flesh and Spirit as that struggle is carried out on the day of Christ's death. The judges of
Israel insist on their rights of passage through the middle of the
street with a painful insistence. Meanwhile Jesus, as He who is
unclean, is regarded as being good enough for the unclean house
of the pagan procurator. The Jewish judges, those epigones of
Moses, Aaron, and Solomon, and of all the prophets, took great
pains not to lose the privilege of passing through the high-flung
gate along the highway of the clean. But they see to it that Christ
is thrown outside of the gate as one accursed. This, too, is His
passion. His people deliver Him at Pilate's door, but keep their
own hands clean in their dealings with the heathen. This people—
and they are His own people—now sanction a method of interpretation of the law which is a contradiction of itself. Only a caricature of that law remains. The Word is at bottom cut loose from its
Speaker, the symbol from the law, the letter from the spirit.

That, therefore, which pushes Christ over the borderline is a
conscious insistence upon the line of demarcation which separates
the profane province of heathendom from the holy province of Israel. No one given to removing landmarks could ever grieve Him
as severely as these spiritual rangers are doing here. All the symbols of the law were calling for Him, but He is cast out in the
name of that very symbolical service. As a monster born of God's
fruitful people, He is brutally thrown out of the fellowship of the
temple.

Nevertheless, it is not becoming for us to begin criticising the
Jews now, for all those who have shared in the threefold guilt of
externalization, of a distortion of the Scriptures, and of self-assertion are essentially one with these Jews, even though in themselves
they have not the power, like the Jews, to demonstrate the perverse
logic of their own sins.

No, there is but one thing for us to do. We must stretch our
hands out to the Surety of our souls. He allowed Himself to be
accursed by all that is law in our stead. By suffering the passion
of that curse, fully aware of its intensest implications, and in obedience to His heavenly, that is, to His perfectly exacting Judge, He

entered into the great self-concealment which permanently keeps the messianic suffering from being mitigated or tempered. It is in concealment, that He Himself in His strong love publicly makes His debut for the faith. The visible wall of external shadows and signs, to which the Jews have added more and more stays, again becomes transparent to him who believes, for Christ's great light shines through it from the inside. Jesus endures the suffering when they throw Him behind the gate of the heathen court, even though they themselves refuse even to pass through it. He endures being classified with barbarians. For He has great plans in mind. Presently He will show Simon Peter a vision from heaven. A great sheet will be lowered from heaven in which both clean and unclean animals will be presented as food (Acts 10). That event will prove that the Surety who endured being segregated with the "sect" of the barbarians is transferring those barbarians, together with the believing Jews, to a new communion, to the universal world-unity of the new messianic humanity, which will make all fleshly partakers of the Passover Lamb a "sect." At the same time in which Christ is being pushed behind the curtains of a pagan house, He earns the right to rend the veil in the temple. He achieves the right to break down the middle wall of partition, and to give to the former barbarians, to the unclean pariahs, and to the abandoned heathen the fellowship of the Messiah of the Scriptures. Accordingly, the hour in which the laws of Moses cast out the Christ was an hour of world-renovating significance. The primary cry no longer is, "Separate yourselves from the palaces of pagans." The call now is, "Separate yourselves from the essence of sin."

This moment caused schisms, yes. The lawyers of Moses segregate themselves from Christ. They thrust Him out of their fellowship. Naturally, their fellowship failed to flourish then, and that is a comfort to no one. But there is another comfort now. It is that God has achieved this schism through the Jews. It is to their detriment, but to the good of those who are of Christ, for these all can flourish now by virtue of their genuine root. With His own hand God cast Christ outside of the sphere of law. God Himself kept the Jews back at the threshold of Pilate's judgment hall. For the whole law must make its demands on Jesus, in order that the whole law presently may harmonize with the gospel.

Whoever has read the letter to the Galatians will appreciate why the Jews shunned the judgment hall into which they threw the Christ. In this way, room could be made in the Bible for the statement: "Christ has redeemed us from the curse of the law, being made a curse for us." Thus, too, room could also be made for those other statements: "When the fullness of the time was come, God sent out His son, made of a woman, made under the law, to redeem them that were under the law, that we might receive the adoption of sons. And because we are sons, God hath sent forth the Spirit of His Son into your hearts, crying, Abba, Father. Wherefore thou art no more a servant, but a Son; and if a Son, then an heir of God through Christ." "Stand fast therefore in the liberty wherewith Christ has made us free, and be not entangled again with the yoke of bondage." "Christ is become of no effect unto you, whosoever of you are justified by the law; ye are fallen from grace. For we through the spirit wait for the hope of righteousness by faith. For in Jesus Christ neither circumcision availeth anything, nor uncircumcision; but faith which worketh by love." "For in Christ Jesus neither circumcision availeth anything nor uncircumcision, but a new creature and as many as walk according to this rule, peace be on them and mercy, and upon the Israel of God."

Let us keep the feast in the palace of a pagan then, in the prætorium of Pilate, for there we were born. The place was good enough for God to use as the place in which to regenerate us through Christ's Spirit. Let us keep the feast in the court of the pagan, for it was there also that the Passover was slain for us, the Passover who is Christ Jesus. It was slain on this side of the threshold; it segregates us from those who are seeking Abraham's house of bondage. O incomparable irony! The Jews seek the house of bondage, but they make pretensions to cleanness by calling that house unclean, and by shunning it. Now they can keep the feast no longer. The house without which they cannot live is barred to them: who, then, can keep the feast? As for us, we are led out of the house of bondage and into the house of the Father. Let us then keep the feast, not in the old leaven, or in the leaven of evil and of wickedness, but in the unleavened bread of integrity and truth.

For the account of Christ's excommunication through the law-
givers of Moses also serves as the Form written by God Himself
for our acceptance by Jesus Christ our Lord. God Himself wrote
that Form, and our High Priest, who was called leprous and unclean, read it to us Himself. He is the clean Priest of God; He
stands in the inner sanctuary—there where He brought the loot of
barbarians. A very great host they were, and Moses did not reject
them.

Christ Being Raised Above the Sphere of Mosaic Law

CHAPTER FIFTEEN

Christ Being Raised Above the Sphere of Mosaic Law

● *Pilate went out unto them, and said, What accusation bring ye against this man? They answered and said unto him, If he were not a malefactor, we would not have delivered him up unto thee. Then said Pilate unto them, Take ye him, and judge him according to your law. The Jews therefore said unto him, It is not lawful for us to put any man to death: that the saying of Jesus might be fulfilled, which he spake, signifying what death he should die.*
JOHN 18:29-32.

ALL the evil that men contrive in this crooked world, God turns into good. The very announcement which was given the brothers of Joseph is given to His brethren today by a Greater than Joseph: "Ye thought evil against me; but God meant it unto good." This is just one more reason for saying to those who do not dare to come near Him because of their sins: "Fear not, for I am in the place of God" (Compare Genesis 50:19).

You sense the point we want to make. We want to point out the harmony, the unity of thought, between the preceding chapter and this one. In that chapter we noticed that they are placing Christ outside of the sphere of Mosaic law. That narrow place is altogether too holy for the profanest of Nazarenes. Therefore: Cast Him out, cast Him out. But while that is going on, God, through whom that same Son is lifted above the far too narrow sphere of the law and of the dispensation of Moses, achieves another accomplishment for His Son. The Jews say, "He stands outside of the law." God replies, "He transcends the law." He who

291

casts out degrades; He who lifts up, transcends. Thus did God exalt His Son in the hour of His humiliation. Yes, it is true that the shadow of humiliation is already falling upon the Son of man; even as it does so, however, it appears that He is the exalted One. He is exalted by the death on the cross, exalted presently above the clouds, exalted in order that all who believe may not perish but may have everlasting life in Him.

This Nazarene, God announces, cannot be kept within the narrow sphere of Moses. Just as Moses raised the serpent—in the wilderness, it is true—so must the Son of man be raised, not in a wilderness in which a small congregation is hidden away, but in full view of the world. He must be raised on a cross, and lifted high above the highest heavens. He Himself announced this, signifying what manner of death He should die (John 12:32-33; 3:14). This it is which God confirms now as He arranges and directs the history of the coming together of the Jews and the Romans in such a way that the saying of His Son is fulfilled, signifying what death He should die.

We need not reproduce the narrative of the event at great length. The fastidious Jews came to deliver Jesus up to the judge. When they reached the front of Pilate's praetorium they came to a halt, not daring to enter. Pilate soon knew what they wanted. He went out to meet them; the judge came out to meet the accusers. He did not insist upon himself, did not haughtily demand that they should come to him when they wanted something. No, as a good diplomat, as one who knows his business, he follows the customs of Rome's colonial policy which instructed its representatives not to ignore unnecessarily the fine points in the religion of its vanquished peoples, but to reckon with these carefully. Hence Pilate is not above coming out of doors and asking what they want.

We must say however, that this was a pathetic beginning of the day. Pilate overlooks Moses, and honors the specific kind of religion which is called Judaism. Such is his diplomatic art. But he fails to inquire into the essence of religion. After a while he will ask, "What is truth?" "Moses" may continue to occupy his little corner of the world as long as he does not interfere with Rome. But there is no room for Christ today, for Christ comes to reveal the hidden significance of Moses. He has come to set the essence of the cult free from its ancient "forms"—and it is this rôle which will cost Him His life today.

Yes, this is the pathetic beginning of Pilate's gloomy day. He ignores all religions but *the* religion. He honors all religions but fails to ask Him who is the essence of religion any questions except the dubious, "What is truth?"

But before Pilate reaches the point of asking even this question, he squirms and twists himself into many contortions in an effort to rid himself of the case of Jesus. At first he is inclined to revert the question which has been appealed to him, to the Jews themselves. Not that he feels unqualified to take care of the matter. No, not that. But all of these issues which arise out of the Jewish religion are really too trivial and mean for his attention. Hence he asks the Jews just what the charge against the man is. Now this was not merely a formal question designed to get the proceedings under way. It is plain that Pilate is really eager to return the issue to the Jews themselves. This becomes obvious even before they have told him what the charge against the Nazarene is. Plainly, then, when Pilate asks for their formulation of the charge, he is, as becomes apparent later, trying to rid himself of the whole matter.

But the Jews refuse to go in that direction. They have staked everything on the attempt to have Jesus condemned as a traitor to the state. Surely, it is not for nothing that they have held that early morning session with a view to formulating the charge.

We know that the morning session of the Sanhedrin (Matthew 27:1; Mark 15:1a; and Luke 22:66) was designed to plan as exactly as possible how to have the sentence imposed by the Sanhedren carried out by Roman authority. They had looked for the most expedient way of inducing Pilate to condemn Jesus as a traitor to the state. The Jews do not want Jesus' incompatibility with the law of Moses or with the theology of Judaism pushed to the fore as the sole *casus belli*. They know very well that Pilate will not allow himself to be hitched to a wagon of the Jewish theologians. And even if he could be constrained to deliver Jesus up for purely theological reasons, the responsibility for His death then would remain squarely on the shoulders of the Jewish authorities. And who could predict how the people would react if the Nazarene should be delivered up solely upon the authority of their spir-

itual leaders? Who can tell? Today or tomorrow the people
might say: Why did you do that? No, no one could predict what
capricious turn the temper of the people might suddenly take.
Therefore the Jews feel that the more cautious thing to do is to
place the responsibility for the final decision into Pilate's hands.
The conclusive argument, then, which they could use to vindicate
the death of the Nazarene to each and every eventual critic, would
be that of the Roman governor himself, the one which none other
than he had officially brought into the foreground.

This gives us the reason at once for which the Jews do not wish
to tell Pilate precisely which final conclusion the Sanhedrin had
reached. Under the direction of Caiaphas that session had found
Jesus guilty of blasphemy. But blasphemy is a theological issue,
and what does Pilate care about theology? No, they must give
matters a different turn, must carefully lead Pilate into another direction. Jesus must be condemned not because He has blasphemed
God, but because He has subverted the state.

Mark their tactics. They do not give a straightforward answer
to Pilate's question. They present no legal paper upon which Caiaphas' sentence has been tersely and effectively epitomized. Instead,
they evade Pilate's question for the moment. They say in effect:
If this man were not really a malefactor (suggesting that He is
one, even according to Roman law), we would not have brought
Him to you. Now this sounds very much as if they were telling
Pilate: Go ahead; investigate the matter thoroughly, and you will
find that He is indeed a transgressor of the law which you as the
Roman authority are pledged to protect and uphold.

And now begins that bidding against each other which is to
characterize the activity of the whole day. Pilate who fears very
much that he will trap himself in the snares which are lying about
abundantly, tells the Jews that they may take Jesus and judge Him
according to their own law. Understand that this is not an ironical
utterance by which the haughty Roman more or less sarcastically
wanted to mock those who were seething around him. He was not
trying to suggest to them that they could not do anything without
him anyhow. No, this is a serious gesture on his part; he wants to
have done with the case. He gives the Jews the authority to act
according to their own findings, and then to give him a record of
their decision, a petition for a writ of capital punishment—de-

manded in that case, of course by the Jewish law—for his signa-
ture. Note that he is not yielding an inch of his authority—to do
that might prove very costly later. But he wants to leave the tedious proceedings entirely in the hands of the Jews. According to
its own findings the Sanhedrin may on the basis of its own prece-
dent draw up the charge and fix the penalty. Pilate can see later,
then, whether the sentence can eventually be sustained.[1]

In short Pilate gives them a free rein. But it is just this free
rein which they do not want now. For if they are to be allowed to
take the law into their own hands, the Roman authority resting
satisfied meanwhile with a "fiat," their whole programme as
drawn up in the morning assembly would be nullified not only,
but the plan on which they had deliberated for weeks could then be
said to have practically failed. Not since morning but since weeks
ago, they have intended to see to it that Jesus be brought into conflict with Roman law. This is very apparent from Luke 20:19, 20.
What we read there proves beyond a doubt that the Jewish leaders
long ago understood that because of the people they would have
to proceed very carefully. The question about whether Jesus was
of God or of Satan might become an embarrassing one. Hence
they "took note of Him then." They kept spies around Him in the
secret hope that these would find reasons for delivering Him up
into the hands of the procurator and the rulers of the city. Now
it seems as if this carefully contrived programme is to be nullified
in a moment by the suggestion of the haughty Pilate. No, no, they
do not want that. The "royal" gesture of this Roman official is
altogether too objectionable to these servile natures. They do not
want to cast Jesus out on their own authority; hence they insist
upon a formal, disciplinary investigation against Jesus. It is designed by all means to put him to death under the Roman yoke.
Hence they reply just as formally as Pilate spoke, that they have
not the authority to put anyone to death. Very diplomatically they
insist upon strictly legal procedure. A comparison of their atti-

---

1. This interpretation removes the objections which some have against saying
that Pilate's statement was seriously intended. It avoids the solution according
to which Pilate spoke sarcastically on this occasion, a solution very hard to sustain, and also harmonizes with the data of the text concerning the manner of
Christ's death. If the Jews had been compelled to sentence Jesus on their own
responsibility, stoning would have resulted, and Pilate would officially have
allowed that. Concerning this issue, read also the rest of the chapter.

tude at this time with the one they carry out against Stephen, who was stoned by the Jews, proves beyond a doubt that they were not morally sincere in this insistence.

Bidding against each other, turning and twisting about—surely, all this is a very petty business, and yet in this, too, the wisdom, and counsel, and majesty of God are apparent. For John adds to his account of the event: "And this took place in order that the saying of Jesus might be fulfilled, which He spake, signifying what death He should die."

What death . . . what manner of death. It is in reference to this that their humanly contrived machination again touches on the solid bottom and carefully arranged plan of divine prophecy. Right now, at this first contact between the Jews and Pilate, the shadow of the cross falls upon the corridors of the praetorium. And it is God Himself who puts the sun of prophecy, the passion of Christ, and this madding of the Jews into such an integral relationship with each other that the shadow of the cross must indeed fall upon this palace. For, in the counsel of God, the issue in this matter is the manner of the death which the Christ should die. Suppose for a moment that Jesus had actually been put to death without a direct participation in the trial on the part of the Roman authorities as represented in Pilate. Then Jesus would have been *stoned* but not *crucified*.

Stoning, we know, was the Jewish method of execution; crucifixion was that of the Romans. From God's point of view, the question now is whether Jesus is to be sent to His death by the bastard sons of Moses, or by the nails of the soldiers of Rome, that typical Beast of the world. Is the death of Jesus to be carried out solely within the narrow walls of the house of Moses, the house in which his bastard sons are rising up against the faithful Interpreter and Fulfillment of Moses? Or is the death of Christ, which is to include all heaven in its sweep, also to perturb and move the whole earth, not excluding the heathen? Is the brass serpent to be raised only in the restricted and degraded area of the malicious Jews, or is that serpent, in the form of its counter-image in the Son of man, to be raised on the horizon of all nations, and of all men? Is the death of Christ to be the act of a sect—the Jews are just that at the very moment in which they put their king-Messiah to death—or is it to be the sentence of the whole world, the universal finding of Jews and barbarians together? Indeed, God cannot do without the barbarians : all flesh must put the Son to death. Just at this time, just when a combination is effected at the door of God's house, God intervenes and directs the wicked business which each is conducting to its own ends for opportunistic reasons, to the end which He Himself has in mind..

Jesus is to die. Yes, but in the manner which God has appointed for Him. He must be lifted up so that all may see Him. His cross must be raised, not in the gloom of a Jewish temple, or of a rabbinical college, but under the full sun of the world and of world economy. His cross must be raised at the crossroads of the world where the nations meet and pass.

Just that is the meaning of our text which tells us that Jesus' own statement still had to be fulfilled, His saying, signifying what death He should die. Now the concept of revelation which God gives us in this text will become meaningful to us the moment we relate it to what we were told earlier in the Gospel. There are several utterances of Christ which point in the same direction as this one recorded by John. We all think in this connection, for instance, of John 13 :14, 15 : "And as Moses lifted up the serpent in the wilderness, even so must the Son of man be lifted up : that whosoever believeth on Him should not perish, but have everlasting life." We also think of John 12 :31a, 32, and 33, where Jesus says : "Now is the judgment of this world ; and I, if I be lifted from the earth, will draw all men unto me ; this He said signifying what (manner of) death He should die." Moreover, in this connection a light is also shed upon Matthew 20 :18, 19 : "Behold, we go up to Jerusalem, and the Son of man shall be betrayed unto the chief priests and unto the Scribes, and they shall condemn Him to death, and shall deliver Him to the Gentiles, to mock, and to scourge, and to crucify Him, and the third day He shall rise again (See Mark 10 :33, 34 ; Luke 18 :32, 33).

Now if we put these scattered statements into relation with each other (as is the duty of any exegesis that is faithful to the Scriptures), we see that the manner of Christ's death is not an accidental one ; it is not a merely regional or historical particular, hardly essential to the whole, but it responds fully to the logic of God, and to the logic of the events as they are described here, and are arranged and governed by the history of special revelation. Jesus might not and could not be stoned within the limits of Mosaic law, for He wanted to be *lifted up*.

To be lifted up. In other words, He must be advertised; He would have world-wide publicity. He would be a universal sign. The journal kept by a decaying Sanhedrin is too trivial for Him; His name and the proceedings of His trial must be taken down in the annals of the world. Men must be able to see Him from all sides. In a time of world-crisis, He would "be lifted up from the earth." For He affects everyone. Therefore He must go to the heathen. He must be raised on the cross, He must be "lifted up." The phrase is rich in meaning. On the one hand, it gives expression to the fact that one who is crucified is raised from the earth, is put on display above the heads of the spectators, is made a "spectacle" to those who would see it. In this sense, the phrase represents a very concrete expression of the manner of Christ's death, and nothing more than that. In another sense, it transcends the scope of concrete language. The idea of "being lifted up" must also be developed in a theological sense. It may be true that the raising, the public manifestation, of the crucified Jesus is an act of men, but it is also an exaltation on the part of God, the God of the whole world. He and He first of all is the one who exhibits the crucified Son to the whole world. Moses raised the brazen serpent on a rod in order that a whole people, a whole community of those who were wrapped in death's folds, might see it. That serpent had to shine forth above the white tents of those who had been summoned to die, and even over the curtains of the temple behind which God dwelt, but dwelt in concealment. Just so Jesus must be lifted up today, and publicly exhibited (Colossians 2:14, 15). For Jesus is the sign of redemption who affects everyone in His death. God points to Him as such a sign, points to Him as He hangs suspended above the white tents of the children of death, and above the wasted and abandoned temple. Therefore we can say that the lifting up of Christ on the cross is indeed an indication of the world-wide significance of the cross. God cannot be contained within a stone temple; nor is there a temple court to which God can be restricted when He comes to die in His human nature. The law of Moses rejects the Christ; that much we saw in our preceding chapter. But the rejection was really His own doing. He did not wish to die in solitary confinement, in a sectarian corner in which the company of Moses—according to the flesh—was old, decadent, and about to fade away. No, there is no esoteric sect, no part of the globe, within whose confines one can limit Jesus, or within which He can be sent to an anonymous death.

Indeed He is cast outside of the sphere of Mosaic law, but it is precisely by such rejection that He is glorified, for by means of it He reaches His own destination. Above the narrow confines which the yardstick of God or of Satan has marked out in the past Christ would be lifted up as a sign to the whole world.

This cycle of thought leads us even higher. We can work out the phraseology of Christ's being "lifted up" on the cross in still another direction. The Bible passes from a consideration of the concept of world-wide manifestation to the idea of Christ's being exalted above the earth in heavenly glory. In John 3:14 Christ demonstrated that His cross was a world-symbol. In John 12:32 He presents it as the beginning of His permanent glorification. *Via crucis via lucis.* Even in death the way of triumph over the world is also the way of world-vanquishment unto life. And in John 3:14 Jesus presents Himself to us as the sign of the brass serpent—but in fulfillment, of course. Now we know that this consummated serpent has not been raised to the right or to the left of a little alley, or of our own street, but that it stands highly exalted as a world-symbol at the very extremity of our horizons.

But that which stands at the extreme end of our horizon merges with the heaven of God's glory even as we watch it. Everything which rises above the earth raises its crest into heaven. Thus Jesus passes from John 3:14 to John 12:32. Therefore it is not only in an eschatological sense that for him who looks at it in faith the cross of Christ stands at the extremity of his horizon, but it is also true that in an axiomatic sense it stretches out as a symbol of victory into the highest heaven. As such the cross is indeed the beginning of the resurrection, the ascension, the being raised to God's right hand, the second coming, and the final judgment. Thus the great God who confines the wise in their conceits directs this competitive bidding of the anxious Jews and the cautious Romans to His own end. It is God Himself who rescues Jesus from the far too narrow sphere of Moses. The Jews may reject Him—as we saw in our preceding chapter. It could not be otherwise, for Jesus Christ had long outgrown the narrow confines of Mosaic restric-

tion. The stream of redemption could not be restricted to the
slender trickle of a private fountain, to initiates in the holy corridors of Moses. Christ had to break through the bonds of Moses;
He had to stand at the extremity of the wide horizon of Moses'
ancient jurisdiction. Every demagogue in Israel cries aloud: Cast
Him out, cast Him out! God says: He is beyond it already. And
everything that these excommunicants plan for His humiliation
God turns to good. He makes it the beginning of glorification. A
heavenly light falls on the crooked transaction going on between
the Jews and the Romans. "Come to His glory, all ye people, and
worship it, O my soul."

The Jews are sealing their own fate. They thrust Jesus out of
the cabinet of Moses but in spite of themselves, they lead Him to
the place where He had to be. For He wished to be on the inclusive, world-wide domain of Romans, Greeks, of the dwellers in Asia
Minor, of Europeans, of Batavians, and of those on the faraway
isles. They bring Jesus to His own destination, for His destination is the world. They drive Jesus out to His *profanum vulgus*.
Praise God for that, for now we are His concern, we are the *profanum vulgus,* and we understand very well that He who was
bound, governed those who bound Him. The province over which
Pilate has authority has placed Jesus and the "common people"
under one and the same sign, and has done so by the will of the
Lord. Wist ye not that He must be in the province of His brethren? He had to be lifted up, and even those on the most distant
shores shall see Him and be satisfied.

All this was God's work. The calendar-wisdom taught us in the
grammar school has a way of beginning the story of our national
history with the coming of the Batavians to our shores, and of
passing on then to the Roman invasion. But the background even
of this national history must be found in the realm of the Spirit.
No one can tell the truth about that history unless he has understood John 18:29-32. There the Jews bring Jesus to the realm of
the Romans — and of the Batavians. Presently the praetorium of
Pilate will become the crucial point of the world empire as it is to
reveal itself through the centuries, and as it will grow in all the
spheres of mundane culture and of wicked world unity.

Whoever has seen these things in this light—for this is the line
of prophecy which relates Rome to Babylon, the Cæsar to the An-

tichrist, and the chair of Pilate to that sea of nations mentioned in Revelation 13 — will understand that the dignified Jews, those who bound my Lord Jesus, are themselves bound by the ropes of God. They bring Jesus the Christ to the realm over which the Antichrist will some day rule. He too will stand at the extremity of the world's horizon. He too will say: I am the Son of Man and must be lifted up; I must be exalted; I must be ever exalted. And He will add: I shall do this *directly*—no cross, no humiliation, and no ascension for me. I shall do it in my own strength.

Now we thank Thee, Lord of heaven and earth, that Thou didst constrain the Jews to bring Jesus to His own place. We thank Thee, Father of all nations, that Thou didst base the feast of Pentecost on this unworthy human business. We thank Thee for protecting missions by keeping the Jews from yielding to Pilate when He wanted to rid himself of Jesus. Teach us to tremble before Thee, Father, for all those who still cast Jesus out of the narrow confines of their own selves are merely bringing Him to His own spacious destination. Jesus can be seen only as one raised above every sphere—He falls, and sits, and hangs, and is enthroned above the globe. The condemnation is not a private but a universal matter. Therefore it becomes personal, as personal as life, and as God, and as — grace.

And we thank Thee for another thing. We thank Thee for light, for the light which shines through the gloom of this sombre transaction. The rays of the ascension of Jesus Christ and of His high exaltation are playing upon this night of sins and sects. Jesus must be lifted up. The manner of His death, although it is fully informed by the curse, must be such as to make a world symbol of that death. And this is to mark Christ's transcendence over the vicious circle of temporal and earthly restrictions and is to make us know that the Saviour is great in His eternal strength. He is being delivered up to profane heathendom but even as this takes place, He as the Son of man annexes unto Himself the host of God's elect. He becomes the Kurios, the Lord. His thorn-crowned head touches on heaven; it reaches the horizon. Now He draws all angels unto Himself. He becomes the Kurios. He is raised to the Father's right hand. Thence He places His own hand on the great domain of the whole Cosmos, a cosmos which can be governed only from the most exalted of thrones. He becomes the Kurios; buffeted, cast out as He is, He will draw all men unto Him. He is rejected; He is cut loose from Moses. He will draw all men, will be the magnetic center of His own realm. Isaiah, Isaiah, they are barring Him from the Testimony, but He confirms His instruction among His disciples. He draws them, calls them out of the snare.

For God so loved the world that He gave His Only-Begotten Son, so that all those who are bitten by the snake, and therefore struggling with death now, might look up to the cross of Jesus, and thus—not by a miraculous but by a true saving faith—have eternal life in the exalted Christ.

There are these crucial points in the Bible which we may not ignore.

The Jews say to Pilate: We may not put Him to death. Do you decide His case on the basis of your world authority. And it is just this decision which rescues the feast of Pentecost, the missions of my church, the victory of the kingdom of heaven, the triumph of the Spirit over the Beast, the universal significance of the struggle of those last witnesses who will prophesy in the spiritual Sodom and Egypt, and the return unto judgment. Just as the lightning cannot be kept within the domain of Moses or within the sphere of any other man, but must shine from the East to the West, lightening the whole sky, so shall the coming of the Son of man be. Today He Himself has indicated and has had reported in the universe of God what manner of death He should die. His death is not to be the act of a peculiar sect any more than God's lightning is that, and all who excommunicate Jesus, the universal Son of man—surely all these are but a sect.

But I believe the holy catholic Christian Church. Why? For many reasons. But also for this one: He suffered under *Pontius Pilate*. I hope to remember this at church next Sunday night.

Christ Accused Upon the Royal Mountain

CHAPTER SIXTEEN

Christ Accused Upon the Royal Mountain

> ● *And they began to accuse him saying, We*
> *found this fellow subverting the nations, and*
> *forbidding to give tribute to Caesar, saying*
> *that he himself is Christ, a King.*
> LUKE 23:2.

WE know then that everything that took place had to lead to Christ's being lifted up *on the cross*. Now, however, the question arises: along what avenues, by what channels, does God conduct Christ to this particular kind of death? Just how does it come about that the cross does indeed become the culmination point?

The answer can be very briefly stated. In order to bring Christ Jesus to the cross, God allowed Him to be accused upon *the royal mountain*. Christ is placed over against Caesar. Caesar has wood and Caesar has nails. He protects his crown and his cup by a series of crosses. In this way Satan goads Caesar on to build his crucifixes. And thus the Lord also provokes Caesar to construct his crosses. For of this circumstance it is also true that although human beings carry it out, although human beings buffet Christ with the cudgel of the kingship He boasts of, it is God Himself who realizes His will through those human beings, and who through their agency directs things in such a way that they achieve His purpose. That purpose, we know, was the cross. It was also the *being lifted up*, the *exaltation* on that cross.

Let us note first how the people look upon this matter. Just what are the Jewish authorities doing? Just what have they in mind? Now it is quite in accordance with what went before that the Jews, in their accusation of Christ, bring the element of the kingship into the foreground. When they were together in their

305

own assembly, they charged the Christ with blasphemy, and mocked and despised Him as a prophet. But on this occasion they strike a different chord. From their point of view, there were good reasons for the change. Just what, indeed, could they hope to gain by talking of blasphemy to Pilate?

Not that blasphemy is not a serious breach of law. But as a charge against a prisoner in this case, it certainly had its disadvantages, for blasphemy is a crime committed against the name of Jaweh. And, unfortunate as it may be for them, the name of Jaweh was written only upon the *first* table of Israel's law. And the matters contained in the first table of the law are such as the tolerance of rulers is perfectly willing to countenance. What people, we might ask, have not a "first" and "second" table of laws? The first table pertains "only" to religion. It is the second which has a wider relevance and more practical implications. Such is the argument of the world's usurpers; such is also the argument of Rome. If the Jews report that Jesus is sinning against the third commandment of the law of Jaweh, Pilate can hardly be expected to listen to them. After all, that third commandment concerns the name of Jaweh "merely." Surely Pilate cannot be said to have much concern about the name of the god of all Jews. That is simply a question of theology, of Jewish theology, you understand.

But what substitute charge is there at hand? If the charge of blasphemy will prove ineffective, what alternative is there? *Prophecy,* perhaps?

No, prophecy will not do. If they push Christ to the foreground as a *prophet,* that is, as a prophet in His own estimation of Himself, and if they make that the accusation against Him, Pilate will be as little impressed as if they use the accusation of blasphemy. After all, prophets are perfectly harmless creatures as long as they engage in their nebulous activity of draping the clouds. They become dangerous only when they lay their hands upon the curtains of king's palaces and of worldly tribunals, in an attempt to arrange and fold these, or to open and close them. No, the self-arrogated prophetic rôle of the Nazarene, too, will not serve as a suitable accusation. If only these two charges which the Sanhedrin finally have left, those of blasphemy and of prophecy, are to be raised in the debate before Pilate, the action of the Sanhedrin and the politics of the day are, if you will, foredoomed to fail.

No, no, they must draw up a more concrete charge than those. Somehow they will have to pass from the first to the second table of the law. For just as easily as Rome leaves the matters contained in the first table of the law to God and the gods, just so punctiliously does mortal man insist upon the rights set down in the second table as he sees and manipulates them for himself. Especially insistent is he when the matter concerns the commandments of the second table as they are when they are isolated from those of the first. Mortal men understand very well that the case of Jesus must be presented to Pilate very differently from the way in which it was presented to the Sanhedrin.

That is why the fifth commandment is substituted for the third, and is placed in the foreground by these armor-bearers of the law of the Lord. The third commandment makes mention of the name of the Lord and it is that name which Jesus is supposed to have blasphemed. But to tell Pilate this would be to leave him quite unaffected. The fifth commandment, however, deals with the concept of authority, and puts the Son of man into a certain relationship over against the government. Now "government" is a term to which Pilate can easily respond; especially so if the first predication of the second table (the one pertaining to authority) is isolated from the first table of the law. For Pilate regards himself as a ruler, not by the grace of the Supreme Lawgiver of all Jews, nor of their God Jaweh, who wrote the first table of the law of Moses and who allows no Caesar or governor any authority except as it is derived from Him. No, Pilate would be ruler by the grace of his own self-sufficient person, by the grace of Rome, and of its theomorphic Caesar.

Therefore, if Jesus of Nazareth and His cause is to affect Pilate at all, if Pilate is to be moved to act against Jesus quickly, no better charge is available than the one that Jesus is a rebel to the government, is a rebel to the sovereignty of Rome and of all of her subjects. Once the case of the Nazarene has been successfully transferred from the first to the second table of the law, the charge against Him can be formulated quickly. "We found Him," they say, "forbidding to give tribute to Caesar. Why does He forbid it, you wonder? Because He says that He Himself is 'Christ, a King'."

This nicely formulated charge fits into the framework of the deliberations of the Sanhedrin perfectly. Once the case of Jesus has been transposed from the first to the second table of the law, the Jews had to degenerate to this way of "interpreting" the concept of the Messiah. You remember that when the issue of Jesus' Messiahship had been raised for discussion in the Sanhedrin, it had been explained in terms of these two concepts: the name of God, and prophecy. But now that they have to make the notion of the Messiah vivid and concrete to the mind of Pilate, that same Sanhedrin explains the term as one which refers to those other two concepts: the name of the king and the kingship. Thus did the Bearer of the loftiest conceivable majesty suffer the accusation of having blasphemed majesty. He who was sent out by the supreme authority of the world, and who was clothed in that same authority, is delivered up as a rebel against authority; He is introduced to the secular judge by His own people as a subverter of the nation. He is said to be an enemy of the state and this is their interpretation of the Messiah, mark you, not of Jesus of Nazareth, but of the Messiah as He was essentially. "He says He is the Messiah," they say, and they add, "That implies that He thinks of Himself as a King. Draw your own conclusions, representative of Rome and friend of Caesar."

We may not ignore this last element. Prompted by a hatred for Jesus of Nazareth, Israel appeals to the sense of authority inherent in a Roman governor, and does not hesitate in its conflict with this bearer of the messianic idea to deny that very idea itself. By so doing, Israel forfeits its innocence; every last bit of it. This proves that it was not an intellectual error but an ethical perversion which delivered Jesus into pagan hands. These are not Sauls, breathing out threatenings and slaughter against Jesus, while continuing to hold high the idea of the Messiah, for these Jews are selling the Messiah without regard to any other forms of revelation in which He might appear. It is plain: A Messiah wants to be king—hence He is a threat to the state. Away with Him: take Him away. Can we say that this is the work of zealots? No, it is that of politicians who know what they are doing. Formally they adhere to their point of departure, yes. In the official session of the Sanhedrin, Jesus had indeed been condemned as one who arrogated the name of the Messiah to Himself. But now that they are in Pilate's presence, they explain the conclusion they have come to, not in their own theological sense of it, but as it will make its best appeal to Pilate's political way of thinking.

Besides, they introduce evidence to prove their contention. Observe how they proceed. They immediately strike the *formal* note. We *found*—those are their words. After due investigation, they suggest, we are compelled to conclude that this man is a traitor to the state. That is the sense of their charge.

This charge they proceed to substantiate by various subordinate arguments. The fact that Jesus proclaimed Himself to be a king has had two effects, they allege. The first is that He has provoked a tumult among the people ("subverts the nation"). The second is that He has forbidden giving tribute to Caesar. They assert that Jesus, because of His messianic pretensions, stands as an obstacle in the way of the regular collection of taxes. It is worth remarking here that the sense of their accusation is not that Jesus merely excites dissatisfaction among the Jews in the matter of taxation, but that He actually is an obstacle to the collection of taxes.

These were serious charges and are such as directly affect Pilate. Just how cleverly the Jews set this trap appears from the fact that in their reference to "subverting the *nation*," they use a word in which Israel is described not as a spiritual, religious community, far exalted above other peoples, but simply as a political unit such as those other nations over which the Roman scepter holds sway.[1] They are glad to humiliate themselves before Pilate, to play the rôle of a condescending province of Rome. They are only a political unit, one which like others enjoys a place in the Roman scheme. They rest in that rôle gladly, for, now that they deliver up the Christ "an sich," they also sell themselves. They come with the complaint that Jesus is stirring up the people and that He is interfering with the orderly collection of the taxes. Can you not see, Cæsar, that the province is in danger?

Now he who sees things spiritually and has an eye for what is going on in the Kingdom of heaven, knows that the passion of Christ in suffering these things was a terrible one. His is a great suffering. Nevertheless God wished it. *God's counsel* was realizing itself in this crooked human transaction. We must note that now.

---

1. Compare Nebe, *op. cit.*, pp. 2, 37, 435.

We said that Christ was being accused upon His *royal mountain*. That is using figurative language, which, as you have surmised, corresponds to that other figurative description which induced us to point to Christ on the *prophetic mountain*.[1]

We are concerned here with Christ's kingship, and also with His prophecy. He is not the *first* king, but He is the *pleromatic* king of Israel. No, not the first. From Christ's point of view Israel has had many kings. But He is the pleromatic king. The theocratic kingship was given its pleroma, its fulfillment, in the Christ. He completely fulfilled the law of the office of the kingship in this God-founded messianic state. Completely and genuinely He preserved the real life, the pure essence of the kingly office by means of His messianic work. Moreover, He gave an appropriate revelation to this latent essence. This He did so faithfully and so fully, that He completely fulfills and expresses the law of the kingship.

Therefore we say that Christ is standing on the mountain of Israel's kingship. He stands on its very peak. But that is something which no one will ever see from a carnal point of view. It is a part of Christ's passion and obedience that the zenith, as the language of the angels would designate it, is a nadir in human language, that is, in the language of unbelieving men.

We know that the person who can only see the tangible and obvious thinks of the kingship as an office with a great deal of external glamour. To him the king is one who can be seen from a great distance. One of the terms used to designate a king in the Hebrew language gives expression to this external obviousness of the king's rank.[2] But in Israel, the people of revelation, God, the Sovereign of kings, has said other things, sublimer things, things touching on redemption about the king and his office. In the messianic, theocratic state the essence of the kingship resides in precisely that which is not obvious to the eye. The external glamour—a crown, a throne, a diadem, a palace, a great host of people—is merely the shell, the husk. But the mystery of faith, the great, messianic mystery, the message of revelation, which makes the king a type of the Messiah—these all are the core, the kernel, the fruit contained within the shell.

1. Chapter 9.
2. Nagid, root n-g-d.

Therefore the history of Israel's kingship, and of the house of David to a certain extent, cannot be written as it should be unless these last considerations are placed in the foreground. Observed from the viewpoint of the flesh, the king is the chosen one, the gracious, the rich, the heavily armed. But from the point of view of the theocratic word and programme the king is the heavily laden one (he comes not to be served but to serve), the oppressed one among the oppressed many, the meek and lowly and defenceless one of whom the prophet Zechariah said such glorious things, that is, poor things.[1] When the flesh essays to write an epic about the Highest King on the royal mountain you will hear the strophes of war resounding in sonorous cadences. You will be presented with a picture of a king at the head of his army, of one who counts his soldiers by the thousands, of one who occupies the pre-eminent position in the world. The "royal mountain" becomes a king of projection of human size and scope. But when the Spirit sings its songs about the Highest King, as He stands upon the mountain of all kings taken together, the great mystery is revealed. Then it appears that the king of the consummated royal power can achieve His theocratic zenith only if He can and will at the same time pass through His nadir—His nadir as the world sees it. He must be poor, defenceless, servile, heavy-laden. Not that this king will be unable to transcend these: for from now on, from this nadir on, we shall see Him—familiar words[2]—in His power, a power which will also have an external expression in the form of mighty and irresistible works. But He must experience the kingship first in the dark, deep valley of annihilation—for it is there that victory begins for Him. That is His nadir—that is the offence and foolishness.

The important question therefore is whether His suffering, His disrobing, His disarming, is recognized as being His pleroma. Whoever has appreciated the law of revelation in this matter knows that the pleromatic Prince of Israel will achieve His zenith in this way, even though the world says that He has been cast into the pit of utmost limitation. He, however, who does not understand that law reserves a place in the nadir of humility, in the deep abyss of nakedness and ministration, only for the slaves. And He

---

1. *Christ in His Suffering*, chapter 8, p. 127 f. and 136 f.
2. This volume, p. 139 f.

points the way of such a servant to a grave diametrically opposed to those of the hero-princes of the realm of David. Meanwhile, of course, he melts the iron for a chariot of war and also the gold for the diadem of his chosen ruler.

These two lines have crossed each other throughout the centuries. From the time of David to the time of his Son the one line looks for the peak of the pleromatic David—there where the world seeks out and finds its zeniths. That is the first line. The other seeks the zenith in the service, the surrender—for the Spirit calls this nadir the true zenith. That is the second line. The first line follows Saul in his desire to be autonomous; it drinks the blood of God's faithful priests; or it hurls its spear—perhaps its invectives—at the man chosen by God and by the Word. And the same line, the line of the flesh, follows David as he counts the people, as he compares his rank with the kings of the world, as he measures himself with a worldly yardstick, and weighs himself in a worldly scale—so many soldiers, so many wagons, so many arsenals, so many subjects. That line also took the course of all those, either inside or outside of David's house who reckoned the worth of Israel's crown in terms of its gold content, and compared it with the other crowns of leading Asiatic powers of the day. All these have defied Israel, the bride of God, with their eyes, and have degraded the theocratic king. He had to be a friend of the bridegroom, a friend of the Lord Himself. A friend rejoices in and is proud of the fact that the groom has his bride and he himself can reverently recede. The friend comes to serve, not to be served. But here the friend of the groom becomes his enemy: he steals the bride for himself after he has defiled her.[1]

But the second and better line, the line of the Spirit and of the history of redemption, was pursued by Samuel and the prophets. It was followed also by David when he sang those psalms of the King of glory, who comes to the world in poverty, it is true, but also full of grace. It pursues David as he weeps his tears on Ornan's threshing floor and as he refuses to sacrifice unless he himself ministers the sacrifice.

In this moment of the darkest gloom, then, these two lines bisect each other. Jesus stands at the point of bisection. He must

---

1. See John 3:29.

keep His course unimpaired to the end. Commit Thy royal way to the Lord, O Christ, and do not ask whether He shall bring it to pass.[1] Perhaps someone will say that this has happened before. It has, and in this same passion week. The line of the flesh and the line of the spirit have met in enmity before. We referred to it then.[2] This first conflict took place at the time of the triumphal entry into Jerusalem but that occasion and this one are not the same. Then it was Christ who took the initiative and who, by means of a genuine preaching of the true king of meekness, spread the gospel among His strayed and foolish people.

But now this study has reached its second volume. In this one it is a *bound* Christ who stands over against the government. His is no more the privilege of free speech. No, the occasions are not alike. Then it was the Christ Himself who could and had to unravel the skein of the thought of His "fleshly" people. If He had not done so, He would have had to take the responsibility Himself for the heresy which is nailing Him to the accursed tree.

Today the problem is a more complicated one for Christ. He sees the knot into which the foolish thoughts of all these people have become complicated. He may not leave it as it is. In Pilate's presence, by means of his active obedience, He must again trace the straight line in defining His kingship—that is, the straight line of prophecy. And this must be done in a manner which not only keeps Him caged in by that skein, but also in a manner which makes Him the sacrifice in the clash between Spirit and flesh which ensues when each represents the kingship in its own way.

Yes, Christ, it is very difficult climbing on this mountain of all the kings of the theocratic realm. Thou hast been pushed very far into the valley of humiliation. So far that now the privilege of taking the initiative — surely a privilege peculiarly a king's prerogative and glory — is no longer Thine. Dost Thou still remember, O Christ, how blessed that experience was for Thee? To be able to take the initiative, when Thou — it was but a very short time ago — badest the sick to come to Thee and when Thou didst keep the royal feast, the feast of a lowly and defenceless prince, with

---

1. See Psalm 37:5.
2. *Christ in His Suffering*, Chapter 8.

the miserable ones in Jerusalem.[1] Dost Thou remember? But how forget? Thou thinkest all things, and rememberest all. Therefore taste now, stop and taste now, O Jesus Christ, here on the top of the mountain of Israel's kings, how bitter are the dregs of this subordination, of this utter restriction. The right of initiative is Thine no longer. Thou canst no longer present Thy problem independently, O Evangelist of Jerusalem.

Yes, all that is past now, all that is gone. Our second volume sees Christ in a different legal relationship than our first saw Him. In these two lines there is much source material for the church and for its dogmatics. Christ stands on the royal mountain, but it is precisely there that He stands in *statu servi,* in the form of a servant — nay, in the guise of a *slave.* To the law He is a slave. The clash between the prophecy of His Spirit and the description of the caricaturists of His true kingship sprang from Himself when He triumphantly entered into Jerusalem. That is why we discussed so long and so eagerly the "circumlocution" which He effected there.[2] Yes, He did the deed, Father in heaven. The delight in the deed was His then. But now there is only suffering. The deed, the right to do the deed rests with those who blaspheme God's holy, prophetic mountain. And now, my Lord and my God, they come to profane the *kingly* mountain. Father, Father of princes, Thou who dost give kings their office, why dost Thou forsake me? It is dark here, Father, on the top of David's house, as dark as in the deepest abyss. There is no sun here, save for the sun of truth and of divine justice. Is this what Thou dost call the *lamp* of David? Are these Thy rays, O Father of heroes?

Thereupon a profound voice responded in Jesus. It said that all would be *provided* on the mountain of the Lord, but that first of all everything must be fulfilled on the mountain of the Lord's kings. Stoop low, stoop very low. Thine is not the right of initiative. There is nothing for Thee to look forward to now, O Christ, save Thy *degradation.* That, afflicted Servant of servants, is the only appropriate gift here on the top of Israel's royal mountain. Didst Thou not know that Thou hadst climbed the mountain where that word is fulfilled which says that the king in the theoc-

---

1. *Christ in His Suffering:* "Christ Relating Children's Games to Universal Prophecy," p. 144.
2. *Christ in His Suffering,* "Christ's Necessary 'Circumlocution'"

racy *comes not to be served but to serve?* Yes, Thou knowest that.
Accept it now. Accept the burden of the royal service. Art Thou
the prophet now? Then Thou canst only ask Why. Thou knowest naught Thyself, and canst but ask, but ask. Art Thou the
priest now? Then Thou Thyself must be the sacrifice, the
bruised one, the empty one. And art Thou the King? Then Thou
must be the slave. Thou hast no right of initiative in the world.
In the ministration of office every zenith is a nadir — or else God
has created the theocracy in vain.

Thy nadir, then. The royal mountain witnesses its most becoming gift: the gift of degradation.

Thus we learn to tremble as we become aware of the perfected
law of Christ on the royal mountain. Thus He had to be returned
from the first table of the law to the second. This passion had to
be His. This pain was a proper part of His suffering. Thus the
degradation became complete.

The distance from the Sanhedrin to Pilate was a short one. But
much happened to Christ en route. When He was led out of the
hall of the Sanhedrin He was still regarded as a transgressor of
the first table of the law. An incomparable honor, that. He was
worth so much concern that the first table of the law accused Him.
Blasphemy: the third commandment: the name of the Lord.
The charge read that He had sinned against Jaweh.

But when He appeared before Pilate — could He believe His
own ears — He had become much less worthy of concern. He
had become that as He labored up His exalted hill. He was counted now as a transgressor of the second table. Disrespect for authority: the fifth commandment: the name of Caesar. He had
sinned against Caesar.

Know now that a person is most maligned when he is regarded
as least valuable, least worthy of concern. Hence my Saviour is
being maligned terribly now. From the defiance heaped upon Him
on the prophetic mountain His accusers pass to negation. Presently they will negate Him as He is in the absolute ministration of
the office in the kingdom of truth. On the way from defiance to
negation, degradation always has a place. The three constitute a
gruesome harmony, a mighty conception on the part of Satan, ever
great as he is in invention.

But we do not want to conclude this discussion of the royal mountain of all kings by pointing to Satan. God is here; the Anointer of kings is on His holy hill. This too was God's counsel. The fact that Christ gradually and imperceptibly was led from the higher to the lower plane, from the first to the second table of the law, was also God's will. Only thus can Christ be disowned essentially and that is precisely what must happen to a slave. Give God what is God's, Caesar what is Caesar's, and slaves that which belongs to slaves. To slaves — *plural?* Yes, a slave is not a single individual — he is but a fragment of this or that mass of perdition. Only thus can Christ be essentially disowned. O church, bewail thy many sins. The royal mountain has looked upon its slave. Only in this way could the law of the great concealment be realized in Christ.

He who is the Author and Sustainer of the law is degraded in the name of the law. And Caesar, it seems, is the last word of that law. For we hear a prayer resounding through the atmosphere: O God, protect Caesar; we, the sons of Abraham, do not want to harm him with the messianic hope. Just what was the phrasing of that line again which said something about Christ as the end of the law? The letter of the text seems very distant, very strange today.

Now, indeed, He is under the law of the great concealment. As they conduct Him from the first to the second table of the law, classifying His "case" in that way, the great truth that every commandment blesses and curses Him in turn is concealed. The truth that He sustains both tables of the law and keeps them together in Himself remains hidden. It is easier for them to rage and to jeer against the Christ than to make Him of less importance, of less concern, than this. But such things happen when one begins measuring and comparing matters in His presence.

Christ before Pilate: this is a new phase. We look back again. When He stood before the *Sanhedrin* they began with the *first* table of the law. The result: defiance, the outlaw, Christ insulted on the prophetic mountain; the mocking phrase, "Prophesy unto us, Christ, who was he that struck thee?"

Now He is in *Pilate's* presence. Here they begin with the *second* table. The result: defiance, the outlaw, Christ insulted on the royal mountain, a crown of thorns, the gorgeous robe, the reed; the scornful greeting, "Hail, King of the Jews."

Again, therefore, Christ must climb the mountain of shame; *again* He must become an outlaw.

He took account of Himself. He could do nothing else. He took account of Himself and His people. He found that in a single hour He had been terribly degraded. Much had happened since the cock had crowed. He had sunk to the rank of a rebel against the state. A crowned head, somewhere yonder in Rome, had been raised above Him. The man was Caesar. He was surrounded with flowers, and with many women. He lay on cushions — watching a charming dancer. A vial of wine stood beside him. He laughed — steeped in delight.

Oh, the cock's crowing! Being a malefactor against God's *universe* — what a blessedness that is in comparison with being a malefactor to that man in Rome. O Sanhedrin, how you have wounded Him, with your charge of *crimen laesae Majestatis,* blasphemer of the majesty of the Lord. But here is Pilate with his *crimen laesae majestatis,* blasphemer of kings. No capital letter here. Caesar has been blasphemed. Degradation, sudden descent of the waters.

But mark how He thanks His Father because *everything* in the world has a capital letter when God governs it. Blessed sermon on the mount. Caesar, too, represents authority. Authority means: God. Foolish Jews! *You will never remove Him from the first table.* He is Himself. He who spoke the sermon on the mount, He submit to measurement and degradation? He stands on His exalted hills and remains Himself, hallelujah, amen. *Ave Caesar, moriturus te salutat,* in the name of the Father and of the uncreated Son and of the Holy Ghost. Caesar, you may keep your capital letter. Jesus will accept it, for there is a *crimen laesae Majestatis.* There is Authority. The fifth commandment is unthinkable without the first table. The Scriptures cannot be broken. For this purpose He redeemed us. He lifts the slaves up to His royal heights.

Christ's Apology For His Kingship

CHAPTER SEVENTEEN

Christ's Apology For His Kingship

● *Then Pilate entered into the judgment hall
again, and called Jesus, and said unto him,
Art thou the King of the Jews? Jesus answered
him, Sayest thou this of thyself, or did others
tell it thee of me? Pilate answered, Am I a
Jew? Thine own nation and the chief priests
have delivered thee unto me: what hast thou
done? Jesus answered, My kingdom is not
of this world: if my kingdom were of this
world, then would my servants fight, that I
should not be delivered to the Jews: but now
is my kingdom not from hence. Pilate therefore said unto him, Art thou a king then?
Jesus answered, Thou sayest that I am a king.
To this end was I born, and for this cause
came I into the world, that I should bear witness unto the truth. Every one that is of the
truth heareth my voice.*

JOHN 18:33-38.

IN THIS manner, then, Christ was delivered into the hands of
Pilate. He was the "little shoot" on the "little horn;" for
Pilate — as we have observed before[1] — is a representative of
Rome, and Rome is not merely a geographically or politically defined unit, but is the realm out of which the "little horn," the Antichrist, will spring. Accordingly, Rome is named in this connection
not as a politically circumscribed entity, but as an unspiritual
world-empire. The prophecy of Daniel[2] has a bearing on all of
these matters.

---

1. See p. 222.
2. See p. 140 f.

321

To go on now, Pilate attempted to divest himself of responsibility in the case of the accused Nazarene but did not succeed in this. He simply had to attend to the trial. He had to attend to it because two charges which affected him had been filed against Jesus: first, that He subverted the people; second, that He stood in the way of the collection of taxes for Caesar. Naturally, both of these charges compelled the procurator to give immediate attention to this matter which had been officially presented for his consideration.

Now it is obvious, in the first place, that Caesar wished that there be as little uprising among the people of the province as possible. And although, as we know, the Roman government left as much self-jurisdiction in things religious to the provinces which it had conquered as possible, it could not go so far as to allow this or that sect or zealot to work the people up to a pitch of excitement which might prove dangerous to the political equilibrium. Jesus, or for that matter, anyone, could think as he pleased, and could see whatever visions he chose to see, for — well, what was truth anyhow? But he could not propagandize his ideas in such a way or give them such a turn that they would endanger the political structure. In this respect, Rome simply brooked no disturbance.

Then there was that second charge. According to the plaintiffs, Jesus' active opposition to the orderly collection of taxes was causing others to take part in the same active opposition. This charge, too, Pilate simply cannot nonchalantly ignore, for it is one which very definitely and directly affects the dignity and prestige of the Roman authority. Yes, we know that when the Jews accuse Jesus of withholding from the Romans what is their due they are misrepresenting the facts. When, sometime before, as a result of a surreptitiously plotted, Pharisaic action against Jesus, certain Herodians had approached Him, and, acting as though the matter were a purely academic issue, had asked Him whether the orthodox Israelite was allowed to pay taxes to Caesar, or whether he should, following the example of "the pious Hezekiah," refuse in the name of the Lord to pay tribute to any of the Babylonian tyrants, Jesus had answered that the question of what was Caesar's due should not be determined until both head and heart had attended to doing *God* justice. Whoever gave God what was His, Jesus said in effect, would give Caesar his due also. In other words, Jesus had immediately put the religious question in front of the incidental political one, and had averred that all revolution against Caesar was indeed revolution if at the center of its thought and activity it did not begin by acknowledging God. The Jews know this very well, but in spite of that fact, they ask Pilate whether he, too, does not feel that a person who presents himself as a king is doing Caesar an injustice. Instead of placing the kingship of Christ, as He proclaimed it in His messianic self-presentation, in the light of prophecy, and in the light of Jesus' own teaching and public activity, they place it in the light of Pilate's own predilection. They know that Jesus means something very different by, and sees something quite different in, the kingship of the Messiah than will be apparent to Pilate. They know that if they hold up Jesus' proclamation under the clouded spectacles of the Roman procurator, he, when he hears the word king mentioned, will think, not of a theocracy, but of "his majesty, the Caesar, and of his political world empire." Hence, without attempting to remove Pilate's erroneous predilections, and without inquiring carefully into what Jesus meant by His kingship, these Jews deliberately make it appear as if Jesus explains the title of king in the same way that the Roman government does. They say to Pilate: you must do your duty over against your patron in Rome. In this way, you see, Pilate was virtually compelled to give Jesus a hearing. Especially so, if he was inclined to give any thought to the past at all. For the question which was being raised now had been publicly raised among the Jews before this time. At the time when Jesus was still a lad, at about the time when He was first allowed to accompany His parents in their pilgrimages to the temple, a great tumult had arisen among the Jews. It had been caused by the appearance of a certain "Judas the Galilean, the son of Ezechias." This Judas, of whom we read also in Acts 5:37, had become the leader of a rebellion caused by a refusal to pay taxes at the time when Quirinius had taken over the registration in the province of Judea in the interest of the Roman government. This Judas of Galilee had put himself at the head of those rebelling against taxation, had recruited a large company in the neighborhood of Sepphoris in Galilee, had armed his followers with munitions taken from the royal arsenal, and had, in short, put the whole of Galilee into a state of tumult. It was said, in fact, that he had wanted to be made king. In this revolution a well-known Pharisee whose

name was Sadduk had been his accomplice. By an appeal to the
religion of the forefathers and to Israel's immemorial messianic
expectations, these two had preached the revolution. True, their
"success" had been a meager one. The movement was soon smothered in blood. Nevertheless, their brief effort had left a deep impression upon the people. Hence it was no wonder that Roman
authority, after those turbulent days, had kept an even sharper eye
open for every religiously motivated agitation which in its effect
might prove to be a threat to the government.[1] Indeed, there was
good reason for caution in this matter. The rebellion of the Galilean Judas had even served as an impetus to the formation of a
new party, a group which aligned itself with the Pharisees — the
so-called party of *Zealots*. These were committed to a program of
abandoning the current laissez-faire policy in favor of active rebellion against the despised Roman authority.

But think no longer about the Jews. Ignore the fact that they
themselves often argued about whether or not Israel was obliged
to pay taxes. Ignore also the fact that the Zealots among the Pharisees would have liked to do precisely what, with much ado, they
now name a capital offense in Jesus. Such considerations, after
all, lead us no farther, and awaken in us nothing except a sense of
regret because of this flagrant lack of integrity. We must keep our
eyes fastened upon Pilate. Naturally, when Jesus was placed before him as heavily charged as he was, Pilate simply had to "sit
up and take notice;" he simply had to take an active interest in the
case. The vivid recollection of the affair of Judas the Galilean
served to make restless now. There was no gainsaying the fact
that secret influences — working unobtrusively, of course — were
operative among these people. These underground forces might
explode at any moment. Moreover, there was a striking resemblance between the figure of the Galilean Judas and this Jesus of
Nazareth. Judas came from Galilee and had conducted the revolt
in Judea;[2] and, remarkably enough, this Jesus, too, hailed from
Galilee and had labored in Judea. Was the resemblance a mere
coincidence? Or — but no, that Pilate does not yet know. Still,
Jesus' name is already being coupled with another. Judas-Jesus:

---

1. See Schürer, *Geschichte des Jüdischen Volkes*, 3rd and 4th edition, 1901,
Volume 1, p. 486.

2. Schürer, *op. cit.*, pp. 526-527.

that is the first pairing of names in which Jesus is involved. A little later His name will appear on a second ballot: Barabbas-Jesus. Those who name these persons as a pair are casually saying that they regard the two as equal. Really, this is a difficult situation for Pilate. That awkward affair of Judas the Galilean had, after all, been officially registered. Time and again restlessness and revolution had broken out among the Jews. Pilate cannot overlook that fact. Gradually, you see, the question of Jesus' kingship becomes an issue in the litigation against Him. This consideration provides an ampler screen for us against which to view the ensuing scenes: those, namely, in which Christ's name is coupled with that of Barabbas, in which the soldiers mock the tax-chiseler from Galilee, and in which they put on a mock play in ridicule of the self-vaunted king hailing from Nazareth. The same consideration gives a deeper insight also into the pathetic culmination of the trial, as it is expressed in the superscription raised over the crucified head: Jesus of Nazareth, the king of the Jews.

If we remember these things, we will be able to appreciate better how Pilate opens the hearing which he gives Jesus, and how Jesus responds to this judge. Pilate enters the room and asks, "Art thou the king of the Jews?" Now note the answer carefully. Jesus says, "Sayest thou this thing of thyself, or did others tell it thee of me?" By means of this single question Jesus at once touches the core of the issue; He puts His finger on the truth, and gives Pilate the profound majesty of that truth to think about. This one question immediately wrenches the issue out of the complication of subtleties in which the Jewish accusers have involved it. Jesus charges Pilate to go for his explanation of the concept "kingship" to the accused person himself. Thus Jesus suggests that if he had really been a king in the sense in which the Jews suggest it, Pilate, surely, would have heard of it long ago. If the Nazarene had really constituted a threat to the state, if He had really instigated revolution, and if, in the guise of a rebel, He had really placed Himself between the tax-paying citizens and the tax-exacting Caesar — surely, then Pilate would long ago have heard of Him. Then Pilate would long ago, and on his own initiative, have made it a point to inquire what this Galilean Joshua meant by His "kingship." Yes, the procurator knows right well that his information is based on hearsay, that others have "told him of Jesus." Therefore, if he is to deal honestly now, he must in determining whether Jesus' kingship is or is not dangerous be guided not by the subtly suggested words of the plaintiffs but by what Jesus Himself has to say about that concept.

This merciless realignment of the issues on the part of the fearless Defendant touches the conscience of Pilate. Acrimoniously he answered, "Am I a Jew?" By this statement, the proud Roman acknowledges that a purely Jewish-religious problem lies at the basis of Jesus' "kingship;" but he prefers to say that Jesus' own people, the chief priests, had delivered Jesus into his hand, and that he is therefore compelled by virtue of his office to ask what Jesus has done.

And again we see Jesus as He is in His unique self-revelation. He acknowledges the powers that be, also the authority of Pilate. In other words, He gives Caesar what is Caesar's. Meanwhile, however, He gives God what is God's; He professes the truth; He makes the confession of His kingship before Pilate. He straightway indicates that the whole catalogue of charges filed against Him by His accusers is beside the point. This He does by that single and primary declaration: "My kingdom is not of this world."

Yes, says Jesus, My kingdom does exist. Observe that He makes no effort to avoid using the word "kingship" or to evade the term "kingdom." On the contrary, He assumes responsibility for a term which, to say the least, is very dangerous for Him.

On the other hand, Jesus also states that His kingship is not of this world. The kingdom He alludes to is a kingdom of heaven. It does not intend to make a revolutionary attack upon the existing political order. It has its own peculiar essence, and expresses itself in its own peculiar form. It constitutes a spiritual community consisting of the members of the family of God. And although this kingdom of heaven enjoins a law upon its citizens which has bearing upon the whole of human life, operating in and through all of it, its essential essence is something other than a politically organized world empire. Accordingly, this heavenly kingdom will never approach the matter of whether taxes ought or ought not to be paid the Roman Caesar in an external way. Hence also it can never be a threat to any existing political structure, can never want to effect its purposes by a drastic revolution. The kingdom of Christ is not of this world. The kingdom which was the objective of those Zealots to which, you remember, we alluded previously, was a kingdom of this world. But Christ's kingdom comes in a spiritual way. It cannot possibly be called Zionistic, or given any other name suitable for a political movement. Christ's kingdom wants to foster no rebellion against the state, but it does reform all existing ordinances. It carries no sword of steel, but holds in its hand the two-edged sword of the Spirit.

By a striking reference to recent happenings, Jesus points out that His statement is not a loose generality which to Pilate might seem pernicious enough because in its consequences the idea of revolution in a practical sense lay embedded in it. Can it be, Jesus suggests, that His servants, those who went in and out with Him, those who lived with His thoughts continually — can it be that these who obeyed His command in Gethsemane just a few moments ago were engaged in open battle? Had they ever incited a rebellion? Certainly not. Just a short time ago when one had attempted to "argue" with a sword, Jesus Himself had reprimanded this wielder of the weapon, and had healed the ear of the man injured by him. That surely is proof of the fact that Christ's kingship and kingdom do not want to establish themselves by means of worldly methods or permit themselves to be classified with a purely worldly scheme of things, but that, on the contrary, His kingdom is of the other world. Of the other world, even though it operates in the existing world in order to realize itself in it.

Pilate listens to Jesus and, although he does not understand everything, he does remember that Jesus has called Himself a "king." "Art thou a king, then?" he asks. That question, put in that way, shows us immediately that it is Christ who is in charge of the trial up to this time. The first time Pilate had approached Jesus, he had asked in astonishment: "Art thou the king of the Jews?" Then it had seemed to him a very strange circumstance that a person like the prisoner standing bound before him should bear the title — *king of the Jews*. Accordingly, the word which he emphasized in his question was the pronoun "thou."

But now, after Pilate has understood that this king somehow or other does not want to be defined — also inasmuch as His kingdom is concerned — according to external standards of measurement, his question has the connotation of this one: "But you are, nevertheless, in some sense or other a king?" This question takes us closer to our purpose, for at its basis there is a latent acknowledgment that Jesus' kingship, whatever it may mean, does signify something different from what is usually understood by the terms king and kingship.

Pilate, you see, is coming closer to the real issue: Christ has constrained him.

At this point Christ rises to His full stature. He has compelled Pilate to judge, not on the basis of what others say, but to look — as a judge should look — at the issue objectively in accordance with Christ's own definition of His kingship. And Christ Himself will make a declaration. Note what He says: It is, indeed, as you say: I am a king. But I am the king, not of a realm representing mundane power or visible conquests of war, but of the kingdom of *truth*. My kingdom is a community of truth; it is not one which is based on the right of the strongest, but, on the contrary, it is one in which the strength of right would reveal itself. It wants to see nothing realized which is not conformable to the truth of God. It despises worldly force; it will never taint swords with blood; it will never usurp authority nor accept taxes in the form of minted silver and gold. Hence it cannot possibly give rise to the issue of taxation as a purely political and national question. The only citizens it desires are those who belong to the kingdom because they are in communion with the truth. The Roman world empire which Pilate is representing here, is a usurping power. Irrespective of whether one is motivated by its principles, it throws its net around everyone who can possibly serve as its prey. It demands taxes; it demands them also from those who are unwilling to pay. The threat of the mailed fist supports the open hand which is asking for revenues.

But if a person is to be a citizen in the realm of Christ, his life must issue from the truth. Those whose lives do issue from this truth hear Jesus' voice, for in the innermost recesses of their being they are assured of His eternal right to rule. Thus the kingdom of Christ's truth does realize itself, but its scheme is that of the other world. Of that other world Pilate has never dreamed. Christ's kingdom is coming directly under Pilate's eyes, but he does not recognize it. For Pilate's life does not issue from the truth.

Thus did Christ make the good confession concerning His kingship before Pilate. In the presence of this *secular* court of justice, He follows the very same procedure which He took a little earlier in the presence of the spiritual court. When He is forbidden to speak by the law of His own kingdom, He is silent; but when speaking is required of Him for God's sake, He speaks. Thou sayest — that is the confession inspired by His active obedience. By this confidence He gives God what is God's and Caesar what is Caesar's due. Although He is the Lawgiver in the realm of truth, He allows Himself to be placed *under* the law and consequently under the power of secular authority. God so commanded Him; God has Him bow before authority. True, the servants He has have not been allowed to fight, but that is only a *negative* matter. Besides, they are only *servants*. Today, however, the *positive* command comes to Christ, to Him who is the king Himself in the realm of truth, not only to avoid conflict with those in authority but consciously to acknowledge and maintain the dignity and status of such authority, even when it comes to cast Him down "into the dust of death."

That single statement, *Thou sayest,* or *It is as thou sayest* is the assurance of our salvation. He who speaks is the servant of the Lord. He obeys the laws of His time, acknowledges the powers that be, and testifies to the truth. He does not hesitate to pronounce the word which spells danger for Himself. In this way, as the second Adam, He would be both servant and subject in the world *as He finds it,* and so begins the ascent to the height of His kingdom. Only because of this degradation for the sake of the truth will He achieve His triumph. And again for the sake of the truth He will celebrate those triumphs over every form of authority conceivable in the world.

Therefore this confession of Christ concerning His kingship brings us good tidings. For, in making the confession that He is King in the Realm of Truth, Christ is professing that He is *the Messiah.* That is the confession which He now makes before Pilate, even as He made it a little earlier before the Sanhedrin.

No, this is not saying that He himself used the word "Messiah." He did not. That word had no place in the dictionary of the pagan Pilate. It is a word which belonged to Israel peculiarly. However, Christ does condescend to explain things to Pilate. He explains the great mystery of Israel to this Roman, and He does it in his own language. Christ enters into Pilate's own world of ideas, makes use of his own ways of thinking; thus He presents to the pagan a paraphrase of the Israelitish concept of the "Messiah," by way of making Pilate sense the significance of the word.

Farther than that Jesus cannot go at this time. The hour of the mission of Pentecost has not yet come; and it is the Spirit of Pentecost who will explain to heathendom the great works of God as they are in Christ. That Spirit will explain fully, will do it in the language of heathendom, and will do it unto conversion. The Spirit of Christ, the Spirit of Pentecost, later, will knead the language of the pagans, will so conquer it, and thus irresistibly proclaim the Council of God.

We must know that Christ does not present this paraphrase of the term "Messiah-King" to Pilate in an effort to convert him. To convert people, to convert pagans — *that* is a work of God. Before Christ can do that, He must have dedicated Himself to His people. Nevertheless, He wants to give Pilate, who is His *judge,* the opportunity to judge Him. Therefore, He gives the name Messiah the explanation which comes closest to the phraseology of the Roman political economy. This He does in order that Pilate may determine whether that political system demands death or not. Now this represents the acquiescence of Christ. If He wants to, He can coerce Pilate by a glance of His eye, just as He once constrained Simon Peter. He can charm Pilate with His eyes, can mesmerize him, can cause him to retreat — who in this connection does not think of Gethsemane? By means of the potency of His thoroughgoing humanity He can do all these things if He wants to. Thus Christ, should He choose to, can be silent over against Pilate, can leave him to Satan; by sheer force, by the puissance of His humanity, He can rid Himself of this judge. He who can force Lazarus out of the grave, can force Pilate back of the curtains — there to be advised by his wife: "Have thou nothing to do with this man."

But Christ does not do this. He is obedient. He does not mesmerize; He does not constrain; He does not struggle with God for the conversion of Pilate, as though the hour had come to cast the bread of the children — alas, such children! — before those "dogs," the heathen.

Instead He addresses Himself to His judge and does him justice. Today He is not speaking in parables or in riddles, for the riddle is appropriate only to that sphere of special revelation in which revelation itself has pronounced its unequivocal word. The maschil — we are referring to it repeatedly in this study — can be pronounced in Israel only by order of the Sanhedrin. Among the *heathen,* under Pilate's roof, the maschil is unwarranted as yet, for up to this time the heathen have not heard the Counsel of God unto salvation preached to them. Hence, no maschil, no riddle.

On the other hand, there is no silence here, no secrecy designed to keep the heathen excluded from the mysteries of Israel. This particular pagan is the judge; hence Christ must explain Himself to Pilate in language which the judge can understand.

From Christ's point of view, His explanation represents a looking into the commandment. It represents also a "being blind"[1] to the future. For — and this is the other side of the matter — even though Christ as He presents that paraphrase of the term "Messiah," condescends to come as close as possible to Pilate's capacity for apperception, Pilate will not succeed in appreciating exactly what Christ means or in being quite certain that there is no conflict between this Jesus who is called Christ and Rome's great Caesar.

After all, the mind of the pagan will remain alien to the mysteries of the Messiah of God as long as it is not conquered by the Spirit of Christ. Can anyone suppose that an "explanation" of the concepts of revelation, an explanation, we must know, which makes use of the words and thought patterns which are current in heathendom can give anyone an appreciation of the Christ? Surely such an appreciation is possible only as the result of a conquest of the heart, and of a victory over the false thinking and the whole personality of man by the Spirit of Christ. That is why Pilate can do more than to guess, to grope, to conjecture. That is why the best he can get is a mere impression.

For Pilate, problems and riddles will remain. To his mind the word *king* must continue to be to a certain extent interchangeable with such words as *despot* and *usurper.* For the oriental man, the word *king* simply carried such connotation, irrespective of who

---

1. Naturally "being blind" is used here in the sense of not trying to escape from the consequences.

the king might happen to be. To the oriental mind king meant potentate, autocrat, despot; that is, one who never serves but is always served.

It is true that much cause for anxiety seemed to be removed for Pilate by the qualification that only those who are "of the truth" follow this shackled "king." Apparently the relationship in which this Nazarene wished to stand over against His subjects was a religious relationship. But even that modification could not avail to put Pilate quite at ease. Remember that it was precisely during these days — and that not by accident — that Caesar, who was also called king, was being honored as a god. The Caesar-kingship had the status of a religious phenomenon; not only in Jerusalem but also in Rome the title of king had a religious significance. In a certain sense, therefore, each "king," each "Caesar" could wish to repeat these words: *Everyone who is of the truth heareth my voice.*

It was in precisely such a world that God revealed His Son and summoned Him to justice. There is no such thing as chance, as accident in the world. If ever any exegesis of the concept "king" could because of the complicated social relationships, and because of the cast of the political and religious situation, have confused anyone, that explanation would be one which was made in the days of Pilate. It is true that his Caesar, Tiberius, had taken more vehement exception to the deification of the living ruler than Augustus had, but it is also true that "officially the *cultus* of the deceased and *senatorially canonized Caesar* was being *universally acknowledged* . . . Such deification by the decision of the Senate was . . . . the result of the Roman custom of having all contact with things supernatural take place *according to officially determined regulations.*"[1]

How in such an intellectual climate could Pilate possibly get a true conception of what this particular "king" had in mind? How could he get a true appreciation of the bearing of His office? This is a king who wants to be a religious despot . . . Yes, but just such a king resides in Rome also. It was precisely the government of Tiberius, Pilate's brutal and difficult patron, which laid down the official regulations concerning the religious significance of the

---

1. Dr. J. de Zwaan, *Jesus, Paulus en Rome*, Amsterdam, 1927, p. 17.

kingship . . . Indeed, it was not easy for Pilate to apprehend Jesus' meaning.

It is our duty in this matter to bow before the counsel of God. He had the Son make the good confession concerning the messianic kingship at this peculiar time. The royal title which Christ bore had to reach the thought patterns, the political and religious mind set of the Roman and pagan world. It is good that this was so. It is a fact that Christ reaches everything; He leaves nothing untouched. In fact, He would object to putting it in that way.

Just because this is our view of this event, we are able to penetrate so much more deeply into the love and the majesty of Christ. Christ knew that the name king would carry the connotation of political threat in Pilate's ears; He knew that this would be so for Pilate, not because of direct pretensions on His part, perhaps, but because of potential consequences of which Pilate had premonitions. We can appreciate more profoundly the love and majesty of that Christ who knew also that His putting the "religious" character of His kingship into the foreground would aggravate rather than mitigate the severity of the conflict. For we understand that Christ, by making the good confession before Pilate, was being obedient. He did not compromise His claims nor conceal the universal, world-conquering character of His dominion. In His self-confession He rendered to God what was God's and to Caesar what was Caesar's.

To God what was God's — for His exegesis was the true one. To Caesar what was Caesar's — for He presented that exegesis in Caesar's own language. And when He had done so, He knew that for Him this meant death. However, He had concealed nothing, had not forcibly thrust the governor aside. To his pretensions to the throne of the world and to the title of the absolute kingship, which precisely because it is religious reaches through to the world — to these pretensions He laid full claim. Had He Himself not so directed events that "in the fulness of time" — a time which He as the Logos had Himself chosen — should proclaim to the very Caesar to whom He had subjected Himself the religious and world-pervasive character of His kingship? Having Himself selected that time, how could He take exception to Himself now? How could He possibly classify Himself now with the things that do not touch the Caesar of all nations? No, Christ's kingdom did not, by an appeal to its religious nature, slink away into the highways and byways or into the hermitages and inner chambers of men, but, instead, asserted itself as a kingship which, precisely by its religion, by its truth, reaches the whole world. It touches all kingdoms. "Everyone that is of the truth," — such is international language.

Once, in the desert, Christ turned Satan away from Him when Satan showed Him "all the kingdoms;" this Christ did, not because He did not long for every kingdom, but because He did not want to acquire these in a way forbidden by God. At this point, however, He returns His more essential answer to Satan. On the one side, we see Tiberius; that is, Tiberius, the Caesar, Rome, the beast, the "king" who has a religious title which represents a world-symbol. This Tiberius arrogantly asserts: "Everyone that is of the truth heareth my voice." On the other side, we see the Christ; that is, the Messiah, the Feast of Pentecost, the Spirit, the "King" who has a religious title, and we hear His humble apologetic and expository voice saying: "Everyone that is of the truth heareth my voice." We thank Thee most gratefully, Lord Jesus. Thou didst take up Thy cross, but didst also emphatically insist upon Thy world-inclusive claims. Thus, by taking up Thy cross, Thou didst redeem Thy feast of Pentecost. Thy answer vindicates and explains Thee over against this ancient trio of days. There will be flames soon in Jerusalem, and tongues of fire, a whirlwind and a voice addressing itself to the inmost heart. Yes, addressing itself to the innermost hearts, too, later on, of the subjects of Tiberius. To them too the voice will be saying that Thou art the King and that everyone who is of the truth heareth Thy voice. That voice will be the voice of the irresistible Spirit of Pentecost.

We thank Thee. As the Son of man Thou didst not forget the Logos, for Thou didst understand the meaning of "the fulness of time" and didst persevere through the difficult course of the fulfilled time. This Thou didst do by telling Pilate what was necessary for Thee to tell him, and by giving Thy exegesis of the kingship in the language of Tiberius while preserving faithfully the interpretation of God. Ah, Saviour, the sublimity of Thy exalted exposition is quite transporting. It makes room in the *acta Pilati* for the Acts of the Apostles; that is, for the Acts of the Holy Spirit. Satan, remember this: Christ looked behind Pilate to Tiberius and saw all the kingdoms of the world. Surely he will not leave Tiberius unperturbed, for what is more inclusive than the truth? "Everyone that is born of the truth" — yes, that sounds personal, sounds individual, suggests something narrow and exclusive. The prediction has the very tang of Election itself in it. But, really, is any word more universal than *truth?*

Pilate, beware. He has by no means said that He is not dangerous. For, what is truth? In any case, it is a troublesome, dangerous thing, and certainly international in scope. Have a care, Pilate. He is to enlist the whole world. You have heard an ecumenical word pronounced — it dropped from His lips just now, here in the praetorium.

Christ Being Negated Upon the Royal and Prophetic Mountain

CHAPTER EIGHTEEN

Christ Being Negated Upon the Royal and Prophetic Mountain

● *Pilate saith unto Him, What is truth?*
    JOHN 18:38a.

C HRIST while upon the kingly and prophetic mountain is either being defied or else — in the entirety of His official ministration — He is being negated. The flesh is always wavering between these two: between insult and negation. That this is true becomes plainly apparent also in Christ's trial.

We have already noticed how Christ was being defied on His prophetic mountain while He was in the presence of Caiaphas. Today, in the presence of Pilate, He is to be negated while He is standing upon the mountain of all prophets and upon the mountain of all the kings of Israel.

Defiance and negation, we said. But do not think that we want to fix an antithesis between what Caiaphas, together with his insulting company, does and what Pilate accomplished by his personal negation. Essentially the "flesh" is always consistent. At bottom mockery and negation are one. Caiaphas had allowed the Lord Jesus Christ to be insulted upon the mountain of the prophets, but before the defiance took place there had been a complete ignoring and an absolute negation of His position upon that highest of all prophetic heights. We still remember, doubtless, that Caiaphas by demanding an oath of Christ seemed to be sinning against Him by the sin of negation. At the basis of Caiaphas' emphatic request that Jesus swear an oath lay the assumption, we observed, that although He was fully informed of God and heavily laden, Jesus was standing outside of the sphere of serious rele-

339

vance, and outside of the pale of God's presence. In the case of
Caiaphas also, therefore, the negation had preceded the defiance.

In Pilate the "flesh" takes this same course. We hear him asking: "What is truth?" Such a statement is an instance of negation. In making it, Pilate is placing Christ outside of the sphere
of those who are to be taken seriously. Obviously if truth cannot
be known anyhow, if the true knowledge of God is unattainable,
then its chief "Prophet" is both the most amusing and the most
piteous idler attending the world's vanity fair. That is negation.
But from negation Pilate and those with him pass on to defiance.
The end of the matter is that the question, What is truth? inspires
the other inquiry, What is justice? It is after Pilate has asked
that second question that he gives Jesus up to death. Everyone
knows what happened after that: Insult, a defiance of Christ upon
the mountain of all kings. What follows is a mock-drama performed in disdain of a presumptuous king: a purple robe, a crown
of thorns, a sponge of vinegar supported by a reed and manipulated by sneering soldiers.

This culmination, therefore, is just another confirmation of an
immemorial truth. It is part and parcel of the sound content of
our faith that Christ must always be condemned in advance by the
"flesh," that He must be rejected by those who are born of the
flesh and not of the Spirit. As Paul has told us there is that old
struggle between the "flesh" and the "Spirit." Flesh cannot appropriate, is not even susceptible to, that which belongs to the Spirit
of God.

Because this general law of perpetual conflict between flesh and
Spirit is true, it must also assert itself definitely and emphatically
in the trial of Christ. For in the trial the line of demarcation between flesh and Spirit is delineated as plainly as it is anywhere. It
was not solely because of his fear of the Jews that Pilate at the
very beginning of this terrible process of law goes awry in principle. No, it was not solely because of his fear of the Jews, nor because of personal indifference, or indolence, nor because of his
erroneous conclusions about the nature and purpose of Christ's
kingship in the realm of truth—it was not solely because of these
that Pilate yielded Jesus to the arbitrary will of the Jews. By the
question, "What is truth?" he demonstrated that at bottom he was
alien to the life of Christ Jesus, and alien to His office and to His

spiritual life. He reached the point of negation, for the natural man cannot appropriate, cannot even receive, the things of the Spirit of God (1 Corinthians 2).

Our text tells us that Christ, while standing before Pilate, testified of His kingdom. His was a kingdom of truth. In it power and truth cooperate. Each moves in the direction of the other. By virtue of the power of His kingship, Christ stands upon the mountain of the king. And by reason of His power in the realm of truth, Christ stands upon the mountain of the prophet. Christ caused the peaks of both mountains to come together as He spoke of His "kingdom" of "truth." This has been His last word. He said that He had come to testify of the truth, and so to obtain subjects (those who "hear" his "voice"). As a king He wants to do nothing which would be opposed to the will of a prophet, or which would be taking place outside of either the will or the calling of a prophet. To this definite uniting of the kingship and of the proclamation of truth, to this merging of the mountain of the king and the mountain of the prophet, Pilate responds with a shrug of the shoulders, and with his dubious, "What is truth?"

Much has been written about the meaning of these words of Pilate. In an effort to trace the background out of which the question arose, one commentator says this, another that. The one claims that Pilate appears here as a sincere seeker for truth, as one who is eager to know what truth is and where it may be found, as one who, although seeking, has not yet found, and therefore now gives expression to his despair and to his repressed dissatisfaction. Others assert that Pilate's statement is by no means to be taken as being as serious as that. He must be thought of, these aver, as the skeptic, as the indifferent and impatient governor who puts the question with a sneer and with a shrug of the shoulders. According to this view Pilate is nothing but a dispassionate, indifferent and proud Roman who wants nothing to do with this bother on the part of the Jews about what constitutes truth, and accordingly, nothing to do with the Nazarene's passion for truth. It simply is not worth the trouble, and is at best very boring.

One observer, you see, looks for a profound philosophical background for Pilate's question, as though this Roman were a philosopher, one who had drunk deep of every cup which the thinkers of his day had prepared. Another thinks that Pilate's query was not

at all prompted by a philosophical interest, and that he must be regarded simply as the haughty, practical, common-sense man of
affairs who laughs any seeking for truth out of court as a sheer
waste of time.

We think it unnecessary to choose one of these interpretations as the correct one. In order to make a just selection we
should have to know more about Pilate than we do know. True,
we get the impression that we can hardly speak of a profound ethical seriousness in connection with Pilate, be it in reference to his
struggle for truth, or in reference to his eventual (conscious) denial of the possibility of finding the truth. Had he really been sincere in his seeking or in his denial, he would hardly have broken
off the discussion as abruptly as he did, or as hastily have given
the Jews his first impression.

As a matter of fact, then, we do not know just what the state
of mind of Pilate is. Moreover, it is not necessary that we be exactly informed about Pilate's philosophical background and about
the nature of his intellectual conflicts. The question is not whether
we can test the spirit of Pilate. The question is whether we can
see Christ as He is being thrust into this sphere of absolute unbelief in which the "flesh" at bottom refuses to respond to and appropriate the "Spirit."

From this point of view we see that Pilate and his "What is
truth?" plainly point us to *the severity of Christ's suffering* and to
the *absolute negation* to which He is subjected.

Whether Pilate was a serious man or a light-hearted fool, a
noble seeker after wisdom or a wolf, whether he puts the question
after many years of tantalizing search, or as a disavowal of such
seeking—all of these questions have no importance for us inasmuch as we definitely know the really significant thing; namely,
that Christ was negated as He stood upon the mountain of His
official career, upon the mountain of His theocratic kingship and
of His messianic prophecy. Pilate negates the mountain and negates Him who is standing upon it. Hence he laughs, or weeps—
what matter to us which?—about every person who claims to see
a royal or a prophetic mountain, about everyone who undertakes
to climb such a mountain of the messianic office, about everyone
who would say that he had reached the top. Pilate and his question name any searching which proceeds upon the basis of having

already found, sheer vanity. By proclaiming that, Pilate does injustice to a revelation which comes authoritatively from above, and which relates all of our new questions to the answer which God once gave. Irrespective of whether Pilate thinks of Christ as a flower growing in the garden of Israel or as a detrimental weed flourishing in the nursery of the world's culture, it is perfectly plain that at bottom he is alien to the official essence of Christ, the Prophet and the King of God. Pilate overlooks Christ and overlooks even the *idea* of His office. According to Pilate, Christ's office does not exist; it is a presumption and a vanity.

The conclusion is obvious now. If there is no such reality as truth, or if Christ has not given expression to it perfectly, Christ's kingship in the realm of truth is a piece of folly, a mere fiction. Christ related His prophecy to His kingship, and His kingship to His prophecy. And that, according to Pilate, is His "bad luck." A kingship which had loosened its firm grip on truth might have met with Pilate's "tolerance," especially in view of the "poor results" which that kingship had been able to "show" up to this time. Or, had Pilate tolerated it, in that case he might, because of the dangerous element which lurked or might lurk in it, have opposed it for the sake of Caesar. But a kingdom which glories in the maintenance of truth is so unreal to Pilate that it is no better than the maintenance of truth itself. "What is truth?" he asks and his question does injustice to our chief Prophet and eternal King. Hence it is inevitable that the second question, What is justice? follow the first.

There is, accordingly, a pathetic correspondence between the depth of insult and humiliation into which Christ is plunged by this secular judge and that other depth into which He was thrust by Caiaphas, the spiritual judge, when Caiaphas told Him: I adjure thee by the living God that thou tell me the truth. For, irrespective of how greatly Caiaphas' cry *I adjure thee* may differ from Pilate's shoulder-shrugging *What is truth?* the first represents to Christ the nadir of His trial before his spiritual judge, and the second the depth of His trial before the secular judge.

Now if we will but turn away from the *"psychology"* of Caiaphas and Pilate, and turn to the *theology* of Christ, in other words, if we will but stop studying the souls of Caiaphas and of Pilate and simply ask what Christ as our Surety and Mediator is suffer-

ing at this time, we will have eyes to see the awful parallelism logically constructed by God between the depth of Christ's trial
before the spiritual and before the secular judge.

When Caiaphas demanded that Christ take an oath, he was denying Christ's abiding presence with God. His continuous tarry-
ing, His unintermittent watching and praying upon the prophetic
mountain—that Caiaphas denied. In short, the act of Caiaphas
was an act of negation.

Now Pilate asks, What is truth? This question is also a denial
of Christ's continuous presence with God, of Christ's constant tar-
rying, and watching and praying upon the mountain of the king
and of the prophet. This again represents negation.

Yes, Caiaphas and Pilate are separate individuals, are quite different from eath other. The one comes from the Orient, the other
from the Occident. The first has his seat upon the mountain of
Jerusalem; the second upon the peaks of Rome. The first wears
the robe of a priest; the second a Roman toga. The one anoints
his head with ointment taken from the temple; the other anoints
his with perfumes taken from the palace. The first moves under
the burden of learned folios; the second whets his sword, and discriminates between his pearls and his golden rings. The first sim-
ulates unusual earnestness, twists and bends himself into a thousand convolutions in an effort to arrive eventually at the point of
rest—the point at which he can condemn Christ to death in terms
of the most expedient plan. The other begins with perfect calm
and with unruffled poise, and only later contorts himself into many
convolutions, only later grows restive and tense, aggravating the
burden of his life even to the point of death.

How complete the contrast between these two types. How far
apart each stands from the other.

Nevertheless, in relation to Jesus Christ, *both* proceed from
the principle of negation. That is the element they have in common. In the last analysis, the flesh is always the same, no matter
where in the world it is found. Yes, the one may resemble God's
thunderstorm in his vehement attack upon Jesus and in his passion-
fraught demand: Swear that Thou speakest the truth! And it may
be that the other mutters but half audibly: Alack, man, what is
truth, anyhow? Do stop talking. But both of these begin with

negation, for the flesh is not susceptible to the things of the Spirit of God.

Caiaphas, for instance, proceeds upon the assumption that the Christ knows nothing about the consuming fire of truth. God and the consuming fire—these are simply not to be found in Jesus. He must be forcibly conducted to the throne of God in order to take a precious oath there. No, *the consuming fire of truth cannot be found with Jesus.*

And Pilate makes the same reply that Caiaphas makes in response to the claim which Jesus makes to the effect that he lives next to a consuming fire. Pilate asserts that there is no fire which consumes the world. In other words, he says that the consuming fire cannot be found in Jesus.

Says Caiaphas: You are not the Messiah; you are just an ordinary Jew. By means of the oath you must be "taught" that there is still something like an atmosphere of eternity left in the world.

Says Pilate, proceeding to the same point, but beginning at the opposite pole: You are not the Messiah, for it is folly to argue that there is such a thing as an atmosphere of eternity in which we human beings could possibly move and have our being; you are but an ordinary Jew; you are but one of these madding thousands.

Caiaphas says to Jesus: You are but a man of the plains, not of the heights. And Caiaphas confirms his statement by negating Christ's revelation of Himself as One who stands upon the mountain of all prophecy and of the one great community of kings.

Caiaphas by demanding the oath asserts that Christ is standing outside of the pale of truth, forced upon him, and he blames Christ for being outside of it. Pilate declares that there is no such thing as the circle of the coercive truth of God. Come to your senses, he seems to be saying: cease wearying yourselves with what is beyond you and unreal to me.

But both of these persons overlook the Lord, both pass by Him on the other side. And, deep within His heart, the Lord knew that this was so. His being concealed was not concealed from Him. All of the profound depths of His suffering were known to Him; they were known to the Logos from eternity. He is the Stranger upon the earth. Again negation was emphatically proclaimed to His soul in order that He should obtain His reasons for the great affirmation of God and of His elect brethren solely from God and from Himself.

In this way, then, Pilate also placed Christ inside of the bootless struggle of human life, mechanical and purely utilitarian as it is. Pilate supposes that this kind of placement is a just one. He could not believe that Christ came to break the endless tedium of the vicious circle; Pilate simply could not believe that. He passed by Jesus on the other side.

In the very year in which this book is being written—1929— a congress of Jewish jurists has raised the question whether the time has not come to re-examine the trial of Jesus of Nazareth and to acknowledge, finally, perhaps, that the Sanhedrin did Him an injustice. The Jewish conscience, this group maintains, must pass in review once more the "case" of the Nazarene, and must do it this time without bias. And it is true that the same question might very well be raised by those who study Roman jurisprudence.

However, even though at any time the Jewish people, or any Jewish organization should openly acknowledge that Caiaphas had unnecessarily delivered up "Jesus," the historical person, and that Pilate had done the same for no coercive reasons, even then Christ would continue to be regarded as an exile by this crooked world. Those who allow "Jesus" to go where He pleases in this world because He is not a dangerous character, or because He does the cause of truth no harm, or because in the depths of His longing heart He did not defile the oaths of Israel, pious and faithful to tradition as they were, but who, for the rest, do not acknowledge Christ as standing at the very top of the prophetic and royal mountain—those, we say, still deny Him. They deny and negate Him as He is in essence. This is an issue which is not conditioned by ideas which our own minds have worked out; it is a question of grasping the command which comes to us along the avenues of the God of revelation—a command which is ever exhorting us: Hear him, hear him. Christ does not want to argue with us about what truth is, what life is, and what God is. He wants to lay upon us with a most palpable authority His truth, and His life, and His God. The passionate qualities of the questions which Caiaphas puts as well as the dispassionate character of those which Pilate asks are irrelevant to the real essence of Christ inasmuch as they do not touch the real meaning of Christ as He is in His office. He

Himself wishes to inform us fully by means of the significant content of His words, and thus to implant in us the tension of the kingdom of heaven. For the kingdom of heaven is one which does not allow itself to be put on a level with a kingdom whose power and significance are mundane in character.

We shall leave Pilate to his haughty supercilious inquiries, just as we left Caiaphas in his state of excitement. We shall go straight to Jesus and see how severely He is *being humiliated*. Now that Pilate has negated His royal and prophetic mountain in its entirety, the case of Jesus Christ cannot possibly be conducted along proper lines. Now it is the "fate" of Christ Jesus, now it is the necessity of our Surety and Saviour that He be appointed for death from the very beginning.

This He Himself felt. He felt it as deeply, as grievously, as is conceivable. Jesus had ever known this. But now He *experienced* that when Pilate put the question, What is truth? and turned his back to Him, everything was and would remain essentially ruined.

When He, a man of like passions with us, grievously experienced that nothing could be expected from this judge, He still confronted the severest task of all. He had to give Pilate every moment that was due him, and had to give God everything after a while that was God's due. This was His sublime majesty: To see Pilate as one absolutely blind, as the plaything of his own fears, and nevertheless to honor God as the Father of spirits, who created the eye, and upon whom every eye must be directed; who sends out His Spirit so that everyone called a servant may be filled with that Spirit, and may constantly seek Him. This was a difficult seeking, this searching for God among the conspirators against Him. This was a hard day, this day in which He had to see His Father's house of justice turned into a den of murderers, and to be unable to fashion a whip with His fingers. For His were the hands which had once fashioned a whip with which to sweep the temple clean.

Christ Being Silent Before Pilate

CHAPTER NINETEEN

Christ Being Silent Before Pilate

● *And when he had said this, he went out again unto the Jews, and saith unto them, I find no fault in this man.*

JOHN 18:38b.

And they were the more fierce, saying, He stirreth up the people, teaching throughout all Jewry, beginning from Galilee to this place.

LUKE 23.5.

And when he was accused of the chief priests and elders, he said nothing. Then said Pilate unto him, Hearest thou not how many things they witness against thee? And he answered him never a word; insomuch that the governor marvelled greatly.

MATTHEW 27:12-14.

OUR preceding chapter closed with the remark that Christ, when He knew definitely that no justice could be expected from Pilate, stood before the difficult task of having to turn away from this judge, and to give His case into the hands of that God who judges justly, and who nevertheless—or shall we say in the language of faith *therefore*—opposes Jesus and proceeds to forsake Him.

Now, however, we must go on. This question forces itself upon us, and there is no escaping it: In what manner did Christ, in view of these circumstances, fulfill His calling over against His God? The answer to that question is as follows: *Christ held His peace.* He held his peace before Caiaphas first; now He stands mute before Pilate also.

When Pilate learned from Christ that His was a kingdom which aimed not at being a secular organization based upon force but at being the dwelling and the working place of truth, He immediately concluded with finality that this manacled Jew did not constitute an immediate threat to the state. Even though it were true—we refer you here to the conclusion of Chapter 17—that the eventual effects of the principles—whichever they might be, which this odd "king" was propagating might have a detrimental effect upon the state in the future,—still, these represented no acute danger for the present. After all, the millstones of "the truth" always do their grinding *slowly*. And Pilate did not care to look far beyond the present. This whole "case" was troublesome enough, and if he could be rid of it now, it would probably "wear off" in time. As a matter of fact, the procurator of Rome, especially one such as Pilate was, is a decadent manifestation; and living in a decadent time, Pilate troubled himself very little about the *future* of the empire. Yes, the whole thing would wear off in time. For the present this strange dreamer who always did His work in the full light of day could not be an immediate danger.

For that reason Pilate, who had turned away brusquely as he asked, "What is truth?" now rather impatiently turns to the Jews, and tells them his tentative conclusion: *I find no fault in him.*

By that Pilate did not mean to say with finality that he regarded Jesus as an innocent man. No, Pilate is not as incautious as that. By this reply he was merely stating that in his official investigation as a judge he had not yet been able to confirm any guilt. Pilate stays in safe territory; he makes only a negative declaration. He says that he has been unable to confirm their allegation of guilt. In response to the official charge of the Jewish plaintiffs which read "We have found," Pilate postulates the equally formal temporary report: "I find."

The discriminating ears of the tensely listening Jewish authorities observe quickly enough that, irrespective of how formally the tentative conclusion had been announced, it was merely an introductory opinion and that it was purely negative. They grasp the situation at once. They know that Pilate is unfavorably disposed towards their wishes, but they know also that he has not yet barred the door against them.

Immediately the Jewish chief priests and scribes rush in to take advantage of this definite position. They quickly thrust their foot into the opening of the door still standing ajar. No, no, the matter cannot be dispatched as readily as that. They mean to discuss it further with Pilate and begin that discussion at once.

In response to Pilate's negative reply they submit a long list of formidable and positively phrased charges against Jesus. What, they say to Pilate, you say you are unable to confirm any guilt in Him. Can you actually think that He is no more than a harmless dreamer who, because of His theological approach to things, and because of His religious aspirations, and because of His prophesying of the truth, is impervious to questions pertaining to the Roman government and to the world empire? If so, we can inform you differently.

And they begin presenting the information.

In the confident hope that they can make this irresolute gover nor serve their own purposes, inasmuch as his policies had proved variable on other occasions, they now proceed to make more vehement accusations against Jesus than they had done at any time before this.

Of course, they persist in upholding their first charges, for they must continue to give these a political color. Had they suddenly introduced a set of new charges into the case, their evil design would have become obvious and they would have damaged their "chances" immeasurably. Hence, although they insist on the counts included in their first complaint, they now proceed to aggravate these charges with redoubled vehemence. We read that they now testify "many things" against Jesus. They bring in the "details"; they give the particulars. Perhaps they carry into the discussion a report of the event which had happened to Jesus about a week before when He had entered the city *as a king*. That they do everything in their power to make the alleged breach of law on the part of the Prophet of Nazarene as convincing as possible becomes apparent even from their *choice of words*. Very carefully they let the impression prevail that not only is there good reason for naming Jesus a threat to the state but that His movement is being supported by a mass-psychology which has succeeded in getting the people—as an Israelite, as a religious group—into its grip, and is threatening to electrify it.[1] Moreover the charge, phrased in general terms at first, to the effect that Jesus was leading the people astray is now intensified and made to assert that He "stirred up" the people. In this way, then, Pilate is asked anew to investigate the case. Surely, they advise, the safety of the state must not be endangered by any personal leniency.

As for Christ? When he is accused of these many serious sins against the Roman state and of these many attacks upon the peace of the citizenry, Pilate approaches Him and asks Him to explain Himself further.

But Jesus said not a word.

It seems that Pilate conducted Jesus out of doors, placed Him before the mixed company which had gathered in front of the praetorium, and asked Him to give detailed answers to all of the charges in the presence of the plaintiffs. At least he asks Jesus whether He does not now "hear how many things these witness against Him."

But Jesus said not a word.

Why did He hold His peace? Many reply that Jesus maintained a silence because speaking had not availed Him anything anyhow. The most elaborate defensive speech would not have changed the attitude of the Jews at all or have affected the conclusion of Pilate in the least. And inasmuch as, according to human reckoning, no beneficial effect could possibly attend an apology, Jesus, according to this interpretation, thought it better to say nothing.

However, it is better not to accept this explanation of Jesus' silence. In fact, the interpretation irritates us a little. Just what is implied in it? May we suppose that such deliberate and casual thoughts were being pondered in the heart of Jesus? Have we found it to be the rule for Christ that He does only those things which, according to human standards, can net Him some benefit? Surely, His whole life, all of His prophecy, everything he does and witnesses and teaches, represents a continuous opposition to the main stream, represents an endeavor, a striving after that which, humanly speaking, is impossible and foolish. Would the

---

1. We observed in Chapter 11 that they first used the word *ethnos* and not the word *laos* in referring to "the people." This time the word *laos* is indeed used. See Nebe, *op. cit.*, p. 56.

Christ who uttered the sermon on the mount, who made the demand that everything must be perfect as God in heaven is perfect binding for the whole world, who always opposed what people think is beneficial to what God thinks is necessary—would that Christ have ceased speaking because it would not have been *profitable* for Him to speak?

To put the question is to answer it. Precisely because a more elaborate amplification of details could have meant much and could have made the outcome of that Friday very different from what the outcome proved to be—precisely because of that, Jesus holds His peace. His hour has indeed come, the hour in which He is to die. Therefore He does not want to be kept from the cross by any speech which would be inspired by something else than His *sense of office*. Nor does He, now that His hour has come, want to postpone or avoid that cross by any such speech.

Who can deny that, viewed precisely from a human standpoint, anything He might say at this point about these new particulars would have achieved much for Christ and would have helped Him a great deal in directing the case so that He would not have to make the sacrifice, or at least not have to make it on this Friday?

Suppose we reflect upon it further. Let us suppose for a moment that Christ had indeed more or less elaborately responded to all of the details of the argument which was being vehemently brought against Him. What would have happened in that case? At the very least Christ could have succeeded in embarrassing Pilate. He could have forced His judge to make a more thorough, a more searching, investigation. Had Pilate ordered such an investigation, the official thoroughness of the reports telling of his jurisdiction over the case would affect these very favorably. In any case, Christ by speaking at this time, prompted by the abundance of the perfect knowledge which was His and by His infinite passion for truth, could have *postponed* the sentence. True, he did not have the right of a Roman citizen, and accordingly, He could not like Paul appeal to a higher tribunal. Nevertheless, postponement was possible to Him in any case.

As a matter of fact, we can safely say that this represents a temptation to Christ, a satanic temptation. A speech given according to human standards would have " benefited" Him greatly at this time. Not that it would have altered the disposition of the

Jewish accusers. But it certainly would have induced Pilate, the judge, to exercise extreme caution.

We referred just now to a satanic temptation. We did it for good reasons. For, had Jesus allowed Himself to be tempted into a response to the accusations raised by the Jews, and had He done this fully conscious of the main issue which He had Himself raised and which Pilate had neglected, He would thereby have committed sin against the kingdom of truth, of which He Himself is the head, the prince, the cornerstone, and of which He later is to be the sacrifice and foundation.

Two possibilities of transgression were open to Him on this occasion. He would have availed Himself of the first possibility to transgress if He had been silent about the *good* confession which He *had to* proclaim. But the second Adam did not fall into this sin, for He declared before Pilate that He was indeed the king of the realm of truth.

Meanwhile, a second sin, humanly speaking, lay at the door. We have in mind the possibility that Christ, even though He had named in so many words the main issue concerned in the matter, would be silent about that issue now, and in this way do injustice to its majesty by negating it, and by talking about side issues in the meanwhile.

Thanks to the genuine working of His sinless soul, Christ escapes from this second sin also. He who is accused of blaspheming majesty, did not blaspheme it; He did not defile the majesty of Caesar, *nor the majesty of Himself.* He did no evil thing to the world of secular authority; neither did He do injustice to His own kingdom. Least of all does He do injustice to Himself. The truth which gives being to His kingdom never wants to be negated. Christ may be in a condition of slavery, He may walk about in bonds, but He nevertheless asserts Himself as a king in His own realm of truth, refuses to be diverted to bypaths as long as the thoroughfares upon which He in His previous confession has placed Pilate and Himself are not being traversed but are being frivolously negated. What good does it do us, what right have we, yes, what right has even Christ Himself, to segregate any side issue from the main issue or any detail in the kingdom of truth from the general truth? Who gives the Son the right to discuss or to submit for discussion anything pertaining to His deeds, discourses, or teachings, before honest deliberation has been given to the essential, basic idea which underlies all those deeds, those discourses, and those teachings? Had Christ approved of a situation in which the basic ideas of the kingdom of His truth and of the truth of His kingdom had officially been negated, but in which the details of these kingdoms had officially been studied, He would have departed from the highway which God had appointed for Him. He would then have pursued that zigzag course, that road of enmity, which at the prompting of a private and perverse will, and by reason of stark blankness, wants to coerce Him to take every bypath from which it can gain some profit for the flesh. No, indeed; those who follow the desperado-diplomacy of the people who cannot sustain life in their own strength may follow such a source, but the majesty of the eternal King in the realm of truth is a different majesty. He wants to tell Pilate the whole truth, and to tell the Jews the whole truth, but He will not do this as long as these negate Him there. Besides, He cannot say anything except what is purposeful for the kingdom of truth in the eyes of God, for such purposiveness is the sole objective of the speaking Christ. No, He can say nothing more. He cannot, for anything Jesus says cannot be seen in its proper light until the light of revelation is shed upon it. And Pilate has no interest in even looking for that light.

Hence it was because of *obedience to God* that Christ kept silence before Pilate and now holds His peace before the Jews. His silence did not represent a failure to act. It was not a reaction, and still less a negative attack upon or revolution against anything, but it was sheer obedience. It was the fidelity of the Prophet to the One who sent Him. For He who sent Him told Him that He might not segregate a single spoken word or piece of work from the central word and from the whole task for which He had been sent into the world. Our Chief Prophet is so faithful not only to the content but also the method of His speaking and witnessing that He will not exchange a word with people who are willing to talk with Him about the objective "details" of His testimonies, teachings, and manifestations but are willing to do that only while overlooking the single, dominating, underlying *idea* of which all these details are an expression. Christ will remain faithful to the method which God has instituted in the kingdom of truth even though He must sacrifice His life for such fidelity.

Christ's silence before Pilate, then, is a *deed* of extreme and powerful obedience. The prophet and king labors, and sweats, and apportions His speaking and His silence in such a way that the priest in Him can arrive at the definite sacrifice, the evening-sacrifice to be offered upon Good Friday. He did not avert His death by means of a cheap, a humanly "profitable" change in the schedule of His witnessing, but He accepted the burden of the sacrifice before His God by the very act of remaining faithful to the method of His prophetic testimony.

By doing this Christ threw off the tempter and preserved His kingdom of truth. He would not give away to false appearances for a moment, not even in respect to Himself.

Just suppose for a moment that Christ had not kept silence, but that He had spoken, and that He had answered punctually each of the questions which the Jews raised. Imagine besides that He by such an apology, which would indeed have been very easy for Him to make, had escaped from the sentence which He could indeed have averted by His words. What, then, would have been the status of Christ throughout the days in which He was still to live upon earth? Understand, we are speaking after a human fashion.

But one answer is possible to this question. Had Christ allowed Himself to be acquitted upon the basis of the fact that a prophet-of-truth did not represent a threat to the Roman empire, at least not a "threat" in Pilate's and Caesar's sense of that word, then Christ would have tolerated the lie, and would have made use of it to lengthen His days.

Remember that Christ most certainly represents a "threat" to the Roman empire and precisely in the sense in which Pilate and Caesar understand the word. He spells the disintegration of that world-kingdom, that kingdom of anti-Christian tendencies, that bestial kingdom in which the "Beast" of the Revelation of John has already in idea been conceived and out of which—according to apocalyptic prognosis—it will presently be born. True, Christ's kingdom enters the world having no physical form and He Himself enters Jerusalem as a "poor and defenceless" king, but in His work and being lies a power which will cause Rome to crumble. The integration effected by the Spirit of Christ introduces a disintegration into the limbs of the Beast, that is, into the constitution of the sinful world. The *regeneration* which Christ works, in souls first and thereupon in the Church, in the ecumenical church, in the new world, has no choice but to battle against everything which lives solely by virtue of natural *birth* and which, besides, is permeated with sin and with human perversity. Even though Christ does not oppose an external, physical force to the kingdoms of the world, and even though He does not beat down the gate of a single world city, He does do something, for He works from within outward. He works a new life in human souls, an irresistible life. He weaves the pattern of a heavenly kingdom in human hearts. That heavenly kingdom writes its mottoes "in the clouds" not only, but in the hearts of men also. It takes its course throughout the whole world. True, it comes from heaven, but it nevertheless works its way down to the world and into the world in order to make all things in the world new. Indeed, the kingdom of Christ *is* not of this world, as He Himself has told us, but it nevertheless *comes to* this world.

You see, then, that Christ does represent a "threat" to Rome.

It is true that Christ's kingdom is regarded by Pilate, practical or theoretical skeptic that he is, as a paradoxical whim; it may be that Jesus—Pilate is not sure—thinks of it as dangerous, but in any case it does not constitute a practical threat to the empire. What, pray, can such an abstract, invisible, Nazarene kingdom of truth avail against the actuality of Rome's political organization and of Pilate's praetorship? Nothing, of course.

But we who have heard His words coming from Christ's own lips have a different view of their meaning.

We know that Christ's kingdom, precisely because it comes to the world from above, has, not by revolution but by reformation, not by mere cultural forces but through regeneration by the Spirit of God, so altered the complexion of the world that the flesh, and the Beast, and such culture as puts itself in the service of sin, cannot have one moment of peace with it. The realm of Christ is not an "innocent," paradoxical whim which can be apperceived only by one standing in the spiritual world and able to read the writing in the clouds. The kingdom of Christ makes its protests against and lays its claims upon every existing order which puts itself in the service of sin. The kingdom of Christ seeks a different man-

kind among visible mankind, and it makes binding upon the natural and historical order of the created world its own peculiar scheme
of things. And precisely because it does these things, the visible
effectuation of the kingdom of Christ will indeed eventually spell
harm for any kingdom which is of the world. "Harm," that is,
according to the logic of all flesh.

Knowing this, Christ did not want to plead for acquittal over
against the charges of the Jews for one moment. Had Christ made
such a plea, He would have *lied*.

The Jewish plaintiffs are telling lies themselves. They try to
give Pilate the impression that Christ is fostering revolution, that
He makes use of force, that is, of fire and the sword. For we must
know that over against these suggestive lies stands the great truth
that Christ comes only with reformation and with regeneration;
that He comes with the Holy Ghost, and with the sword of the
heart-vanquishing Word. Moreover, these plaintiffs lie when they
say that Christ is opposed to Caesar; for, in the last analysis, He
favors Caesar and favors everyone who is willing to confess and
seek that which is for his real good. And again, the Jews are telling a falsehood when they suggest to Pilate that Christ sets up
Himself as the final end and goal of His unremitting verbal battle
against the kingdom of the world. For the truth, we know, is that
Christ has constantly been having His work proceed from God
and that He will ever cause it to return to God.

Thus far then, the Jews have been making false statements
about Christ.

Now Christ might have refuted all of these false charges. He
might have made use of this overwhelming rebuttal-material and
for the rest have been silent about the undeniable fact that in very
truth He came to change the whole complexion of the world and
to interpose into the history of the world, as that history had heretofore spent itself, a reign which should make all things new. *But
even if He had done only that,* Christ would have gone through
the world without interference on Rome's part, it is true, but as a
rejected exile of God. He would in that case have received a writ
of acquittal from Pilate, but He would have been struck down by
the lightning of God. Then He would not have become a king of
the world but a beggar who had succeeded in getting from the
hand of Rome a lease on a few more days of life, and one who had

done this at the expense of the right of His God. Then the chief
Prophet of the kingdom of truth would have stifled the prophecy
of Daniel which had said that the stone of the Messiah should destroy the kingdoms of the world and utterly annihilate the titanic
display of worldly power.

Now draw your own conclusion. Could Jesus have been a Saviour to us, and a King of the realm of truth if we knew of Him
that before the Sanhedrin He had especially emphasized the prophecy of Daniel (recall His own statement about the Son of man)
but that before Pilate He had subtly buried that same prophecy by
His silence? No, our great Samson does not cut off His hair nor
dally with His secrets. His statements express obedience. Now
His silence expresses the same. His silence gives expression to a
positive lordship; it is a sacrifice, it is an obedience; it asserts the
validity of the whole of prophecy inasmuch as it refuses to accept
every favor of Rome available to Him only at the expense of
a forthright acknowledgment of the axiom He Himself pronounced: *My kingdom is a kingdom of truth.* My realm, He said,
is a *kingdom of truth.* The accent on both terms is equally pronounced. Jesus does not want to accentuate the word *truth* so
sharply that Pilate will forget to notice the word *kingdom.* My
kingdom, says Christ, is not *of* this world, it is true, but most certainly is *in* this world. Whoever is of the truth hears my voice.

That, certainly, spells danger for the state.

For it is quite in line with these things that Constantine the
Great caused an evil day to dawn upon the Roman empire, an
"evil day," that is, according to the Beast of Rome. Some have
supposed that Christ wrote the command to rule upon the clouds
for Constantine to read but all believe that Christ wrote that command upon his heart. Writing upon the clouds — that, Pilate, is
a relatively harmless thing, but beware of Him who can write
upon the tables of the heart!

Hence it cannot be doubted by those who accept what is written above as the truth that Christ both in what He said and in
what He did not say does exactly the same thing, builds the same
edifice of truth, gives expression to the same peculiar style before
Pilate which He does and builds and expresses before Caiaphas.

Those who take no pains in thinking through these matters regard it a paradoxical thing that Christ should say first, "I came

to bear witness to the truth," and a few moments later should say not one word in testimony to that truth, but be silent and obstinately hold His peace.

We must not take exception only to that first group of people who — as we observed above — want to explain Jesus' silence by reference to such human arguments as are designed to show that, after all, Christ failed to speak because no human benefit could possibly issue from anything He might say anyhow.

We must also take exception to another group who read the Bible, to those, in other words, who interpret Christ's silence before Pilate as a departure from the line which He at first had drawn when He named it His calling and the purpose of His mission to bear witness to the truth.

Remember, it is not in spite of His calling but precisely because of that calling that Christ maintains a silence before Pilate. True, we sometimes think that "to bear witness" means simply to heap up words, and that "to give testimony" represents a kind of nervous repartee being carried on among the ready speakers and the silent ones of the world. But at bottom bearing witness to the truth means forcing subsidiary issues back to the main issue and things of the periphery back to the center. To refuse to say more may be a form of bearing witness to the truth and is that when we are asked to say things at the expense of the genuine method which God makes binding upon those who testify of Him. To bear witness to the truth is not the same as to exhaust the truth. Nor is it the same as to particularize the truth, and so to cut its garment into pieces. To bear witness to the truth means to follow Christ who proclaims His theme, which is all-inclusive, once and for all and who now forbids us to segregate a single detail, a single feature of that broad and inclusive preaching from the basic idea which lies contained within that theme.

Looking at the matter in this way, we too can ask — but in a sense quite *different* from that of those to whom we alluded above: What good would it have done Jesus to have spoken at this time? After all, His truth is not an aggregation of gnostic sayings or epithets which can be distributed on separate bits of paper, and so serve as a kind of daily almanac for those who choose to read. His truth is a principle of life, it is a *power*, it is a unity. Either we are inside of His truth or we are outside of it. We must be regenerated in principle; an overwhelming absorption must take possession of our whole personality; we must be completely filled with the theme which He has proclaimed; a thoroughgoing, an essential and radical renewal of eye and heart by the Spirit of truth Himself must take place in us. How, then, could it benefit Christ to "explain" His entry into Jerusalem as an activity which could hardly constitute a threat to Pilate's status; how could it profit Him to lay His finger upon those paragraphs of the Roman *corpus juris* or, for that matter, even upon the text of Israel's own prophets, in an effort to prove that He had transgressed not as much as a single rule of law? For we can see His entry into the city and all of His royal words and royal deeds in the proper light only if we have internally, that is if we have by an "internal calling," listened to the one word of His absolute command and laid at His feet the summary call to the beneficences of His kingdom.

In this way, then, Christ did justice to His *Father*.

His Father is the God of *truth*. And to the truth Christ bore complete witness, both by His speaking and His silence.

He did justice to Pilate also. For Pilate, too, may not stumble upon the Christ unless the stumbling takes place because of his own fault. You remember that in Chapters 4 and 5 we spoke of the maschil of Christ which He left unexplained in His appearance before the Sanhedrin. If you remember that fact and also the reasons which induced us to say that Christ by an untimely explanation of His maschil would have caused the Sanhedrin to sin, and would have damaged His own kingdom, you will be able to understand how, to a certain extent, the same consideration holds in reference to the relationship in which Christ stands to Pilate. Suppose Christ had explained to Pilate in detail that His kingdom could become effectual only by means of death on the cross. Then Pilate could have escaped from the annoying responsibility of this case. In that case Pilate would virtually have been invited by Christ to appeal not to the revealed legal code which God in His general grace had permitted Rome to retain but to the hidden things of the Lord which God's special grace had kept secret even from Israel. Then Christ would have played the game of destruction with His kingdom which, as we pointed out at the time, would have been the inevitable result of a premature explanation of Jesus' maschil about His prophecy.

It is true that Christ's kingship *must* achieve victory only *by means of death*. But that does not mean that Christ Himself is going to debase this kingship by inviting Pilate — so to say — to "take a chance" with the imprisoned Galilean, a chance, that is, designed to determine whether or not Jesus would actually arise from the dead in His royal power. For Pilate, too, the truth holds that this silent king has no room for *experimentation* in the closed circle of God's holy justice and strict truth.

We will conclude, therefore, by taking a glance at the terrible harmony which obtains between the court-session of Caiaphas and that of Pilate. We stated in the preceding chapter that there was a nadir in the litigation of Caiaphas which corresponded to one in that of Pilate. It was the nadir in which both of the judges sank out of sight at the very beginning of the legal proceeding.

But to point out that correspondence is not to complete the parallelism. Next to those nadirs in which the human being on his part sinks from view stands a twofold zenith on which Christ, by virtue of His own strength and sovereignty, stands most gloriously. That zenith of the exalted Man of sorrows upon which He makes the whole court of Caiaphas converge consists of the fact that the silent Christ maintained His maschil and His parables.

He does the same thing in the court of Pilate. There, too, Jesus holds His peace. Now inasmuch as this second silence on the part of Christ represents a second silence over against the Jews, we need to say nothing more about it. We all feel that Christ persisted in the attitude which He had once and for all taken in reference to them, and that He still does not want to explain His maschil. As for Pilate, over against him, too, Christ maintains the great mystery of His being and of His work.

Such was the law of the transcendent revelation of the King in the realm of truth. He comes from above, and — He proclaims that He does. He works irresistibly into the life and being of what is found below, and — He proclaims that. He gave basic and honest expression to the transcendence of His being and of His work in all of His speaking. And He does the same in all of His silence. He does not allow a single one of His transcendent miracles to be cut out of His heart by letting as much as a single sliver or single shaving of the tree of knowledge be cut off from that tree itself.

And only by strictly insisting upon His transcendence in the coming of revelation was He able to preserve the immanence of the grace of revelation for us. The tree of life, that tree of grace, must continue to throw out its roots before our eyes, and to fasten them not in the soil of this earthly life, nor in the prepared field of our false reason, nor in the circumscribed area of the world's vicious circle, but in that eternal soil which the infinite God of revelation has in His sovereign way prepared for the flourishing of His conquering truth.

So Christ prevented time from imbibing death from the troubled fountains of human reason. This is a manifestation of His immanent grace. Nevertheless He gave this world of the vicious circle an opportunity to seek and to find in our world those fountains of revealed truth which God has opened there, and an opportunity for it to drink life from these. This, too, is an instance of the immanent grace of that speaking and silent witness to revelation, Jesus Christ. We want to see Him, both as He is in His speaking and as He is in His silence, entirely true to Himself, to His God, and to His people. Speaking and silent, He is the one, the unmoved, whose work endures into eternity.

When Christ had kept silence, also before Pilate, God in heaven wrote in the books that He would grant His Son the complete judgment. The king of the realm of truth had not *played* with His crown for a single second. Hence He could in perfect *earnestness* now permit that crown to be wrenched from His head. A king who dallies with his crown will let it drop to the ground without any conceivable profit but he who forgoes playing with the crowns of kings, he who preserves sincerity both in speaking and in keeping silence is able to lose infinitely and forever; the loss will never harm him, for he has preserved himself in righteousness.

The silent Christ refused to accept the crown which was offered Him as a gift of worldly tolerance. When He refused, the intolerance of all the worlds came and struck His crown from His head. The blow was vehemently dealt, and God struck more vehemently than they all.

There He stood. It was night. He was forsaken. His was an uncrowned head.

But such was the law of truth. Thus did He remain king in the realm of truth. Whoever is of the truth hears His voice even though — on this night — it sings a lamentation about the uncrowned head.

Christ Before Herod: Israel Before Esau

CHAPTER TWENTY

Christ Before Herod: Israel Before Esau

● *When Pilate heard of Galilee, he asked whether the man were a Galilean. And as soon as he knew that he belonged unto Herod's jurisdiction, he sent him to Herod who himself also was at Jerusalem at that time.*

LUKE 23:6-7.

JURISDICTION over Christ Jesus has already changed hands several times. He passed from Annas to Caiaphas, from Caiaphas to Pilate. Today they will take Him farther — from Pilate to Herod. But even this does not mark the end.

The question arises: Is this recurring shift of jurisdiction merely accidental?

It is not. It is an expression of the wise counsel of God, and also of God's exalted justice. We must know that all things in the world must co-operate in pronouncing the death sentence upon Christ. Every manifestation of human, social life, every classification of the life of the world, every *modus vivendi* must say to the Christ: Do Thou go out and die.

That is why it is necessary for Him to appear before Annas and Caiaphas; that is, before the older and the younger generation in Israel. That is why He must appear before Pilate, the representative of Rome, the world empire. And that is also the reason for which He must appear in the presence of Herod, the false *brother*. Herod, remember, is an Idumean; we must think of him as belonging to the line of Edom, and must in our thinking associate him with *Esau*.

Christ's appearance before Herod, therefore, represents the appearance in judgment of Jacob, who is called Israel, before Esau. Had Esau's voice been silent in that last chorus of all the

369

great singers in the oratorio of death, who, tearless, gnashing their teeth and mocking, take their places presently at the grave of Jesus — had Esau's voice been silent among those, the judgment of the world and of the flesh against the elect of God would have been incomplete.

We all know the history of the situation. Pilate had heard that Christ had begun His activity in Galilee; mention had been made of that fact by the accusing voices of the Sanhedrin. A person who finds himself in an embarrassing situation develops a keen sense of hearing, and Pilate, too, has a discriminating ear at this time. For he finds himself in circumstances which are very annoying. Hence he is heartily glad that the place of Jesus' origin, namely Galilee, allows him an opportunity according to the letter of the law to escape from the responsibility of this case. He makes it a point to ask again and to ask definitely whether it is really true that Jesus comes from Galilee, or whether He at least belongs to the legal jurisdiction of that province. And when it appears that the Nazarene by reason of his background and early activity, both of which were centered in Galilee, could officially be regarded as a Galilean, Pilate decides to call Herod into this strange case.

Now Herod, or more exactly, Herod Antipas, was a tetrarch, a governor of Galilee and Perea, even though he bore the name of king officiously rather than officially.

As it happened, there was a regulation at the time which had it that an accused person might be tried in any of three places: at the place of his birth, at the place where he established his residence, or at the place in which he had committed his crime. According to this regulation, more than one basis could be named to justify calling the tetrarch of Galilee into the trial of Jesus. Accordingly, Pilate, who is eager to take that course decides to have Jesus appear before Herod. Now it happens that Herod is in Jerusalem at this time. The Passover is about to be celebrated and Herod has expressed an eagerness to celebrate it with the Jews. In this way Pilate, even if he cannot escape from responsibility in the case altogether, can at least share it with the other official.

Thus Jesus appears before Herod. Now, as we have stated already, we discover a parallel in this meeting: *Christ* appears before *Herod;* in other words, *Jacob-Israel* is ushered into the presence of *Herod-Esau.*

Christ-Jacob. Herod-Esau. Those are the contrasts, those the parallelisms. Have they been arbitrarily contrasted? Many thinkers have spoken and written in the sense of such parallels. Herod has often been associated with Esau, Christ with Jacob-Israel. And there is good reason for such alignments.

The name *Herod* is not entirely strange to us. The Bible never uses that word without bordering it with crepe. The Herods all belonged to a renowned family who were of an Idumean origin. If we remember, now, that the term Idumean is identical in meaning with the term Edomite, and if we recall also that the name Edom is identical with the name Esau, it will not seem strange to us to learn that theologians long ago associated Herod with Esau in their thinking, and that a parallelism was pointed out between Jesus-Herod and Jacob-Esau.

We should, however, be doing truth an injustice if we failed to raise objections against this method of thinking about the gospel of the passion and against the habit of looking for parallelisms on the part of those who discover them too facilely. There are people who cannot keep from smiling when they see these efforts at relating the conflict between Jesus and Herod to the ancient dualism between Jacob and Esau. How many centuries — so these proud observers like to say — have not elapsed since Jacob and Esau quarrelled about their birthright?

Besides, they add, who can actually prove that Herod the Idumean, or if you wish, the Edomite, was a descendant of Esau? Remember, they suggest, that the Peoples of the Old Testament were dispersed over the whole world. Not only is their genealogy uncertain, therefore, but many of those who belonged to one country have mingled with the people of another. Hence no one can say definitely that this or that people has sprung from a given ancestor. So goes the clever, dispassionately scientific argument of these observers.

Counter contentions follow in quick succession. For instance, it is said that Herod belongs to a generation which presumably came from Ashkelon. That would mean that the Herods were descendants of the Philistines. And it would certainly be difficult — so runs the argument of one commentator — to point out the

genealogical continuity between the Philistines and Esau. Comes
another who remarks very learnedly: As for those Edomites . . .
yes, it may be that Esau was called Edom for various reasons,
but the Bible itself points out that by no means all of the Edomites
were genuine descendants of Esau, even though the "sons of
Esau" are subsumed under that head. A third critic calls our attention to the fact that Amalek, for example, is also associated
with Edom in certain references of the Bible (This accounts for
the fact that the conflict between Amalek and Israel is regarded
by many as an after-effect and continuation of the old Esau-
Jacob struggle), but — this critic goes on — in other references
the Bible proves to us that there were Amalekites who were in no
way related to Esau by ties of blood.

After all of these arguments have been presented to you in a
scientifically "objective" manner, you are asked whether you are
not going too far afield when you state that a parallelism exists
between the meeting of Christ with Herod and that ancient struggle between Jacob and Esau.

We feel inclined to reply that the Bible knows all that very
well. The very fact that the Bible itself presents the data raised
in these arguments should make all those who use such contentions against the traditional reference of Herod to Esau very
cautious, for if such reference of what is taking place here in this
unique moment between Jesus and Herod to the conflict of Jacob
and Esau were the product purely of human allegorizations or of
the arbitrary habit of seeking out "parallelisms," we should indeed have to protest strongly against looking so far back for the
beginning of the threads of history.

But it is obvious that the Scriptures themselves, not only in this
particular moment but throughout the centuries, see in this conflict between Israel, on the one hand, and the Edomites, or the
Idumeans, on the other, a recurrence, or better, a continuation and
culmination of the old conflict between Jacob and Esau.

This is no wonder, surely. The Bible, in delineating the methods of revelation employed by the Spirit, does not limit itself to
ties of blood, as though the spheres of revelation juxtapose precisely with those of the blood or permit themselves to be bound
by the limitations of the flesh. No, natural birth, flesh and blood,
do not circumscribe the domain of election and reprobation. The

opposite is true. The God who is present in that antithesis between election and reprobation, faith and unbelief, spirit and flesh, the seed of the woman and the seed of the serpent — that God circumscribes the boundaries of flesh and blood. He makes the paths of the Spirit manifest in the meandering ways of natural life; He makes the whole of nature the working-ground of the Spirit. All of the antitheses named above may be discovered in nature, if only we explain nature in terms of the spirit, and not the spirit in terms of nature. Because the clash between Jacob and Esau has found an historical, a predestined sequel in each successive age, therefore the record of that clash must run through all of their generations. That is why in the evolution of tribes and nations, groups will define themselves according to the same law of antithesis which operated in Jacob, the chosen one, and in Esau, the reprobate.

Yet the Bible itself knows very well that the collective title *Amalek* includes others besides the sons of Esau, and others besides the sons of Edom. The Bible knows that there is such a thing as a spiritual communion which inheres in successive generations, and that a choice must be made for good or for evil; the Bible knows that there is an entering into fellowship with the seed of the woman or a coming into communion with the seed of the serpent.

It is precisely because the prophetic Spirit is operative in history, and because the Bible hears that Spirit testify in history, that the Bible does not allow the blueprints for the building of the Spirit to be drawn up by a pen of the blood, but, on the contrary, has it prepared by the Spirit Himself. Such — in the language of men — is the haughtiness of the Spirit of prophecy. The flesh — to speak in the terms of evolution — does not govern the Spirit, but the Spirit — to speak in the terms of revelation — rules over the flesh. That is why the "gathering together of Esau" in the broadest sense of the phrase is opposing itself to Israel. Under the name of Esau or of Edom the Bible groups together all those who have in the course of history moved in Esau's direction, have intermarried with him, or have formed a coalition with him against the God of Israel. And this grouping together of all those tribes and fragments of peoples under the general title *Esau* is not a genealogical coincidence, but a prophetic infallibility.

Hence, because of the Spirit, that was a true interpretation of the course of events which Israel's historiography gave when it named the conflict which God had appointed between Jacob and Esau the one and thoroughgoing conflict of the succeeding generations. Such it was designated to be, both in the apocryphal[1] and in the canonical writings.

We should have to go too far afield if we were to point out every instance in which that immemorial conflict between Jacob-Israel and Edom-Esau manifested itself in these successive generations. It suffices here to call attention to the struggle between Amalek and Israel; to the warfare conducted by the Midianites, a people belonging to the classification of "Edom," against Israel; to the war carried on by Doeg against David; to the conflict waged by Hadad against the throne of David; to many revolutions, constantly occurring, on the part of Edom against David's rule; to the prophecy of Isaiah in which an oppressed voice from Seir, Esau's hill country, asks when the night will cease in which the prophet must tell the mountain dwellers of Edom that for them morning has not yet dawned; and, finally, to that very remarkable struggle between Haman and Mordecai.

In reference to this last conflict, we must state that in the book of Esther Haman is called an Agagite. Now Agag is also to be associated with Edom. For a long time the Amalekites were subject to a royal house whose members all officially bore the collective title of Agagites. Hence the conflict between Haman the Agagite and Mordecai is a revival, and a sharply accentuated one at that, of the old antithesis between Israel and Esau, a conflict in which Israel, who properly belongs to the classification of Edom, forms the historical connecting link. This fact is so obvious that in the apocryphal as well as in the canonical books the fierce struggle between Haman and Mordecai is set down in the light of that ancient and immemorial struggle. In the apocryphal literature, the bitter hatred obtaining between the Agagite, Haman, and the Jew, Mordecai, is depicted as a battle between dragons. In other words, the struggle between those two is in that literature set down as having gigantic proportions; it is transposed from the small domain of human malice and jealousy to the broader spheres

---

1. In these, too, "remnants" of revealed truth are contained.

of the immemorial conflict between the primal powers of the world. Can anyone say, moreover, that the Bible itself in the canonical book of Esther does anything less than this? No, indeed. This book opens up similar perspectives. In this small book Israel's kingship is indeed depicted as having degenerated and been destroyed according to the flesh; but note that it tells us also, when the hewn-down stem of Israel's kingship, of Jacob's beautiful inheritance, seems to be left alone, unfruitful, and twice dead, God discovers the marvelous influences of His extraordinary providence. The spirit of Esau-Agag-Haman may attempt to destroy Jacob but it cannot succeed in the attempt. Mordecai who bears within himself the flesh of "Jacob" and the spirit of "Israel" triumphs over Haman after a while. He triumphs over Esau. Esau may demand Jacob's birthright again and again, and it may be that this birthright sometimes reverts to Esau entirely on this or that occasion, but by way of faith and repentance, and by way of a spiritual struggle for the real essence of the seed of the woman, that birthright will remain Jacob's, Israel's into all eternity.

Yes, by way of the Messiah, the birthright will remain Israel's.

Balaam once said something which is quite in harmony with these truths. When Balaam had to prophesy for Balak, he saw and described the struggle in which Israel was involved in the concrete embodiments which that struggle took in his own time. His vision was authentic as the vision of prophets is, even of those who are prophets against their own will. Amalek's attack upon Israel's retreating camp had taken place but a short time before. Agag — taken now as the collective title for all of the kings of Amalek — had taken up the sword against Israel. In other words, and in a deeper sense, Esau had again attempted to get his birthright back from Jacob. For "Esau" cannot reconcile himself to the fact that he has given his birthright away. The transaction which took place between Jacob and Esau, by which Jacob won the birthright, was ever lamented by Esau, and the prophetic record of history never tires of showing how in the conflict of Israel against "greater Edom" the old feud between Jacob and his brother is revived again and again.

Just what are these two quarreling about? We have already indicated the answer: The feud concerns the birthright. According to the good pleasure of God's sovereign election that birth-right was Jacob's due. But Esau cannot reconcile himself to Jacob's having it. When the Spirit of prophecy acting through Balaam's agency presently thunders, it announces *that Israel's kingship shall be exalted above that of Agag.*

That, surely, was a significant prophecy. Somewhere down in the valley there might be found a little group of disordered Is-raelites. Nomads, exiles they were, without any certain political affiliation, without a fixed dwelling place, their property stolen. Nevertheless Balaam sees these robbed and roving people develop into a nation having a well-ordered political system. He notices that this people will receive a king, and he also sees that this king-ship of Israel's future will far transcend the power of Agag, and greatly supersede the strength of Amalek·and of Edom. He ob-its prerogatives over against Esau.

> Edom's fires of wrath may flame
> Against the glory of God's name,
> But God will bow his head in shame;
> And Edom, all his boasting done,
> Will see the crowned Jacob's Son.

In other words, the prophecy of Balaam may be interpreted in this way: In the future the generation of Jacob — thanks to its eschatological king—will possess the birthright and will exercise its prerogatives over against Esau.

We have alluded to but a few instances of this age-old feud be-tween Jacob and Esau. No, this is not a game of allegory; nor is it a far-fetched "type" study. It is the effect of the fact of elec-tion and reprobation. Whoever sees the antithesis of election and reprobation going on between Jacob and Esau, he will be the one to see the real meaning of that conflict. If we can detect in this meeting of Esau and Jacob, of Herod and Jesus, only a chrono-logical continuity, we will not see half as much significance in it, as he who sees the shadow of Jacob and Esau playing behind Jesus and Herod. But if we acknowledge according to the rule of faith that the Logos and the Spirit use all that history brings forth as a stage and sphere of operation for the law of election and repro-bation, we shall be guilty of gross ignorance, if we fail to find in this meeting of Herod and Christ a fulfillment of the former meeting of Esau and Jacob. What, pray, is Jacob's rôle in the

world, if God's purpose for him is not related to the appearing of
the Christ? The womb of the seed of the woman gives him birth
solely in order that in and through him Christ may make His
appearance.

Thus it is that the Logos drives Jesus into Esau's presence.
Jacob's great Son stands in the presence of the epigone of Esau.
He stands there bound and fettered. The concealment of God in
the man Christ Jesus, in the incarnation of the Word, is now
having its effects. It is expressing itself more specifically in this
concealment of Jacob's birthright, of the birthright of the first-
born, in the man Christ Jesus. God, and the seed of the woman,
and the Spirit of election, and the Word of God's sovereign good
pleasure, and the calling by the free grace of God — all these are
contained in the humanity of Jesus. The wind blows under the
canvases of the tent in which Jacob once dealt with Esau about
the birthright. The tent pins are being jerked away. Alas, Jacob
stands empty-handed under the naked sky. There is nothing
which he can call his inheritance.

Now something must happen to Jacob. Just as Jacob once
trembled as he awaited the coming of Esau after Jacob had
squandered the birthright, and just as he could regain that right
only by a struggle with God at Peniel, so Christ stands before
Herod. He is bound; He bears the burdens of His father Jacob,
and is able to achieve His birthright only by a struggle with God.
Come, Father, struggle against Him: *veni pugnator spiritus.*
Hurl Jacob to the ground, Father; He must experience His Peniel.
God must attack Him. O God of all history, wrench more than
His thigh out of joint; bruise His heels, for He is a Jacob having
no rights. Esau rules in Herod now. And Jacob in Christ Jesus
is a poor, robbed, manacled, and despised Man. Moreover this
Christ-Jacob has no rights in the world; He can make no claims.
He stands in Edom's presence, and can only wait. Does Esau
come in peace? Alas, he is heavily armed. But the Christ is the
outlaw. He stands in the presence of Esau: see, His cheeks are
still burning. He who is the Bearer of the birthright had to enter
the world as one having no form or comeliness, as a foolish and
offensive one, as the butt of ridicule to the Esau who has only
carnal eyes with which to look upon the flesh. For Esau lives in

that vicious circle described by a life whose boundaries are drawn up in terms of the flesh.

Today Jacob appears quite naked. Thou art very beautiful, Thou Man of sorrows, Thou art very beautiful. For Thou art here to bear the burdens of Jacob. Therefore Thou hast neither form today nor beauty. That face which has been spat upon, that head which has been bent low, and that humiliated body is nothing but the limping thigh of Jacob. But — O divine Grace — this is Jacob's thigh removed from the course of that vicious circle which bandied Father Jacob and his lost generation to and fro for centuries in that interminable struggle with Esau, Edom Amalek, Doeg, Haman, and Balaam. For it is evident, O great Son of Jacob, that Thou must enter into an absolute death. The tedious round of the strife between Jacob and Esau will be broken now. Whether it fail or succeed the attack will be conclusive. Esau must see that God is punishing Thee today. Yes, he himself may raise the sword against Thee, O Thou great Son of Israel.

Remember this: Esau must know that Jacob *is not chosen for Jacob's sake*. Esau must know that Jacob has been chosen because of the good pleasure of God, and he must know that God punishes all of Jacob's sins in Jesus Christ who is Jacob's Son and Lord. Yes, Esau must acknowledge that this is not merely a verbal truth, must confess that election comes solely by reason of God's good pleasure. And this, of course, means that God can not find as much as one of His reasons for choosing Jacob in Jacob himself. Therefore everything that is Jacob's must enter into an absolute death today. Heaven and earth must testify now that Jacob can keep nothing because of the strength of his own hands, or in virtue of his own powers. The limping thigh with which Jacob began his journey to the land of his inheritance was the beginning of the history of the passion. For Jacob and Christ are one. Hence that history of the passion must reach its culmination today in the bruised heels with which Jacob in Christ Jesus will finish his course.

Yes, Esau must see and must acknowledge today that *to be chosen means to be heavily laden.*

That is why Esau may put the great Son of Jacob to death. For it was this Son with whom God was concerned long ago in the tent in which Jacob prepared the mess of pottage and in which

Esau consumed it. For Esau has too long forgotten that God calls His Jacob — to be blessed, yes, but also to serve. The *elect* — that is a title of honor. But that honorable name has this synonym also: *the heavily laden one*. And this is the translation, the all too faithful one, which occupied the mind of Jacob too little, which was never understood by Esau, and which is neither appreciated nor understood by Jacob's carnal posterity today. Does not every Jew cry aloud: We are the *chosen* people? And do you hear any voice which adds the conclusion: Therefore we are the heavily burdened people? Nevertheless, election means calling, privilege implies task, "to may" is "to must," or, as the Germans say, *Gabe ist Aufgabe*. But Jacob in the persons of his Christ-accusing sons is still priding himself in the flesh.

But of all those children of Jacob there is that one who does understand that election involves service, obligation, and the burden of the Lord. That One is the Christ, the great Son of Jacob.

Accordingly, He must wrestle with God. He must experience His Peniel. And remember that Peniel is the place of the spiritual wrestling for the gifts of the sovereign election.

What we are witnessing today, therefore, is the entrance of Peniel into Herod's house. The mystery of Peniel re-enacts itself in the courtroom of Herod. There it reaches its denouement; there it comes to rest. When Peniel still had its place near the Jabbok, God did indeed struggle against Jacob, but Esau stood at a distance. That was an instance of the grace of God which allowed Jacob to have done with God before entering into judgment with Esau.

But here in the place of Herod Antipas, Esau stands directly in front of Jacob. Again God struggles with Jacob in Christ, inasmuch as He has been made the curse because of Jacob's sin. But today the law of Peniel becomes even more difficult to understand than it was long ago at the side of the Jabbok. In this hour of Christ's presence before Herod-Esau, God does not begin to punish and to bruise, for God on this occasion is terrible in His silence. Esau scolds and gnashes his teeth; he grimly gnashes his teeth, and he will not put up the sword of his tongue.

Now the great task of Christ as the absolute Son of father Jacob is that in His spirit He will be so perfectly occupied with God, will so see things from a theocentric point of view and so live them, that He will see Himself standing behind Herod, will hear God's own voice speaking in Herod's verdict, and will feel the hand of God in the blows of Esau which are wounding His thigh and bruising His heel.

Peniel, O incomparable grace. Here I see Jacob quailing and Jesus trembling. Oh, blows of God! O matchless grace! It is better for Thee, Jacob's Son, to fall into God's hands than into the hands of men. In Peniel, God struck thee, O Jacob, and it was a magnanimous grace. It is better to be beaten by God than by Esau, is it not, father Jacob? But today God conceals Himself and lets Herod persist in the beating, and God tells Thee Thou Son of Jacob, that Thou must be silent in the presence of Thy judge, inasmuch as He who is beating Thee through the agency of Herod-Esau is none other than Thy God. In this resplendent palace in which the reeking stench of sin and uprighteousness is striking Thee full in the face, Thou must experience Thy Peniel, and must say to Thy God: I will be silent, I will not open my mouth. But I shall not let Thee go until Thou bless me. I shall not let Thee go until Thou prepare the room of the Passover for me, and a first-born from the dead. . . .

The allegory is a striking one, is it not? Still, we have not plumbed its deepest, deepest depths. The deepest depth of Christ's suffering in its absolute mystery is that God is not beating Himself, is punishing and warring against Himself. And that same mystery we witness here now.

Just who, after all, was it that wrenched Jacob's thigh out of place at Peniel and struggled with Him until dawn? Who else but the Logos, the Eternal Word, The Son, as He made His appearance and worked His influence among the children of special revelation before His appearance in the flesh? Yes, it was the second person of the holy Trinity that wounded Jacob in the dark hour of Peniel. He struck Jacob's flesh in order to emancipate the Spirit of Israel from Jacob. But now the Son must bear His own burden. Taking Jacob's place today He must approach Esau and say to him: Beat me, I pray, beat me. In Herod-Esau He must see the God who is legally punishing Him. Hence He must inflict blows upon Himself—God is punishing God. No, that is not too far-fetched, for these matters lie ready at hand in the suffering Christ. Just as the priest and the sacrifice become one in

Jesus Christ, so the smiting Judge and smitten flesh become one in Him. Just as in Christ He who offers, offers Himself, so the night of Peniel is being fulfilled there where the Son inflicts the blows upon Himself which once He inflicted upon Jacob.

This is the great joy, and this is the great grief. This is the exalted mystery, by which God assigns to Himself the blows which He inflicted upon the flesh of Jacob. For Jacob was called into being and was beaten solely because he bore the Christ in his loins. The sprained thigh, the bruised heel, Jacob, Christ, Esau and Jacob, Herod and the great God, the eternal absolute good pleasure and the full round of life—these all can be grouped together, for the Word was made flesh, and the incarnation of the Word is the only interpretive principle of all the mystery of this world.

Bow low, bow very low, O son of man, before the mystery of redemption which is in Christ Jesus. God is in hiding; zenith and nadir, the climbing of official heights and the bending low in the vale of the martyrs are one and the same thing. Do you yourselves say now whether such nonsense to the unregenerate mind is not an expression of the vision of God? Can it astonish you, then, that the kingship of Israel is exalted above that of Agag in the very moment in which that kingship was humiliated before it? Ah, Mordecai must be sent to the gallows: I mean that Mordecai's Mediator must be nailed to the tree of disgrace. Only then will Haman who also is Esau walk before Christ's white horse. Only then will the red horse of Esau's vaunt of war lead in the victory march of Christ's white horse of triumph. Who would miss Herod's intermezzo? For all the threads of history come together in it.

Christ Being Silent Before Herod and Being Mocked in the Vale of Martyrs

CHAPTER TWENTY-ONE

Christ Being Silent Before Herod and Being Mocked in the Vale of Martyrs

● *And when Herod saw Jesus, he was exceeding glad: for he was desirous to see him of a long season, because he had heard many things of him; and he hoped to have seen some miracle done by him. Then he questioned with him in many words; but he answered him nothing. And the chief priests and scribes stood and vehemently accused him. And Herod with his men of war set him at naught, and mocked him, and arrayed him in a gorgeous robe, and sent him again to Pilate. And the same day Pilate and Herod were made friends together: for before they were at enmity between themselves.*

LUKE 23:8-12.

WE concluded in the preceding chapter that for Christ zeniths are nadirs. When He stands at the very top of the royal and prophetic mountain, He stands at the very zenith of His glory; and that zenith corresponds perfectly to the nadir of His humiliation.

This correspondence manifests itself also in Christ's meeting with Herod. He stands upon the heights, upon the mountain of Jacob's blessing of the first-born. That, then, according to the logic of the incarnation of the Word means that Christ is entering into the vale of martyrs, laden as it is with mockery and disdain. Only in this way can He achieve glory for the faith. Consequently we shall not speak in the interests of that faith in terms of parables at this place either.

385

Yes, when Christ is being conducted before Herod, He is entering the vale of martyrdom. Herod Antipas, the Edomite, feared for a long time—and to this fact we will allude again later—that Jesus was none other than the murdered Baptist, who, he supposed, had arisen from the dead. To his wondering anxiety, therefore, Jesus is a resurrected martyr. In fact, the Baptist is the greatest martyr of the Old Testament: "Among them that are born of women there has not arisen a greater than he." Those are the words Christ Himself used when, taking full cognizance of the wide circle of great men referred to in the Old Testament, He ascribed that high place to John the Baptist. Hence, when Herod sees the figure of the murdered Baptist who was put to death at the very end of Israel's wall of mourning, still playing before his eyes—decadent kings very often labor under the burden of such a diseased imagination—he sees Christ approaching Him as one coming from those who have witnessed with their blood. Is it he, or is it not he? Herod cannot be sure, but in any case Jesus is enveloped in the cloud of all martyred witnesses, is enfolded within the reeking vapor of their shed blood. As Jesus enters Herod's palace, that judge reckons with the possibility that the spirit of the Baptist resides in Him, that this spirit is looking for a new outlet in the world, some very secret channel, perhaps, but in any case bent upon Herod's destruction.

Now the thing that moves us, and the thing that causes Christ to suffer is this: Herod has assigned to Christ a place in the dark vale of martyrs. Seeing Jesus, Herod saw blood; he detected the vapor of the souls of martyred men in Him. Nevertheless, even in that greatly dreaded vale of martyrs, Christ is being despised by Herod. Christ enters Herod's palace as an "eventual" martyr, but He is ushered out of it a little later wearing the garment of mockery.[1] In other words, Christ is entering into mockery and disdain in the company of all His martyrs and blood-witnesses, that is, in the company of the whole of the martyred seed of the woman.

My God, what hast Thou done to Him?

---

1. This is the strongest possible evidence thus far for the fact that, even though someone should arise from the dead—and Herod thinks John has so arisen—a person cannot be converted without the Word and the Spirit. Stronger evidence for this follows in Matthew 27:53.

There is still one opportunity for Jesus to gain some renown in the eyes of "the world"; He can obtain the martyr's crown. That crown is as becoming to those who with Pilate ask what truth is, as it is to those who with the Sanhedrin say: He is, speaking theoretically, worthy of death. Obviously, if Jesus is purely a martyr, He still has a reasonably good chance in this world. But if even the crown of the martyrs cannot protect His head from slime and venom, surely then His last chance in this world is taken away from Him.

No, even that cloud of reeking martyrs' blood will not serve to protect Jesus. Christ may enter any given house in the world which is filled with sin and lying as a Mountain Climber who has scaled peaks higher than any prophets or kings before Him have, or He can enter as a Dweller-in-the-valley who, in the company of the martyrs, is laid away in the dust of the grave. It does not matter how or where He goes. What matters is that He has ever entered these houses and will never be able to escape from the roundelay of death.

We have already observed in what manner Christ was conducted into Herod's presence. This new feature of the process of His passion represents a remarkable moment in His suffering. When He was before the Sanhedrin, Jesus had to battle against the false and carnal exegesis which the unregenerated heart gave of the Messiah. In the presence of Pilate, He stands over against the fact of unbelief. Today, as He stands in the presence of Herod, it is superstition which casts its dull reflections upon Him.

As for this superstition, the Bible mentions the fact that Herod Antipas,[1] who now sees the Saviour standing before him, had for a long time been struggling with the question as to who Jesus, the Nazarene, really was.

A long history of suffering lies behind this question which is agitating the king. Time was when this same ruler had had John the Baptist killed. That murder had in part been the result of a false sense of shame owing to the fact that Herod had not had the courage to refuse the "favor" which his daughter Salome had asked of him. We remember that he had promised to give her

---

1. In the preceding chapter we regard Herod as a typical representative of Esau. But there is room, too, — and that is why this separate chapter is devoted to it — for the consideration which Herod as a *person* devotes to Christ.

whatever she should ask, when she danced before him at the celebration of his birthday. Spurred on by her mother, Salome had on that occasion asked for the head of the Baptist. In part this murder, the plan of which had been carefully worked out in the mind of Salome's mother, Herodias, had had a political significance. We know this from the fact that the Baptist had been imprisoned for a while before his death. John, then, was beheaded in his cell, and the ball in celebration of the king's birthday was brought to a conclusion by this atrocious act.

After that day, however, Herod had never again felt at rest. This is not surprising. We must know that before the Baptist was beheaded, Herod had had a good deal to do with him. In secret, you see, he acknowledged that the Baptist, even though he had been imprisoned, was guilty of no misconduct, but was, on the contrary, a holy and righteous man, a prophet whose credentials were indisputable. That is why Herod, during the time in which the Baptist was being held captive, secretly visited him more than once, in order to talk with him. These lone conversations between the weak prince with his troubled conscience and the quiet witness-bearer of God had made a deep impression upon the soul of Herod. How eagerly he would have refused to grant the request of the frivolous dancer when she required the head of that much-hated man. But to refuse he dared not. He dared not because of the people who were standing by and who noticed that he had given Salome an indefinite promise. Is it any wonder then that the restiveness which had consumed his troubled conscience before the gruesome murder continued to tantalize him afterwards? No, that can readily be understood. Accordingly we read that after this time Herod Antipas could not rid himself of thoughts about John the Baptist. A tantalized conscience, a smothered voice of conscience, a superstitious obsession, a suppressed anxiety, and a rather vague notion about what becomes of the dead after their departure from this life (the question of the state of the soul was a much mooted issue among several factions in those days)—these all combined to greatly disturb Herod's peace of mind. Secretly he feared that the Baptist might return some day.

Then Jesus of Nazareth went through the country doing wonders and preaching a message which in all of its earnestness greatly resembled that call to repentance which the Baptist had sounded. Moreover, when Jesus, just as John before him, showed no respect of persons, the king felt intuitively that the line of the Baptist had not been cut off in the sombre cells of the prison where his head had fallen to the ground, but that this line of his prophetic work was being continued by Jesus of Nazareth. This thought never left Herod: a troubled conscience cannot easily be put to rest. That is why, then, Herod again and again imagines that he recognizes the beheaded Baptist in the miracle-working Jesus. Sometimes he rejects the thought as unworthy of acceptance (Luke 9:9), but on other occasions he simply cannot escape from the depressing possibility (Matthew 14:1-2, Mark 6:14-16). Hence Jesus existed as a vaguely understood mystery in the mind of Herod Antipas. Moreover, Herod was not the only one who, in a vague sort of way, felt that the murdered Baptist had returned to the world in one form or another, be it in the guise of the prophet of Nazareth or in some other form (Luke 9:7). Hence Jesus was regarded by many as a hidden mystery, as an unexplained visitor from the other world, possibly an angel of wrath. Jesus' good works and preaching were regarded as sombre threats by the king and the court. But especially alarmed was Herod himself,—poor Herod, against whom a wreaking judgment should unexpectedly be released later.

However, even this does not tell the whole story. We read that when Jesus returned to Galilee somewhat later, certain Pharisees warned Him in a quasi-friendly way that Herod wanted to put Him to death; and they added the advice that the best thing He could do was to remove Himself from the province of that king.

It becomes apparent from the very peculiar reply which Jesus gave to these "friendly" advisers that the Pharisees had mingled truth with falsehood. It was true that they were eager to have Jesus remove Himself from Herod's province. It was not true that Herod wanted to put Jesus to death. He would not have *dared* to do that. The king feared the influence of Jesus. The threatening storm cloud was approaching ever nearer, and the king did not know what he had to think of it. It is obvious, accordingly, that he had arranged with these Pharisees that they should make use of these means of intimidation in an effort to get rid of Jesus. This arrangement was just another manifestation in Herod of that mingling of hope and fear which had long possessed his soul, and which was stirred up as often as he thought of Jesus in connection with John the Baptist. Quietly but persistently the longing grew in his soul to see the remarkable Jesus face to face. On the one hand, he shied away from any such need; no one could tell when the storm might break loose, when the spirit of the murdered Baptist might leap forth from the body of the Nazarene, when John's hand might reach out to grasp Herod's throat. . . . But, on the other hand, the king wanted to have as much certainty as was at all possible. He had to rid himself of his anxiousness; he simply could not go on living with this tantalizing conscience.

Hence it is easy to see why Herod is as happy as a child to know that today Pilate has referred Jesus to him. The opportunity for meeting Jesus has unexpectedly come at last. That which the king had not dared to coerce was suddenly achieved for him through an agency with which he himself had had nothing to do. The question to which he himself could give no reply—should he engage Jesus in conversation or shun Him?—was suddenly answered for him.

Besides, the manner in which Jesus was presented to the king immediately alleviated much of his anxiety. For Jesus made His appearance in bonds. He was quite defenceless. No, that does not mean to say that Herod supposes no danger at all remains now; superstition is not put to rest as easily as that. But at least the first threat of danger seemed to be allayed for the time being. As long as the Nazarene stands before him bound, the arrow of death will very likely not leap at the king's throat. Accordingly, Herod was very glad when he saw Jesus.

We can appreciate his feelings in the matter even better if we remember that the last word which Jesus spoke to him had never ceased to trouble him. We refer to the answer which Jesus had given those Pharisees to whom we alluded a moment ago.

In response to their friendly warning, advising Him to leave Herod's province, Jesus had replied: "Go ye and tell that fox, Behold, I cast out devils, and I do cures today and tomorrow, and the third day I shall be perfected. Nevertheless I must walk today, and tomorrow, and the day following: for it cannot be that a prophet perish out of Jerusalem." With this message Jesus had dispatched His advisers.

But the sublime irony contained in that statement had long continued to make the king's life difficult for him. The statement gave expression to a spiritual superiority which offered the king a good deal to think about. It was plain that the Nazarene was not afraid. That in the first place.

And this besides: Just what did the statement mean? It seemed to be a kind of riddle. Yes, to a considerable extent it represented a kind of international conundrum, the kind in fact to which we have had occasion to refer frequently in this book. What did Jesus mean when He said: "On the third day I shall be perfected?" Did He mean to say that He would have completed His work after a few days? Or could it be that this statement contained a hidden allusion to His death? And, in case this last meaning were the real intent of the utterance, could it be that Jesus wanted to mock the king by telling him in effect that he could kill Him, but that the death would in no sense harm Him; that He will complete His own work in His own way in spite of the murder; that His death would represent a *perfecting?* And that other idea, too, implying that Jesus wanted to complete His schedule of activities in His own manner first, and that then, if the king chose, he might take Him, perhaps in . . . *Jerusalem*—what could that possibly mean? It just does not happen, it is quite impossible, said Jesus, that a prophet is killed *outside* of Jerusalem, and is He giving expression to the fact that He knows such a death will be the culmination of everything? Can it be that Jesus is telling Herod that He, as the very crown of the prophets, standing upon the prophetic mountain, wants also to assume the fate of those prophets who in a general way were never understood by the people and, consequently, were each in turn, be it literally or figuratively, put to death? When Jesus says that He is going to Jerusalem, the city whose privilege it has been to murder prophets, He seems to be relying on the fact that He will have a place in the vale of martyrs. In any case, however, this statement, which might then be fairly called a cynical one, is an instance of haughtiness on the part of a citizen of Nazareth against his majesty, the king.

Now it was certainly a most difficult thing to know what Jesus' statement might mean. We say this seriously. We do not hesitate to say that we notice a kind of maschil in this ironical speech of Jesus. We do not mean to say that it was a general riddle such as accompanied Jesus' usual prophesying, but do mean that it was a conundrum directed to a specific address.

The more we think about it, the more delicate and the more devastating the irony of Christ seems to us to have been. For Herod on his own part has already feared that Jesus has taken his place heretofore in the valley of martyrs—recall the Baptist again. Mark now: Jesus, He who tried human hearts, seems to fall in line with those peculiar, restless thoughts of the king who is the prey of folly, and by means of His well-chosen and pointed words He seems to join in with the trend of those thoughts. He appears to be quietly playing with the secret anxieties of Herod. Can it be that He actually is the Baptist? And does that man know everything?

Ah yes, this was indeed an instance of sublime majesty. On the one hand, Jesus did not repudiate the truth of what the king feared, but couched His meaning in such phrases as would give the king's anxieties new stuff to feed on. But, on the other hand, Jesus also showed very plainly that He goes His own way quite independently, and that He, when He is ready to enter the city which kills the prophets, will make His entry not as an embarrassed and shy candidate for the privilege of martyrdom but as a king who follows His own schedule, and who will not be diverted from it by this old fox.

Hence you need not ask what impression this last message which Christ had conveyed to Herod made upon the king. He must have felt a sense of defeat. The sublime irony of the Christ was simply too much for him. His spiritual superiority weighed down very oppressively upon Herod.

Nevertheless, the matter was not one of spiritual superiority solely. Christ was standing over against Herod not merely as a human being but as a prophet, as a revealer of God, and Herod had been caught in the snares of Jesus Christ, the Christ who bears witness to revelation. Christ had taken the king captive in

His maschil, in His intentional conundrum, in His riddle directed to "that fox".

We refer to a maschil, and do so with good reason, we believe. Remember that a maschil is characterized by two elements: first, it represents a concealment of the truth; and, second, a thorough-going penetration in the direction of the truth. Both of these elements characterize Jesus' reply to "that fox".

On the one hand Christ had purposely couched His meaning in the form of a conundrum. To that we referred above, and hence we will not discuss it here.

On the other hand, however, Christ had also constrained Herod; in fact, had constrained him to a seeking of the truth which had hitherto remained a mystery to him in the matter of the Nazarene. By naming Jerusalem the official city for the murdering of prophets and by declaring outright that Herod, *if* he indeed wanted to rid himself of the Nazarene in whom the Baptist possibly was hidden had better wait until both of them were in Jerusalem, Christ had given the king a very definite hint. He had clearly indicated to him that for the present the Nazarene did not expect any persecution on the part of Herod. But He had indicated also that He nevertheless expected an outburst of enmity against His own life work. Christ had not tried to conceal the fact that a persecution of life and death was not only a natural consequence of Herod's own life but would also serve as the very crown of the tribulation of martyrs, which had accrued to all the prophets of God throughout the centuries. By naming Jerusalem as the place of the murder of prophets, and by awaiting Herod in Jerusalem, Jesus had included Himself in the company of all the martyrs. He proved that He thoroughly understood Herod, that He knew him to be a dyed-in-the-wool Edomite, an enemy of the true seed of Jacob-Israel. This, too, was a painful reprimand for Herod, the more so because he was doing his best to be acknowledged among the Jews as a pious prince, one who was being faithful to all the traditions. That he had been eagerly active in attaining this purpose becomes obvious from his restorations of the temple, later from his battle against Pilate's religious plunderings, and now from his presence in Jerusalem for the purpose of attending the Passover together with all orthodox Jews.

You see that the man was eager to be popular when such popularity was expedient for him.

In this way, then, Christ had caught Herod in the net of His revelation.

Thereupon Herod came to the city at once with a heavy heart. What can he do? His superstition gives him no answer. On the contrary, superstition always makes one lose one's way. In fact, a superstitious person cannot even read such directions as point out the road to take. Yes, what can Herod do in the city? Conform himself to its manner of life? Join with the others in singing the feast-day songs, and so drown out the groanings of the murdered prophets in this "official" vale of martyrs? Or should he proclaim judgment to the city? Had not the Nazarene truly said that the murdering of prophets had grown to be the habit here?

And at the feast itself: What must the king do there? The whole city is talking about the Nazarene. Naturally Herod, too, has heard the rumors about his triumphal entry. Hence they are both in the same neighborhood, Herod and the Nazarene miracle-worker, Herod and the man who has been an irksome problem in his mind these last years, Herod and the man who has been writing on the wall of his festal ball-room. Secret writing indeed and bearing a message which seemed to say *mene, mene, tekel* . . . Ah, yes, what must Herod do at this feast? Shall he carefully avoid any conflict with the Nazarene and move about at the feast as unobtrusively as is possible for a king? Or shall he try to lay hands on the Nazarene and prove that the lofty utterances of the ruler of Galilee and Iturea are not a bluff? The Pharisees had not forgotten the agreement: they would be there to see whether he "could hold his own" over against the Nazarene, now that He had dared to come to the city in which prophets were murdered.

Yes, Herod's is a very difficult situation. Too many eyes are kept upon him to allow him a sense of ease. The eyes of the Pharisees, and more particularly—the eyes of John the Baptist.

But mark now: God suddenly removes Herod's perplexities. All of a sudden the Nazarene is placed before him. This is a pleasant surprise—a *surprise* inasmuch as the detention of Jesus had occurred in secret and inasmuch as the events had followed each other in astonishingly rapid succession.

Can we wonder at the fact that Herod is surprised? And *pleasantly* surprised. Some say that Herod was glad solely because Pilate granted him the honor of a share in the procedure. Others maintain that Herod's joy was as exuberant as it was because the situation gave him an opportunity to put Jesus to death. A third group contends that Herod's tantalized conscience felt much better now because of the fact that the formidable, depressing uncertainty which had made life so difficult for him these many years would give way at last to certainty about whether this man were really the Baptist or simply an ordinary man of flesh and blood.

You see that there are three interpretations. Must we choose one of the three? We believe that is not necessary. The one cannot possibly be separated from the other two. Psychological conflicts are always complicated. On the one hand Herod must have leaped for joy at the thought that his unformulated problem—after all, a person always feels ashamed of his superstition—was suddenly removed in an unanticipated manner. At least, he thinks that it will be removed. On the other hand, it must have been particularly pleasant for Herod, inasmuch as he was always pathetically wanting in self-assurance—and the man standing before him there was to a large extent "responsible" for that—to know that some official attention was given him at Pilate's behest. And, finally, he can positively rejoice at the fact that the man whom he feared so much is dependent upon him now.

Nevertheless, uncertainty dominates the situation. A feeling of abiding uncertainty claims dominance over the rising sense of exuberant gladness. The question mark remains; the secret writing remains, its letters almost standing out as large now as Herod himself. Yes, the question mark and the writing on the wall both have been introduced into the court.

Hereupon Herod reveals himself as he truly is. He asks for a sign. That is revealing himself as he is, his asking for a sign. It may be that faith first asks for the Word, but superstition would rather have a sign. Hence Herod demands one of Jesus. He wants a sign, he wants a miracle to be performed. He wants something miraculous to happen. From the Nazarene's answer to the question whether or not he can perform a miracle it will appear whether he is the much-feared Baptist or not.

The king asks for a sign. He hopes that this will give him some assurance as to the identity of this mysterious person.

Quick as lightning he makes the request: Perform a miracle.[1] Naturally this question greatly increases the tenseness of the atmosphere in the court. Visualize the situation. Here is Herod. He vehemently demands that a wonder be performed. The conflict he has suffered during the past months gives his request an impassioned violence. There, on the other side, are Jesus' accusers, the high priests and the scribes. These, for their own part, want no such sign to be displayed. Suppose the Nazarene should comply with the request—that would be merely a waste of time. Besides it would weaken their "chances," for the Nazarene would get more prominence because of it. As long as Jesus' signs simply provide the stuff for folk-tales to feed upon, they have no objections. After all, such tales, . . . well, they are merely the gossip of the masses. But it will be a harder thing to erase from the public mind the impression which would be created by a sign given in this court. Had they not when they were in the presence of the Sanhedrin carefully avoided every inquiry about miracles?

Yes, the atmosphere is growing tense in the court.

Herod and the Jewish authorities stand there over against each other. The one is eager to see a sign, the others want to do everything in their power to prevent one. The one makes his wishes known by expressing them aloud; the others make violent and persistent accusations their forte. By the clamor of their vitriolic accusations they would hinder Herod from asking and Jesus from demanding attention for an impressive sign.

What of Jesus Himself? What does He do? We can put it this way: He sees the temptation, but He conquers it.

Yes, this was a temptation for Christ. This is the third time during the process of law affecting Him that a temptation has come to Him. Had Jesus explained His maschil to the Sanhedrin He would have placed the meeting in great embarrassment and have been able to postpone the day of His death. But He would

---

1. True, this is not stated in so many words in the Biblical account, but it is evident from that account that much was said on this occasion; and the eager desire of the king must naturally have arisen to the surface.

have done that independent of God's justice and truth.[1] That was the first temptation.

Moreover, if He, just a moment ago, had disclosed His official and personal secret to Pilate, in spite of the fact that Pilate had brazenly overlooked the all-important question as to what the essence of Christ was (that is, when he asked: What is truth?), Christ would also have embarrassed Pilate greatly, would have forced the suit at law, and would have postponed the day of His death. But that too, He would have to do, then, independent of God's justice and truth. That was the second temptation.[2]

In the presence of the Sanhedrin Christ conquered the first temptation: He held His peace.

In the presence of Pilate Christ conquered the second temptation: He held His peace there a second time.

In the presence of Herod Christ conquered the third temptation: He stood mute a third time.

Yes, this occasion was indeed a temptation for Him. You can arrive at that conclusion yourself. How easy, how very easy,—we talk after the manner of men—it would have been for Christ by means of some suggestive hint or by means of busy argument to escape from His own fate, which is the fate His Father assigned to Him, or at least to postpone the decision to a later time.

In the first place, Christ could have made use of the principle employed by tyrants: Keep factions alive, and rule. A perfect opportunity was given Him to drive a wedge between Herod and the scribes. The one wanted a sign, and the others did not. Besides, Herod, who had so often catered to the Jews and was doing so even now by attending the Passover, had also on occasion bitterly provoked and offended the Jews. Everyone knew that such was the fact, and Christ was the first to know it. What could be easier, therefore, than to play off Herod against the scribes? Life is so good, and He was a man of like passions with us!

In the second place, the opportunity was an especially favorable one for Jesus, because the soul of Herod was particularly impressionable. If ever anyone—and again we speak after the fashion of men—was susceptible to receiving a good "impression" which

---

1. Compare Chapter 5 of this volume, especially pp. 115 f.
2. Compare this volume, p. 356.

nevertheless would involve him in difficulties, that man was Herod. A psychological conflict which lasts months and years suffices to make the human personality very pliable. It might be that Jesus was the Baptist in very fact. But Herod himself knew very well that the Baptist was a "holy and righteous" man. Hence, as long as he reckons with the possibility that the Baptist has returned in the form of Jesus, so long he must necessarily think of the Christ who is standing before him as one who is "holy and righteous". And it is not true that a single dazzling sign would have strengthened that thought in Herod immeasurably. Was the Nazarene a messenger from heaven? An angel of wrath? Or a token of God's utmost long-suffering? A messenger from heaven, in other words, whose coming was ushered in with peace? One who showed a stern countenance, but nevertheless had no will to condemn? This wandering mystery—might something still be expected of him? If so, O Jesus, Jesus, help Herod then. He will be grateful to Thee if Thou canst heal his sickness. He will move about much easier then, there in his position above the tombstone of the accursed Baptist, that good and holy, but very troublesome man. He will do everything in his power then to change Pilate's point of view. He will be glad to bear the discomfort of a break between him and the scribes if he may know that the weight of the burden resting upon his conscience will be lifted today. O Christ, do show a sign!

But Jesus held His peace.

Again in this matter we worship Christ's passive obedience, an obedience which rests in His Father's good pleasure. We must worship Christ's active obedience as He manifests it in the silence which He maintains before Herod quite as much as His passive obedience. Jesus recognizes that the temptation is here, but in all of His responses to what confronts Him in this world he acts purely and genuinely, and He does so also in His response to this situation.

Yes, He knows very well that a sign, humanly speaking, will save His life. O Christ, Christ, Thou hast saved others by Thy miracles: canst Thou not save Thyself? By Thy signs and miracles Thou didst give much to many. Mayest Thou not in this Thy dire need give Thyself anything? Christ, Thou crown of Moses, Thou prince of Aaron, convert Thy staff into a serpent, put Thy hand—have it loosened a moment—into Thy bosom so that it may become leprous and then well again, have Thy almond reed burst into bloom, perform a wonder for Thy own benefit in order that Thy enemies may in their wrath and much to their regret, observe how God comforts and delivers Thee.

But Jesus held His peace. He did not reply to a single word. He performed no miracle, precisely because He is more than Moses. Yes, "more than Moses"; there are two ways in which that phrase can be explained. Satan has his own exposition. He tells Jesus: If you really are more than Moses show a greater sign than Moses ever revealed. But God has an explanation too. His exegesis of the messianic appeal, "being more than Moses," is a different one. God says: Because Thou art more than Moses, perform no miracle on this occasion. For Moses performed his wonders in order to escape from the house of bondage. In the company of his people, of course, but also in order that he himself might escape. But Christ is a greater than Moses. And He performs no miracle, He shows no sign, on this occasion, for the specific reason that His people will emerge from the house of bondage at the very place at which he, Christ Himself, must all alone enter into that house of bondage and be swallowed up by it.

That is what "being more than Moses" means. It means to refuse to show a sign, whenever the demonstration of it would benefit only Himself; to refuse to understand, in order that He might show those signs which will convey some of the gifts of the peace of God and the power of salvation to the others, to the oppressed and heavily laden.

No, Christ knows very well that if He were to show a sign, here in the presence of this man at this specific moment, He would be sinning. For Christ, that is, the *man* Christ, is not the chief Lord of wonders, even though He demonstrated His signs time and again. His task is to be the *servant* of the Lord. Now a servant may never play with the signs and with the powers of the kingdom of his Sender. Had Christ in this moment demonstrated a sign which had not been commanded Him He would have been playing with the powers of the world to come.

The signs which Christ demonstrates must find their purpose in His God and not in Himself, for He is a servant. The sign He demonstrates must reveal the power of redemption, not as that power pertains to Himself but as it pertains to the people to whom He has been sent. Obviously, then, if Christ had showed a sign, the only purpose of which had been to glory in the presence of Herod, or to redeem Himself from this maelstrom of death and curse, He would Himself have taken the central position; He would have thrust God out of that position. Then He would have placed Himself at the very end of His course in an effort to save Himself from death, and to throw the responsibility for our illnesses off His shoulders; He would have thrust His people aside.

That, then, is why He shows no sign. Had He done so the Christ of God would have fallen into sin. He will not stretch out His hand to the tree of life, before God's time has come. He will not eat a fruit which God has refused Him, in all eternity He will not.

This is so perfectly true that, to go on, we can safely say that Christ was *unable* to perform a wonder. In order to perform a miracle, faith is necessary, faith in the fellowship with God in this specific hour and for this specific purpose. As often as in any given instance this faith is not present in Him, He cannot show a sign.

That faith is not present in Him here. Christ has no faith in the fact that it is possible for Him to perform a wonder here. He has no faith in it because He knows that any wonder which He might perform now could profit only Himself. But He knows that He may not be the end and purpose of the powers which God sends into the world. That is why Christ was *unable* to show a sign on this occasion. To say that He did not *want* to is to tell the truth. And to say that He could not do it is to present the other side of that perfect truth.

Hence the moment in which Christ refuses to perform a wonder for Herod is just as momentous as the one which came to Him in the wilderness at the very beginning of His official ministry. In one sense this whole episode resembles a kind of intermezzo; in one sense Christ's hearing before Herod seems hardly more important than the sudden flash which induced Pilate, who was eager to have done with the matter, to give the case into the hands of another. Nevertheless, Christ's stay in Herod's house is a perfect counterpart to His temptation in the wilderness. At the beginning, in the wilderness, and at the end, here in Herod's court, Satan tried to tempt Christ to perform an extra-official wonder.

The parallelisms in these two events are not hard to discover. When Satan invited Christ to show a sign in the wilderness, the question at issue was whether or not Christ would be willing to show a sign within a "closed circle," that is, in the wilderness with none there to see except Satan and Jesus Christ. By this sign, then, Christ would have served Himself the miracle-bread, apart from the favor and outside of the fellowship of God. For it was God who had caused Him to hunger. The same implications hold for the temptation which followed, in which Satan advised Christ that He leap down from the pinnacles of the temple. Even though this last sign would not have been as conspicuously limited to a closed circle (for the temple was a public place), Christ by this sign, too, would have been serving Himself. He would have been curtailing the tedious road which He must take in revealing Himself as the Messiah, by personally deciding to forego the suffering. This dispossessing sign would not have served His God nor God's people, but would have remained a service of self. In this way, according to the Satanic prediction, the way of the Servant of the Lord would have taken a direct route to world conquest: "I will give thee all the kingdoms."

This same evil prompting of satanic temptation returns at this time. Would Christ not be willing, just for one moment, to show a sign in an *exclusive* society? If need be, Herod and Jesus can step into the king's apartment for a moment,—the two can be quite alone there. Or, if the secretiveness need not be as far-reaching as that, would Jesus not be willing to show the sign in the somewhat larger but still limited circle of Herod and the scribes and the chief priests? He must remember, of course, that in both events the sign which He shows will be demonstrated for the benefit of the accused Himself; it will help Him greatly in obtaining His freedom. True, this demonstration of a wonder will not this time be directly referred to God, nor to God's people, and it will not be done with a strictly evangelical purpose, nor be full of blessing for the poor and the miserable—but, after all, Christ has blessed these so very often before. This time it concerns Himself. Yes, indeed, have Him perform a miracle; perhaps the wonder will not lead to world conquest, but it will at

least insure a longer life. It may be that the cross will recede. . . .
The offer sounds attractive, does it not, Lord Jesus?
But Jesus held His peace.

He will perform no miracles in an exclusive circle, but will
show His signs only along the ways traversed by God's church-
forming redemption. The Christ will perform no miracles in a
secluded corner, but only along the public way which has been
made smooth and traversable for God, only along the highway by
which God seeks His people in love. The servant never makes
himself the purpose of his actions. Hence Christ refuses to show
the requested sign.

How now, Christ, do you really want to make that choice? You
have come to appear before Esau today; a new Jacob stands before a new Esau. What has become of your *birthright,* Christ?
Is it not true that to show signs, to master the forces of nature, to
manipulate the forces of the kingdom of heaven as you will, are
some of the highest prerogatives which belong to the birthright
of the estate of God's covenant of grace? Come, Christ, appropriate Thy birthright, work it out, cause it to shine in splendour.
But Christ held His peace.

For He is not Jacob, but *Israel.* He is paying the penalty for
Jacob's sins. When he robbed Esau of his birthright — we return
to this matter once more — he reached for the promise, but he
overreached himself in reference to the commandments. He separated the blessing of the birthright from the duty of the birthright and made himself, instead of God, the purpose of God's
promises. He refused to take the roundabout way of suffering in
his journey to glory. In that moment Jacob, who had been called
a prince, became a beggar; he had to beg for his life — from
Esau. He fled from the spot and later purchased Esau's favor at
the cost of half of his capital; he had already closed the deal in his
soul before that.

Now see the Christ standing before Esau. He makes God, and
not Himself, the purpose of life and of work. He does not beg
Esau for a day of life. He does no dickering in the house of God.
If there is anyone who thinks such language irreverent, we ask
him to remember that prophecy itself reaches one of its high points
when it is able to say: *"There shall be no more the Canaanite
(that is, the bargainer, the dickerer) in the house of the Lord of*

Hosts (Zechariah 14:21). This statement has the sound of music in the ears of the prophets. For the history of Israel began by a "dickering." Think of the wiles of Jacob, of how Esau sold his birthright, and of many instances besides. Spiritual goods have very frequently been offered for sale in the markets of the unworthy.[1] But today that spirit of Esau and that deceit on Jacob's part will be entirely wiped out and atoned for by Christ. The Christ who refused to perform a miracle, earns His birthright by remaining faithful to the commandments. By His refusal He not only persisted in the purification of the temple which He began when He threw the "dickerers" out of the house of God, but He also earned His right to the feast of the Passover and related to Himself the powers of the world to come. By refusing to abuse the forces of nature for an arbitrary personal wonder, He earned for Himself the mastery of the forces of all natural life. He earned His reward; presently He will be given all power in heaven and on earth. In Him the power of the blessing of the birthright will be perfectly conjoined with the prerogatives which that birthright gives. O Jacob, here only will you be able to find rest.

On this occasion, then, the steadfastness of the manner of Christ's perfect justice becomes manifest. This third instance of His silence is again an assertion of the maschil, of the greatest mystery. Again the desire to conceal, apparent here and now, points to the manifest character of His revelation.[2]

We remember that the last word which Christ had conveyed to the king before this time was the marvellous message: "I do cures today and tomorrow, and the third day I shall be perfected." Now this maschil was even richer than the first which Christ pronounced to the Jews in the vicinity of the temple. You remember it; He spoke of breaking down the temple and rebuilding it in three days.

But this second maschil, directed to Herod, refers unmistakably to His humiliation, to His death. Prophets are put to death only in Jerusalem, and the Christ numbers Himself among them.

---

1. Compare this volume, p. 79.
2. Compare this volume, p. 87 f. In order to circumvent too much repetition we simply allude in passing to what was treated in greater detail in connection with Christ's first assertion of the maschil.

In this way, then, Herod saw Christ consciously entering into the vale of martyrs.

But the problem remained. In the statement directed to Herod, Christ had put two truths in juxtaposition with each other. He had referred to the persecution, to the fact that He was awaiting the fate of prophets ("I shall not perish outside of Jerusalem"). Next to that He had put the truth that He would complete His own work in His own way and would brook no interference on the part of anyone ("I shall be perfected"). Now by placing these two truths next to each other Christ had given Herod a difficult problem to solve. And He had done more. He had constrained Herod — precisely as in the previous instance He had constrained the Jews — to come out into the open, to lay bare his feelings. What will Herod do? Abuse the maschil by riding over it rough-shod, by brutally and indifferently ignoring it? Or will he take refuge in the Word, shamefacedly and with embarrassment? Will He mock Jesus, or will he precisely because he cannot explain the maschil, inquire into the secret of His mission?

Yes, Herod too, has been caught in the snares of the messenger of God who speaks in riddles. Now Herod's position must be made public.

It was made public. It appears later that Herod has no will to inquire; that again he deftly steps over the stumbling-block of the maschil. It becomes apparent that he does ask for a sign, for the unknown, but only in order to escape from the Word, from the known.

Thereupon Christ asserted His maschil over against him also. Everything we have said about that maschil heretofore[1] applies in this instance also. For Christ did Herod justice, He did Himself justice, and above all He did justice to God the Lord. The key to the explanation of the maschil (which called the death of prophets the perfecting of prophets) lay in the knowledge that Jesus' per-fecting, Jesus' complete florescence, was contained in the martyr's crown, in His going down to death as one of the many belonging to the martyred seed of the woman. However, Christ did not give Herod the key. The maschil remained unexposed. Herod was simply directed to the Word of God and to the birthright of Jacob-

---

1. Chapter 5; "Christ Being Silent Before the Sanhedrin."

Israel, and that was enough for him. Note how austerely strict the style of Jesus is. Three times He holds His peace. He is always perfectly consistent with Himself.

We must say more. Christ asserts His maschil not only, but also His irony. He not only remains true to His style, but in using it He always remains beautiful, the most beautiful among the children of men.

We have said already that Christ's statement to "that fox" was an ironical one. Moreover, we have previously made the point that irony in Christ represents the fact that His thoughts have reached a point of rest.[1] This holds true also of the poignant, ironical utterance with which He caused Herod to reflect upon His status. The statement gave expression to the fact that Christ had reached a point of rest in His heavily laden life.

If anyone should ask whether Christ, who was very man, after He had been abused by three judges, could still maintain His poise, we would reply: Yes! Christ has appeared before Caiaphas, before Pilate and before Herod and, even though the tension for Him was never as oppressive as it was in Herod's presence, inasmuch as — humanly speaking — the chances for living were His for the taking, He even there perfectly retained His equilibrium. He even maintained it over against the tantalized conscience of Herod which He thoroughly penetrated.

Such is a crushing majesty, for none of us can avoid thinking of the fact that Jesus can maintain an equal poise over against our own tantalizing conscience. He who thinks of this is wise.

But it is also a *saving* majesty. Remember that Christ has now reached the end of His hearing at the court. After this time He will not be heard further, not even by Pilate.[2] It was His own will that it should be so. And the fact that He retains the irony with which He had addressed Herod and upon which He now lets him continue to brood, proves to us that His will to sacrifice is extremely great. We can say that He has already prepared the wood for that sacrifice Himself, has done it even now. When, after a while, He is conducted out of Herod's palace — never in all eternity to

---

1. Compare *Christ in His Suffering*, p. 383 ff, 391-392.
2. The question "Whence art Thou?" which we will discuss later, does not represent a legal hearing.

be given another hearing, for it is so that He thinks of it — His soul calmly says to God: Father, the wood has been laid ready; I think everything has been prepared. In Herod's presence I gave Satan no chance to lay His hands upon me; Father, it was still possible for me to see Thee. I thank thee, Father.

As for ourselves, all that we can do is to worship Him. One who after three hearings before as many judges is still able to express His irony is able also to make the state of equilibrium which He achieves on the prophetic mountain correspond to the nadir of the vale of martyrs. By means of His irony, that is, by the superiority of His soul, Christ preserved a state of equilibrium in the presence of Herod. In doing this, Christ, by reaching backward, maintained the sense of the sublime statement which He had made in Gethsemane: Sleep on now and rest.[1] In addition, by reaching ahead, He achieved for Himself the prerogative to say to weeping children later: Weep not for me, but for yourselves, and for your children.

In the meantime, however, the irony of prophets when asserted over against kings meets with the penalty of death. Hence Christ will not be able to escape from His punishment. In fact, we can say that He has let "His last chance" escape. His last chance had been to cling fast to Herod's restlessness and to the disparity between him and the scribes. When Jesus failed to take advantage of this opportunity, the decision against Him was quickly made.

Herod feels provoked and humiliated. The question mark in his mind refuses to become an explanation point. The wandering mystery he had yearned to know refused to disclose itself. What is more, that accursed "Jacob" simply persists in refusing to beg from "Esau."

But now Herod succeeds in getting past his "dead center." He "gets a grip on himself." He succeeds in mastering his doubt; succeeds because of the law for all sinners: his mind has not reached clarity, not a single question has been answered for him, but he acts nevertheless as though he knew the answer, he acts as though he knew everything about it, and goes on to try to suppress his fears by arranging a mock comedy. The kings of his day understood the art of arranging these. They lived close to the

---

1. See *Christ in His Suffering*, p. 379 f.

actors of their time, especially when they kept up close contact with Rome. Herod Antipas, for instance, retained in his splendid palace such luxuries as a theatre gave. Now, accompanied by his whole court, by his entire retinue — for that is the implication of the word used in the original—he begins to flay and to mock Jesus. Jesus had entered the hall as an eventual martyr in Herod's own eyes; He had announced Himself to Herod as a probable martyr beforehand. But Herod, who takes the fact of Christ's candidacy for martyrdom from His own lips, does not want to let Him leave as a martyr. Sin is always changing its own ways of regarding things. Hence he refuses to wound Jesus and does not condemn Him. As a matter of fact, he does not even talk threateningly to Him, nor sign a death warrant against Him. He simply proceeds to mock Him.

When he did that, Christ — this was His fate — took the lowest place in the vale of martyrs. He became a lesser one than all others who had been beaten down in it.

After all, the martyr was struck down in the name of the law, but we have observed repeatedly that the outlaw is thrust outside of the pale of the law. Hence Herod unites with the Sanhedrin in making Christ an outlawed Christ, one, that is, who stands outside of the scope of the law. He arranges a mock comedy which in its devilish purport and brutal sarcasm is by no means second to that arranged by the Sanhedrin. He and his courtiers jeeringly move to and fro around the Christ. Thereupon they put a gorgeous robe on Him. Some think that the word *gorgeous* tells us nothing about the color of the robe, which, they maintain, might have been red or white or any other hue. But others, and these very likely upon a sound basis, believe that what is indicated is a white garment, a glistening white robe.

What is the significance of this gorgeous robe?

Many have felt that Herod put it on Christ as a kind of caricature of the so-called *toga candida* in which according to the Roman custom those persons were dressed who presented themselves as candidates for this or that official office. If this interpretation is correct, Herod would have been mocking Christ by ludicrously making Him a candidate for the kingship. Naturally the motivation for such conduct would have to be found in the charge of the high priest that Christ had wanted to regard himself as a king.

At the same time it must be said, however, that it is highly unlikely that Herod thought of this Roman usage on the spur of the moment, or that he chose to make use of this device here in this particular vicinity. In Jerusalem the *toga candida* was not used for such purposes. Accordingly, the Jews would not have understood the satire conveyed by the scheme. Hence, the interpretation that Herod wanted to mock Jesus as a pretender to the crown must remain an unlikely one. Herod did not want to mock Christ as a pretender to the king's crown but as the caricature of a king. The robe in which he decked Jesus was a princely garment.

This phenomenon teaches us the *nature of sin* and simultaneously conveys to us the meaning of Christ's suffering *as the Surety*.

Yes, this manifestation reveals the *nature of sin* to us. When Jesus first came, Herod began by giving his own problems first consideration but he concluded by joining in with the others and by agreeing with the charges and formulae of complaint drawn up by the priest's party and by the scribes. When Jesus first entered, Herod began his inquiry by asking whether or not Jesus was a mysterious prophet. Now, as the session is dismissed he acts as if he is certain that Jesus is a self-vaunted king.

You see that in a single moment Herod has abandoned all of his own problems. He has completely bared himself, and revealed the pathetic nakedness of his blinded understanding and perverse will. When Jesus first came to him, he thought: You are perhaps a *mystery;* I do not understand you yet. Now that he dismisses Jesus he shouts after Him: In your own eyes you are a sun, but I call you darkness. As Jesus entered the court, he thought: This may be a messenger from heaven. Now that he sends Him away, he says: You are called *the* messenger of heaven, but that is impossible. At the beginning he thought he recognized in Christ *a* mystery; but at the conclusion he denies in Him *the* mystery. Herod began by acknowledging the possibility that Christ was *a reincarnation* of a *human being,* in this case, of the Baptist. But at the close of the session he haughtily ignores the preaching that Christ truly was *the* incarnation of the *living God.*[1] And although Herod had at first suspected that Christ was *an* angel of wrath,

---

1. The many and violent charges which the priest sounded doubtless included what Christ had professed in the presence of the Sanhedrin: I am the Son of the living God.

now he resorts to mocking Him in order to escape from the message that Christ is *the* angel, of love certainly, and of grace, but also of God's perfect wrath.

Such is man, of course. I like to think at present that the Holy Spirit, who thinks of all things, also thought of Herod Antipas when He had the evangelist write that men would not repent even though one should return from the dead. For Herod troubled himself about that issue — God knows how long. But this moment suddenly marked the end of his meditation, of his thinking, and of his anxious temptation.

Such is man: he would see a sign, so that he might have certainty, and closed his eyes to those possibilities which he feared had begun to become realities.

> Herod still lives and lifts the sword
> Of mockery against his Lord.[1]

But what good does it do us to regard Herod's sin? It is our sin also. Hence we must turn our eyes aside from Herod and ourselves and search out our Surety.

He is here. Our Surety and Mediator is here. He is in the vale of His martyrdom. He suffers the reproach of mockery, and is humiliated as the Christ who stands outside the pale of law. Observe Him now as He sinks beneath the plane of all martyrs; observe Him as He enters upon a fate which is a thousand times worse than that of John the Baptist.

Yes, worse. For it was at least the Baptist's privilege to be put to death by the sword, and to be put in prison as a dangerous character. In fact, he was taken seriously by the king, who visited him repeatedly in order to talk with him.

Christ is not taken as seriously as this. He gets only mockery and disdain. They belittle Him. He sinks beneath the plane of the Baptist. Certainly a prison, and a vindictive woman, and an embarrassed ruler are better than the mockery of an entire court. This all constituted His suffering. Never before was the fact so unmistakably proclaimed to Him that even the very idea of the Messiah was thought of as perfectly despicable. Here was the man who, of all those concerned in the legal process, appeared to be the most susceptible to the teaching of the Great Mystery. But this

---

1. Guido Gezelle.

man also washes his hands of the Christ as soon as the messianic message reaches his conscience. For Christ this means that even the crown of the martyrs which Herod had seen resting upon His head when Jesus entered, does not serve as a recommendation to the world for Him, as long as the spirit does not intervene to vanquish the heart by His irresistible power. The spirit only can conquer the heart and make it susceptible to the truth that Christ is not a martyr, even though He is mocked in the vale of the martyrs, for when He was in the depth of that valley, He bore them all within Him; He was no longer one of them, but became their surety, the Lord and Head of them all.

In all this we honor God's plan. Herod mocked and despised the Christ, but he went no farther than the mockery and disdain. He was not allowed to write the death sentence. He was not allowed to, because God gave him no permission. The same God who first prevented Christ's being limited to and being put to death by the narrow circle of Moses' last Jews[1] also prevented Jesus' being put to death now within the restricted area of Galilee, the province over which Antipas swayed the sceptre. Herod was not allowed to dismiss the case of Jesus once and for all. Christ must go to Rome, to the empire which circumscribed the whole world. Pilate, and Rome, and Caesar, in short, the world, will not succeed in getting rid of Christ. Christ must be made a sign before the broad gates of Rome and of the world-tribunal, and not merely inside of the narrow enclosure of Galilee, nor before the narrower door of Esau-Herod. The brazen serpent must be raised to a height where every eye may see.[2] For Christ will continue to affect the world. The same God who exalted and raised Him above the circle of Moses-Jacob, also lifted Him above the plane of Esau.

Accordingly, Herod had to send Christ back to Pilate.

It may be that these two will become good friends today. If so, the friendship will only prove that hatred against Christ and against the birthright of Jacob-Israel, serves to unite the false brother (Esau) with Sodom and Egypt, that is, with Rome and the world-empire.[3] Herod and Pilate become friends, and that is a good thing. For it proves that Herod's friendship with the Jews

---

1. See this volume, pp. 297-298.
2. See this volume, p. 298 f.
3. See Revelation 11.

and with Moses, whose Passover he has been eager to celebrate, is broken because of Jesus of Nazareth. He celebrates the feast of the Jews, but he thanks the *pagan* for the pleasant time he has had at the feast. By this fact, then, the great, unique, all-inclusive schism of the world proves to be conditioned and circumscribed by the antithesis between the seed of the woman and the seed of the church, between election and reprobation, between Christ and Antichrist, between faith and unbelief. By that antithesis the great schism is determined, and not by the fluctuations of natural birth, by cultural problems and their various fortunes, or by any force which can be explained in terms of purely mundane phenomena.

Presently Christ leaves Herod's palace wearing his gorgeous robe. God has laid His king's crown and His martyr's crown in a place above all prophets and kings, and in a place below the deepest catacombs of all the martyrs. The seed of the woman, adorned with that double crown, is now being led for the last time through the broad gates of the empire of the world by God Himself.

O Thou King of the gorgeous robe, Thou wearest the garment of mockery in front of the eyes of all the powers of the world. It is good that this is so. Thus it will be possible for Thee to wear the white robe, which God will give Thee, in the presence of all people. If a king's crown and a martyr's crown are identical to Thee, then the white robe of Thy perfected mockery will also be the white robe of Thy perfected glory. Thou wilt return. On Patmos Thou wilt return. Patmos belongs to Rome's domain. There Thou shalt wear the white robe, and in it dominate the world. I hear Herod saying: "There goes the king with the white robe." I hear the angels singing: "We see Him already crowned with glory and honor." And all of the martyrs are awaiting their white robe and their summons to the great rest.[1] They await the hour of Patmos in which John will see Thee in Thy shining white robe as the Son of man. Here, O church, is the Son of man as John saw Him and described Him:

> His robe was long, His waist encircled quite
> With golden belt. As white as wool, as snow
> His flowing hair; His glance a flaming fire;
> Like dazzling bronze in burning oven bleached,
> So were His feet; His voice the voice

---

1. Revelation 6:11; also 1:13, 14.

Of many waters. . . His left hand
Held seven stars aloft; and from His mouth
Issued a sharp, a two-edged sword. Like
Dazzling sun, haloed in mid-day splendor,
His face . . . .[1]

But first it will be necessary for Thee, Saviour, to pay God a price. Thou wilt be required to look upon Thy gorgeous robe of mockery, and to recall Thy dazzling form upon the mountain of metamorphosis.[2] It will be necessary for Thee to see both of these two white robes around Thine own body at once. Then, Lord, Thou wilt Thyself confess that it seems as if the Lord God up there — upon the mountain — has had Thy shining raiment trampled upon by the angels or the satyrs. Does it matter much in this world which?

I ask no further questions: I see His eye fixed upon me, as though He wanted to say: Behind me, Satan.

I believe it, Lord. I believe that Thou understandest heaven and its strange mode of doing things. I believe that Thou wilt be able presently to watch soldiers raffling off Thy robes. Lord, I believe that no raffling is going on between heaven and earth in the whole world. Help Thou my unbelief.

He will go on His way. But all the souls beneath the altar will have to confess that He did not leave John the Baptist in the lurch. He did not forget the deceased friend of the bridegroom; the bridegroom confessed this friend before Herod and the Father. That is a great thing: there are some who name the remembrance of a departed one the greatest act possible to love.[3] He placed no sign upon the Baptist's grave in order to release Herod from painful memories of John, and thus to shake Himself loose from the fingers of death which were reaching for Him. What? No sign? No matter, soon Thou wilt be with the Baptist; such is law in the vale of martyrs — surely, it would not be proper for a prophet to die outside of Jerusalem.

Finally, this:

Herod still lives and lifts the sword
Of mockery against his Lord.
Up Christians, rise, hear duty call,
Proclaim Christ's glory unto all.

---

1. Louis Couperus: *Fragmenten Uit Johannes' Apocalyps* (Williswinde).
2. See *Christ in His Suffering*, p. 83 f.
3. Kierkegaard.

CHAPTER TWENTY-TWO

Christ Jesus Completely Outlawed

> *And Pilate, when he had called together the chief priests and the rulers and the people, said unto them, Ye have brought this man unto me, as one that perverteth the people: and, behold, I, having examined him before you, have found no fault in this man touching those things whereof ye accuse him: No, nor yet Herod: for I sent you to him; and, lo, nothing worthy of death is done unto him. I will therefore chastise him, and release him.*
>
> LUKE 23:13-16.

CHRIST, still wearing His gorgeous robe, was sent back from Herod to Pilate. Herod did not complete the consideration of the charges which were named against Him. True, he did say to God — think of the mock comedy which he staged — that he would have nothing more to do with this man, but he carefully avoided telling Pilate as much. He undertook to deal brutally with Jesus in the world of spiritual things, a world seen by angels and similar powers, but he did not dare to set down his conclusion on official state papers. State papers, after all, will be read by man; and men are more dangerous than angels. And Herod did not dare to write on such a document the verdict "He is guilty," nor the verdict "He is not guilty." His conclusion in the presence of the people amounts to a simple *non liquet* : I do not know. It is easier to reach a conclusion about Christ in the presence of God than in the presence of the people. Had Herod given his conclusions in terms of secular law, or in terms of the rules of government as they functioned at that time, he would have had to draw up a written formulation which would have reached the public eye. That he did not want to do. He succeeded in dismissing Jesus from his own conscience but not from the "popular conscience." Hence he sent Jesus back unaccompanied by a writ of advice, be it in the direction of an acquittal or of condemnation. He did not make use of his right to handle and to despatch this "case" from Galilee.

Thus it is that Christ appears before Pilate a second time. What will happen now? The verdict cannot be withheld much longer.

The answer to this question comes quickly. It is this: Jesus is made Christ the outlaw.[1] He had been that before. *Now* he becomes that completely.

Things happened in this way. In the earlier stages of this trial, Pilate had already made an important mistake. He had already officially declared that he could find no fault in Jesus, but he went on, nevertheless, to actions which were incompatible with this declaration. That mistake comes back with a vengeance now. He has involved Herod in the case, but his conduct in this respect does not have the desired result. Hence he must reach his own conclusion, and the case is now more difficult than before. If he releases Jesus, he may be blamed for having taken upon himself the prerogative of engaging in the preliminary hearing. Just suppose for a moment that those troublesome Jews decide to appeal the case to a higher court. That would weaken Pilate's position immeasurably. However, if without any further formality, he condemns Christ to death, he is inconsistent, for his formal official declaration stated that he had not yet found legal grounds for such action. Add to this the fact that his own conscience does not quite allow him to take this drastic step.

Moreover, it may be that a kind of indefinite fear of the people constitutes a third difficulty in his present consideration of the case. Pilate knew that there were many among the people who esteemed the Nazarene very highly and lauded Him unstintedly. The Pharisees had themselves openly declared that Christ was indeed exercising a great influence upon the people. Besides, the reports of Jesus' triumphal entry into Jerusalem a few days before were evidence enough to confirm the fact that He was very palpably affecting the mass mind. Now a death sentence based upon superficial reasons in such circumstances might very well get Pilate

---

1. See footnote, p. 53.

into difficulty with the people. If he issued a death sentence he might continue to live in harmony with the leaders, but would do so at the expense of the favor of the masses themselves. Not that Pilate dreaded this greatly — many a time he had provoked and annoyed the people — but, in the last analysis, what does one do when one wants, above all things, to have peace? What must a Pilate do who is unable to follow the profound discussions as to the nature of truth? One who asks "What is truth?" must, as we have said before, also ask that other question: "What is justice?"

That second question raises itself at once. In his confusion, Pilate calls the whole assembly together again. Yes, he wants to talk with the leaders once more, for these after all were the original accusers; but he also wants to call the people into this troublesome case. Our text tells us plainly that he brought the people, the masses, whose curiosity had induced them to gather in one place in order to await the final decision, into his second hearing. We remember that once before this Pilate had personally conducted Christ out of the praetorium, in order to question Him there in the presence of the people who were with Him. Pilate does not neglect to make use of the same means now. He appeals in particular to that moment in the preceding hearing, in which the case had been dealt with publicly. He recapitulates the course of the proceedings, and emphatically states that even if he should put the accusation in its acutest form, its untenability would be obvious. At least — this was a milder and more cautious way of putting it — he had to deny that a clear presentation of evidence had accompanied the charges. You have presented this man to me, he tells the masses, as one who perverts the people. Note, in this connection, that Pilate puts the charge which is stated mildly in the second verse of our chapter in more acute form. The sense of the word used in the second verse of the chapter is that He merely made the people restless, that He excited their emotions, and that He raised problems which in the long run might prove dangerous for the peace of mind of the people. The sense of the word used in Verse 23 has a sharper directness. It says that Jesus *perverts* the people. That is the equivalent of saying that Jesus is teaching revolution and that He has already an incipient revolutionary movement under way. Naturally Pilate bases his choice of this word upon the various debates which gradually amplified the original charge. In the course of the discussions that original accusation had taken on ever severer connotations. Hence the thrust of Pilate's statement now is this: Even though I accept your accusation at its worst, I cannot prove His guilt. I have heard nothing of the fact that He has stirred up a revolution. Moreover, Herod, he adds, is of the same mind as I. I have had Herod consider the case.[1] He, too, has not advised condemnation. He has not told me expressly that I may justly sentence Him, to say nothing of sentencing Him to death. And Pilate goes on: Is not that fact significant? Personally I know only about what has happened in Jerusalem and in the neighboring vicinity of Judea. As a matter of fact, it might have been possible that the accused man conducted Himself differently in Galilee where Herod has jurisdiction than in this capital or in this neighborhood. But Herod, too, has not regarded Him as worthy of death. Now if it were true that the defendant had disturbed the people in Galilee or begun revolutionary movements there, Herod could not have ignored that fact. Hence, my conclusion is that He has done nothing wrong; surely nothing worthy of the death penalty.

Now if Pilate had been a ruler who was aware of the implications of his office, and had lived up to the demands it made upon him, this, as far as Jesus was concerned, would have been the irrevocable conclusion of the matter. Christ would have been set free for no other reason than a lack of evidence against Him. But the terrible truth is that Pilate does not stop at this. He goes on. In his attempt to satisfy all parties concerned, he says: I will chastise Him, and set Him free.

Observe that by the statement "I will chastise Him," Pilate is saying nothing about the nature of the chastisement which he has in mind for Jesus. It is not necessary to suppose that this has reference to the scourging which was inflicted upon Jesus later. The word which Pilate uses and which has been translated "chastises" is in the original a very general term. It may designate a light chastisement or a severe one. Pilate does not state which he means

---

1. There is some difference of opinion about how Verse 15 should be read. Our official state translation has it: I have sent you to him. But other manuscripts have a different version; for example: I have sent Him (Jesus) to him (Herod); and: He (Herod) has sent Him (Jesus) to us. Which of these versions is the original one is a question that has no bearing upon our argument, however, and with this we drop the matter.

to inflict. The only thing which is definite is that he wishes to give Jesus a lesson which He will remember. Moreover, it will be a painful lesson, and will be given in such a way that Jesus' life as a leader of the people will in the future be impossible. That, then, must be the last to be heard of the case.

Those who wish to marvel at the cleverness, at the craftiness to which an embarrassed man can sometimes resort will find abundant matter here. Moreover, remember that the device to which Pilate resorted was "from his point of view" a desirable one. By chastising Jesus, Pilate hoped to save the prestige of the *leaders* of the people. These members of Israel's highest tribunal would thus be spared the reproach which would have been theirs as the result of a futile appeal to Pilate. Moreover, Jesus' influence among the people would by the same act be given a serious blow. On the other hand, those among them who were kindly disposed towards Jesus would be unable to blame Pilate for having sentenced a righteous man to death. In spite of those considerations, however, his idea of compromise places Jesus officially and definitely outside of the province of the law. Even if the chastisement were to consist of a single stroke of the whip, or of a mere public reprimand, even so slight an act of discipline would be taking place outside of what was officially legal, and would be inflicted upon Jesus only for the sake of Pilate and the Jews. They must vindicate themselves, and assert themselves; and Jesus by foul means or fair must be made to serve *this* purpose. That is why this occasion marks a new stage in the history of Christ's passion.

Now we know that the idea of the Christ, of the outlaw, has demanded our attention again and again. The first time was when the servant, in the presence of Annas and with his consent, struck Christ. Later we observed that Christ was made an outlaw in the presence of the Sanhedrin which mocked Him. Thereupon Herod, too, insulted the Christ as an outlaw by mocking Him and by giving Him the "gorgeous robe" to wear. Now, however, the torture of this suffering becomes a perfect torture. Now Christ is being named an outlaw by Pilate also, by Roman justice, by the government of the official world empire. Publicly declared to be such? No, not that exactly, but amounting to that just the same. Proclamations, after all, cost the price of the paper on which they are written, and the name of an *outlaw* does not appear on paper. The only ones to write about such a man will eventually prove to be the Spirit of God and a few fisher-folk, and, possibly, a disciple of Gamaliel.

However, we look upon the Christ as the Surety. Hence we recognize in the concept of Christ the outlaw not merely the vindictiveness of men but also the penalty which God's own justice inflicted upon Him as the Mediator. Therefore *we* particularly may not overlook this event. We must give it adequate attention, for, irrespective of what Pilate may plan or perform in the future, as long as he fails to rescind the statement he has made, Christ's status officially remains that of one placed outside of the province of law.

And Pilate did *not* rescind his statement.

Therefore our Saviour was thrust outside of the reach of all laws, and was by the whole world declared to be an outlaw.

He is the outlaw to the Jews, that is to Abraham and to Moses.

He is the outlaw to Esau, that is to the false brother.

He is, in the last analysis, the outlaw to Rome, to the *corpus juris* of the world empire, to godless culture, to the power and the realm of the Beast.

Therefore summon every law to testify against Jesus, summon existing laws and conceivable laws, profane laws and holy laws, religious and cultural laws, utilitarian and divine laws, *consilia evangelica* and *humana,* summon the *fas* of divine justice and the *jus* of human justice,—summon these all, and you will find that not a single law in the whole world will fail to testify against Christ by saying: I do not know Thee, whence Thou art; I never knew Thee; depart, and be as one who is accursed. For even the last, the most inclusive pale of law into which Christ was finally coerced (the law of Rome) has now definitely declared: Law has nothing further to say of that man; He stands outside of the scope of law.

On this occasion Christ is an outlaw not only as the Christ, as the Messiah, as He declared Himself to be in the presence of the Sanhedrin, but also as Jesus, as the historical personage, as a citizen of Rome, as one enrolled in the registers of the world. What we see here, then, is *Jesus Christ officially and definitively* named an exile to the domain of law.

In God's dictionary such a status is named a *curse*. It is a curse to the extent at least to which human beings can express and develop one. And the curse of God against His Son is involved in this curse of men.[1]

Pilate's godless proposal therefore represents a most bitter experience of spiritual suffering to the Christ. The scourgings which are to follow will surely be unable to injure Him as much as this compromise of Pilate which, as the last and most inclusive legal jurisdiction, names Him an outlaw. Yes, Christ knew this was coming before this happened. We repeat,[2] however, that although He knew it beforehand, He first *experiences* it now. It is this experience of the curse which constitutes a new suffering for the Man of sorrows. The severest part of that suffering does not consist of the formal surrender of Christ to death, as that surrender follows later, but consists of this official placement of Christ outside of the law. The rest is a logical outcome of this.

Those of us who read this story of Jesus' suffering with fear and trembling can only feel a profound sense of shame on this occasion. For Christ who as the Surety was excommunicated by all known laws proved by this to be the *second Adam*. His excommunication pictures our own. Here all authority, all conceivable authority including the authority of God, stands over against us with an unsheathed sword and says to the lost sinner: Depart, for you there is no room left anywhere. The writing of laws happens quite without reference to your being lost.

The unsheathed sword — the first Adam knew of that when he was driven from Paradise. But today the curse, the suffering, is even more severe. For when the first man was driven from Paradise, he was still lighted on his way by the sun of God's mercy. He entered into the wide world, but before him lay the expansive history of many centuries, in which he would, of course, have to suffer the curse of sin, but in which common grace[3] would temper that curse, and would give him a life which would be made bearable by law and order. The first Adam, although driven out of his Paradise, can still proceed under the protection of an evangelical

1. Concerning the relationship of God's justice *and* that of men in reference to Christ the outlaw we shall say something in the next volume of this work.
2. We mentioned it also in Chapter 10, p. 201 f.
3. See page 152 f.

power, of a divine love which is ever seeking the Messiah, and which ever and again mitigates the curse by the power and the will of the God of all grace. Hence Adam receives a great gift in his lost country: the gift of a natural law and order and of a preservative jurisprudence.

But the institution of this general history, which by means of common grace still gives our human life the possibility of existence and of development, has been awaiting this terrible hour in which the second Adam should be made the outlaw completely.

When Cain was given the *"sign"* assuring him that no lawlessness would be allowed to destroy him, and that he should never find himself out of the province of law, even he was already tasting of the fruits of this hour in Christ's suffering. And Cain did not even desire this life which issues from the Christ of God.

Hence we should be on guard. Those living in the world *today* should be wary. The question is not whether the sign of Cain will protect us, but whether or not we are truly *redeemed* by Christ the outlaw, and are born into that circle of law whose boundaries are circumscribed by grace. Christ the outlaw shows us plainly what will one day become of the man who has not chosen Him as his Saviour. Just behind the gate of the other life the devil stands ready to make the man who was satisfied to let Christ remain an outlaw realize what the nature of his corrupt choice has been.

Now we know, of course, that the status of the outlaw will not obtain in hell[1] (for God asserts himself there also as a Maintainer of law), but it is true, nevertheless that those in hell feel that they are outlaws both to themselves and to others. The order of laws which human beings on earth know will be irrelevant to them there. And inasmuch as sin on earth has seized upon human law in an effort to escape from divine law, the bane of the thoughts of those in hell will consist of the fact that God will give them no other law to manipulate save that law of God which lost man eternally despises.

Viewed from God's side, therefore, the status of the outlaw does not exist in hell, but from the human point of view it most certainly does exist. Man's own laws will betray him there; that precisely will be his suffering: his own laws will mock him.

---

1. See p. 184.

That will be Satan's way of eternally vexing those whom he has destroyed. In the abyss of sin and death God does not really recognize the status of the outlaw, but Satan will continue gloating over the concept of the outlaw. In hell man is outlaw to himself and the mockery and insult of that, Satan will always be hurling into the faces of his victims.

It was not for nothing that Pilate, the last speaker for all earthly tribunals, degraded Christ to the level of an outlaw. The second Adam, was, by the bastard sons of the first Adam, deprived of the privileges which even Cain was allowed to retain.

This fact the Supreme Assize of heaven will not forget in all eternity. Tremble, son of man, for the Supreme Assize and the Judge conclude alike inasmuch as they are one. In the last day verdict and charge will coincide and will support each other eternally.

Chastisement to God is a blessing, and a fruit of the "release" pleaded for by Christ, or else it is a chastisement of penalty for unrighteousness.

The Court can pronounce one of two sentences in judging us: The sentence of acquittal, "I will chastise you because I have released you," saith the Lord; or the sentence of condemnation, "Hence I will chastise you and never again release you," saith the Lord Almighty. In the one case the chastisement comes according to the law of *grace* and in the other according to the law of the curse and of death.

Christ the outlaw is identical with a world turned upside down. Say not in thine heart: who *shall ascend* into God's domain of law? (that is, to *bring Christ up* from below and rescue Him from the hands of Pilate.)[1]

Comfort ye, comfort ye my people, saith my God. Near you is the law; the law is in your mouth and in your heart. The law has been brought you in the gospel of Christ the outlaw. Hear ye this . . . for this is the Word which is preached among us.

---

1. See Romans 10:6.

Christ the Outlaw and His Forgotten Chapter

CHAPTER TWENTY-THREE

Christ the Outlaw and His Forgotten Chapter

● *For of necessity he must release one unto them at the feast.*

LUKE 23:17.

But ye have a custom, that I should release unto you one at the passover: will ye therefore that I release unto you the King of the Jews?

JOHN 18:39.

SATAN knows very well which moments are the strategic ones for him. He chooses them painstakingly. Do not, therefore admire him without first and primarily glorifying God.

For Satan owes his ability to choose his times and circumstances strategically solely to the fact that he has dwelt with *God.* He has been endowed by his creator with great gifts, and has remembered so much of the sublime manner of heaven that even his own Satanic work is still characterized by the style which is excellent, amazing, austerely patterned. Again: Do not admire Satan's style, but marvel at *God's* style, and then tremble before the gruesome regularity of whatever is satanic in its being. After all, Satan is able to achieve an artistic manner in his work because he bases it upon the work of *God.* God puts His sublime, His divine style into His exalted work, and Satan is ever bound to that.

This will become apparent to us as we probe further into the story of the passion of our Lord Jesus Christ. In the preceding chapter we observed that Christ who was previously made an exile to the law now becomes the complete outlaw. At this point we might ask the question: why should that perfect rejection from the pale of law take place *just now?* Why should the complete and definitive realization of the concept of *Christ the outlaw* occur at this particular time? The answer which the assumption of faith gives to this question can be outlined as follows: A. One chapter in the litigation against Christ at this time had been forgotten. That chapter is entitled "The priestly office of Christ." B. That "forgotten chapter" now makes itself seen; just for a moment, for a very short moment—but it makes itself seen. C. But even before the concept of Christ's being a priest is taken up for discussion, He has already completely been made an outlaw. His priesthood, His sacrifice, everything in Him which urges Him to make atonement, was discussed and dispatched, even as far as the concept was concerned, outside of the sphere of law. D. By this we were humbled, the world judged, and the Man of sorrows, the High Priest of our confession, deeply humiliated.

Let us consider what can be said of this. Remember that assumptions have the right of way here; but who, wishing to *believe,* is ashamed of an *assumption?*

A. In amplification of that first thought this can be said: The prophetic office and the kingly office have come up for discussion, but up to this time not a single word has been devoted to the *priestly office.* The office of the priest is not raised in discussion by the Sanhedrin, by Pilate, or by Herod, and it is not made a part of the superscription over the cross. But the *whole* Scripture does call Christ's priestly office an essential part of His official messianic task. Besides, throughout the course of the Old Testament the priesthood is continually presented as being messianic in its essence and implications. Nevertheless, here in the litigation against Christ, this office remains in the background. It has been completely ignored by everyone. There was good reason for this. *God* willed that it should be so; and men also willed that it should be so.

Yes, the people also wished it, and that is a discomforting thought. They were guilty of completely negating the priesthood of Christ during the process of the litigation against Him.

Was this the result of an oversight? Was it due to ignorance? Is it being too facilely and undeservedly censorious to criticize the murderers of the Saviour now, so many centuries later, by saying that this was a serious omission?

We think not. These same Jews who were so eager to be called scholars of the Scriptures might have troubled themselves to become acquainted with those Scriptures. They might well have made themselves familiar with the prophecies to which Christ pointed again and again—as has become evident repeatedly in this book—during the last week of the life of humiliation which He lived upon earth. They might have taken pains to know that prophecy, and to earn it by the struggle of their thoughts. They might have followed that prophecy most punctiliously, placing their finger upon the very letter of the law, just as they boasted of doing in other instances, and just as they had done, for example, when the Magi of the Orient had inquired at the court of Herod where the Messiah had to be born according to the prediction of prophecy. Now if the Jews had actually done all this, which after all was quite in their line of activity, they would have been unable, and that simply upon the basis of ordinary human honesty, to have segregated the priesthood of Christ from the kingship of Christ in the course of their trial of the Saviour.

It is important that we remember certain things. The first is this that they knew that Jesus called Himself a king. And the second is that they knew that He derived His kingship from His Messiahship. Knowing that, they should also have known, and pondered, and proclaimed that according to their sacred Scriptures the messianic *king* was most intimately connected with the messianic *priest*.

Surely, they should have been convinced of that intimate relationship. Had not the prophet Zechariah—to limit ourselves to but one prophet—openly declared that a close relationship, a covenant of peace, an official unity would obtain between the eschatological messianic kingship and the similarly eschatological messianic priesthood? Read Chapter 6 of Zechariah. You will notice that Israel's hope for the future is outlined here. God presents that hope by giving a concrete picture of it. Joshua, the high-*priest,* you will notice, is given a crown, the ornament which a *king* wears upon his head.

Now note this distinction. Joshua is presented as a priest wearing the crown of a king. He is not presented as a king wearing the cowl of a priest. It is that last picture, a king's head adorned with a priest's cowl, which is the ideal of the heathendom of the day. Such a thing Pilate, too, can appreciate. We have had occasion to point out repeatedly that such was precisely the direction in which the Rome of Pilate's time wished to go. The priestship was subject to the secular authority of Rome. Caesar, by virtue of his office, was also regarded as *pontifex maximus*. He figured prominently on occasion in the temple-service. He was the chief authority in things religious as well as in things secular.

Now Israel's expectation for the future was diametrically opposed to this. The ideal which beckoned to them from the blue distance was that of a priest wearing the king's crown. Surely, the royal office would remain in Israel. Authority guarantees liberty when the authority is just and merciful. Hence authority will not be wanting in the messianic state. But the king's crown there will rest on a priest's head, and that priestly head will carry out its commands with a priest's hand—united with a priest's heart. What the prophet simply wants to say is that the authority in the messianic state will not be tyrannical or despotic in character, but will rule in the spirit of love and in a service which is the product of a glad surrender.

Now this priestly authority, this close relationship between the office of the king and the office of the priest, incipiently figured forth in Joshua, will appear, perfectly developed, in the coming of the Messiah. In that Messiah the kingship of *David* will be retained. But in that period of messianic florescence there will be no jealousy, no animosity, no rivalry between the king (secular authority) and the priest (spiritual authority). Peace will obtain between those two; peace will unite them into one. Priest and king, grace and culture, the service of love and the lordship of authority, the service of atonement and the service of protection, communion with God and orientation on earth,—those are the things which in the messianic period are to exist side by side.

We remarked that because of this relationship, *David* and *his* kingship would be retained. Remember that from Zechariah's point of view David was no longer extant. Zechariah does his prophesying after the captivity. Hence he stands beside the ruins of David.

David has no longer anything to say in the world. David's house no longer has any right to demand service of the people. He will no longer do great things. The last king of the house of David has entered into captivity, a blind weakling, dethroned once and for all. His princes have been put to death in his presence.

That was the last thing his eyes were permitted to see; thereupon the enemy thrust them through. Hence David is no longer being served. All that he can do now is *to serve, always and only to serve.*

That is why the sublime sweep of Zechariah's prophecy is so particularly eschatological. When David's house had degenerated so far that in the future it could *only serve,* David no longer existed in the minds of men. But the kingdom of God and the word of God still had a task for David. The priest must be intimately united with the king. In that way the one who serves becomes closely related to the one who is served. Love, condescending love, becomes wedded with authority. Hence not only the grace of truth (the prophet) is gladly greeted, but peace, too, is also met with the kiss of a king's authority. Hence David has after all been served. Serving is not a strange but an entirely natural thing for the perfect messianic King. Just as a priest is poor and defenceless among poor and defenceless people, so the king, too, has become one with the priest of the messianic era.

It is in this way, then, that the prophecy of Zechariah directly related the messianic kingship to the messianic priesthood. Remember that this prophecy was not written in vain; since this prophecy has been written, no one may say of Him who announces Himself as the Messiah that He is a king, without for the sake of the Scriptures also saying of Him: If you are a king in the messianic sense, you are also a priest.

Hence if the Jews take their knowledge of the Scriptures seriously today, they may not in the litigation against Jesus, inasmuch as the kingship has not proved to be a forgotten chapter, regard the priesthood as a *forgotten chapter.* If the scribes search prophecy just as painstakingly now as they did in the time when Herod was visited by the Magi of the Orient they must, if they are to be consistent, dare Him to bring the issue of His *priesthood* to the fore.

They have already insulted the *prophet* in Christ. This they did in connection with Christ's self-proclamation: I am the Messiah. They have also seen the king in Christ being defied, have, in fact, shared in the defiance just a few moments ago in the presence of Herod. This, too, they did in connection with Christ's self-proclamation: I am the Messiah. As a matter of fact, it was while defying Him on this count that they presented Him to Pilate.

Come now, scribes, come, you scholars of the Scriptures, what of the office of the priest? Come, people at large, you all who have gathered here, what are you doing with the *priest*? The whole subject has not been raised yet. Who will be the first to raise that point?

But there is not *a single one present there who is willing to begin that discussion.* They all ignore the subject.

To a certain extent this is due to *enmity.* We have had occasion previously to refer to the fact that the Jewish nation was not disposed to accept the prophecies of Zechariah. When Christ, poor and defenceless, triumphantly entered the city of David, the Jews did not understand Him. But they did not *want* to understand Him. Their perversity taught them to live without the Scriptures, because the evil heart of man wrests the Scriptures into whatever shape it will, and accepts only those truths which are compatible with its thinking.

But to a certain extent—and now we are thinking particularly of the crowd—this neglect is also owing in part to abysmal ignorance, to absurd misunderstanding. The prophecy of Zechariah stood miles away from what Jewish pride, from what the theology of Judas, from what the chauvinism of the Jewish spirit expected, —and learned from its leaders.

It is in this sense and to this extent that we can speak of the *"forgotten chapter."* The *priesthood* was that forgotten chapter. The leaders of the people had first neglected it, had reasoned it out of existence at the prompting of the evil choice of the heart. Those leaders did not want a king who was quite defenceless and as poor as a priest. The result was that the *neglected* chapter became a *forgotten* chapter.

Consequently this was an oppressive hour for the Christ. His great soul, ever alert to the sense of the prophet, is as heavily oppressed now as it was when He triumphantly entered into Jerusalem. At that time the madding thousands of the people also segregated the priest from the king. They wanted to regard Him as a militant general, as one who is being served, and not as one who related authority to humility and to a defenceless and unremunerative priesthood.

The same thing happens here. True,—viewed from the outside —there is a great difference between *this* moment and the one which marked Christ's entry into Jerusalem. Then there was a milling crowd, the plaudit of the masses, the kiss of the sun; now there are bonds, silence, quietude, and a sultriness in the atmosphere. But *again* the king is separated from the priest. Again the curse is proclaimed against a king who is *humble*. In the last analysis the attitude expressed now is therefore the same as the one voiced then.

Christ feels that His official life has been torn apart. His "bowels" feel the pang, for it is in His "bowels" that He bears the law and the prophets. For He Himself experiences the unity, the fusion of priest and king in this very moment. Once Joshua, the ancient Joshua, had lived. Now Joshua reappears. That is His name,—Jesus, Joshua. This Joshua knows that He follows in the line of Zechariah. That is precisely the reason for which He kept silence so essentially as He did in the presence of the Sanhedrin, and of Pilate and of Herod. He did not want to be segregated from the priesthood when He was being maligned for His awareness of being a prophet and for His pretentions to being a king.

He knows clearly and profoundly, however, that the masses must make a selection. Yes, you say—for you know the story almost by heart — yes, they must choose between *Barabbas* and *Jesus*. However, do not forget this: that choice which will take place presently, that pairing of names, simply makes manifest what in principle is obvious already. But even if there had been no Barabbas available in that vicinity, the people would still have had to make a selection. They would have had to choose between the official priests who are accusing Jesus today, on the one hand, and Jesus, on the other. They would have had to choose between the Priest-King in the realm of the Spirit and the Caesar-priest in the realm of the Beast.

To the extent that King Jesus has related his kingship to the priestly concept of love and tender service—even to the point of self-sacrifice, — those priests who are standing there shrieking their accusations against Him, have sold their priestly soul to the king's crown of the Caesar who dwells in Rome, to the usurper who will come now to tread upon the neck of the Jews, and—upon their sacred scroll. Yes, he will tread upon the book which tells the story of the priest-king.

What did the chief priests care about David? Zechariah's abstract prediction — prophets can be so annoyingly abstract, such arch-dreamers!—could send the priest of the future into captivity behind David, if it wished to, but the priests of Pilate's day will not hear of that. They have deaf ears for anything referring to captivity. They simply cannot understand how anything can be expected from a trunk which has been hewn down, much less how something resembling the double effect of a priesthood and kingship in one can be expected of it. They have cut loose the future of the priesthood from the fate of David. They have said farewell to that disinherited ruler. After all, one cannot keep on writing epitaphs forever. Today they prefer to bow in obeisance to Caesar. Caesar is not a priest wearing a king's emblem. He is a king wearing the emblem of a priest. That which Saul had been, against which Samuel had stormed, and for which Jaweh had deposed Saul, substituting David for Him—to that they now make obeisance. It was so long ago that Saul had been deposed; that had long been history. And who can believe that history can prophesy?

Thus it was, then, that the priests of Jaweh in Israel had refused to humble themselves with David, and in that humility to wait for the coming Messiah-of-lowliness. Accordingly, they sell their souls today to the despot of Rome. "Learn of him," they say, "for he is neither meek nor lowly."

In this way their priestly service has become a willing tool in the hands of the secular power. They prefer to bow in obeisance to Rome's power for a time rather than always to unite the crown with a priest who had to remain in captivity with David because the barrier of His body supposedly was the condition for the resurrection of His spirit. Once and for all they had refused to enter the grave with David; in other words, they had once and for all segregated themselves from David's house. They displayed themselves to the world ostentatiously and expressed themselves as willing to work under the auspices of any king, or any usurper, who would allow them to live an easy life, while still retaining the knife of sacrifice. The priesthood had become the willing tool of the secular authority. The spiritual messianic struggle of the office in

Israel, an office which in its tripartite implication (king, prophet, and priest) had to conduct the battle of spirit against flesh, and of the preservation of its hidden sense against the temptation of an outward show,—that struggle had been given up once and for all.

How, now, can they be expected to deal differently with David's Son at this time than they dealt with David in times gone by? They have no choice but to negate a priestship which seeks David's grave and which gives the crown to a defenceless Joshua. The forgotten chapter!

Accordingly, it is inevitable that Jesus Christ be denied and by His own scribes. For He *is* the Joshua of Zechariah's prophecy. He will maintain His priesthood today, not only by offering a sacrifice but by being that sacrifice Himself. Such a thought is gross folly and an intolerable offense to all priests who can no longer tolerate the idea of a David who is a trunk which has been hewn down. For a priest to become the sacrifice himself is in the absolute sense of the word a complete departure on the part of priesthood from the law of the flesh, which would always make its appearance an external one. The priest who himself becomes the sacrifice enters completely into the sombre law of the hewn-down trunk. No, the priests of Israel cannot bear the thought that Jesus is called a "priest." The idea of a priestly law which makes the priest identical with the sacrifice has never occured to them. Therefore they separate the concept of priest and king. They have seen Jesus the Nazarene make His appearance in the visible world, and as a prophet and king take exception to the existing order of things, but they have not the vaguest suspicion of what His priesthood may mean. That the death of the Nazarene must be the fulfillment of His priestly deed, that He must be the sacrifice and not merely the one who sacrifices, is a thought which they have never pondered.

Now it must be said further that not only the logic of the people kept the priesthood of Christ concealed but that Christ's own will would have it remain a great mystery. The mystery of His true priesthood will not allow itself to be profaned for a moment any more than will His prophetic or His kingly office. In *all* of His official work Christ is a *mystery*.

To Pilate He is a prophet who cannot come with an "outward appearance," for in response to Pilate's question, What is truth?

He does not give a logically argued refutation based upon human wisdom; and when the Sanhedrin mocked Him upon the prophetic mountain He chose to be silent. His prophecy is not of this world. That prophecy, too, just as He Himself, is obedient to the law of the hewn-down trunk.

The same holds true of Christ's kingship. My kingdom, Jesus is compelled to say, is not of this world. My servants, He says, do not employ physical force; in other words, they do not come with outward appearance. My kingship maintains, just as I myself maintain, the law of the hewn-down trunk.

Hence when Christ as a prophet and king enters into the dire stress of David, His degenerated father, and with him enters into captivity, Christ must also as a priest fulfill His priesthood according to that same law of florescence out of the hewn-down trunk. As a priest, too, He enters into hiding, into humiliation. Why should He raise the forgotten chapter for discussion here? The other chapters have been denied; and who could possibly gain anything from a *fragment* taken from the book of Christ's offices?

In this way, then, Christ's priestship remained entirely concealed during the very period of time in which satisfaction and atonement were achieved by His ample priestly suffering. The people who were seated in darkness and who knew no priests except those who were the willing servants of false prophets and usurping kings, were unable to do as much as raise a question about Melchizedek's priesthood. Christ as the high priest according to the order of Melchizedek continued to be the great unknown. He takes His position there as the unknown quantity. Thus He stands between the satellites of Rome who in the name of Aaron induce Caesar to put David's *king* to death. Dispossessed souls these are who invite Pontius Pilate, who as the denier of all the fathers' prophecies asks, "What is truth?" to put the prophet of David's messianic psalms to death. It was impossible for Him to be anything but the great Unknown to them. Did He wish one day to be the well-known and the well-beloved of His people He must now in His priesthood completely fulfill the law of sacrifice. Accordingly, that priesthood must be kept quite concealed, just at midday, the moment when God's justice is burning at its hottest. This too was sacrifice. This also was self-annihilation. This terrible silence also was the acceptance of the trunk which was hewn down.

Christ, then, at midday of the Lord's great day was completely ignored as priest. . . . As priest He was completely neglected. . . . But that—that is God's holy programme for this moment.

The Sanhedrin mentioned His *prophecy; but Jesus held His peace.* Pilate was troubled about Christ's *kingship; but Jesus held His peace.* Everyone is silent on the issue of His *priesthood. But Jesus held His peace,* for flesh did not see Him, and blood did not know Him. God, revealed in the flesh, must first be seen only by the angels; and only thereupon He will be *believed* on in the world (I Timothy 3:16). This, to be an ignored, neglected, overlooked priest, is an offense which was spared Aaron. Yes, Aaron was spared the offense; but He who is here belongs to another order: He is the priest according to the manner of Melchizedek.

Now Melchizedek never parades publicly in the world. His lot is one of *isolation.* Prophets of falsehood sometimes make up a stately, martial company; they sometimes incorporate themselves within the retinue of honor who parade ostentatiously in the company of the celebrities making up the kingship of the world (for which reason Isaiah calls them prophets of the *tail*). The priests of Aaron, or of his ilk, may organize a parade by reason of the fact that they can confer their office upon their posterity, a worldly king may sometimes go storming over David's grave on his way to the distant future of the promiscuity of Babel, Rome, Jerusalem and Athens. But among these all there is the unique Melchizedek. Without father. Without mother. Without heirs. Without a son to inherit his priestly clothes after his death. He is Melchizedek, the solitary one.

What we wanted simply to say therefore, was that Christ's priesthood was ignored by the spiritual and secular courts because He had to bear the griefs of Melchizedek, that great and solitary figure in the busy, multiform world. For Melchizedek is very poor. He would have been forgotten long ago, if he had not once met a certain Abraham, or better, a certain Levi, who was still contained in Abraham's loins. Except for that, he would have been quite forgotten.

Jesus Christ shares his fate. The crowd is growing in size, but each new visitor who makes his appearance upon the square aggravates Christ's crucial solitude. Besides, Jesus - Melchizedek knows that many others who are also forgetting Him are still contained in the loins of that crowd.

His forgotten chapter lies exposed before Him: if only someone would begin criticising that chapter. But they do not. They are silent on the matter. They talk about the head (the attractive king and Caesar) and about the tail (the prophet who teaches falsehood), but that which lies between is overlooked altogether.

B. We made reference to a second thought: namely, *that the forgotten chapter of Christ's gospel of suffering does, nevertheless, make its appearance for a moment.* This was owing to a certain Barabbas.

The priesthood of which we spoke sustains the service of *mercy* in Israel. It is the office in which God gives abiding "service" to love and to atonement. The service of atonement finds expression particularly in the sacrifices. However, we would be very superficial if we observed the functioning of the priesthood only in the offer which was presented each day, at a stipulated time, and according to fixed rules. For the priestly service of love, the office of the shedding abroad of the mercy of God, had permeated the whole of Israel's life. The Love of God did not limit itself to raising its song of praise above the groans of the animals of sacrifice in the temple, but also loudly sang its song at the corners and in the squares of the city. Its incense permeated all of natural life, too. The main theme of the priesthood, the redeeming love of the atoning God, is given expression also in the institution of the year of jubilee, concerning which we had occasion to say something before.[1] This year is a part of the cycle of Israel's holy festivals as much as is the feast of the Passover, of the Great Day of Atonement, and others. The love manifested in the atonement, the answered prayers of the priests for peace, these are reflected in all of the laws of the theocratic people. It is also reflected in the laws of the citizens, in the governmental laws which, we know, cannot for a moment be segregated from, though they can be differentiated from, the laws of Israel's religious life and the laws of its ceremonial service. Now this idea of the irresistible love and mercy of God, which spoke to Israel through all the usages

---

1. See *Christ in His Suffering*, pp. 404, 418, and 429.

and institutions mentioned above, was manifested also in the custom, to which the text refers,—that of granting the people the privilege of releasing a prisoner on the feast day.

The text tells us that Pilate, according to an established custom, could regard himself as being obligated more or less to set free a prisoner on the feast of the Passover. We must know that this custom did not hold true for every feast day, but for the Passover in particular. Apparently the people were very insistent on this privilege. It is obvious that the custom was of reasonably long standing, and was highly valued by the people. It must not be thought that this was a special Roman custom introduced by the Romans without regard at all to the Jewish mind. Such a notion would not be compatible with Pilate's statement: Ye have a custom, that I should release unto you one at the Passover. From that statement it appears that this usage is one which had its origin in Israel's own life, was sustained by uniquely Jewish thought and in which a deeply rooted longing and firmly established conviction of the Jewish people itself came to expression. Now it is remarkable that when we read the writings of rabbis in the Talmud or in related books, we observe that no mention is made of such a practice.[1] This fact shows that we are dealing with one of those many "institutions" under which, according to Christ's own statement, the Pharisees had buried God's commandment, but one which had its roots in Israel's peculiar religious consciousness. Many suppose that this practice arose in the time of the Maccabees, a time in which Israel had to fight for its spiritual-religious freedom. However this may be, it is very likely that this practice of an annual amnesty gave expression to the Biblical proclamation which announces generally the coming of freedom for the oppressed in Israel. The message of the law in which God includes all of His elect people had cast an evangelical light upon the condition of the slaves, and, in general, upon all oppressed and unfor-

---

1. Strack-Billerbeck, in his well-known commentary, tries to illuminate the New Testament by means of the Talmud and Midrasch, and says, in agreement with Schürer, that the custom according to which the procurator of Israel released a prisoner to the people on the Passover naturally had to be based upon a special enactment of Caesar. But he adds that no additional historical evidence or explanatory notice of this custom can be found in the Jewish literature. This fact is particularly significant for us, — the more so because this particular commentator finds analogies and parallel passages for almost every text of the New Testament in all the possible corners and crevices of the rabbinical literature.

tunate ones among Abraham's children. The institution of the
year of jubilee is a strong confirmation of this fact, but there are
many other less prominent features of Israel's community life
which serve as reminders of that love of God which sheds its rays
upon all the bondmen of Israel. All of these features—too numerous to mention—are so many signs pointing to the fact that the
practice of releasing a prisoner on the Passover is reminiscent of
the actual Passover event itself.[1] In this connection we must recall the statement made in Chapter 5 of Deuteronomy in which an
explanation is made of the Sabbath-keeping commandment (In
Chapter 20 of Exodus the institution of the day of rest is founded
upon God's own rest on the seventh day after creation). Deuteronomy 5 points out the relationship between Israel's day of rest,
which provided a respite from the hard labor of the days of the
week, and the general redemption of the people from the slavery
of Egypt. Besides, the law commanded that Israel had to release
the slaves again after a while. This custom served to remind the
people that they themselves had once been slaves in Egypt and had
been set free. The light of grace played upon the whole domain of
natural and community life. Even the threshing oxen were regarded by Israel as standing under the sun of grace (Deuteronomy 25:4; see I Corinthians 9:9).

If we keep all this in mind, we may indicate a connection between the main idea of the Passover—the redemption of the people from the tyranny of Egypt and the atonement of the people
by the blood of the Passover lamb, on the one hand, and the release of the prisoner on the Passover day, on the other hand. Was
not prophecy—think of Isaiah, and of Jesus' first sermon—quite
permeated by the thought that the messianic day, to which all of
Israel was looking forward, should also set free all prisoners?
And ever and again Israel's dreams had gone back to that departure out of the house of bondage in Egypt, had they not? Was
not the exodus out of the Egyptian prison the beginning of Israel's
whole expectation for the future? Hence the particular manner in
which the custom of setting a prisoner free on the Passover ob-

---

1. Nebe, *op. cit.*, p. 84, calls our attention to the story which is told us in I
Samuel 14:24 f. It is possible that such an analogy can be found: the people
ask Saul not to spoil the glad day of Israel's redemption by punishing Jonathan.
In any case, however, this can be but a weak analogy.

tained its legalization does not concern us much. The thing that is important for us is that Israel's national sense and the passion for freedom which ever recurring tyranny whetted in it had to place this custom, once it existed, in the light of its own ideal of freedom. That ideal was the ideal of a fulfilled Passover sometime in the form of Israel's perfect liberty.

Accordingly, the prisoner who was set free upon the Passover naturally became the popular hero, a prominent figure of the Jewish Chiliasm. This one man who was annually released on the feast of the Passover was thought of as a kind of epitome of a longing people who, like him, would sometime regain a former freedom. This one man became the symbol of Israel's whole future. In the active imaginations of the crowd this one act of amnesty was sublimated into the festal gift of the advent of a messianic era which would sometime lead all of God's captives out of the house of bondage. An ardent Passover fire of reconciliation and of freedom illuminated his path between the prison and the temple.

And is it not true now, as we said a moment ago, that in this manner, at the very moment in which the matter of the annual amnesty is being raised in the Passover programme, the *priestly* element looks around the corner?

We know that is rather a mild statement of the fact. But we put it so advisedly, for we would be guilty of making false inferences, and of arbitrarily distorting the historical data which we have and which are very meager, if we accepted as absolute certainty the fact that the people attached the whole Passover concept and the whole Passover reality to the custom of releasing a prisoner on the feast day. We may say no more than we can be sure of. Besides, we ought to take time to ponder how very seldom the masses related the forms of their festivals to the original idea which gave birth to them. This surging mob who come with a great deal of bluster to demand the release of a prisoner do not represent a group of upright keepers of the Passover. Not all of them are wont to wrestle with Israel's theology and eschatology. Their cry for freedom, their demand that the prison doors be flung wide, their summoning of the Passover hero is a trifle bold. The angels sensed that their cry had a raw and rasping sound.

But what of that, in the last analysis? What does it matter to us whether the people understood very little of the original Passover concept expressed in the ceremony of the Passover amnesty? Whether the people understood little or none of it does not affect the issue. The great question is: How much did Christ understand of that concept? The important matter is what thoughts the annual release of a prisoner upon the feast day called forth in *Him*.

Now we can be perfectly sure that Christ who always lived by the Scriptures always did and now also establishes a relationship between the joyous event of the day and the whole of the preaching of freedom contained in the Old Testament. Christ preached His official sermon to His people upon the basis of Isaiah 6:1, in which the opening of prisons is referred to as the great festal climax of the messianic day. Hence, He must very consciously have established a relationship between this element of the Passover programme, and the entire service of the love of God as it was shadowed forth among Israel by the law, and was preached by the word. Is it plausible to suppose that He would forget His first sermon now that, at the close of His career, He is condemned to silence? No, indeed, all of His sermons become part and parcel of His inner experience. All the longings of Isaiah, all of the lyrics written by the poets of God and of Israel, and the whole of the profound concept of eventual victory, of eventual freedom, for God's troubled people, also become an integral part of His personal experience. Jesus kept His silence, but He is listening, is listening profoundly. He listens in on the body of the prophets. In the sensitive awareness of Christ the priestly idea of reconciliation and of peace does not merely come "looking around the corner" as it does for the people, but rejoices aloud in His translucent spirit.

Just what course things took in that crowd is not yet entirely plain to us. There are two possibilities. The first is that Pilate himself hit upon the idea that he might profit from the aforementioned Passover custom, and that he thereupon decided to present Jesus as the candidate for freedom. This is not implausible possibility. We remember that Pilate was suffering embarrassment. It is just possible that in the reasonably long interval during which Jesus was in Herod's hearing, he made use of his time to ponder upon what attitude he should take over against the matter in case Herod should refuse to condemn Jesus or to acquit Him. During that time Pilate might have concluded to make the people the offer of severely chastising Jesus and to suggest to them that thereafter they should no longer molest Him. Such a proposal would be much more acceptable in the event that Pilate could relate Jesus' eventual release to the annual custom alluded to above. Much could be said in favor of such a "solution," and would probably satisfy His enemies. If Jesus were publicly chastised first, and released afterwards, His activity would prove quite harmless in the future. Never in His life would He be able to shake off the odium of having once deserved punishment and of having escaped from the judge and from the death sentence only by a most fortuitous circumstance. Such a solution would give everyone his way, and Pilate would be rid of the troublesome matter.

If this was indeed the course which Pilate's thoughts took, then he at his own prompting hit upon the plan of relating Jesus' chastisement and subsequent release to the customary amnesty accompanying the day of the Passover.

But there is a second possibility. It may be that Pilate rather accidentally took the course he did take. We get the impression that, while Pilate is busy with the process of the trial, a mob suddenly makes its appearance upon the scene and informs Pilate by means of a delegate that it wishes the annual amnesty to be granted it at once.[1] Some add to this possibility the fact that the crowd which appeared immediately suggested the name of Barabbas; but this addendum is not necessary to the possibility. It is more than likely that among that crowd there were many who wanted to give Jesus this happy opportunity, those many, in other words, who continued to honor Jesus as a popular hero or as a

1. This construction of the facts is based upon a very plausible interpretation of the text given in Mark 15:8. The King James version has it that the crowd was "crying aloud." But the original can also be translated: "and the crowd drew near." Naturally, this rendering of the text supports the interpretation that the people suddenly make their appearance.

beloved prophet.[1] Now it is quite possible that Pilate, being suddenly reminded of the amnesty, at once concluded to profit from the circumstances by suggesting that Jesus be the candidate.

Be that as it may, the crowd is making a demand. They want their Passover hero. You may as well say it in a whisper: the idea of the priesthood, the idea of freedom and reconciliation, just manages to look around the corner.

For Christ in this same hour the whole of the Scriptures are an open book. See the thousand-headed mob which is demanding its hero. How many are there among those who relate this Passover tradition to the whole of prophecy, How many of them will hesitate when asked to decide *whose* release they wish? Besides, how many of those who wish to grant Christ the favor, want to do it because they see the priest in Him, the supreme Bearer of God's mercy, by which He seeks His longing people?

It is certain that these will be few. And even those few will be making a mistake. For this is the day of the strange, paradoxical meeting of appearance and reality.

Suppose for a moment that Christ had been released on the feast day, that as the bearer of God's love, as the priest of reconciliation, He had been set free? In that case an injustice would have been done to His priesthood. Christ may not receive the great amnesty as a gift on this day; He must earn it as a right for others. He may not be the object of amnesty; He must be the cause which deserves it. This very day is the end and purpose of all of Israel's forward-looking laws. This day must provide the legal basis for Israel's regulations affecting freedom. Hence only by yielding Christ up to death and by denying Him the amnesty can this mark the deliverance of Abraham's bondmen.

---

1. Dr. J. A. C. Van Leeuwen (*Het Evangelie Naar Markus, Korte Verklaring van de Heilige Schrift*, Kampen, J. H. Kok, p. 195) thinks it likely that the crowd immediately and unanimously hit upon the name of Barabbas. However, we feel that there is not enough evidence for this opinion, and that according to our rendering of the text (see the immediately preceding note), it is not necessary to accept this interpretation. Had the crowd been unanimously in favor of the release of Barabbas, it would not have been necessary for the leaders of the people to influence it to choose against Jesus and in favor of Barabbas. It is likely that some came to demand the amnesty without having a particular person in mind, that others wanted to suggest the name of Barabbas, and still others that of the Nazarene.

Yes, Christ, this is Thy forgotten chapter: Thy priestly ministration. Thy beautiful office of honor, which Thou wilt fulfill on
this day by Thy descent into hell, and by Thy complete sacrifice,
is being entirely ignored. It is true that Thou art standing upon
the mountain of all kings, of all prophets and also of all priests.
But all those who pronounce judgment upon Thee, and all those
who come to plead for Thee have quite forgotten Thy priestly
office. Thou wast mocked as a king, despised as a prophet, negated
as a king and prophet, but there is another grief which has been
reserved for Thy exalted spirit. The priesthood, forgotten chapter as it is, although it has been very active in Thy soul throughout the day, will make a brief and slight appearance now. Very
brief and very slight. The faint outline of its image will appear,
no more. But even in full cognizance of that fact, Thou Thyself
must confess that this crowd, even in making its loud petition, is
deaf and blind to Thy priestly ministration. Thou Thyself must
confess that they are overlooking Thee, precisely as Thou art in
Thy reconciling sacrifice. Jesus, dost Thou sense that? The priestly sun is rising; — in response a myriad-headed crowd stintedly
turn up the wick in its lamp. Should the light be extinguished, all
would be gone. Is this not a negation of the priest! The office of
the priest is giving its greatest gift today; it is giving the true
Passover bread. But Israel is quarrelling about one crumb which
the dogs—the heathen!—have left behind under the table of the
children.

Negation of the priest! The Priest's love is pouring the vessels
full of wine, but in response the children of Abraham cry out to
Pilate, to Caesar, to moisten the tip of their tongue with a drop of
water. Negation of the priest! Even for the best of those in the
crowd who still retain an inkling of the relationship of the Passover amnesty to the true concept of the theocratic-messianic priestship, only two possibilities are open. If they persevere in keeping
their Scriptural ideas unimpaired, they cannot beg the favor this
day for Thee, Saviour, for the very institution of the priestship
would be stranded on the amnesty of Christ Jesus. And if they,
motivated by their love for "Jesus," beg for Thy release from
Thy bonds, then their love has succeeded in honoring Thee according to Thy historical manifestation, but not according to Thy
office. Then, although loving "Jesus," they will be negating

"Christ." In other words, they will be tearing Thy life apart, for "Jesus" does not want to be segregated from "Christ."

How ironical this day is! How painful it is for Thee.

Moreover, it is difficult, O Christ, for all those who hear Thee and love Thee. For all these this day is difficult. It is hard for them to keep from stumbling as they follow the course of love. When their love prompts them to ask that their Jesus be released, that He be made a symbol of Israel's future day of redemption, they negate Thee as Thou art on Thy priestly mountain, and do just what Pilate did. On the contrary, if they do not implore the judge to grant Thee the day's favor, they will be voting for Barabbas, or for some other person; in that case they will be voting against Thee, and will be certainly driving Thee to Thy death. Thou, my Saviour, art in a terrible dilemma: not to vote for Thee means to vote against Thee, and to vote for Thee means to deny Thee. Yes, even Pilate discovered the dilemma; he could not regard the situation from the vantage point of the law and, consequently from the vantage point of the gospel. We canot escape from this dilemma, Lord, unless Thou dost remove all the ballots from the table, and dost tell us: Blessed is he whom *Thou* hast chosen. . . .

We cannot escape from it. That is certain.

C. And why not? Why are we unable to escape from making the wrong choice?

Certainly, it is a terrible thing to have to make the discovery that even the simplest concept of the priestship, as that concept finds its fulfillment in the Christ but its foreshadowing in the Passover amnesty, can be introduced into the discussion by Pilate only after Christ has been completely made an outlaw.

When we think of that, we know that the important question is not how much or how little the people understand of the priestly element in the custom of releasing a prisoner on the feast day. Then we know, too, that the important question is not how much the love for *Jesus* which obtained in the crowd is able to understand of the concept of *Christ* the true High Priest. For it is plain now that every view of the priesthood, inasmuch as it pertains to Christ, to Barabbas, or to any other acquitted prisoner, is arrived at quite outside of the procedure and the justice of law.

Christ is the outlaw; irrespective, therefore, of whether His priest-ship is thoroughly fathomed or but slightly noticed, nothing more can be done. Pilate has declared Him to be irrelevant to law, and the forgotten chapter of Christ's priestly love will never regain its position. Irrespective of whether He enters into His death or continues to live, of whether He is named together with another as a candidate for amnesty or whether He is overlooked for that favor, He will have to fulfill His priestly ministration from now on quite alone. He will be supported by nothing, sustained by no one. Even if He should be released presently on the basis of the usage customary to the feast day, even if it could be said of Him that He represented an embodied image of the promise of priestly reconciliation and redemption in Israel, He would gain nothing. He cannot present Himself as the symbol, to say nothing of the fulfillment of the symbol. He is the outlaw even before His name is coupled with that of Barabbas. Moreover, He is that to the whole world.[1] He stands outside of the pale of law even be-fore He can become a priestly emblem as the one who was set free on the feast day. What, indeed, can that priest possibly do on earth? It is precisely in terms of His office, and in terms of the office of priest that He has been thrust into extreme isolation. The very idea of the priesthood, if realized in Him in its weakest form —as an emancipated delinquent—will never get the acknowledg-ment which even human laws are willing to contribute. He is the outlaw, the completely outlawed one. He is rejected, excommun-icated by every ordinance. From your and my point of view God's love is impotent over against this. The love of His people can do nothing for Him. The best which they could demand of the judge in His favor would only serve to malign Him, for the request would be granted only upon the condition that Christ is being re-garded as the outlaw. Whoever would grant Him His life upon that condition, would be maligning, would be negating Him while He stands upon His own priestly mountain. And whoever allows no harm to come to Jesus' soul on this day would be allowing harm to accrue to his own soul.

This is an agonizing irony in which God has involved us.

Consequently, only one possibility is left us if we are not to

---

1. See pp. 419-420.

offend Christ with our "love." We can be silent, just as He was silent. We can concern ourselves with Christ, not according to any human law, not within the circle circumscribed by any human ordinance, but by including Him and ourselves solely and purely within the fellowship and within the province of the law of God. That law is the law of eternal justice, and of a self-revealing love which comes from above. Lord, there is no room for Him in me. Even my frailest images are of no relevance to Him according to my point of view and in terms of my law. Lord God, I see no way in which I can assign a place to Him and His symbols. . . . Lord, He is the outlaw, and unless Thou dost Thyself fulfill the symbol, all the temples of the world will hold their peace.

D. Naturally, the significance of all these considerations should serve to humble us. Human love and human "sympathy" proved unable to do anything for Jesus on this occasion. We see that to vote for "Jesus" at this time is to vote against "Christ." Whoever chooses to vote in this way wishes to impart life to the Chief Priest, the most generous of givers, in patronizing generosity, and to forget the sacrifice entirely.

Has this any significance for us?

Indeed, it has. The chapter of Christ's priesthood which was forgotten at this time is frequently forgotten by us also. To give attention to the prophet and to the king in Jesus, but to ignore the priest is a fault which is not peculiar to the judges who promoted the litigation against Jesus. It is our error also. There are many to whom the priestly service of Christ amounts to a forgotten chapter. They are willing to accept Him as a prophet and a king, but they reject Him as a priest. They reject Him and His symbols. Their thoughts, their actions, and the choices and laws of their life never give any attention to the priest in Christ.

In response I hear someone say that those who so neglect the priesthood of Christ are the liberals; that we are the orthodox; that we devote full attention to the Suretyship and sacrifice of Christ; that among us His priestship is not a forgotten chapter.

I am not convinced that such is the case. I am not sure that you assign a rightful place to the priest in Christ. For why do you, orthodox man, often say, sometimes with a kind of unctuousness in your voice, that "the world" refuses to acknowledge the priest of your confession because the priest humiliates it, because salvation by grace, by perfect satisfaction, humiliates it. Do you mean by that, that as a prophet and a king Christ does *not* humiliate the world and us? Do you mean that in these two offices He does *not* crucify us, and does not put us to death?

Surely, if you fix such an antithesis as this between the offices of the Christ, you are wrenching Him apart! Then you become like the world as it is represented here before Pilate. For Pilate also thinks that he can talk about the king and the prophet without any reference at all to the priesthood, as though the three offices could be separated from each other. No, no. He represents humiliation and exaltation in all His offices; in each of His offices He is an outlaw according to the flesh, one who determines His own laws for Himself! The very humiliation which Christ places upon us as a priest is the same which annihilates us in His prophetic and kingly activities. As a *prophet* He must have banished falsehood from us, must have called us liars, before He can communicate a single word of truth to us. As a king He must first reduce us to the plane of slaves and rebels, before He can let a single drop of myrrh fall upon us from His royal hand. Yes, even in our own thoughts, it is a great error to suppose that the humiliating element accrues to us only from Christ's priesthood. Nevertheless, the truth is that in each of His offices He can exalt us only by first humiliating us. Not only as priest, but also as prophet and as king Christ is foolishness and an offence to us. Any theology which recognizes humiliation in Christ's priesthood alone may call itself ever so orthodox, but as a matter of fact it stands on the same plane as Pilate, and the Sanhedrin, and the whole of this poor Jewish people. For these three, too, have completely overlooked Christ's priesthood. Why, you ask? Because they nurtured the foolish illusion that Jesus of Nazareth does affect prophecy, does have bearing upon the kingship, but that His priesthood can be ignored.

The Jews first gave Christ as a prophet a hearing. Only after the hearing did they pronounce Him as a king an outlaw.

But the whole of this gathering of tyrants did not once give Christ as a priest a hearing. As a priest they immediately pronounced Him an outlaw. The Fulfiller, the Intercessor of all the prayers of all the priests had been placed outside of the pale of the law at the time when the last children of Abraham came to present their poorest beggar-prayers, at the time when these came to the "dog," Pilate, to beg for one small Passover loaf which they might give to one of Abraham's misformed children, be it to Barabbas or to Jesus.

O Lord, how Thou didst humiliate me,—for I also was among them—when Thou didst open my eyes to this fact. I did not want to be humiliated. And that is why I ignored the priest, supposing that I could obtain the full benefit of the king and of the prophet without Him.

Save my church and save me from this basic heresy. Prevent me from supposing that Christ humiliates me less as prophet and as king, as the preacher of truth and the guide of my life, than He does as priest. Lord, only when the entire Christ completely crushes me will the judgment of the flesh against Christ be completely repudiated by Thee in the courtroom of my conscience. Not until then will the transaction which took place before Pilate seem as foolish to me as a world turned upside down.

For the orthodox church, too, there is reason for being humble. Not always is it able to escape from the error of Pilate and of the Jews.[1] To go on, however. The world, too, is being judged and *condemned* on this day. The whole world is being condemned. By negating Christ as a priest, and by busying itself with His other offices, it maligned Him greatly. It tore Him as the Messiah into pieces. In this respect Rome, as well as Israel and Esau, becomes subject to judgment. The world declared Him to be an outlaw before He was able to say: I am the lamb of the Passover. It declared Him to be an outlaw before He could ask: May I repeat my first sermon, here at the close; may I repeat my first sermon about the amnesty which will accrue to the prisoners of God?[2] Satan could not contain his laughter when that happened, when the mercy of God which opens the prison gates of Israel was not even given a hearing, when Christ stood before Pilate and wanted to be a priest. As for Israel, it wanted to be led out of the house of bondage, of course, and demanded that a prisoner be released who should serve as a greatly desired symbol of Israel's dream of freedom. But before Israel made that request, it had led its own re-

---

1. Partly because it has been more concerned with the structure than with the content of its thinking.
2. See p. 442.

deemer back to the house of bondage. We have mentioned that already.[3] This foolish people discussed the burning question of whether Jesus Christ was the object or the author of Israel's liberties without referring the question to His own laws and to the teachings of the Scriptures. When this people did that, it was doomed. Barabbas—regarded as a type now—was also doomed. They thought of him too late. Who trembles in the presence of this doom? Who trembles in the presence of this annihilating judgment? Surely he will tremble who lets the priestly love of Christ Jesus be proclaimed to him by the law of God and by it alone.

For the Man of sorrows the humiliation of this forgotten chapter was very severe. At the very hour in which He was earning and fulfilling Israel's priestly privileges (for which He was giving His blood on this day) His priestly love could not say one word in defence of His priesthood or of Israel's privileges. This was a deep humiliation for Him. He was being wrenched apart. Only in the pain of the dismemberment is He able to find Himself again. His priestly heart suffers grievously. But the prophet in Him suffers no less. O God, is this the result of my first sermon? Moreover, the king is being humiliated also: Barabbas, the rebel, is more than I, for Barabbas has not been thrust outside of the province of law. His prison is at least a place in which men embody serious intent. . . . O Christ, who wearest the crown of thorns,—we see the thorn enveloping Thee already. We notice that the whole world has not developed a single system of thought or form of doctrine which systematically raises the issue of the priestly shedding of Thy blood into its discussion. Thy forgotten chapter can be spoken of only outside of the law of Cain, and of Esau, of Moses and of Augustus.

Whence may I know my misery?

Out of the law of God.

Not out of my own laws?

No, for they silenced Him completely. That is the greatest sorrow and there is none that will take it to heart. Christ the outlaw, the Suretyship, is explained by no earthly laws. Thou wast forgotten, Saviour, The shedding of Thy blood was separated before-

---

3. See Chapter 11.

hand from the feasts of Barabbas, from the law of Moses, and from the forum of Rome. That is the bitter bread which was given Thee to eat on this day. Thy blood is pouring from Thee and no single earthly book of law makes any note of it. The justice of God alone observes it.

Later the Spirit of Christ calls this: Being in the form of a servant. The servant is the outlaw; if He is that no longer He bears a different name. In other words, the name of Christ's situation here is *slavery*. This is His humiliation, His offence, His foolishness.

Early in the morning Pilate respected Moses.[1] At noon he still respected him.[2] He respected the symbols, and had no eye for the embodiment. We cannot say too much about it. It is terribly difficult to see such things in a world which is held together by a superfluity of laws.

---

1.   P. 292.
2.   P. 544 f., Chapter 29.

Christ · or · Barabbas

CHAPTER TWENTY-FOUR

Christ - or - Barabbas

> ● *And they had then a notable prisoner, called Barabbas. Therefore when they were gathered together, Pilate said unto them, Whom will ye that I release unto you? Barabbas, or Jesus which is called Christ? For he knew that for envy they had delivered him.*
>
> MATTHEW 27:16-18.

S IN always betrays its real character after a while. It cannot avoid doing that. Sin is consummate folly. Hence it is that the praise of folly is sounded again and again in the drama of sin.

This holds particularly true of the litigation conducted against God's own Son by the world. Logic and justice are absent in this litigation. Not only is the process of law an atrocity of injustice on the part of the people, but it is also a piece of folly. Hence what we say now will be less a counterpart than a fulfillment of what was said at the beginning of the preceding chapter. We stated there that Satan knows which particular periods of time are strategic for him, that he makes good use of those periods, and that in all of his sombre activities he knows how to attain to an awful and horrible mode of procedure. And this holds especially true in his sombre work of condemning Jesus Christ.

We persist in saying that this is true. We may not subtract an iota from this truth, for, as has been said already, satanic whims and impulses are constantly forced to fit into the scheme of God's ordained plan. He who wrecks the palace—that is, he who wants to wreck it—simply is unable to work in disregard of the plans followed by its builders.

Accordingly, if we keep our eyes fixed on the confusion of the litigation of Jesus, if we examine the structure, the scheme of the activity going on in it at the prompting of the invisible world, be it that of divine justice or of devilish injustice, we cannot fail to discover that an awesome logic, a sublime display of inevitable sequence, an integrally interrelated system of death and curse and of basic perdition is delineated in it.

However, heaven and hell, although invisible forces, take their course straight through the visible world. Now that visible world is populated by crooked people, foolish putterers, triflers, and dickerers surging around the chair of God, and the wooden throne on which the prince of darkness is pluming himself. And these people are not capable of an artistically authentic mode of procedure, of an austere and integrally interrelated style of activity. Their sin is incapable of reaching the level of Satan's artistic fòrm. It represents an uncertain drifting, a failure to keep to the course on the lakes planted between the mountains which limit their horizons and which hide the awful abysses. They are merely dallying on these lakes quite purposelessly. There is no system in their work, and consequently they do not comprehend the satanic scheme and satanic system. Why not, you ask? Because they do not know of *God.* Did they know God in faith, they would be able to understand a little of Satan's sublime mode of procedure. For Satan adapts himself to the style and to the system of God to the extent he knows these or to the extent that he can recollect them from his observation. But they do not know God; and Satan himself, of course, does not reveal his thoughts to them. He does not teach his disciples the way he plans to go. Is it not written that he comes as an angel of light? And is his *parousia* not an *ap-ousia,* and his manifestation not a concealment of his essential intent? Indeed, no one will ever learn Satan's ways from Satan. Only in the school of God is that psalm taught which says:

> He who bows before His throne,
> *To him shall all His ways be known.*

It is impossible, consequently, for people who are willing tools in Satan's hand not to know that in their very follies a scheme, a *plan,* conducted by both hell and heaven, is realizing itself. Hence, too, it is quite possible for them to be inconsistent in their actions. It is possible for them to drift about purposelessly on the deep lakes between the mountain cliffs delimiting their horizons. Purposelessly drifting, yes, until a treacherous squall rushes down from the cliffs and destroys them.

Such was the case of Pilate on this occasion. We have observed that his proposal to *chastise* Christ first and to set Him free then, caused Christ to become an outlaw. Now if Pilate had drawn this atrocious evil to its logical conclusion, he would never have coupled Christ's name with that of Barabbas and have submitted both to the people for a selection. Had he followed his intent to its logical conclusion he would have coupled Christ's name with no other name, and certainly not with that of Barabbas, of whom we have spoken in the preceding chapter.

For it is logical, surely, to say that an outlaw must be an *exception* in the world. He is one who is cast outside of the province of law, and who consequently becomes the prey of the arbitrary will of one and all. Obviously, if Pilate's action is to make sense at all, and if it is to become apparent that its sense is clear to the man who performs it, then that man must be willing to pursue his conduct to its logical conclusions. And one of those logical conclusions naturally must be that the man who is named an outlaw—whoever he may be—can in no sense be placed on a par with another person not thrust outside of the province of law. The two simply do not brook comparison.

But Pilate coupled the names. He presents a pair of names and adds the announcement: whom will you have, Barabbas or Jesus who is called Messiah?

Now if this pairing of names had taken place before Christ had been declared an outlaw, it would, from Pilate's point of view, have been a less serious and offensive piece of conduct than it is now. Barabbas, we must know, had not yet been placed outside of the sphere of law. On the contrary, he had just been treated and punished according to the regulations of law. Now if Jesus had not yet been thrust outside of the rules and the governance of law, this pairing of names, humanly speaking, would have made sense.

But that is not the course Pilate pursues. Barabbas has been treated according to the law. He was a rebel; Peter afterwards calls him a murderer. The law of authority condemns him; the law keeps him prisoner; and when he passes through the gates of the prison to his freedom today, even that will take place in accordance with the law. Think, for instance, of what the preceding chapter stressed in this connection.

But Jesus has become an outlaw; and it is after He has become this, that His name is paired with that of Barabbas. This, surely, is an instance of Pilate's inconsistency. It sounds the praise of folly. From Pilate's own point of view the names of two individuals, each of whose case is quite different from that of the other, are named together as though they were of the same rank.

The fact is that we are not afraid to say that even according to human law, and according to Pilate's own preliminary declaration, the juxtaposing, the coordinating of the names of Barabbas and of the Nazarene represents a humiliation for Barabbas.

Take note of this last-named particular, shocking as it may sound. What we usually say is this: How Jesus is being humiliated by this event! In fact, there are those who would be disposed to congratulate Barabbas upon his promotion supposing that he has been singularly raised from the gutter. There have even been serious commentators who have gone beyond their proper limits in an unworthy play of allegory which ever since ancient times—conceivably for want of ideas—has presented Barabbas as a symbol of the sinner who is granted his freedom by Christ's mediatorial work. And this allegorical conclusion is thereupon amplified by many an edifying rationale. Often it is presented thus: Jesus is going to His death; Barabbas is recalled to life; and we must all become Barabbases who by reason of Jesus' entrance into death can ourselves escape from death. Thus we all can be gloriously ushered into life again,—hallelujah, so be it.

Such allegorization, certainly, is incompatible with the Bible. In the first place, Barabbas was not released because Christ served as his Surety. The complete holiness of Christ protested against this emancipation. When Christ presently sees Barabbas entering into his freedom, He does not plead with God for the man, or later give His blood for him. In saying this we are, naturally, speaking of Barabbas as he is revealed to us in history; for the rest the hidden things belong to the Lord. In the second place, we may not transfer that which Pilate approves in opposition to all regulations of law to the conclusion of God's good pleasure, which is pleased to justify the ungodly for Christ's sake. Therefore we are justified in saying that from Pilate's point of view, and even from a general, human point of view, the pairing of the name of Barabbas with that of Jesus constitutes a humiliation for Barabbas. In the estimation of men, Barabbas was not an outlaw, and Christ was. In other words, a person who is unworthy in the sight of human law is placed next to a person who is very worthy; a man having no rights is placed next to a man having rights, and a figure who is no longer taken seriously is placed next to a figure whose case has been and is being given close scrutiny by the law. This most strange and most shocking of all pairings would have lost its humiliating features for Barabbas only if Pilate had first retracted his ungodly proposal to chastise a guiltless Christ first and to "let Him go" then. In other words, Barabbas would not have been disconcerted by this coupling of names if Pilate had re-built the litigation from the very bottom, and if in the rebuilding he had followed the established plan of his own human sense of justice. Inasmuch as Pilate did not so rebuild the case, this pairing of names is a shameful humiliation for Barabbas.

We have pointed out earlier in this study[1] that not long ago certain noble leaders of the Jewish people suggested that the litigation against Jesus be re-examined and that, should the investigation warrant it, Jesus be rescued from the odium which his people placed upon Him. Well, in all seriousness we wish to state that if this committee for reconstructing that ancient case of law should want to do its work adequately and well, it would also have to re-investigate the litigation against Barabbas. For he, too, may lay claim to vindication. The issue in his case is not what God thinks about Jesus. This issue is contained in the question: According to which human ordinances of law is Jesus being released? Now these ordinances of law were so humiliating for Jesus that Barabbas, had he had a fine ethical sense, would have refused to be regarded as belonging to the same class as that to which Jesus belonged.

You ask why we introduce this matter? Naturally we do so in order to point to the state of Christ's humiliation. It is only when we devote special attention to these plain but frequently neglected

---

1. See p. 346.

matters that we get a true insight into the overwhelming logic of heaven and of hell. Only then do we realize how atrociously and profoundly Christ was humiliated. He who stands before the world as an outlaw now becomes a shame and a byword to all. To this, Isaiah had reference when he said: He is without form and comeliness. This is what Isaiah on another occasion called: being the rejected of men. This is the beginning of the descent into hell. The servant of the Lord was made the least among men, and an example of shame to all. Abel becomes a shame even before Cain. Indeed, this is an oppressive, a sublimely oppressive burden of logical truth.

This is also the great *concealment*. God passes into hiding: Jesus, as outlaw too, is the Son of God. Our throats become constricted as we think the thought that we might have been Barabbas; that our names might have been paired with that of . . . Jesus; and that we, accordingly, from a purely human point of view and on the basis of human ordinances of law, might then have said: Spare me such humiliation. He who feels no lump in his throat at this does not know himself. The man who reflects upon these matters in the obedience of faith will confess to his God that sin is the greatest nonsense of the world, that it turns the world topsy-turvy, that it turns even me upside down, although — alas — never inside out. Such a person will confess to God: Father, they must prefer me to Jesus: help me, Father, lest I perish because of this honor. Barabbas shares the bread of the Passover with me; he urges me to take it, saying: Take, for this is food for you also. But for me to eat his Passover bread is to invite my death. Give me manna, Lord. He who has seen these things right will beseech his God that he may despise this foolish, this human, this altogether too human pairing of names in its very essence, and that he may see the Christ solely as the One who mocks all comparisons and who can be compared with no one.

Only then will he hear a voice sounding from above: To whom then will ye liken God? or what likeness will ye compare unto Him? So say God *and* Satan. Only after hearing that will we sense that the great concealment of the essence and of the honor of God — a concealment which drew its references from the law of the incarnation of the Word — proves to be just as foolish and offensive and unreasonable to the flesh as does the entire Gospel. A premium was placed upon folly not only when Barabbas left the prison in the evening as a free man, while Jesus was faltering under the weight of the cross, but when the two names, Jesus-or-Barabbas, were placed in juxtaposition. What do you think of such language? Just pass out the ballots. What do you think of such language, free people; what do you think of it, children of Abraham?

We have advisedly put these matters as we did. In our opinion we have placed the emphasis upon the right thing. Naturally, we do not mean to say that the further particulars have no significance. But these additional details can be given their proper place only if the other matters have been properly assigned to their places first. Bearing that in mind, we can say that the additional particulars which demand attention are numerous.

In the first place the figure of Pilate attracts attention. This man by pursuing his characteristically wavering policies of state, by choosing the way of escape which we have just seen him enter, attempted a last time to rid himself of Jesus, but in the very moment of his doing it he became completely captive to the might of the Jews. From this time on it will be impossible for him to recede.

In the second place, the person of Barabbas is a mysterious figure. All that we know of him is that he had committed a murder, and that he had done this on the occasion of a revolution in the city. Some think it may be safely supposed that Barabbas played no rôle in the periodically recurring displays of animosity on the part of the Jews against the Roman people. These argue that it would certainly have been difficult for Pilate to present as a candidate for freedom a man who had openly taken part in a revolution against Rome.

However, we want to say that this contention is not a properly argued one. In the first place Pilate was not one who was strictly dutiful in acquitting himself of his responsibility. In the second place, Jesus Himself was one who was being accused of fostering rebellion against the state. That tells us enough. The pairing of Jesus (after this accusation) with Barabbas makes it very likely that Barabbas had also been sentenced by the Roman authority for being a rebel. Now the situation is that Pilate wants to do everything in his power to remain friendly with the Jews. You see the connection. Placing Jesus' name next to that of Barabbas would prove a better instance of catering to the popular wishes, and to the roaring lion of Jewish chauvinism, would serve, indeed, as a stop-gap for the time being, if Barabbas too had been involved in an anti-Roman movement just as it was said Jesus had been.

However, we have no absolute certainty about this. Nor need we have. For Barabbas became a kind of popular hero the moment he was incarcerated. The reputations of heroes are as cheap as popularity is, and as far as Barabbas was concerned, a revolution of any kind, irrespective of how it arose, would always be a revolution against Roman authority. Those nameless ones who were involved in such revolutions would always to a certain extent have an opportunity to cool their hatred against the despicable empire of Rome by pondering this incident of Barabbas. Add to this the fact that in any case everyone hated the Roman and that any imprisonment of a son of Abraham at the hands of Rome caused the children of Abraham to feel their subservience very keenly. In connection with this think of the Passover custom which will presently give the man who is to be released from prison an ovation in the form of the sacrifices of Israel's self worship. You can easily understand that Barabbas, irrespective of his antecedents, and irrespective of who he may be as a person, does certainly in this moment elicit the sympathy of the people as a symbol by virtue of his candidacy for deliverance.

To this we must add another thought. His name is: Bar-abbas. Literally this means: son of his father. It is almost self-evident that this was not a common family name inasmuch as every human being is a son of his father. There is reason for supposing, as some have maintained, that the "abbas" alluded to was a rabbi. In that case Barabbas was one who sprang from a family of rabbis. Now a rabbi, a teacher of the people, was officially addressed by the name, *father*. If this supposition represents the truth Barabbas was a man of noble descent. In that case, too, his being taken captive affected a prominent rabbinical family. His case, then, was not merely a penalty applied to this or that street rebel. His was an action against Rome in which rabbinical pride, Jewish theology, and ancestral tradition might be found. In this connection we think of Judas Iscariot who had also given his heart and hand to the rabbis and who for that reason could no longer endure

Jesus.[1] Even if Barabbas had been taken captive for a reason which had no conceivable connection with Jewish patriotism, he would have become a hero on this day the moment he was named for the amnesty. We read that he was "notable." We need not doubt for a moment that he became a popular hero. All we have to do is to follow the crooked line of the popular rationale and the whimsical ways of the popular favor to be convinced of this, even though not as much as a single particular about Barabbas' criminal past is historically verifiable.

For all of these reasons, then, we are quite right in saying that the pairing of names in question here represents an antithesis of the false freedom which Israel sought to the true freedom which Christ promised. Can you suppose that Judas is the only one who betrayed Jesus, and that the thirty pieces of silver changed hands between him and the chief priests only? That cannot be. Such would have been a humiliation too meager for Christ the outlaw. When Judas betrayed him, we notice that one of His twelve left Him.[2] Now one of twelve can hardly be said to amount to much. But on this day Christ experiences something which, numerically considered, is far worse. We all will betray Him. The protest which Judas filed against Jesus takes tangible form in this pairing of names. On this day the name of Barabbas becomes a motto, a party slogan. To the heated phantasy of the people he becomes the bearer of the typical and genuinely Jewish ideal. Hence he immediately wins from Jesus of Nazareth in the ensuing election. Barabbas fights for a freedom which is immediate. Jesus of Nazareth, . . . ah, He is the pioneer of a freedom which is ever looking to the future, to the morrow. As for that morrow, . . . well, it never comes. Barabbas represents the emancipation of Israel from the bonds of Rome, and that is a far more practical thing than the work of Jesus who is always talking about emancipation from the slavery of sin. Barabbas, even though he himself may be unaware of it, is being appropriated by the Jews' illusion of freedom and he allows himself to be appropriated in this fashion, especially perhaps because he is still safely seated behind the gate of the prison. There Barabbas is pliable as is every bearer of an ideal — every bearer, that is, who has no mouth with which to affirm or to pro-

---

1. See *Christ in His Suffering*, p. 168.
2. See *Christ in His Suffering*, Chapter 23, p. 407 f.

test. But Jesus was ever antagonizing people. Nothing pleased Him. At one time He deliberately refused to accept the king's crown. Barabbas represents revolution; Jesus, the Gospel. Barabbas is carnal; Jesus spiritual. Barabbas belongs to the line of Lamech-Cain; Jesus to that of Seth-Abel. Barabbas wants to subjugate; Jesus to deserve. Barabbas will not let his sword rest unburnished; but Jesus has no work for a sword to do. Barabbas is a hero; Jesus a worm on which we must necessarily walk, though we tread ever so lightly. Of Jesus we feel like saying: Ecce homo. Not so of Barabbas.

Perhaps there is another particular which deserves attention here. There are many manuscripts, by no means unfaithful witnesses, which give Barabbas the name *Jesus*. We shall devote no attention to that question in textual criticism which busies itself with which of these manuscripts deserves preference, that which includes or those which exclude the name of Jesus. Suffice it to say that there is much to be said in favor of the opinion that Barabbas was also called Jesus, or Joshua.

If this interpretation is a correct one, we have here two Joshuas, two people who go by the name of Jesus. Their names are placed on a single ballot: Joshua-Barabbas and Joshua of Nazareth. And was this juxtaposing of names not a revelation of God rather than an accident of chance?

The people who are called Jesus: in that statement is contained the whole problem of the incarnation of the Word. What we have in mind is this. The incarnation of the Word represents a concealment of God, and of God's majesty. It represents a hiding behind the meager humanity of Christ. In the incarnation the Logos is lost to view behind the veil of a humiliating human nature. Now this incarnation of the Word followed its divine style to its logical conclusion, even to the point of the name which Christ accepted. For His name is called Jesus, or Joshua. And the remarkable thing about the name Joshua, Jesus, is that it is in no sense unusual. In those days there were thousands who bore the same name. There still are. Many a Joshua, many a Jesus, can be found in the markets of any great city, and among the hucksters and cattle buyers of many a smudgy village. You see that it is a very common name.

Now it is a very ordinary name which suits the incarnate Word. If it had been necessary for Jesus to take a name (supposing this could be done) which would give perfect and adequate expression to His essence and being, God would not have made the selection from a human register. For Jesus is unique. Accordingly, a name which would have given complete expression to His being or which would have approximated such adequacy of expression most nearly, would have been understood by no one and would have left us God's incarnate Son without a means by which we could appropriate Him. Therefore the incarnate Word had to bear a name which fitted His mission and His purpose. It had to be a name which the people could sense, a name in which revelation appeared demonstrably. The name of Jesus Christ simply had to be an ordinary, oft-recurring name. Christ, too, is like us in all things, sin excepted. Hence He does not come to us bearing a more than aristocratic name which no one beside Him could ever have in the world. Instead He is presented to us with the name which a man of the street might also bear. This is part and parcel of His humiliation, of His commonness. In this respect, too, God's thoughts differ from those of men. Jewish writers had a way of creating dazzlingly unique names[1] for the Messiah, but God gave Him the common name of Joshua, a name as usual as John or Peter is in our own language. But the choice of this name had its bearing upon salvation and judgment. We know that the name Joshua means: *the Lord saves*. The rich significance of this name might escape the attention of the countless Joshuas who were making the markets unsafe places to be, but in Jesus of Nazareth the name was fulfilled perfectly. Evaluate Him in terms of His name

---

1. A few of these Jewish fictions created the following names for the Messiah: Sjalôm (peace); Risjôn (the first); Jinnon (because he exists from eternity or because he has the dead arise again); Chanina ("grace"); Menachem ben Chisqijja (comforter, son of Hezekiah); Chiwwará debê Rabbi (the white one, i.e., the leprous one, of the house of the Rabbi—see Isaiah 53:4); Jahweh; Tsèmach (sprout or shoot); Natrona or Netirutha (the watcher or the watching one); Menachem (comforter); Bar-Næphlê (son of a degenerate one—see Amos 9:11); Nehora (light); Anani (he who comes with the cloud); Ephraim (perhaps to be explained by reference to Jeremiah 31:9 and 20); Menachem ben Ammiël (comforter, son of Ammiël). Inasmuch as these names which the Jews ascribed to the Messiah are not names currently known and used at the time, they are characteristic to the extent that they differ from the Biblical revelation of the matter, according to which Jesus had a common name which was quite in accordance with His humiliation and its effects. For a discussion of these names themselves, see Strack-Billerbeck *Kommentaar op Mattheus*, pp. 64-67.

and you will discover that it fits Him appropriately, that it fits Him only, and that it fits Him completely. Thus it was that the name which Jesus bore was itself a means of revelation. True, this revelation, too, was not adequate, but it was genuine. Whoever believed and whoever struggled with the name of Joshua would eventually discover in Jesus of Nazareth the fulfillment of the truth revealed by that name (the truth that Jaweh saves). And this is a fulfillment which can be discovered in no one else; and he who does not believe is one who "hearing doth not hear."

To return now to Pilate's ballot of two names. If it is true that Barabbas also bore the name Joshua, the naming of him as well as the naming of the Son of Mary and of David takes on a particular significance which is not discovered until this moment in the presence of Pilate. The one name of Joshua is now developed into two different directions through these two "candidates." Jesus of Nazareth redeems from sin, does the redeeming by means of justice, and by earning that justice in a strenuous struggle with God; and Jesus-Barabbas redeems from worldly tyranny, does the redeeming by means of imposed force (rebellion), and without once thinking about earning redemption in a struggle with God or of the requisite of satisfying God. Jesus of Nazareth first effects a spiritual redemption, and only after that has taken place does His renewing power realize itself in the visible world; but the "redemption" of Barabbas is a purely pragmatic incident which takes place according to the law of the flesh.

This pairing of the two names represents the great concealment of the Word of God: One can distinguish the true from the false Jesus only by faith and according to the Word. Joshua-Barabbas and Joshua of Nazareth are listed together. These names constitute a ballot in which self-redemption by means of one's own power and redemption through grace are placed next to each other. Salvation without humiliation and salvation by way of humiliation are placed in juxtaposition. Barabbas sacrifices others; the Nazarene sacrifices Himself. The one acts in the visible world; the other in the invisible. The first stands for revolution; the second for satisfaction. The former pleases the heart; the latter offends it. All this the heart of Pilate and of whatever is human puts together upon a single ballot.

You ask whom they will choose after a while? Ah, man, that makes no difference: His own did not accept Him; even though they vote for Him, even though each and all choose in His favor, they will have denied Him already. The fault inheres in the ballot itself.

Do not burst into tears, then, when after a while the popular vote proves to go against Him. For the ballot itself is a cursing of the Messiah. Instead, greet and worship the Surety of your soul for the labor which He bore for you. He was dumb in His response to this pairing of names, His silence represents a singular greatness. For that screaming mob out of doors the name Joshua-Jesus may have lost every feature of its specific content. But Jesus of Nazareth has detected the voice of His God behind His name. The several letters of His name, even as He read them upon the ballot, bore down upon Him with the weight of eternity. He pondered the content of His name in the presence of Barabbas and of His heavenly Father. That caricature — Barabbas — did not cause Him to lose hold of Himself.

Seeing the ballot, Joshua of Nazareth thought to Himself: They must do what they will; my calling is to be Joshua: let them draw up their lists.

They drew them up.

When Jesus saw that the logic of sin had put itself in the service of the choice of the flesh against the spirit, he understood all. At the beginning the case had read: Jesus superior to Barabbas; I find no fault in Him. At the conclusion the situation declared: Jesus beside Barabbas; the two are a pair. And the result of that was: Jesus beneath Barabbas; crucify Him and give us Barabbas. Yes, He had understood it all, and He did not move from His place. He found that His task was as simple as His name, used as it was a thousand times, for He had previously sensed that His name was as hard to bear as was His task in this terrible hour.

Jesus' name was coupled with that of Barabbas.

Who does not shudder at the thought that he is no better than Barabbas, and that therefore the whole world as well as his own flesh would vote against Jesus and in favor of himself? Who does not shudder at the thought that he, just as Barabbas, is named on the ballot of "the flesh" next to God Himself? Whoever ponders this deeply will pray: Lord help me, for I shall go mad un-less Thou dost reveal to me the true sense of the first chapter of John, unless Thou dost teach me the real meaning of the state-ment: In the beginning was the Word, and the Word was with God, and the Word was God. And the Word was made flesh, and dwelt among us, and we beheld his glory, the glory as of the only begotten of the Father, full of grace and truth.

Pilate's ballot: *Moriae encomium,* the praise of folly.

But: the flight from that ballot; refuge in Jesus' arms, the praise of godliness.

Come, ye angels, raise a hymn of praise for Him. It may be that He will not hear it today, but sing it anyhow to yourselves: to whom then shall ye liken Him, or what likeness will ye compare unto Him? saith the Almighty.

Angels, keep your countenance firm over against Him. For God is about to forsake Him. God has already left Him. God left Him when that evil ballot was drawn up. The clouds were not rent, heaven did not break through, the sun was not darkened. But God forsook Him. Jesus, my Surety, why didst Thou endure the ordi-nary name which is borne by the Jew at the market and by me? Lord, help me, for I am sure that I, too, would not have voted for Thee.

Be quiet, He tells me in return. That is just the point. You must not "select" me. I and the Father must have selected your name at the time of election, by sovereign choice and unto salva-tion. A ballot consisting of two names, He tells me further, once existed in the presence of God. The one name included upon it was the old man of sin, the son of perdition, existing in reality. The other name was that of the new man of election, genuine and pure in principle, in idea. The Father and the Son chose the second and greatly desired him; they were governed by their good pleasure in the choosing . . . That is why I can live; that is why I shall not perish. That is why I pass out of the prison house of sin and of Satan by means of Him, by means of Him alone, for the sake of God's sovereign pleasure. Barabbas passes out of the prison, but he leaves the prison standing. Jesus, however, enters into hell but for Him the very prison becomes His loot. O Lord, Thou seest

Thy struggle crowned with gifts for the comfort of men in order that Thy obstinate dear ones might ever dwell with Thee.

He endured the choice of the earth in order to vindicate the choice of God's good pleasure in His death, in His concealment, in His perfect perdition. That is what I read in the Holy Gospel. What must I do?

> "What must I do, Lord; tell me, what?"
>
>   * * *
>
> "Give me my cross, Thy cross, Thy heart,
> Thy love, Thy sorrow, and then go
> The way of grief to Golgotha."[1]

---

1. John H. De Groot, Sprongen.

Christ Is Pleaded for and Travestied

CHAPTER TWENTY-FIVE

Christ Is Pleaded for and Travestied

> *When he was set down on the judgment seat, his wife sent unto him, saying, Have thou nothing to do with that just man: for I have suffered many things this day in a dream because of him.*
>
> MATTHEW 27:19.

THE LIFE of the Son of man, ever alert to God as it was, is on all sides bounded by *dreams*. We find the dream at the *beginning* of His life, and we find it again at its *close*. Joseph, the husband of the woman who introduces Him into life, has a dream; the wife of the man who leads Him out of life also has a dream. Even before Jesus had been laid in the manger an angel tells Joseph in a dream: adopt Him for He shall be righteous. And as He is about to be led to the cross, the spirits say to the wife of Pilate, and God says to her again in a dream: Release Him, for He is a just man. Thus is the life of Christ bounded by dreams. Conscious and unconscious life, day and night, waking and dreaming — each and all of these must testify to Christ, must point to Him as the Just One with whom the world is certainly bound up even though it will not admit it.

The dream of Pilate's wife certainly constitutes a peculiar intermezzo. We hardly know what to make of the frail voice of a woman coming to us through all the clamor of the streets and the excitement of the trial. But Pilate's wife hardly makes her appearance at all; in fact, she does not let herself be seen; she merely sends a messenger.

Nevertheless there is something distinctive about this woman. The message which she has sent to Pilate arrives in the middle of the clamor which broke loose when the ballot, bearing the names of Barabbas and Jesus of Nazareth, had been presented. This, then, is the time which must be given to deliberating upon the choice which ought to be made. The people are being influenced from all sides; each new voice adds to the effect. A very inconvenient hour this is for a woman who wants the attention of her husband for a moment. But it is precisely in this moment that the message of the woman has a tremendous effect upon Pilate's emotion. She throws an obstacle in front of the wheel of the coach in which Pilate is riding to his doom. She tells him that he must have nothing to do with that just man. Why not? Well, last evening she has had a most depressing dream. She has dreamed about "that just man." And that dream is a sufficient motivation for her to say to her husband: "Keep your hands off; do not touch Him. I fear the consequences."

Pilate's wife has gradually become famous in history. She attracted people's attention very early. In fact the records of the transition definitely give her a name. She was called Claudia Procula, sometimes abbreviated to read Procla. This woman whom hereafter we shall call Claudia — without thereby committing ourselves to the historical faithfulness of those transitional records in the matter of this name, a matter which must necessarily remain more or less legendary — this woman, we say, has left an indelible impression upon history. As a matter of fact, the Greek church canonized her; the 27th of October is a day on which the Greek calendar of saints is dedicated to her. Others — the apocryphal gospel of Nicodemus, for instance — tell us that she became a proselyte to Christianity, and that she later took a prominent and honorable position among those who confessed the Christ. So effectively has she charmed the attention of people that she has been made the subject of a whole book.[1] In The Netherlands Frederik van Eeden has written a book on Pilate and his wife. But he himself says that he has done it in the same manner as Anna Catherine Emmerich had. Van Eeden, too, has Claudia become converted to Jesus, and even has Jesus appear in the family to effect a reconciliation between Pilate and his wife.[2]

---

1. G. P. Kits van Heyningen, *Claudia Procula*.

2. Frederik van Eeden, *Uit Jezus' Openbaar Leven*, Chapter 98, p. 194. H. Padberg, S. J: *Frederik van Eeden*, 1925, p. 220 (you will find an inaccurate reference of literary fact there).

Perhaps it will always be difficult to differentiate between fancy and truth. Hence we shall not make an effort at achieving that. We cannot go much further than that which has been officially confirmed. And the little that has been is limited for the most part to the information that Claudia was not unfavorably disposed to the Jews, that she interested herself, for instance, in the building of schools. For the rest, we shall let her figure remain hidden in the twilight in which the Spirit left her. The question for us is not who Claudia is, nor just what she saw in her dreaming,[1] but what place Claudia's dream had *in the story of Christ's suffering*. We do not need to know all of the details of the life of Claudia, but are seeking the relationship of her dream to the passion of the Man of sorrows.

Now one of the first questions which raises itself in this connection is whether Claudia's dream can be "explained" in natural ways, or whether that dream must be regarded as a supernatural one sent by God.

Just as is frequently the case, interpretations differ in this matter.

Some maintain that Claudia's dream can be wholly explained in a perfectly natural way. Who can contradict this contention? Jesus was generally known; during these last days many had been talking about Him. He Himself had appealed to the imagination, especially to the imagination of the women. The romantically colored account of His entry into Jerusalem undoubtedly reached Claudia's ears. Besides, Pilate knew (according to the immediately preceding verse) that for some time a conflict had obtained between the Jews and Jesus, a conflict which could be explained as far as the Jews were concerned by reference to their envy. Add to these facts that the trial of Jesus had called Pilate from his bed early in the morning, and that the restlessness which had arisen on the street in the matter of the Nazarene had therefore penetrated through to the bedroom of Pilate. Think, in addition, of the stir, the clamor, the going to and fro of the mob between Pilate's and Herod's house and you will indeed have matter enough for

---

1. For a discussion of Gustave Dore's presentation of the content of the dream, see Dr. J. C. de Moor, *Genade voor Genade*, Kampen, J. H. Kok. This discussion is a sermon on Claudia.

claiming that the dream of Pilate's wife can easily be explained in a natural way.

Therefore, when *others* maintain that they must ascribe the responsibility for this dream to the *devil,* and to him only, we think they are making a too audacious assertion. In the first place, the devil is not a deus ex machina; to cite his name is not to explain the first cause of an event. Besides, this method of explanation can very easily degenerate into a seeking for allegory or unreal parallelisms. One commentator will say: Just as the devil in Paradise first addressed the woman in order to use her for introducing death into the world, so the devil now first addresses himself to a woman in order to put an obstacle in the way of the death of Christ; that is, to stand in the way of redemption, and to put an obstacle in the way of life. According to these interpretations Claudia's act is looked upon solely from the dark side: it makes Claudia an obstacle, a hindrance in the way of the redemption contained in the death of Christ. How wildly arbitrary such explanations are becomes apparent from the fact that there are others again who read in this apology of the *woman,* Claudia Procula, a kind of compensation for what the *woman* in Paradise had spoiled. For, these argue, in Paradise a woman bore evil testimony over against the first Adam, and now, in the hour of the second Adam, a woman makes recompense by means of a good testimony. She registers her protest against all the evil statements made by all the wicked men. In giving this testimony she, too, is the first.

Naturally, we feel that there is a hitch somewhere. Our recompense is that we must not immediately blame the devil for everything which we cannot readily understand, as if that were a satisfactory conclusion. We know that the devil, too, is bound by the forces which make themselves felt in natural life.

However, there is still a third interpretation. It ascribes Claudia's dream to a direct influence of God. According to these interpreters, Claudia's dream is a kind of dream-revelation,[1] a "warning which God directs to Pilate." Those who hold to this view believe that God intentionally influenced Claudia's soul in order that it might admonish Pilate, or in some other way by means of that dream have a specific effect upon the suffering of Christ.

---

1. Grosheide, *Kommentaar op Mattheus,* p. 344.

What must we say of these various views? Must we choose one of the several interpretations?

As in so many other instances, so in this one it is quite unnecessary to align ourselves with one or the other of these commentaries. To do so would be to suggest that any one of them completely excludes the possibility of any other. But is not the whole of world history and especially the entire trial of Christ a confluence of *three* factors; i.e., a divine, a devilish, and a purely natural one (to the extent that we have erroneously allowed ourselves to name it that). But why should the one interpretation necessarily exclude the others? God often made use of *natural* factors. Whenever He did, however, it has been true of them that they did not explain His work, but, on the contrary, that they were themselves explained in terms of His plan. As for Satan? We know that he is everywhere and immediately present in order to turn towards evil what God is directing towards good, if by any means he is able to do so. The dream of Pilate's wife cannot be explained *solely* in reference to heaven, and even less in reference *solely* to purely psychological complexes. Hell also had a responsibility in the matter. Whoever could wish to keep the several interpretations of this event quite separate from each other would have to construct the whole problem of the providence of God, and of the manner of His government, in fact the whole of dogmatics in a way quite different from that which the Church up to this time has done.

Accordingly we endorse the opinions of those who do not abstract this remarkable intermezzo—for so it seems to be—from the pleasure of the evil one. But we also refuse to accept the proposition that this noteworthy dream simply and suddenly impinged upon the situation as a remarkable wonder which in no sense could be explained by natural phenomena. Above all, however, we may certainly not for one moment place this "incident" *outside* of the structure of God's determinate counsel and providence.

If we cling to these views we can let Claudia retain her position on the plane which she, together with all other people, occupies. Her dream is not typical of her life. She does not become a proselyte by reason of it, and no distinctive nobility of soul can be ascribed to her on the basis of it. Those who would like to explain this unique dream phenomenon in any specific way could much more easily find ground for blaming Claudia for her superstition than for praising her for her faith. We will point out presently that Claudia's dream, in the matter of which God certainly has a sacred purpose in mind, is soon explained by her in such a way that the rankest conceivable egoism is compatible with her interpretation and with the "application" which she infers from it. So much for the natural causes; so much for the "human factor" in her dream.

And this for Satan's share in the matter: certainly we cannot exclude him. We, too, believe that in the sinister play of his hellish wickedness this dream has a part. It is true that Satan avidly longs for the blood and death of the second Adam. But it is also true that hell would derive a kind of satisfaction from the fact that Christ would be released in the world as a result of mere superstition (fear of a dream), and by reason of pragmatic considerations (fear of the evil consequences which might attend the condemnation of the guiltless Jesus). If Christ were set free by Pilate as a result of the bizarre logic or vague intuition of Claudia to the effect that this "just man"[1] if put to death might be avenged by God or by the gods—but not by Himself,—then He will in the future no longer be proclaimed as the Messiah. Had Pilate in this particular set of circumstances, now that Christ had been proclaimed an outlaw anyhow, followed Claudia's advice and eventually given Jesus His freedom, Christ would not have escaped from the odium attaching to Him in the eyes of His people. In this connection we involuntarily think of that slave woman in Philippi who—later—gave the messengers of Christ a diploma of honor by announcing them as people having a good message, as preachers of a noble name. Satan exerted an influence upon that incident also. That slave also called out: Make no mistake about this Jesus Christ, for in my dreams I suffer much on account of that just man. Nevertheless, Paul detects a diabolical influence in her hysterical cries. The thrust of that influence is this: if Jesus gets the right of free passage in Philippi on the authority of this wo-

---

1. The qualification which names Jesus as a just man must not be stressed too strongly. Its meaning goes no further than to allege that Jesus is not as bad as His accusers say He is. Strack-Billerbeck, *Kommentaar op Mattheus*, p. 1032, presents an analogy.

man, He will be entering Philippi not as the one and only Messiah who thrusts all the other gods of Greek phantasy out of the way, and who takes all the people and all who minister in the temples of Philippi captive, but as one among many who, reckoning by human standards, all know how to speak "good and acceptable words." Just so, if Jesus by reason of Claudia's apology had gained His freedom at the hands of Pilate and of those ugly Jews, He would have secured the privilege of free passage into Jerusalem indeed, but then He would have been damaged and dethroned for all time. Claudia can do but one thing: she can give the Gospel only evil services. Just suppose for a moment that Satan has no hand in this affair. Do we know everything about his sinister activity? Is it not compatible with the passion of his sin-steeped being that every "interpretation" of the significance and place of the Nazarene in the world which does injustice to Christ is pleasing to Satan? We hold that the influence is present in this instance also in order immediately to effect this particular movement in the spiritual world. For Satan wants to exert effective influence upon every wave which God dispatches into the world of invisible things. If he cannot succeed in this, he at least tries to set up his loud-speakers in the neighborhood of God's waves in order that he may falsely reproduce the pure sounds intrinsic to them. So much for the devil's influence. We may call this the diabolical factor in the dream.

To go on, however. Above all, we are convinced of the fact that *God Himself,* from the vantage point of His spiritual world, intervened in the trial of Jesus by means of Claudia's dream. Moreover, we believe that He did this with a specific intention. Now anyone who is surprised by the thought that God uses a heathen woman for purposes of revealing His intentions in a dream will certainly have to admit that his Bible contains many another such instrument of revelation. We need only to name Abimelech, Pharaoh, and Nebuchadnezzar among others to indicate that God more than once addressed Himself to heathen in the form of a dream, in order to give expression to a specific working of revelation. Claudia's name must be added to these. Nothing in the trial of Jesus is independent of the influence of God and everything in that trial has its specific significance.

God's intent is, however, so intricately complicated[1] that no one has the right to force it into any one direction. Now the fact that God wanted to admonish Pilate and to do so in Pilate's own language is certainly an element which helps us to understand God's purpose in the dream of Claudia. It would not wholly account for God's intent, but it cannot be properly ignored. There was very little that Pilate could still do; he had already sold himself to the Jews. But perhaps it will be possible for him to be diverted by a dream. True, Pilate has asked, What is truth? but the man who has lost his faith soon tried to sustain himself by superstition and when that is the case, how many a man has not listened to the charming voice of emotional woman? We are all familiar with the somewhat sinister saying: *Cherchez la femme*. Now the fact that this saying does not suffice on this occasion to explain everything to Pilate certainly cannot be ascribed to the governor himself. Had the Jews not annoyed him so much—and in this respect we notice Satan's presence in this matter—Jesus would have been set free. But all Jews and all historians, and indifferent you and I, might have smiled mockingly and said: Yes, He is free, but after all,—*cherchez la femme*. In short, the dream of Pilate's wife is an admonition. God is speaking to Pilate in Pilate's *own language*. That God does so need not surprise us, for He is the same God who once admonished Saul in Saul's own language—the time, you remember, when in the night at Endor God had Samuel speak to him. This is the same God who, during the very moment in which Pilate's wife is dreaming her dream, is prepared to send souls down from heaven to the earth, souls who, later, when Christ has yielded up the spirit, will enter into the body in order that after His resurrection they may appear to many in the holy city. No, those who have become used to the atmosphere of miracles—to the extent it is possible to become used to that—will not be surprised to find that God makes use of Pilate's own language to arouse his sense of responsibility. On the contrary, such a person will remember that God by means of this woman, and by means of her dream, greatly enhanced Pilate's sense of responsibility. A dream never gives respite from the task of being responsible. As

---

1. So it seems to our defective thinking. On the other hand, however, from God's side, His unity also fully informs the decree. From His point of view, the designation "complicated" is sheer foolishness.

quickly as the dream has passed the question arises: What did it mean; what is the explanation of it? That throws everyone back upon his own resources again. Everyone must explain his own dreams himself; and each man seeks the solution in terms of his own life and temperament. Instead, then, of providing relief from responsibility, a dream intensifies the sense of it. A dream gives the human mind a new task. The task is one which the consciousness of waking hours has tried to escape from, or has neglected. Hence we can truly say that God intensified Pilate's sense of responsibility to the highest degree by means of this dream. For this dream we thank Him; it will be the reason for which Pilate will be found without excuse in the last day when Jesus will be the judge instead of the accused, and consequently will be the judge of Pilate also. Because of the dream, Pilate will be unable to say: I did not know; or: You did not talk to me *in my own language.*

Nevertheless, it would be a complete denial of the entire, conscious predilection which is governing the content of this book, if we should drop the discussion at this point. That conscious predilection is that every detail of the gospel of the passion has a definite significance for Christ Himself. Everything has an influence upon the soul of Christ, and each new thing thrusts Him farther into the abyss. For this is now His hour, and the power of darkness. As it is, God simply gives His Son no respite from suffering on this day.

Now as we look for the significance which Claudia's dream, as well as her report of it and the application which she gave of it has for the soul of Christ, we discover several things.

We can put its significance in this way: In the whole of Christ's trial, Claudia's effort to reach out her hand to the Nazarene in an attempt to "rescue" Him is a very noble gesture. Nevertheless, that noblest of gestures also serves to deny, to mock, to misconstrue Christ, and serves only to harm Him.

In the first place, we pause to consider that application of Claudia's dream which reads: *Have thou nothing to do with that just man.* Dost Thou hear that, Jesus? In the very hour in which all the angels and all the devils, in which God Himself and Thy own Spirit adjure the whole world saying: Have *everything* to do with Christ Jesus, release Him, for His is the only voice which still has a good word to sound in this world, comes the dictum: Have *nothing* to do with Him; give Him His freedom, rid yourself of Him. Does that not cause Thee incomparable pain, Thou Prophet of God? Alas, if only this statement came from the strident throats of excited Jews or if only it were the conclusion of the refined diplomacy of the Roman governor, it would not be as bad as it is. But the statement comes from a person who, not without the influence of God, has just returned from the invisible world. Jesus' own text had just echoed in His own soul: I must be raised on the cross,[1] for I affect the whole world; everybody has everything to do with me. Now comes this message from the unseen world: Have nothing to do with this man. Is this not humiliation! And negation again! First from Pilate, and now from his wife!

Yes, the "noble gesture" on Claudia's part can only serve to harm Jesus. She in her manner says precisely what Gamaliel will say later in the council of the Jews: Simply ignore that Nazarene incident; if you consider it, you may burn your fingers. But it is necessary to burn one's fingers on the Christ. Did He not come to bring fire upon the earth? Nevertheless, Claudia says: Stay out of the neighborhood. In this, you see, the Saviour is again being isolated. And this is accomplished through the person who made the noblest gesture in the whole of this ungodly trial. Yes, Claudia, you have insulted Him. It is true that you protested against your husband, but at bottom you are one with him. You, too, declare that this Just Man is an outlaw. Surely if this Nazarene has any rights according to law, Pilate *must* have a great deal to do with Him.

Who, pray, can still dare to speak of a *noble* gesture?

Can you not detect a note of selfishness here? Just who is it that Claudia would save? *The Nazarene?* No, indeed, but she would save *Pilate*. What she fears is that vengeance will one day accrue to him . . . Does not this pain Thee, Jesus? Thy life is being protected, but in a way that takes no cognizance of Thee as God's active avenger; it takes cognizance of Thee only as the outlaw whom men dare not touch because they fear the Nemesis of which Pilate's wife has heard at times. One can never know how much of truth there is in those old sayings! . . . I think of Enoch. He once declared to Noah's contemporaries: The Lord will come, and

1. See Chapter 15, pp. 292 and 297.

when He does His coming will be an *offensive* approach; He will bring myriads of saints with Him and many thousands of angels of vengeance. Now, in this hour of Christ's death, the Lord has indeed made His offensive appearance. Today He comes; the Holy One comes, bringing myriads behind Him. Beware. On this very day someone says: The gods of Greece and Rome, the fates and the furies, may possibly make their approach with a sting of death and with an angel of destruction. Negation this! Again negation! Christ has come to drive all gods out of Greece and Rome. He comes to sweep them all from Olympus by means of the winds of Pentecost. Yet it was only by a hair's-breadth that Jesus escaped from becoming the protegé of the gods of Greece, the very gods He came to destroy, and for whose defeat He had *already thanked the Father*.[1]

This also represented *suffering*. And *temptation*. His way of coming into life was not a matter of indifference to the Son, and He is equally concerned how He passed through it and out of it. Why should a doxology sung by angels mean more to Him than the proposal of Pilate's wife? He does not "figure" the way we do. He is "true" man. Yes, His soul yearns for light and life, but it is compelled to protest against this "noble" gesture, the only thing which would still comfort Him as He stands before the bench. Among all those people there is not one who raises his voice for Him, save this one woman . . . But His whole soul must implore, and cry aloud: Do not listen to her.

Why not, you ask? Had He been set free by reason of *this* advocate, the Chief Priest of Israel would have lived by virtue of the grace of the anachronous gods of Greece. Then the Highest Wisdom would have passed through the gates of freedom by the grace of superstition: that is, by the grace of the most utter folly. Then every rising of the sun after this would have raised a hymn in praise of folly because of this bizarre phenomenon; a Highest Wisdom living by the grace of sheerest folly, and a Passover recollection (the amnesty) manipulated in the name of the remnants of the Greek Olympus to which Claudia attributed the dream. Even Maccabeans would have protested against such a Passover memory; how much more, then, Jesus Christ!

---

1. John 12: 21, 23.

Indeed, this is humiliating. The *highest* revelation which God has given the world now runs the danger of letting its *own* notion of its ways and means be circumscribed by the erroneous notion of the lowest form of revelation of which God makes use in the world: namely the *dream*.[1] True it is that God spoke genuinely to Claudia, but pagan superstition gave the message a wrong interpretation. "God, who aforetime spake through the prophets, has now fulfilled that saying in the Son." But the life and the right of prophecy of that Son—woe to Him, if He should desire it thus— is sustained by a silken thread which was spun by the diseased imagination of a born egoist who has scented something of the sulphur and brimstone which has been ignited on the top of Mt. Olympus.

In this connection we think of the Baptist. Just before his death we witnessed the enmity of a woman, Herodias, and the weakness of a man, Herod. Together they struck off John's head. Here, again, we have the whim of a woman and the weakness of a man, but *on this day* these two are inclined to spare Jesus' head. But to spare Him thus for the day is to humiliate Him forever. Then the Baptist would have served his purpose and attained his end, but Jesus would have been basically defeated. Understand, we are talking from a human point of view. For the author of the sermon on the mount it is a terrible lot to hear it said: Have nothing to do with Him. For the hairs of His head, as well as those of Pilate's head, are all numbered. Jesus *senses* that this is true.

In concluding we can hardly interest ourselves in what became of Claudia, in the conflicts of her soul, or in the manner in which God in the future allowed Pilate to suffer for the sake of the Nazarene. It is said that Pilate died in darkness; it is certain that his life after this time came to be a restless one. Doubtless, he often recalled what his wife had once told him.

But what point can there possibly be in considering such things? The only thing that can be important for us is the terrible humiliation which struck Christ as the bearer of God's highest revelation, which caused Him to feel as keenly as death that His life was made to depend upon the superstition of a pagan woman. The

---

1. Hebrew 1:1.

bearer of God's highest revelation must hold His peace now. And the recipient of God's lowest mode of revelation flutters by: the dream, which is hardly set forth distinctly in a vague nebulosity, is permitted to speak. Meanwhile Jesus Christ must simply bide His time in order to learn what the content and the *effect* of this dream of revelation are. When Claudia told of the fact that she had met God, Jesus also felt Himself forsaken of God. Over against Him all the heavens were silent.

How great Christ is in His perfect obedience! In spite of His intense yearning for life, He refuses to accept it on these terms. He wavered neither to the right nor to the left. It may hurt Him to think that the dreams of Abimelech and of Pharaoh and of Nebuchadnezzar gained more for Abraham, Isaac, and Daniel respectively, than Claudia's dream gains for Him—for Pilate at its behest did not change his mind—but again in this matter He gives Himself up willingly to the counsel of God, holds His peace, and sees that justice is done. And He does this without clinging to the lifeline which superstition threw to the Man of sorrows when He became the victim of the overwhelming stream of God's justice and curse. True, He sighed: *All* thy waves and *all* Thy billows go over me. At that moment Satan threw Him the lifeline saying: Grasp it. But *from this temptation, too,* Christ escaped. Even after Claudia's intervention,[1] and in spite of the fact that as a human being her speech seemed to invite a response, Christ permitted his dark sayings to go unexplained over against Pilate and did not defile or profane His own great mystery by an avid appropriation of Claudia's mysteries. He did not mingle the waters disturbed by Claudia with the pure springs of our delights. He preserved the fountains of God pure and undefiled. Thou art great, Lord, and greatly to be praised. Thou maintainest all the holinesses of God's revelation and dost do it also in spite of the slight breath of hope and life which, as it seemed, for Thy benefit, briefly blew over Thy head from the atmosphere of paganism.

We praise Thee, O God, for Thy name is very dear. Thy wonders are proclaimed even though a decadent daughter of Zeus attempts to cover them with a garment of the Greek gods. O Sav-

---

1. The phrase is repeated again: Jesus answered not a word—not even after this intervening episode.

iour, Thou didst not quail, neither when the naked Satan confronted Thee in the wilderness, nor when he tempted Thee here by
means of a dream. For the truth is that Satan tempted Thee, and
that Thou wast proved by God. However, now that Thou hast
confessed the name of Thy God over against the nebulous dream-
reflexes of an uncertain pagan woman, Thou hast wrought for
Thyself the privilege of having Thy disciples see visions and to
dream Thy own old dreams. Thy spirit of Pentecost has mounted
his highest peaks, O Christ, Thou hast kept the dreams, uncontaminated by the filthy, dirt-laden streams of heathendom. The
revelation of Thy God which proceeds from Thy spirit pure and
undefiled almost became smothered in the sand and mire of pagan
superstition and of late-Roman defeatism.

If Christ had imbedded Himself in these simply to preserve His
life then God's dream of revelation would first have been diverted
and thereupon been smothered in paganism and superstition with
Christ's approval. That which was at stake here was the Word,
the Word, the revelation of the New Testament, and the whole of
Scripture. For a Christ who could permit the revelation of God
to become contaminated by clinging, not to God's purely spoken
word, but to Claudia's impure superstition, could not possibly have
remained our Chief Prophet. The Word is at stake here. Christ
must see to it that the ways of revelation are kept straight, and
may not permit them to digress into the direction of the paganism
of Claudia. The very fact that God was present in her dream
spelled incomparable temptation for Christ. The slightest of God's
actions, and those realized in people separated from Him farth-
est, demand a complete, a genuine, and a well-rounded response
from the Bearer of God's highest revelation. Scrutinize Him closely now. The act of God's revelation inhering in this dream, which
proceeded from Him genuine and pure at first but which was contaminated when received by the pagan woman, is now again received into His own soul in its pure and genuine condition. He introduced no breach into the words which the Spirit had sent out
into the spiritual world. He did not interpose a falsetto note into
those pure sounds, and inasmuch as He had to serve as God's loud-
speaker, He reproduced flawlessly the voice of His God.

Come, Thou spirit of Pentecost, permit the Lord's people to
dream His own dream, and let the people wait upon Him night and

day. Come, Thou spirit of Pentecost, enter in, and force the stream of revelation into its own river bed. To that it has a right, inasmuch as even this dream did His soul no damage nor caused it to quail in this hour of extreme temptation.

And Thou, my Saviour, have patience and bide Thy time, for Thou hast almost arrived at Patmos, the province of Rome's Caesar, Pilate's lord. There Thou wilt permit John to dream his dreams.

There Thou wilt permit him to dream ever and again of Thy might. Even the last dream of revelation which Thou wilt evoke in the spirit of John as recorded in his Revelation, Thou wilt be dreaming Thy "ancient" dreams, Thou wilt be fulfilling the Scriptures, Thou wilt be giving the Bible its concluding testimony, and wilt by Thy voice as expressed in his dreams be saying to the whole world: Have much, have everything, to do with me, that Just Man, who suffered Himself, not in a dream, but in complete reality.

Such is the triumph of Christ over Nemesis; of the Word over the false concept, of Christ over Claudia. For God has *in these last times* spoken through His Son. The dreams which He evokes in the prepared spirit of His people are bitter dreams, a thousand times more bitter, in fact, than was Claudia's dream, but they are also very sweet for they point out the tendencies of the *Gospel*. God approached from Teman, the Word mounted to its heights, and Christ was humiliated and exalted also in the land of dreams. Hence my soul shall wait upon Him night and day; even in the night time He instructs my reins. This He does, not because of Claudia's troubled dream, but because of His pure response to that dream. For when, pray, is He not the Saviour? He rejoices because of the fact that the spirits of dreams are subject to Him. Now He is assured that many names are written in the heavens because of the watch which He kept.

Christ's Blood Esteemed Less
Than That of Abel

CHAPTER TWENTY-SIX

Christ's Blood Esteemed Less Than That of Abel

● *The governor answered and said unto them,
What shall I do then with Jesus which is called
Christ? They all say unto him, Let him be
crucified. And the governor said, Why, what
evil hath he done? But they cried out the
more, saying, Let him be crucified. When
Pilate saw that he could prevail nothing, but
that rather a tumult was made, he took water,
and washed his hands before the multitude,
saying, I am innocent of the blood of this just
person: see ye to it. Then released he Barabbas unto them.*
MATTHEW 27:21-26a.

JESUS-BARABBAS and Jesus-Christ—those are the two
names which we have seen drawn up and heard proclaimed as
constituting a single ballot. The one was a descendant of
Cain; the other of Abel. The first of Cain, yes. He is the murderer, the blood-thirsty one, the usurper of the flesh. The other of
Abel. He is the seed of the woman. He gives his blood as a ran-
som. He has been in the deep valley of the martyred.

You can draw the line farther yourself. Whoever puts the
names of Cain and Abel on one and the same ballot must conclude
by murdering Abel. He robs Abel of the right to exist. Abel may
live in the world only if he is the seed of the woman, and consequently brooks no comparison with Cain. Must Christ then not
sink below the level of Abel?

Alas, nothing else is possible. His blood must be negated. It is
thus that he sinks beneath the plane of Abel. Hence Pilate arises
and says: This blood has no voice crying out against me and rising up to heaven. Hence the Jews rise to say: This blood has no

voice crying out evil against us. That which Cain did not believe about Abel's blood—for he still *believed* that it could cry out to heaven against him—that "Cain" in his generation does not believe about the Greater than Abel. Now, inasmuch as Christ is He who is greater than Abel, He must also become a lesser than he. It was not for nothing that we observed how nadirs are zeniths, and zeniths, nadirs for Him. It is in this connection that the Bible tells us how it came about that Christ's blood was esteemed less than that of Abel. Mark the account well.

In the preceding chapter we listened to the voice of *woman*. She wanted to touch the heart of her husband and by an appeal to fear wanted to restrain him from a terrible murder. However, the voice of the woman was lost in the howling storm which blew over Pilate's house and over David's roofs on the day of Christ's death. The disaster could not be averted. Who, indeed, can check sin in its coming? It is as irresistible in its descent as is a waterfall.

Accordingly, we can say that Pilate no longer has the rudder in his hand. He has listened to what his wife had to say to him. But he says to himself—official people do occasionally like to say it to themselves—: It is easy for her to talk; but meanwhile I am confronting the difficulty. The clash between his desire to release Christ and his fear of rowing against the stream compels him to reach one of his many desperate solutions.

He goes out to face the crowd again. This time he asks them emphatically which of the two they want. When he finds that their choice invariably favors Barabbas he puts them squarely before the question about what then must happen to Jesus who is also called the Messiah. The fact that he adds the designation *Messiah* probably was not intended as an insult but as an accentuation of the *importance* of the case of Jesus, also as evaluated in terms of the logic of the Jews. In effect, Pilate means to say that there must be many a man among the Jews who esteems this person to be greater than a mere human being, who detects something sublime, something issuing from heaven in him. As a judge, Pilate means to say, I must officially reckon with the possibility that there is a hardly insignificant group among your own people who find in this man a kind of satisfaction for their religious longings and a fulfillment of your own Jewish, religious expectations. How else can you account for the fact that the man bears the name Messiah?

Tell me what I must do with Him. Release Barabbas, you say. Yes, that is easily done. But to dispatch the case of this other man, that is more difficult, especially since He seems to be the problem of your own people . . . You see that Pilate, by placing the title of Messiah into the foreground, wants to convince the Jews that he is a humane person who truly wants to take cognizance of all factions of the national life. It may be, he suggests, that Jesus' party is not officially represented on this occasion—at least no one of His disciples is rising to His defence,—but that does not mean that no such party exists. And these are they who see in Jesus of Nazareth a revelation of heavenly forces. Now just what must a man as humane as Pilate is, do? No one can deny that there is such a thing as equitable representation, and that there is such a thing as beneficent neutrality.

However, without any hesitation at all, the whole crowd of people persist in the response: Let Him be crucified.

Some commentators have maintained that Pilate had in mind not only to release Barabbas alone but Jesus also. This Passover festival, then, could have been celebrated as one which marked a double amnesty. Absolute certainty is impossible in this matter. In fact, it is even unlikely that Pilate had a carefully rounded plan in mind. As for the Jews, however, these know *very well* into what direction they wish to steer. They want the *cross* for Jesus.

The demand that Jesus be crucified need not, as some believe, be regarded as an attempt on the part of the crowd to prevent Pilate from saying that they had better put him to death by stoning in the usual Jewish manner. The dilemma with which Pilate confronts them is not that of crucifying or stoning but of condemning or setting free. If Jesus was to be condemned to death, death by crucifixion would under the circumstances and after repudiation of Pilate's own proposal (see page 296), be the natural method. Now we know that the Jewish leaders of the people had already concluded in private caucus that they would not put Jesus to death according to the Jewish custom of stoning. They, too, reckoned with that rather important element among the people which actually honored Jesus as the Messiah or at least left room for the possibility that he was the Messiah. Accordingly, they influenced the people to demand death by crucifixion. This action was quite in line with the course things were taking. Barabbas, too, was in danger of death on the cross. Were he to be released now, Jesus could suitably take his place. By moving the masses into this direction therefore, these leaders of the people carried out the tactics they had agreed to pursue somewhat earlier (page 293). And the people, without understanding everything involved in the matter, put themselves in the service of the leaders.

However, even though the people did not consciously place the possibility of *stoning* over against that of *crucifying,* they did emphatically demand that death on the cross be appointed for Jesus. And that is the new element which this event introduces into the gospel of the passion. What was the nature of this new element, you ask? As we see it, it is *this*: The affair of Christ is now made the affair of the *whole people.*

Yes, in a sense it had been that all the while. The Sanhedrin up to this time had been dealing in a way which was quite compatible with the sense of this blinded people. But now there is an external demonstration of the fact that the masses are agreeing with the intent of the Sanhedrin. "They *all* say unto Pilate: Let him be crucified." *All* is an inclusive word. It refers to the chief priests not only, but to the people also; not only to the Pharisees, but also to the man in the street. Not only to the vengeful enemies, but also to the timid spectators. The fire of hell spreads over the whole crowd, and a mad cry vibrates over the square: *He* must be sent to the cross.

However, Pilate still attempts by means of a formal question to save the situation. He asks the crowd to state what evil Jesus has done. In other words, the judge wants them to progress from generally protested accusations to a specific and concrete charge. He demands that they name facts, facts which can be officially substantiated. But the question goes unanswered. The voice of this weakling blows away. The leaders fan the flames which are sweeping over the masses into a fiercer conflagration. Hoarse throats give utterance to more violent cries: He must be sent to the cross; this thing has lasted long enough. Then Pilate understood that nothing more could be done with this people. Then he knew that he was occupying a position between this people and his "gods." It might be that he did not believe them, but—there was that report his wife had just brought him. Now it is most embarrassing to be in a position between gods and people, if each of these parties wants to go in a different direction. Whoever in such a case chooses against the supernatural world and in favor of the natural has to do something to hide his confusion. Accordingly, Pilate has a basin of water brought in, and washes his hands in the presence of the people. This was a symbolic piece of conduct by which he wished to give expression to his guiltlessness in the matter. He is a man who by the pressure of a fate which he cannot circumvent has arrived at an impasse from which he cannot escape. Circumstances compel him to a deed of which he himself cannot approve. In the presence of the people, and looking out upon the open heavens, Pilate officially asks that they take note of his innocence. He cannot do anything about it, he says.

Was Pilate, when he made use of this ceremony of washing his hands, following a *Roman* custom? Some say that he was. Others suggest that he made use of a custom which was well known in Israel. Fortunately, it is not necessary to place these two interpretations over against each other. It is apparent that the Jews understood the meaning of this symbolic conduct. Had that not been the case, Pilate's gesture in this instance would have been futile. As for the Roman, he too seemed to be familiar with the usage. The ceremony, therefore, must have been in official use outside of the province of the Jews also.

Be that as it may, Pilate by employing this ceremony in this moment at this place appropriated a custom which in Israel was actually circumscribed in the law. The several commentators quite correctly point to Deuteronomy 21:6-9 in this connection. There the rule is stipulated that the eldest of a city near the place in which a murdered person has been found, in case the murderer is not known and no evidence about who it might be is available, must wash their hands. Thus, by making use of a certain ceremony of sacrifice they can testify over against the Lord and the people that they are innocent of the shed blood. Psalm 26, verse 6, seems to make a reference to this ceremony in the words: I will wash mine hands in innocency: so will I compass thine altar, O Lord. And in Psalm 73, verse 13, we read: Verily I have cleansed mine heart in vain, and washed my hands in innocency.

Pilate, therefore, by making this ceremony his own, and by doing so in the presence of the Jewish people thereby wishes to indicate—and the Jews by acting upon this gesture agree to accept the invitation—that he declares himself to be guiltless of the blood of Jesus, that he cannot do anything in the matter, that fate makes his conduct in the case binding for him. This blood, he says, cannot cry out to heaven against him. "Claudia," he assures his wife, "you need have no fears."

In this way, you see, Pilate, who up to this time has been characterized by weakness rather than by outright duplicity, does sink to the level of making a hypocritical gesture. He is not guiltless in this matter. Think of the many swords and staves which are protecting his head. And, even if he had been compelled to take a stand alone, he may not betray his office as he does.

We must add, meanwhile, that Pilate's symbolic deed is accompanied by a statement. He speaks to the people, and says: *See ye to it*. Divesting himself of the responsibility, he places the burden of it upon the shoulders of the Jews.

In this connection we are compelled to recall what was said in verse 4 of this same chapter. When Judas no longer wished to be responsible for the shedding of Jesus' blood, and when he returned the traitor's fee to the chief priests, these stated: *See thou to that*. These same chief priests now hear that very statement addressed to them by Pilate. Thus does the one party transfer the responsibility in the case to the other.

But the case cannot be left in its present condition. Accordingly, we notice that the crowd crosses the bridge. We have observed, to employ another figure, that this people very often cuts those knots into pieces which it cannot succeed in untying. It accepts the burden of responsibility. It is always very easy for a crowd to do that. A crowd is a mere aggregation, a mere gathering together of anonymous entities. It has hit upon the pragmatic fiction of divided responsibility for evil, and attempts to make use of that means to avoid personal responsibility. The crowd, therefore, can easily and does frequently, say: We, we! We will see to it!

In this instance, too, the crowd arrogantly shouts: "His blood be upon us and upon our children." This passionate cry has a threefold implication. Inasmuch as the judge himself is concerned, it represents a taking over on the part of the people of Pilate's symbolic gesture. It represents a taking over of that gesture inasmuch as the Jews are concerned also. Finally, it represents, in

Whenever the situation is such, no one can check the course of sin. Only a moment later Barabbas will be released. Then the candidate of the flesh is desired in preference to Him who fully realizes and fulfills the spirit.

Now there are always those writers and speakers who must always be setting off this panorama before the imaginations of their readers and auditors by delimiting it with a circle of *crosses*. With quivering voices they tell of the crosses on which the Jews were hanged when Jerusalem was devastated. Thus, they add, you see, that the self-accepted curse accrued to them, that His blood *came* upon them and their children. But is that the note we should strike in closing? True, very true it is that quantities of crosses encircled Jerusalem later, and that the children of these various people were indeed crucified upon them. Yes, yes indeed, the Jew is a roamer, a nomad. But is it fitting for us to delimit the place on which the praetorium rests with the *crosses* of Jews? And is it proper to enhance the treatment of the curse accepted by the people by means of a vignette dedicated to the rags, and worn out sandals, and the crooked cane of the *wandering Jew?*

Suppose we give our attention to a better thing. Here is the Christ. He has already been nailed to the cross, He has already been negated according to the idea. Do you know who they are that are assisting in the deed? Do you know who also are calling down His blood upon them and upon their children? Do you know upon whom that blood will come? Those are they who would escape from the implications of the sermon on the mount, those who confuse themselves by inventing the notion of an "insignificant detail," those who *comfort* themselves by tracing out an "indifferent thing." May these all beware, for these all are saying to God: His blood be upon me and upon my children.

May these all read the sermon on the mount, and stand in awe of the Prophet, who, in order to maintain His sermon on the mount and to make it fruitful, was willing as a priest to give His life for that purpose. May they understand that Christ's blood ever is *upon* the world. It comes—yes, at this point someone again arises to a point of order. I hear him saying: That blood comes upon the world in the form of the crosses of those detestable Jews at the destruction of Jerusalem. But we can stay nearer home than that. That blood comes upon the man and woman who may have fainted at the spectacle on Gabbatha, or at least at Golgotha, but who thereupon, in a characteristically human way, negated the Christ as He is even in the idea. Such a person trivializes the Christ. And in making Christ a trifle, he makes God that. He rebels against heaven.

In this chapter we called attention briefly[1] to that study in our first volume in which we saw Christ in Gethsemane as He was being strengthened by an angel. He had seen the angel there, and He understood that heaven was not regarding His blood as a trifle. In thought He remained far above such minimizations; His blood would disquiet the whole world. God was *maintaining* the *sermon on the mount in* reference to its Author. He was a *worm.* Accordingly someone[2] said that He was a mere trifle. He who makes himself a worm must not become angry if someone steps on him. But God addressed Christ and by means of that angel said to Him: Even though Thou art a worm, Thou and Thy shed blood affect the whole world. Thy blood can never be regarded as the blood of an outlaw. The whole law is manifest in every drop of it.

I think of that angel and I say: these people are contradicting him. Now can they ever say to the angel: I have made a mistake, and that is all?[3] Plainly, they contradict the angel.

Who contradicts him? Jerusalem's future candidates for crucifixion? Man, be still. It is you; it is I.

O Jesus, if Thy blood must ever *come* upon us, let it come in grace, and—in order that it may be preserved—in vengeance also. We praise Thee, O Lord, because Thy blood is very near. People are silent about the wonders it has wrought. No, we would not pray to have Thy speaking blood diverted from us, but would pray that it come upon us. Cain, be not a fool, do not stumble over the protective symbols and say: I no longer hear Abel's blood crying aloud; thanks be to God, its voice is silent; it has finally grown dumb. The blood of Abel-Christ still cries aloud. Mark it, Cain. It speaks of justice and of grace. It speaks of the last children to come. It takes a "Christly" vengeance. It avenges itself by giving itself away in love, and by destroying those who cannot bear

1. P. 497.
2. Nietzsche.
3. See Ecclesiastes 5:5.

that love. Listen well, ye lost children of the Jews. No one will be hounded to death by the blood simply because it has been poured out, but only because in the last analysis it was not allowed to *come* upon thee and upon thy children for their peace.

Mark this, Cain. You received the sign on your forehead, not in order that you might forget the blood of Abel but in order that you might still call down upon you for your salvation the blood which speaks better things than that of Abel. Over against that "greater than Abel" you must definitely decide whether you want to commit the murder again or listen to the voice of the blood calling your peace unto you.

> The earth drank blood one day and called for vengeance,
> And Abel's blood four thousand years could not erase.
> The earth drank blood again and called for vengeance
> But Christ's blood was and still remains: pure grace.[1]

Listen. He ever lives in order to pray for us. It is thus that His blood comes upon us and our children provided that we do not "lift up" the name of the Lord and the blood of the Lord "unto vanity."

-----

1. From Guido Gezelle.

Christ's Blood Being Shed by Human Agency the First Time

CHAPTER TWENTY-SEVEN

Christ's Blood Being Shed By Human Agency the First Time

● *Then Pilate therefore took Jesus, and scourged him.*

    And when he had scourged Jesus, he delivered him up to be crucified.

            JOHN 19:1; MATTHEW 27:26b.

WE have now arrived at the *shedding of blood*, without which, according to Biblical testimony, no forgiveness is possible. The story of Christ's suffering in the presence of the judge is hastening to its conclusion. Thereupon will follow the third volume of this study, which is devoted to a consideration of His blood as it flows away into the ground. But even before the subject matter of this third volume is reached, Christ's blood is being driven from Him. It is being driven from Him by men. This is significant.

You have discovered that this study divides the suffering of Christ into three volumes. The first volume presents Christ as He enters upon His suffering. In that volume we observed Him when He was still unbound, and when He went to and fro among men at the behest of His own will, when He had not yet been delivered into the hands of His judges. This second volume considers Him as He passes through His suffering, while standing over against the court. In this study we are devoting our attention to the *bound* Christ upon whose suffering the human will, the will of justice as maintained by the authorities, must make a decision. The third volume will presently deal with Christ as He is at the conclusion of His suffering. It will study Him as He takes upon Himself the results of the sentence pronounced upon Him, and as He drinks the cup of passion to the dregs of death.

Now the remarkable thing is that in each of these three divisions the blood of Jesus Christ was forced out of Him. In the first section we observed that He sweated blood in Gethsemane. In this second section we observe that His blood is pressed out by the scourging, and, as we shall see presently, by the crown of thorns which was used to mock Him. Later, in the third volume, we shall note that His blood is driven from Him when it flows out of His hands and feet, out of the wounds inflicted upon Him, and out of His side when the spear is thrust into it. Obviously, we need not argue for the fact that this does not represent an accident, or the byplay of fate. Accordingly, we shall try to comprehend the meaning of these three moments in the shedding of the blood of Christ.

Before we take up this task, however, we must outline the course which things took in the presence of Pilate. We know from what has been said already that Pilate released Barabbas, and that in this matter he therefore satisfied the wishes of the Jews. Christ's name—to use a phrase which is absurd but nevertheless painfully accurate—was removed from the ballot which had been drawn up and announced. Christ was formally returned to His position at dead center. We noted previously that Pilate resorted to the custom of amnesty in his effort to escape from his uncertainty. He had constantly attempted to rescue himself from the choking grip of the hate and envy of the Jews. Inasmuch as this method did not meet with success he was forced to return to the plan he had originally had in mind, namely that of chastising Jesus first and releasing Him then. As a matter of fact, that too had not been a plan but merely a suggestion. From the cry of the throng which had brutally demanded that the Nazarene be crucified, Pilate became aware of the fact that, unless he added to it, the proposal to chastise Jesus and then release Him would not meet with the approval of the crowd. Accordingly, he does not put the question in the nice form of a dilemma, for he knows that his auditors will be indisposed to listen to that. Anyhow, dilemmas are dangerous on the tongue of spineless people. Nevertheless he proposes to make one more attempt. He issues the command that Jesus be scourged.

Now one difficulty which arises when we try to arrange the several data which the Bible affords in this matter is that we cannot be sure just which chronological order is intended by the narrative as it is related in Matthew, for example. Matthew reports that after Pilate had scourged Jesus he delivered Him up to be crucified; in other words, Matthew relates the scourging and the sentence of death on the cross to each other. The question arises whether this was the formal condemnation which definitely determined that Jesus should die on the cross. If Pilate intended it to be such, we are confronted by the peculiarity that John in the 19th chapter of his account of the gospel plainly indicates that Pilate after he had scourged Christ made another effort to set the Saviour free. According to John, then, a deliberate discussion took place between Pilate and the Jews after the scourging had been inflicted.

This variation in the accounts seems to indicate that the surrender of Christ to death on the cross as it is recorded by Matthew at this point is not to be regarded as the definitive, legally formulated, and official sentencing of Jesus but as a preliminary penalty which, should crucifixion prove to be inevitable for Him, would be a beginning of the infliction of that penalty and would at the same time leave room for substituting a more lenient treatment later.

Hence, in agreement with the opinion of many others, we also interpret the data of the Bible to mean that Pilate was acting more or less officially when, after Barabbas' release, he sentenced Jesus to death by crucifixion. The scourging constituted a suitable part of such a program, for the Romans adhered to the practice of scourging a prisoner before nailing him to a cross. This bloody introduction to the crucifixion is called by one writer: *praeparatio ad crucem* and also *medea mors,* or *medium supplicium.*[1] Interpreted, these phrases mean the formal preparation for the cross sentence and the transitional phase in a process designed to culminate in death. At the same time, we may think it very likely that the judge who hoped by means of this scourging to quiet the excited emotions of the mob, secretly hoped also that he would be able presently to return to the proposal he had suggested at first, and after the severe "chastisement"—which had not been supplanted by this scourging—to set Jesus free. At least, this would account for the fact that when Jesus stands before him later in abject misery, suffering grievously because of the scourging, Pilate accompanies the pathetic figure out of doors and attempts to

---

1. Titus Livius 33, 36. Referred to by Groenen, *op. cit.,* p. 372.

stir the feelings of the crowd by his well known: Behold the man. Only when that last appeal to humanity failed to elicit sympathy did the formal, definitive, and officially registered surrender to death on the cross ensue. Whoever pictures the historical sequence of the several events which took place here to his mind in this relationship will find in them an uncoerced alignment of the Biblical data.

In this way, then, the scourging was inflicted upon Jesus. We must know that this scourging in itself constituted terrible suffering. The Romans had named this the proper punishment for numerous breaches of law, but found the punishment so gruesome that they permitted it to accrue to Roman citizens only in the most extraordinary cases.

The manner in which this punishment was inflicted is not known well enough. We may accept the fact, it is true, that Jesus was not scourged in the Jewish manner (in which case the person being punished lay face forward upon the ground),[1] but in the Roman way. According to the descriptions given in numerous books, the scourged person was stripped down to the loins and was bound fast to a post or pillar in such a way that he had to stand with bent back and with his head bowed toward the ground. "In that way the first stroke had to succeed in drawing blood. Accordingly, we can easily understand that in some descriptions of scourgings which took place, we read that the strokes of the whip sometimes tore the flesh so badly that the human skeleton became visible as a result. . . . In order to aggravate the pain even more, barbs, pieces of bone, or knots were woven into the scourge, and in later periods, during the time of the persecution of the Christians, for instance, leaden bullets were fastened to the thongs."[2] We do not know to what extent these particulars held true of the scourging which was inflicted upon the Saviour. Scripture speaks very soberly of these things. It is not by means of an enhancement of the details of Jesus' physical suffering, but by an accentuation of the majesty, the love, the will to sacrifice on the part of the Christ of God that the Bible tries to delineate the Christ to us. By these means the Scriptures conduct us from the external things which are seen to the spiritual things which are

---

1. Deuteronomy 25:2.
2. Groenen, *op. cit.*, p. 375.

not seen. Spiritually considered, the feature which needs to be accentuated at this time is that now the blood of Christ was for the first time being driven out of Him by men. God had demanded that blood in Gethsemane. Now it is the people who cause it to flow.

Inasmuch as we are speaking about the blood of Christ at this time, it may not be out of place to say a thing or two here about the manner in which the blood of Christ is frequently raised for discussion in the church.

There are those who usually speak of the blood of Jesus Christ in a way which gives us the impression that for these the shedding of blood constitutes the whole of the suffering of Christ. For the spiritual conflict, for the life-long ministration of Christ's offices, for the struggle of His soul, for the tension of His active and passive obedience in such instances as these, which do Him no *physical* harm, these observers have no eye whatever. Always and again they are talking about the blood, about the dear and precious blood. Those other things they regard as merely being aids to the memory jotted down upon the blueprints of Christian dogmatics. But their mystical musing, their meditation and their temptation have no bearing on this.

Such is, however, a gruesome shortcoming. It can be explained in part by that general spiritual apathy which has a keener eye for the visible than for the invisible, and in part by the profound after-effects which the Roman Catholic leaven still exercised in the post-Reformation period. Nor has the epoch in which we live made good the defect. For while, on the one hand, the church has become lax in its dogmatic thinking, on the other hand, a group of "mystical" poets and artists—first by permission, later by request—are placing their esthetic loaves of shewbread upon the table of dedication in those many temples which an extra-ecclesiastical religion has established. In each of these groups a certain, so-called spiritual eroticism resides which prefers to accentuate the blood of Jesus rather than His soul, His soul rather than His spirit, and the humanity of Jesus as it is in its suffering rather than the hidden powers which inhere in Him as the Christ. That this is a disease in fact, we should not hesitate to say a sin, and that this represents a decadence in thinking needs no argument.[1] Hence, when we in this connection point emphatically to *the blood of Jesus Christ* we are not, we hope, thereby committing ourselves to the course pursued by the one-sided observers to which we have just referred. Surely, if we had wanted to go in that direction, we should have been denying the very trend of thought which has governed the content of this book. We would continue to insist on the fact then that the labor of the blood of Christ means nothing more than the labor of His soul. In the Bible those two terms are not separated from each other. If we acknowledge that Christ's passive and active obedience are of equal worth we must be willing to take upon our lips a statement which may sound rather blunt but which should seem very actually true to every Christian among us : namely, that a sermon of Jesus is of no less worth than an impaled hand of Jesus, and that a miracle of healing is as potent a messianic act of redemption as is the sweating and shedding of blood in Gethsemane and at Golgotha respectively. Or, to limit ourselves to the trial : the silence which Jesus maintained no less than three times is not a less influential act of redemption or a less productive act of mediatorship than is His experience of this terrible punishment of scourging. We may not put that asunder which God has joined together. Faith and eroticism may not for one moment be joined together.

Accordingly, when we in spite of these considerations ask that emphatic attention be given to the moment in which Christ's blood was first forcibly driven out of Him, we do so for a good reason and in obedience to the demands of the Scriptures.

We know that we may never segregate Christ from the place, and the time, and the stage of the history of revelation in which He appeared as our Mediator. God did not send Christ into the world at an arbitrarily determined time, but at the time chosen beforehand. Accordingly, God had all epochs issue in Jesus, and had all preceding eras serve as preparatory epochs for the coming of Christ. Just so God did not send Jesus to an arbitrarily determined place in the world, but revealed Him in *Israel*. And that people, too, was introduced in the world by God so that its life and its land might serve as a stage for messianic wonders, and

---

1. See my essay "Eros of Christus," which is included in *Christelijk letterkundige Studien*, Volume 2, U-M. Amsterdam.

in order that Christ might become manifest among that people and outside of it.

Observe from this point of view, Israel's entire service of worship is a shadow-service. Israel's religion had to point to Christ. That is why so much is said of the *sacrifice*. For the idea of sacrifice, the idea of shedding blood, is a separate moment in Israel's liturgy, and as such is strongly accentuated. We cannot for one moment understand the sense and meaning of that dark stream of blood which for centuries painted the road along which Israel traveled a deep red, and which drenched with gore the very ground on which this people had to walk, if we do not acknowledge that all this blood was pointing to Christ. His blood had to be shed, for without the shedding of blood, say the Scriptures, there can be no forgiveness. His blood had to be shed, for, say the Scriptures, *the soul is in the blood.* The blood of the second Adam had to flow, for the blood of the first Adam, say the Scriptures, began to flow the moment the soul entered into the clay-formed human body of the first. When the human body had been created on the sixth day, and God had breathed the soul into it, the blood began to course through its veins at the very moment in which life entered the dust. And just as the blood begins coursing in the human body at birth in a way quite different from the circulation which was present before, so in Genesis 1 the last act of the creation of God was the beginning of the circulation of the blood of humanity. God breathed life into the first Adam, and he thereby became "a living soul."

Nevertheless blood cannot continue flowing forever. The circulation of the blood began in Paradise, but must sometime have an end.

This is an immutable decree. If the person who was created in Paradise is to keep his ways uncontaminated by sin, he must attain to a different form of life. At the end of God's way there is a human being who according to body and spirit is mature. He is the heavenly man, the perfect man, who is no longer in process of becoming, but who *is*. This heavenly man must sometime exist without the earthly, circular movement of his created and pulsing blood. He is the man of the future. And this future man, this man of things perfected and completed, will no longer marry nor eat food. His entire form of life, his whole law of existence will differ from that which he has in time. Hence the circulation of blood will not take place in heaven. Such circulation is properly a part of the beginning of man, but not of his perfection.

Hence, if man had remained in the state of obedience, the circulation of blood would, according to modes of development which God has not revealed to us and concerning which we consequently will make no guesses, have ceased. Then, in a manner known only to God, the circulation of the blood would gradually have stopped, and man would have risen to that consummate form of life in which neither the sexual urge, nor the sense of hunger, nor the pulse-beat of the blood would have been the driving motives of life. The pulse-beat and the heart-beat are appropriate only in a world of time.

God's ideal, then, is a bloodless human being. Until this world has reached its consummation, of course, bloodless man will remain the poor pale human being who has sunk beneath the plane of ordinary life. But the bloodless man who has transcended the need for blood is the full, the rich, the perfect, the healthy man. Had man remained in the state of obedience, God would have visited him in a fatherly way, would have come at His own time to quiet the feverish course of the blood, and to effect the transition of man to a state of immutable *being*. Circulation would then be unnecessary to a man's body, inasmuch as that body would have transcended the need of it.

But—man fell into sin. Hence the stopping of that circulation of the blood which would otherwise have been normal was withheld. The sin which entered man's being kept him from developing into that bloodless condition of perpetual youth.

Accordingly, sin avenges itself very severely upon the human blood. When man had sinned God told him that he should surely die. In other words, God announced that separation would come between the soul and the body. Thus bodily death was instituted. Even in this, however, God's evangelical will unto grace was operative, for God introduced physical death into humanity: that is, God interposed physical death between the first sin and the punishment accruing to that sin, in order that in this way He might make room for a history lasting many epochs, a history consisting of cyclical movements, of the vacillations of life, of the circular course of blood and of those who bleed. And from the very beginning that history was directed to the Christ. That is to say that it was directed to Christ's blood and spirit. For Christ must now make His appearance in history in order that, on the one hand, He may die "in the blood," and on the other, that He may emerge triumphant over that blood. To suffer the penalty in the blood and at the same time to transcend the blood represents positive victory. Christ had to become the bloodless one in the sense that He had to become the absolutely poverty-stricken one. He had to suffer the dire stress of the blood to an infinite extent. But on the other hand He had also to become the bloodless one in that other sense, in that rich sense of the word, in which it refers to a second Adam who no longer is a *"living soul,"* but who becomes a *"life-giving spirit."* The Biblical sense of that phrase is in the main that He, the second Adam, will completely subject the bodily, earthly, temporal, and all that is moving, feverishly active, and in process of becoming, by force of the strong *will* of His perfect spirit.

You see, therefore, that the institution of physical death after the fall is a mighty act on the part of God. For by that act the stream of blood, and its continuous circulation, which originally should have been quieted in the blood-transcendent state of the blessedness of creation according to the covenant of works, is now being diverted to a different direction and is constrained to move toward death. It was God's gracious will that the blood of Adam and Eve should not immediately be parched by the firebrand of the punishment of hell, but that it should be limited to that circular course, to that "vicious circle" concerning which Ecclesiastes very grievously complained and concerning which we have spoken so often.[1] Accordingly we must apply everything that was said about that vicious circle in the preceding chapters of this book to the pulse-beat of the blood inherent in man and in mankind.

Yes, we may bring the whole of the teaching of that vicious circle to bear upon this discussion of human blood.

The circulation of the blood contains all the sorrow of the vicious circle. It represents a postponement of perpetual youth and perfect blessedness. But it also contains the joy and grace of the vicious circle. It represents the removal of perfect death and of existence in hell. Hence we can safely say that the law of the

---

1. See pp. 58 ff., 77, and 137 ff.

blood which governs and serves as a motive force to the life of all physical existence upon earth, is Christological, messianic, and subject to the law of the Gospel which Christ would send out into the world.

From this time on all movement of blood is directed to Christ. He is the first expositor of such movement. Accordingly, also, all shedding of blood from this time on is directed to Christ. Again He is the first expositor of this pouring out of the blood. And the whole of the long way of blood is the highway of my Lord Christ coming into the world.

When God instituted physical death into the world (the *returning* to dust, understand, and not the triumphant transcending together with the dust to the perfectly blessed life such as was promised in the covenant of works), His act was an act of punishment —for it was the result of sin—but it was an act of grace also. It was done for Christ's sake. The separation of soul and body— and this constituted the punishment—came in the place of that which had been promised at first: namely, the metamorphosis of soul and body, the glorification, the regeneration and renewing of both soul and body by the Spirit. But this again contains the element of grace: God fixes that returning to the dust as an inexorable law for many ages in order that in this way He might make room in the world for Christ. *Why room for Christ,* you ask? Because this Christ, later, would suffer the whole of death in His blood; because He would let the way of blood be figured forth in His own being, first through the law of punishment, and afterwards in order that as Prince of the Passover, as the second Adam, He with the "blood" (regarded now as the driving force of our physical life) might rise to victory and thus become the bloodless man of everlasting youth, of infinite power and of sound humanity. Thus would He become the blood-transcendent man of salvation.

That is why the *blood of Christ* is of such great significance. The course of death and life is perfectly described in the shedding of His blood and in its sacrifice. We cannot put the matter in a way which suggests that Christ's suffering consists of "two parts": a bodily—bloody—part, and spiritual-bloodless-part. The course of Christ's "blood" is perfectly governed by the will of His "spirit." "Bloody" and "bloodless" are opposite sides of the same thing. *The soul is in the blood*—that is the way the figurative language of the Old Testament expresses it in connection with the law of sacrifice. The Spirit is *active in the blood*—that is the statement which expresses the perfection of Christ as He *fulfills* the law of sacrifice in Himself and as He, by His blood, puts to rest the service of shadows.

The corollary of this promise naturally is that Christ's blood, therefore, must be seen in relationship to the statements of the Old Testament and in harmony with the language of all those bloody sacrifices which the old covenant demanded. But this premise also protests that Christ's blood speaks a language which far transcends the signs represented by those ancient sacrifices. Christ's *reality* goes higher and farther than the shadow of the Old Testament. Shadows are always more meager than the realities they symbolize.

For this reason, then Christ as Mediator had to give His blood, and had to give it personally, consciously, and spiritually as Mediator. In this respect, too, He must completely work out the task assigned to Him as the second Adam. That task was to again subject the coursing of the blood-stream to the will of God in order that, together with God's people—now included in the second Adam—He might attain to everlasting youth by the power and satisfaction of the sacrifice of Jesus Christ. Thus we can regard the restlessness of the blood of Christ as a separate element in His suffering, provided that we understand its direct relation to the labor of His spirit.

Blood *and* spirit. Both of them. It is in the *blood* that Jesus must fulfill the whole of the law of sacrifices. The circulation of the blood must in Him issue in death, be smothered in the bottomless depths of absolute death. He must descend into hell, and He must do that with the blood. To this extent the shedding of His blood represents passiveness, sacrifice, and the payment of penalty.

But because His eternal spirit must also exert its power in His shedding of blood, the dogma of His *passive* obedience in this matter must again remain united with the doctrine of His *active* obedience. True, His blood was taken; but it is also true that He Himself gave it, shed it, forced it out. He did this by the strength of His *will,* His personal, conscious *will.* Together with His blood, with the blood of the second Adam, with the blood of His whole church, with all the movement in the life of all His own, He labors in the direction of eternal youth, of eternal power, and of a blood-transcendent heaven.   That also is the sense Paul would convey by his significant expression: the second Adam is the *life-giving spirit.* Hence we would not present the moment of Christ's first shedding of blood by reason of the scourging of Pilate, that worldly judge, in a false light. Pilate does the scourging, yes, but *God* also does it. Pilate draws the blood, but God also by means of Pilate draws Jesus' blood. God demands the blood of the *second Adam.* As the first drops of blood stream from the bruised and furrowed back of my Lord Jesus, time is striving towards eternity. The life of the Passover is already pushing its way through the narrow gates of death, is raging through Jesus' swollen veins. Add to this the fact that Jesus sees approaching Him the terrible reality of that suffering which marks Him not only as sacrifice, not only as priest, but *also as temple.* For, according to the significant and well-conceived designation of one writer,[1] the law of sacrifice and its idea is *comprised* perfectly in Him. The concept of sacrifice is so perfectly comprised in Him because Christ is not merely the sacrifice, not merely the one who sacrifices, and not merely the temple in which the sacrifice is brought and in which the offer and the one who offers it come together, but because He is all three of these simultaneously. He is the *sacrifice,* for His blood must enter into death. He is the *one who sacrifices,* for He Himself must force His blood into the state of death. He is the *temple,* for His is not a partial possession of the spirit and consequently He, as the Bible itself tells us, must through the eternal spirit offer Himself up to God blameless.

By revealing to us that Christ is also the temple, the Scriptures teach us the truth of what was said above when we stated that the issue of the blood of Christ may not be separated from the labor of His soul but that the whole struggle of His spirit is contained in His blood. Now there are two ways in which the sacred temple may be defiled. We have alluded to the first already. That is the way of those who speak only of Christ's blood and who never or who at least never consciously speak of the spirit

---

1. Dr. Abraham Kuyper, *Van de Voleinding*, Volume 1, p. 47.

which labors in and through the blood. But we ourselves would be guilty of taking the second way to the profanation of the temple if we in our stress upon Christ's spiritual struggle—think of the outlaw, of the negation, of the mockery on the official mountain, of the vicious circle and its breaking, of the maschil, of His repeated silence—should refuse to see His *blood* streaming from Him. True, we must not take Christ's spirit out of His blood; but it is just as true that we should not take Christ's blood out of His spirit. We must give *both* elements full consideration.

To return now to the beginning. We pointed to the fact that in each of the *three* periods of Christ's suffering (the entering upon it, the passing through it, the conclusion of it), the subject of His blood comes to the foreground. And is there a difference? Yes, there is a difference, and a good reason for it in each instance. The reason is that in no single deed of Christ's suffering may the elements of spiritual labor and of the shedding of blood be silent. As long as Christ is not bound and therefore may move around freely among God's people, in God's world, and in David's city, He must fulfill His passion in spirit and in blood. That is why in the first division, the entire struggle of His passion simply had to be both spiritual and bloody. For it is God, and God alone[1] who drives that blood out of the Christ. Now Christ is bound and is brought before the judge. Again His blood is taken, and again a spiritual struggle has been fulfilled before that blood is shed. After awhile He will be crucified. That cross, too,—think, for instance, of His seven words, of the great stress which soul and spirit undergo because of His being forsaken— represents a spiritual conflict which issues afterwards in the sacrifice of His blood. The harmony, you see, is perfect; spirit and blood, invisible and visible sacrifice—the whole Christ.

Now we can say this besides, about that *difference* between these three instances of the shedding of His blood. In Gethsemane Christ offers His blood only because He confronts the *possibility* of the cross. Upon Golgotha He offers it because of the bitter *actuality* of the cross. Between these two[2] comes the scourging: a situation in which the death on the cross seems to hover over

1. See *Christ in His Suffering*, p. 370.
2. That is why Golgotha also was placed over against Gethsemane in *Christ in His Suffering*, p. 369.

the confines of *possibility* and *actuality*. For we observed, you
remember, that Pilate seemed to be making a *beginning* of the execution of the death sentence, but that he also, both at the time
of the first proposal[1] and the later one wanted to use the scourging
as a means of averting the crucifixion. The cross, accordingly,
remained a mere possibility. But Christ's blood—and well He
knows it—on this occasion falls upon the boundary line between
life and death, between a return to life and a movement in the
direction of death.

We see, then, that Christ strove to the point of shedding blood
for this reason too: namely, that He might, while standing upon
the border line between the two, make the good choice, the choice
of obedience to God, and of faithful love to His people.

How sublimely great this matter! To make the good choice
when He knew that no other was possible—that is difficult, but
it is not the most difficult thing. That had been the situation in
Gethsemane. There He had seen God's might, and He had been
bruised by it. He was compelled to do so. He simply *had* to. That
would be the situation at Golgotha. There He would see the force
of rams and bullocks, a very great host of them, and would be
bruised. He would have to, simply have to choose death. But
now, in the presence of these soldiers, it is *possible* for Him *to
turn back.* He has read the uncertainty written in Pilate's eyes.
He knows it is possible for Him to soften the heart of the man.
Meanwhile, He can now *feel,* keenly, what it means to give one's
blood to man, to dogs. Christ, wouldst Thou turn back still? The
necessity of the crucifixion and the possibility of escape lie side
by side; wouldst Thou still persuade Pilate to release Thee Christ,
O Man, this hour can gratify Thee. Once Thou didst say that
the scourging was most certainly the beginning of the crucifixion,[2]
but it seems now that the scourging may prove to be postponement
first, and complete escape from the cross next. Is this not a pleasant surprise, O Christ? What of one unfulfilled prophecy! That
is quickly forgotten, and life is very sweet. You have read the
message gleaming in Pilate's eye. Just notice—he is perfectly willing to risk another attempt to save Thee. He will tell the Jews:
mark now, there is a law which says: *pars pro toto.*[3] Look, here

---

1. To chastise Jesus first and release Him then, p. 418-19.
2. Matthew 20:19.
3. A part instead of the whole.

is a part of His blood; see, it is gushing down His back—suppose we let this suffice; take the part for the whole: *ecce homo*—let Him go now—make Him a present of the rest of His blood. Pilate is still hesitating, Jesus. But He—nay, not He but God— wishes to keep Thee on that boundary line between necessity and possibility of escape. One word, a single impression upon Pilate's soul, and—the world will go on as before!

Then the whip screamed through the air. The body quivered: thereupon blood, more blood, and excruciatingly tortured flesh.

Christ stood on the boundary line between the land of freedom and the land of necessity, on the dividing line between the possibility of return and the necessity of laboring on to the point of blood. But, even as He stood here He fought the fight according to the Spirit. He said *yea*, to His God, and *yea* to the souls of the sheep. He confronted alternatives, and alternatives are always tantalizing to the human mind. But even as He stands over against those alternatives He makes the one good choice. He makes that choice while He is consciously expunging His blood, His own blood, the blood of all who believe. In this He is great and wonderful. Out of possibilities He creates God's realities. To accept God's will and to preserve God's justice as He makes this choice is to be perfectly obedient as man. To change possibilities into God's actualities, what is that but to be the Son of God, the ever-creating Word? How strangely warm it is becoming here in this public square. The air grows oppressive. I know that I am standing very near my Lord and God. I hear the crash of thunder; an act of creation is taking place. He speaks and it is done. He commands and it stands fast. Think! Suddenly a cross appears. The possibility of His cross which from eternity He has been conceiving, He now makes an actuality. The first word of the Bible has been superseded. What, pray, can a stroke of the whip do to Him now? He makes His angels flaming fires. On flying horses they sail high over the scourging. Protect me from the awfulness of this—a creative act is going on here. Hell is posting theses on its gates about *possibility,* and about Pontius Pilate, cunctator.[1] God be feared: neither the gates nor the ideas of hell have ever prevailed against Him. Not even the ideas, for He

---

1. Play upon the phrase "Fabrius cunctator" — Fabius, the hesitant one who does not know which way to turn.

found that these weighed as heavily as gates. If I conceive it
well, that also was present in my God when He created the world.
Ideas were as concrete and as real as gates. One idea cannot out-
wit the Christ; a possibility cannot divert Him from an actuality.
In His spirit He united possibility and actuality, for as Creator
He first separated these two from each other. How troublesome
He is to you, Pilate. Your wife is possessed of the devil, or is it
of a demon? You feel a draft in your palace. A wind is blowing;
I say it is the wind of the first day. Unless I put it that way, I
cannot believe that I have any faith, any faith. . . . But go now,
Pilate, and go, Claudia, and too, all ye devils. In His creative
power He is perfect as God is perfect. He is that also in the art
of living, of realizing the God He is in His humanity. Perfect in
the art of living—and in the art of dying. His dying will presently become a creative act. The world revolves in its cyclical course.
But the Logos was made flesh. Saint Augustine and the host of
prophets and a small catechism and theology—offense and folly,
power and wisdom.

Be quiet now. Neither the gates nor the ideas of heaven have
ever failed to prevail against Him. He has apprehended by Himself and by His own ideas. That is why He persists so obstinately: the Son of man *must* be delivered to the Gentiles, must be
scourged, and then crucified.[1] Make no further attempts, Pilate;
you have not a chance against God. That which you have in your
hands today is not a living soul but a life-giving spirit. The art of
living! Yes, that is the power of the Creator!

The power of the Creator, indeed. The Creator clings to His
ideas. He will not yield His honor to another, nor His praise to
graven images, for these are but so many pieces of fiction departing from His ideas. I think I know now what a paradox is. If
this Christ is God, is Creator, is one who realizes His own ideas,
then the statement, "I shall give my honor to no other," is now
literally translated into the sense: "I shall give my shame to no
other, nor my cross to Claudia's graven images." I think I can
understand now why He is so determined: I have seen the *Will*
in action. In the beginning this Will created heaven and earth.
The day is void and without form, but something will appear
presently. The story has not yet ended.

---

1. Matthew 20:19.

Christ Caricatured By the World

CHAPTER TWENTY-EIGHT

Christ Caricatured By the World

● *Then the soldiers of the governor took Jesus
into the common hall, and gathered unto him
the whole band of soldiers. And they stripped
him, and put on him a scarlet robe. And when
they had platted a crown of thorns, they put
it upon his head, and a reed in his right hand:
and they bowed the knee before him, and
mocked him, saying Hail, King of the Jews!
And they spit upon him, and took the reed,
and smote him on the head.*
MATTHEW 27:27-30.

WE concluded our previous chapter with a reference to
Christ as one who faithfully works out His own ideas.
Even to say this is a very serious matter. For Christ to
feel it was far more serious still, for it required scourging and
called a cross into being. Very serious, yes. And that is why it
is so severely profaned by the brutal mockery conveyed by the
statement: Christ is being *caricatured*.

Do not shun that word—an admonishment I would give myself
also as I pronounce it. The incarnation of the Word, the concealment of God—those are things accompanied by the most extreme
consequences conceivable. To name the word *caricature* is to be
reminded of cartoons, of libelous pamphlets, and, as we think of
these we do indeed feel like saying: Do not introduce that word
into this discussion. However, you must not forget that the age
of Augustus and of Tiberius was an age in which caricaturists—
and very good ones they were—abounded. Moreover, even if this
had not been the case, the age in which Christ was born knew how
to make use of its own devices for mocking and ridiculing Him.

525

Whoever wants to appreciate the meaning of that mockery is compelled, accordingly, to translate the forms which the soldiers employed to give expression to their enmity against Jesus into the language of his own times. Hence, when I think of those soldiers of Pilate who are busying themselves around the Saviour I think of my own world, of its presses, of its cartoonists, and of its jesters. For one who speaks of the Eternal One-in-Hiding, the scientific repudiation of an "anachronism" is anything but scientific. In the modes of expression of our own day, the game which the soldiers played over against Jesus would have been carried on in the press, on the stage, and in the revue.

Yes, He who realizes, who works out, His own ideas is being caricatured. This must have constituted the severest conceivable suffering for His spirit, for the caricature which is conceived and executed at the prompting of enmity always represents a working out of false ideas, and, in this case, a distortion of the ideas of its suffering victim. In the preceding chapter, we saw the majesty of Christ Jesus subjected to the tyranny of the rod. Now that majesty recedes behind cartoons. This, too, represents the Suretyship; in this also the Word battles against the false word, and God's expressed Image is buried under the symbols of caricature. There is not a single form which life can assume in which the labor of the Surety does not operate.

I hear someone say that this is not the first time Jesus was caricatured. That is true. He was caricatured in the Sanhedrin. There Christ as a prophet was subjected to caricature. But the Sanhedrin is after all only a regional institution; it has no international ramifications. The Sanhedrin was even less than regional in character; on this day we should have to say that it became definitely regionalistic in its insistence upon peculiarly local emphases. Hence Christ cannot be brought into world-caricature before the Sanhedrin. But, says someone, how about Herod-Esau? Yes, he also caricatured Christ. However, Esau, no more than the Sanhedrin, bestrides the world. His gorgeous robes will never be shown at the world's fair, unless . . .

Not unless Rome sends it on—to the world's stage. For Rome is the world empire. We have discussed that before.[1]

---

1. See pp. 222, 298, and 419.

And that is exactly what is about to happen. Christ is being robed in the garments of caricature by the soldiers of Pontius Pilate. It is possible that they have taken over Herod's robe. If they did not actually use his, they certainly imitated it. Hence when Christ is being mocked in this way inside of the private chamber of the official representative of the world-empire and of the world-might, He is being inducted into the world-caricature. Naturally, this does not make sense to a person who says: But a soldier, after all, is only a soldier. However, he who sees that prophecy is active in the passion of Christ will never say that.

The Saviour is inducted into world - caricature. Rome represents the world. And this happens to Him in the moment of perfect seriousness.

In respect to that seriousness, this: the blood of Christ has been forced out of Him. First in Gethsemane, now here. In the garden of Gethsemane God exacted the blood of Jesus in perfect seriousness, in the terrible tension of awful judgment. At that time the angels held their peace, and covered their faces. Such was the holy seriousness of the matter! Now, however, Christ's blood is being taken and driven from Him by human beings. This was the sequel to what had begun in the garden. And now we hear the laughter of mockery. It is diabolical laughter, it is the brutal ridicule of soldiers, and it is mocking the perfect outlaw.

The blood of Christ was first placed under the pressure of God; now it is being laid on the table of Satan. The guests at that table are toasting each other in it. Meanwhile He, who is called Adam, approaches His cross on which He will offer up His blood to God and to people, and on which He will lay it before Satan's eyes in the scales of God. The Bible tells us what happened after the scourging. When Pilate had surrendered Christ for that scourging, and when these "penalties" had been inflicted, the soldiers decided to have some further fun with this prisoner. Why not make a joke out of the event of the day? You can read from their faces the disdain they have for all Jews in general and for this Jew in particular. They arrange a scene in which their eagerness to mock this self-vaunted king can be satisfied. They call together "the whole band of soldiers." This means that they call together all those who happened in that moment to be present in the neighborhood. They are an ingenious lot. Why not caricature that self-arrogated king? Caricatures are cheap. The soldiers hit upon the idea of dressing the Nazarene pretender to the crown in the garb of a king. Why in that of a king, you ask? Well, the trial had repeatedly raised that point. Pilate's interview, the accusation on the part of the Jews, and Christ's own apology all tended to accentuate the office of king in reference to the Christ. A pretty incident, indeed. A prisoner who had wanted to be king. Look! he is a ridiculously pathetic figure. They know all about it.

Just notice. Over there someone is already fetching Him a scarlet robe, a soldier's robe. The garment is not a "new, freshly dyed cloak"[1] but very probably a "worn-out, badly faded and dirty one" whose color—purple or a kind of crimson—could no longer be recognized.[2] Yes, this coarse soldier's uniform makes a rather good imitation of a king's robes. With the help of a little imagination it might very well be regarded as the cloak which a king wears.

Come to think of it, though, a king must have a crown too. Where get the crown? No difficulty about that at all. The neighborhood afforded reeds having barbs on them which would serve the purpose beautifully. It is not unlikely that they made use of "a low, densely thistled reed, which resembles heather, and which grows so rank on the uncultivated bottomland of Palestine that it is used now and was used long ago as fuel. This helps us to understand how the soldiers had those thorns on hand for their purpose.[3] From these reeds one of those present—be careful, man, you might hurt your finger!—begins weaving a crown. It is put on Jesus' head. The idea, in the first place, is not to "cause Jesus pain, but to mock Him by this gift of a king's crown."[4]

But the king is not yet fitted out completely. He has to have a sceptre, too. Otherwise the resemblance is not complete. Accordingly, they give Him an imitation of a sceptre; they put a reed into Jesus' hand; a very neat sceptre it is! Some think that this reed by its very pliability perfected the mockery. After all, a true sceptre always retained its firmness and rigidity. But others sup-

---

1. Groenen, *op. cit.*, p. 382.
2. Ibid.
3. Ibid, p. 383.
4. Grosheide, *op. cit.*, p. 347. He refers to Dalman, *Orte und Wege*, p. 210.

pose that a kind of sea-reed was employed which, in contrast to the reed that grows in swamps such as we know it, is pronouncedly rigid. The fact that the soldiers later used this reed to beat Him makes the second supposition more tenable.

Thus the matter of the caricatured king is quickly "dispatched." The rest of the fun is up to the soldiers. Look, they are already standing at attention; they go through their paces before Jesus; they bow their heads as they pass Him; give Him the military salute. And with a mock display of respect in their voice they shout: "Hail, king of the Jews!"

Notice, Jews, that in the first place this is a defeat for you. You have hardly "won" your game before your joy in the victory returns as a boomerang to strike you. True, these soldiers are mocking the Nazarene, but in Him they are mocking your people. You have rejected Him, but they continue to count Him as one of you.

As for Christ, how does He find it possible to locate His Father among all these murderers? How can His hand find the altar, when His head is being wounded by thorns, and when a reed is being pressed into His hand? It has been said that Christ did not keep the reed in His hand, inasmuch "as Matthew alone tells us that the reed was put into Jesus' hand as a sceptre, Mark speaking only of a reed which was used to strike the Lord. In this respect again we need look for no significant difference between the two presentations. It may be that they attempted to put the reed into the Lord's hand, but He certainly did not want to keep hold on it, inasmuch as in no single respect could He take an active part in the mockery directed against Him. . . . Hence we may suppose that the Lord's refusal to hold the reed in His hand is what induced the soldiers to strike Him on the head with it."[1] This interpretation has its appealing features especially because it shows us how Christ's active obedience immediately leads Him to His passive compliance. For if He does *not* keep the reed in His hand, He is beaten with it.

Now each of the several threads involved in the trial meets at a point in this induction of Christ into world-caricature. Herod is here again. The soldiers have conducted their sport in imitation of Herod. Naturally, a few of the soldiers went along on the

---

1. Groenen, *op. cit.*

visit to Herod, and they told all about it to their fellows. Besides, Herod permitted Jesus to go when the garment of mockery was still hanging over His shoulders. In other words, these Roman soldiers simply take over Herod's method of mocking. That is why this mockery represents a collaboration of Esau with the enemy against Jacob.

In the second place, the idea of Christ, the outlaw, after it has first been officially worked out by the judge, as we noticed before, is now taken over by the soldiers. Pilate should never have allowed this to take place. His discipline should have kept the men from doing it. But Christ has once and for all been placed outside of the law, and the soldiers cannot be expected to deal differently with Him than the others. The trial of Christ begins with the mockery of a servant of Annas, who strikes Him on the cheek. At the conclusion of the trial that one servant has become multiplied. And so have the blows.

In the third place, we have here another instance of the *forgotten chapter* to which we alluded. The only thing the soldiers can think of ridiculing is Christ's *kingship*. Matters concerning kings are more in their line than are matters involving prophets or priests. They are attracted to what is immediately before their eyes. Hence Christ appeals to them solely as an ill-fated *king*. That is all they can understand about Him. Again, you see, only the kingship of Christ's threefold office is given any attention. The Sanhedrin's way of putting the issue, of talking about the messianic question in a purely political sense, has its logical conclusions, for of Christ's three offices only that of the king is now being preserved. And this means that He is being torn asunder, that His soul is being scourged.

In connection with this third point, we should name a fourth. By means of the mockery on the part of the soldiers the universal Christ is being driven into a sectarian corner. Just who is it that is receiving these blows? A second Jacob? A second David? A second Melchizedek? A second Joshua? No, He is the second Adam. Nothing could be more universal, and nothing more cosmical. He wants to be the second Adam, the founder of the new mankind; He wants to be the king, not of a provincial group, not of a sect, not of a closed club, but of the world. He would be king of that new mankind. But all this does not take away the truth that in the world-caricature He appears solely as the king of the Jews. In this feature, you see, Christ's ambition to a universal kingdom is made ridiculous by those who degrade Him to the plane of an ill-fated potentate over a handful of Jews who had already for some time counted for little in the world. Oh, the wonder of clinging to the feast of Pentecost under such circumstances, the wonder of His farewell addresses in all of their cosmopolitan sweep!

In the fifth place, we have in this instance the phenomenon of Christ's first shedding of blood. In our preceding chapter we called this instance of the shedding of the *blood* of Christ the beginning of that divine deed which will reverse the course of the blood and point the way from death back to life. Now the blood of the Lamb begins to flow. This is the meeting place of all epochs, the turning point of the ages. But in this meeting place of the centuries, and at this crossroad of all times in reference to both nature and spirit, Christ finds the company of Psalm 35 in the society of drunkards and scoffers. When this blood *began* to flow, wise men were present, and shepherds, and a star. Now there are only devils around Him; they grin maliciously; and the God of the stars holds His peace. Pray, where is Thy God? It has been said that "the scourging which was inflicted upon Jesus dishonored Him, drove Him out of the society of human beings. Involuntarily we think of the angel which drove Adam and Eve out of Pa.'adise."[1] But if Adam had been here, He would have said to the second Adam: It is better to fall into the hands of God than into those of men. When Adam was driven out of Paradise by the angel, no one was there to mock. The hush of awful seriousness lay on the face of heaven and of earth; the clouds penned a piece of secret writing: *mene, tekel, upharsin*: weighed, numbered, and found wanting. The breach, the break had come but today while the second Adam is being driven out of Paradise, and even out of the wilderness, now that He is shown the door even in the house of common grace, and now that He accordingly is being humiliated far worse than the first Adam was—now heaven makes no threat, and the clouds write nothing. No, the sun shines at its brightest, is eager to make its circuit. Besides, this is the day of the Passover. The seriousness with which the first Adam was sent out far out-

---

1. Grosheide, *op. cit.,* p. 346.

weighs that which overhangs this byplay of mockery with which
the second Adam is accompanied on His journey to a dry and arid
death. Yes, that whip is but an extension of the drawn sword
which defended the gate of Paradise. But this appendage has been
dipped in the poison of Satan and of Cain. Jesus must discern the
sword of *God* in that whip. Here, in this inner room into which
they have conducted Him, He must confess that He is the great
Samson, battling against the angels and the drawn sword, and
laying His hand on the gate of Paradise. Here in this inner room,
the tree of life must beckon Him; He must go there as the second
Adam to eat and to give of His fruit.

That is why *faith* is necessary for Christ when, as the second
Adam, He confesses that He is the Mediator. He must have that
faith now. The Baptist is not here to say: I dare not baptise. Christ
is not in the wilderness where Satan tells Him: Come now, let us
have a serious talk together. The angels and the animals do not
come to Him now to serve Him. Simon Peter does not pose his
satanic objections. Moses and Elias are not here as they were upon the mountain. And, hence, to believe under those circumstances,
that He is the second Adam, the central man, the world symbol,
the greater-than-Abel and the pleroma of all that was real in the
ages gone by—that was very difficult. To believe that when there
is nothing but caricature around Him and when all prophetic,
priestly, and kingly mountains and all accursed and withered fig
trees recede from His sight—yes, that is infinitely difficult. It was
grievously hard labor for Jesus Christ to unravel His faith in His
own importance and in the sublime power of the cross from these
clever caricaturists. This represented a marvelous active obedience governed by passive obedience.

But He believed, nevertheless. Therefore we say of this Surety
and Mediator: *ecce deus.* For even as He stood in that inner court,
and even while He was being mocked by the soldiers, He saw God,
the angels, Paradise, the vistas of open fields and the mountains
and valleys of Genesis 1 and 3. I cannot prove that: fortunately
not. I can only believe it. For He both speaks and holds His
peace about that which He has *seen* and *heard.* He is my God.[1]
Moreover, I can only *believe* that He saw Himself also in the state

---

1. John 3.

of His spiritual nakedness. He believed Himself to be God when He was being made a lesser one than Abel by the soldiers of Pilate. Had it not been told Him long ago that His blood would be counted as less than Abel's blood? He knew that, and He nodded imperceptibly with His head. Now He had become inferior to Abel. God still takes some pains about the blood of Abel; a theophany can issue from that. Glorious Abel, favored of God, beautiful in death. Abel—an appropriate burial, a funeral oration delivered from heaven, and sublime seriousness. But for Jesus? Quiet everywhere, and devoted attention to the caricaturists. My God, my God, why dost Thou forsake me? Nay, do not answer yet: "My mouth shall I not open, while the ungodly is over against me; but a fire is kindled within me; my grief is increased."

Thereupon the Christ took courage, the courage of the Surety's heart. I cannot prove that, fortunately not. I can only believe it. He confronted *His people* so that He might see them. He knew that only upon the condition that this hour should sometime come, had common grace spread out a tolerable bed for Adam to lie upon instead of a bed of thorns. Of this He was very sure. Hence He bore the thorns and kept an awful silence. He would put a judicial basis under the structure of common grace and would kindle the fire of grace under the floor of the common judgment. He bore it all. There He stood in that poor inner court upon which the sun beat down. There He stood, greatly forsaken. Thereupon He in His spirit strode through the whole world and in His spirit saw the great separation. In His vast dream the thorns were being plucked out of every rosebed. Only roses remained. And even the corn poppies were being plucked out of the stubble fields on the other side of the world's area. There only the thorns remained. With a grim earnestness Christ drew His schism through all the worlds. He did it with His will and with His word. Of the mingled sphere of common grace—tough, persisting interplay of thorns and roses as it was—He made a hell and also a heaven, an unmixed hell and also an unmixed heaven, places giving rise solely to thistles and places giving birth only to roses.

Thereupon He was in great haste to reach His cross. To Pilate He had nothing more to say. He felt Himself to be very strong. For He had seen His own. He knew that they were scoffers, foolhardy rebels against God, Satan's objects of caricature. With His eye fixed upon them He said:

> *You* caused me all this pain;
> Know well it was your deed,
> The insult, mockery, disdain,
> The crown of thorns, the reed!

It is true. I have been the one who caused this. For my sake He was mocked. He endured our caricaturing.

Now love, and faith, and hope also proceed to write upon the clouds the sign of the Son of man, and the sign is this: the very head which now wears the crown of thorns, and the very hand which now holds a reed, will some day wear a golden crown and carry a sharp sickle (Revelation 14). Hence we would remember Him long, Him and His crown of thorns. We would weep and would laugh. For His being mocked earns for us the crown of honor. Christ, we will remember Thy crown of thorns, and Thy being caricatured, when we sing

> We raise our heads in confidence
> For we shall wear a crown of glory
> For Thy Name's sake, O Lord, for Thy Name's sake alone.

We would laugh, not in consonance with the soldiers, but in harmony with the believing Abraham.[1]

---

1. The author concludes the chapter with a sonnet of Heiman Dullaart in which the poet presents the spectacle of the caricatured Christ in Herod's court. The authentic art of the poem defies a faithful translation—The Tranlator.

Christ Condemned

CHAPTER TWENTY-NINE

Christ Condemned

● *Pilate therefore went forth again, and saith unto them, Behold, I bring him forth to you, that ye may know that I find no fault in him. Then came Jesus forth, wearing the crown of thorns, and the purple robe. And Pilate saith unto them, Behold the man! When the chief priests therefore and officers saw him, they cried out, saying, Crucify him, crucify him. Pilate saith unto them, Take ye him and crucify him: for I find no fault in him. The Jews answered him, We have a law, and by our law he ought to die because he made himself the Son of God. When Pilate therefore heard that saying, he was the more afraid. And went again into the judgment hall, and saith unto Jesus, Whence are thou? But Jesus gave him no answer. Then saith Pilate unto him, Speakest thou not unto me? knowest thou not that I have power to crucify thee, and have power to release thee? Jesus answered, Thou couldest have no power at all against me, except it were given thee from above: therefore he that delivered me unto thee hath the greater sin. And from thenceforth Pilate sought to release him: but the Jews cried out, saying, If thou let this man go, thou art not Caesar's friend: whosoever maketh himself a king speaketh against Caesar. When Pilate therefore heard that saying, he brought Jesus forth, and sat down in the judgment seat in a place that is called the Pavement, but in the Hebrew, Gabbatha. And it was the preparation of the passover, and about the sixth hour: and he saith unto the Jews, Behold your King! But they cried out, Away with him, away with him, crucify him. Pilate saith unto them, Shall I crucify your King? The chief priests answered, We have no king but Caesar. Then delivered he him therefore unto them to be crucified.*

JOHN 19:4-16a.

THE drama is moving to its conclusion. Our second volume has almost been written. The last step in the action which cursed the Lamb of God as being impure, and that in the very hour in which the passover lambs were being brought into the temple of God, is now approaching.

In the preceding chapter we observed that the mockery on the part of the soldiers but repeated all the leading ideas which had governed the trial of Jesus. The same holds true now. Again there is a recapitulation, a summary of the things which have held our attention throughout. That summary was drawn up for the soldiers in the first instance; for the judge in this last one.

Yes, a recapitulation was presented by the judge. This is a grievous thing. The judge, in his last official action again *passes in review* the entire, tedious course of the passion, accentuating each feature sharply and clearly. To Christ this constitutes a temptation. He is exhausted; His blood has been taken from Him; His soul is groping for something on which to rest—and can find that resting point only in God who withholds Himself from Him. In spite of this, however, He must experience it all *again*. We can say that everything is being done once more. Who would dare to say that Satan, the tempter, is not active in this? And God, He who proves all things? They have their reasons for tempting and proving the Christ. One can always find people in the world who are able to withstand a first temptation of Satan and to sustain the first trial of God, but who invariably succumb when the affliction is repeated. He who would subdue a strong man must make repeated attacks, he must persevere; he must follow the first round by a second, and the second by a third. Had the Christ been a man having finite strength, He would, even though He had withstood the first attack of hell and Satan, certainly have quailed before this recapitulation.

But we shall see that He remained unmoved up to the very end. God's repetitions and Satan's recapitulation harm Him not at all.

Pilate had withdrawn into his palace and had in the meantime surrendered Jesus to the sport of the soldiers. But did he have peace of mind? It may be that his wife discussed the matter of that dream with him further. Certainly his conscience troubled him. Besides—as we suggested before—it is possible that he was

deliberating the plan of making a last attempt to release the Nazarene after the scourging which had been given.

Accordingly he returns after a while and seizes his last opportunity. The Jews have remained on hand to see the outcome of the
affair. As yet they have no definite assurance and they refuse to
believe that their attempt has succeeded until their eyes tell them as
much. And, as a matter of fact, things were pointing in the wrong
direction the moment Pilate made his appearance. For, as a general rule, a person who had been scourged was immediately taken to
the cross and led away. Apparently that is not the course which
events are to take in this instance. The Nazarene is being led out
of doors again. Pilate, then, has not yet concluded to surrender
Him to the brutes who want Him.

What can the man have in mind? Well, they did not have to
wonder long. He has not yet wholly weakened. He accompanies
Jesus out of doors in order to make a display of His misery. He
lets Jesus keep the clothes which the soldiers have put on Him; in
other words, in the very condition in which Pilate found Him, he
takes the Saviour with him outside.

See, the Saviour comes. He comes in the robe of mockery; the
crown of thorns rests on His head; He is bowed down beneath the
force of the scourging. You ask why Pilate did not first have this
robe removed from Him, inasmuch as it loudly protested that in
this hall of justice the grossest arbitrariness of the soldiers was
being officially condoned. The answer is that Pilate hopes to profit
by presenting the pathetic spectacle of this miserable man to the
eyes of the crowd. He wants to present Jesus in all His nakedness,
and accordingly he says to the Jews: Ecce homo, behold, there is
the man. Why does Pilate say this, you ask? One interpretation is
that he wants to excite sympathy. He thinks that a public exhibition of the pathetic figure of the man will amount to pouring oil
upon the waves. Others think less favorably of Pilate. These suppose that Pilate is making a public exhibition of Christ solely to
assure the Jews that in any event they will never again be troubled
by this man. A man who has been decorated in this fashion—such
is Pilate's terminology—and a man who is in a condition as pathetic as this man is will never in all his life succeed in making an
impression. Now, what more do they want? Surely, this had better be the end of the matter.

Again, we need not choose one of these alternative interpretations. The two are not mutually exclusive. Pilate's whole desire is to be rid of the case, to escape its consequences, hence, any means which furthers that end is welcome to him.

But, to go on. Is Pilate "successful"? Does his *ecce homo* help him?

Over against those who think that Pilate erred in his choice of approaches and that he said the wrong thing at this time, we would reply that at first his words did succeed in achieving the expected results. Remember that the 6th verse of Chapter 19 of John's gospel indicates precisely who those were that immediately rebelled against Pilate's plea for sympathy. They were the high priests and the counselors. This specific reference is not the same as that given in Verse 40 of Chapter 18. There an emphatic reference has it: Then cried they all again, saying, *Not this man, but Barabbas.*[1] Accordingly, in that instance it was the people who together with their leaders lifted their voices against Jesus. Now, however, the people seemed to be silent; they seemed somewhat hesitant. Hence the leaders are just so much more eager to have their say. The people have suggested that they are inclined to give way; here and there a wave of sympathy moves over the crowd; a change of attitude can be seen in their faces. Now the leaders, who fear such a shift in popular opinion, immediately react. More vehemently than before they raise the cry, Crucify him, crucify him.[2] But Pilate refuses to let his chance slip away from him as easily as that. Not without pathos—for the people are present here, and whoever would move the people to this or that end gets a long way by means of pathos and sentiment—he once more declares emphatically that he finds no fault in Jesus. Why this concerted demand for a death sentence? Let the leaders take care of the matter themselves. If they want to, why, let them proceed to crucify Jesus. Naturally, Pilate does not mean to say by this that the Jews must or may crucify Jesus upon their own authority (crucifixion was not a Jewish form of punishment), but he means to say that he does not want to shoulder the responsibility which they themselves

---

1. We agree with those who suppose that the word *all* in John 18:40 which is included in certain manuscripts properly belongs there. For arguments in support of this, see among others Zahn, *Das Ev. des Joh.*, 3, 4, 1912, p. 636.
2. See Verse 15 in which the high priest and not the people has the last word.

refuse to accept. To this the Jewish priests and Sanhedrin immediately reply that they are perfectly willing to accept the responsibility. Even though we may not crucify him, they say in effect, it
is true that he has done something which according to our law deserves the death penalty; he has made himself the Son of God.

In this instance truth scores a victory. While studying the out-
set of the transactions between the Jews and Pilate, we observed
that the Jews said nothing about the charge of blasphemy which
in the Sanhedrin had been arrived at as the important accusation.
Instead, the Jews immediately gave a political color to the matter
in Pilate's presence. In other words, they transposed the Messiahship of Jesus from the first to the second table of the law. They
degraded the Saviour.[1] But now that Pilate is making a last effort
to release Him, they take recourse to their last word; they shoot
their last arrow. Now they give expression to the official charge:
Well, yes, according to our law, He is guilty of blasphemy, and
among us that is a capital crime.

This is indeed a victory for truth. Before Jesus is condemned
by the government, He is again transferred from the second table
of the law to the first. Before Pilate's tribunal *also,* acknowledgment is finally made of the fact that Jesus of Nazareth is not concerned in matters affecting Caesar, but that He is concerned in the
cause of the honor and revelation of the living God. Undoubtedly, this acknowledgment gladdened the Christ, even though the
gladness came with trembling. For it is this very acknowledgment
which drives Him immediately to death.

That it does so appears very soon. For *when Pilate heard this
word, he was the more afraid.* Why afraid? Because of superstition? Is he somewhat bound still to the notions of Roman paganism which continued to honor gods and a son of the gods? Does
Pilate have something in common with the centurion who says of
Jesus a little later: Truly this man was the son of God?[2] Or is it
that Pilate fears only the *results,* knowing that as soon as this element becomes a factor in the situation, the fanaticism of the Jews
will become quite uncontrollable.

---

1. See p. 315.
2. See Mark 15:39, and Matthew 27:54. The translation "a son of the gods"
is more faithful to the original than the rendering "the son of God." We shall
discuss this in the next volume of this work.

We dare not make a choice between these possibilities. Pilate's soul has thrown no light upon its inner recesses, and again we need not choose one or the other of the alternatives; again they do not exclude each other.

Instead, we can better attend to the results which followed upon Pilate's increased concern and aggravated fear. He approaches Jesus and says to Him: Whence art thou? That question is not to be regarded as springing from a sincere interest, and even less as an attempt on Pilate's part to personally understand and accept Jesus. Pilate's intent is simply to try to get an understanding of the background to the conflict which obtains between Jesus and the Jews. They call Him the Son of God; He calls Himself that also. It is about that that Pilate wishes to inquire. In effect, his question amounts to this: On what basis can the man's influence be explained? What is the secret of his success?

But Jesus makes no reply. It is precisely because of Jesus' silence that we can know that Pilate's question was not born from a heart which was yearning for salvation, for such a question never reaches God too late. Pilate's question was simply another request for information about the nature of the conflict existing between Jesus and the Jews. But that question *comes too late.* A judge who has first allowed Jesus to be scourged, and has made Him an outlaw, has no business asking a question afterwards. Who, pray, makes the investigation *after* punishment has been meted out?

Accordingly, the Saviour makes no reply.

Now Pilate, all the while marvelling at His silence, advises Jesus that it is dangerous not to reply inasmuch as the judge has the authority to restore His freedom to Him or to assign Him to death. Thereupon Jesus pronounces His last word. Observe that this last word which Jesus pronounces in *the course* of His trial is a reference to the powers that are above. "Thou couldest have no power at all against me, except it were given thee from above." Christ is by this statement indicating that God stands higher than the authority Pilate represents. He assigns to the authority of the government the place of a servant of God. He sees the *first* cause operative in and by means of the *second* cause. And He accepts the consequences of this vision of faith which is fixed upon God.

That is why this *last word* of Christ which was spoken during His trial, this final word before His condemnation, is of great and redeeming significance. This statement about God is the very pillar upon which the trembling thoughts of Christ, the Scourged One,[1] are leaning. His whole soul and spirit are exposed in this reference to the power which is above. This concluding word which Christ speaks is the great torch, the great light of righteousness which shines in this dark night of sin.

Again we see a beautiful harmony in all that Christ does, even at the time when all that men do represents the grossest conceivable discord.

In our first volume—Gethsemane—we saw Christ struggling to keep His vision fixed upon God. As soon in Gethsemane as He had been able to see His God rather than men, He had a sense of well-being, He acquiesced and found that upon which as a man He could lean.[2] This had been the equivalent of His saying: Father, into Thy hands I commend my spirit as I *enter into* my passion.

Now, in this second volume—the trial—we see Christ again struggling to keep His vision fixed upon God. After the meandering course from Annas to Caiaphas, from Caiaphas to Pilate, from Pilate to Herod, from Herod to Pilate, and from Pilate to the people, from the people back to Pilate, from Pilate to the soldiers, from the soldiers back to Pilate, from Pilate back to the people, and from the people who are outside to Pilate who is within—you are not becoming impatient, are you, for this is your bridegroom?—after all these meandering ways, I say, Christ *concludes* the whole trial, and proclaims His patience, His speaking, and His being silent to us in this last word which again turns His attention from the people and fixes it upon His God. Now all is well; now He can rest again; now as a human being He finds His resting place in His God. This is the equivalent of saying: Father, into Thy hands I commend My spirit, now during the *process* of My passion. Presently the *third* volume—the cross—will follow. In it again we will observe Christ struggling, suffering, seeking; we will see His head bowed in the conflict against the dark night of utter forsakenness and judgment. But then, too, He will finally find his resting place in His God, and will exclaim with a loud

1. Not because of Caesar but by the grace of God.
2. See *Christ in His Suffering*, p. 323 and pp. 387 ff.

voice: Father, into Thy hands I commend My spirit, now as I *pass out* of My passion, for "it is finished." Oh incomparable grace, Christ's style ever remains with Him. The temple of holiness and justice stands spiritually erected, a building which cuts its way straight through the crooked dealings of the world.

Thus did Pilate see Christ standing over against Him calmly: God was preaching to Him. Jesus' quietude troubles him. Pilate's *ecce homo* affected the mob but Jesus' *ecce deus* affected Pilate. Hence Pilate—and this is the last time—tries once more to release Jesus.

But he cannot do so now. As soon as the Jews notice his hesitant attitude, they raise their last and best argument and openly exclaim: If thou let this man go, thou art not Caesar's friend. The friend of Caesar. In those days that was a customary title. The Jews are in effect saying this: If you release this man who not only bears the name of our God but also that of your imperial god you are by such conduct indicating that you are no longer a real friend of the emperor, but are indifferent to the Caesar of all Romans. Figure it out for yourself: consequences are sure to follow.

Pilate, in other words, is formally threatened. Pilate succumbs to the threat. Fearing an official investigation—he had done so much which was of a dubious character—he concludes to make this one Galilean the price of his own future and hopes for promotion. Clenching his teeth, he finally concludes to put an end to the matter.

Now it will take place, people, Jesus, world, God. Now it will happen. The judge, the authority, Rome, the world, God, now definitely, once and for all, over against time and eternity, say: I condemn Jesus Christ. Now it is to take place, angels; the judge, God—these curse Him. My justification is about to be pronounced. It is to take place, apostles, patriarchs, and all singers of the *Te Deum,* it is to happen now: the just one will be treated and condemned as the unjust, in order that the unjust and wholly lost may again appear before the tribunal of God as a free and redeemed man, against whom the law can make demands no longer.

It is to take place now.

With great dignity Pilate goes to his judgment chair, to his tribunal, and has it carried out of doors. Moses, Moses, you are still regarded as a responsible person in the world. Pilate wishes to show the Jews a favor and therefore has his judgment seat brought outside, inasmuch as the Jews because of Moses' feasts were not allowed to enter the house of a heathen. Moses, you are being respected, but Jesus Christ is not. You need not move your chair, Moses, up there in heaven, for so it was meet for you to fulfill all righteousness. Is this not exactly what you told him on the mountain of the transfiguration? Besides, the hymn of Moses must be followed, or rather continued, today by the hymn of the Lamb. Hence, Moses, bear the unbearable preferment which is being accorded you. We do not want to sing the hymn of Moses and of the *lion* (lest you take offence at the occasion on which Pilate for your sake has his chair brought out-of-doors and from it, out of respect for you, proceeds to condemn Jesus). But we want to sing the hymn of Moses and the Lamb. After all, can it be that the Lamb should *not* be slain? No, no, the Lamb may not find grace in the world. There is a place for Moses, but for the Lamb there is no place other than the place reserved for it: namely, the altar of *death*.

At this point John's style achieves a certain dignity. This is the great hour. The man who at the time carefully noted the exact hour in which Jesus first met a couple of embarrassed souls,[1] now notes the place and the hour in which the Saviour was sentenced to death. This occurred at the official place which in the Greek language was called *Lithostrotos*—probably because of a pavement laid as a mosaic in front of the palace—which in the Aramaic was called *Gabbatha*—a word which, according to some means "the high place" and according to others something else. There it was that the Saviour surrendered to death. At about noon on a given day—some say that it was the 18th of March in the year 29 A.D.—and if that is true the year in which this book is being written[2] is removed precisely nineteen hundred years from the time Christ was condemned. But no one called for a few moments of silence. Fortunately God did not call for them either. He demands "only" a life-long silence. There, at Lithostrotos, Pilate, although he had definitely concluded to put Jesus to death, addressed the Jews for the last time. His humiliated pride, His sense

---

1. "For it was about the tenth hour." John 1:39.
2. 1929.

of defeat, his pent up anger, the deep disdain with which he in the last analysis condemned the Jews and their Messiah, all these are concealed in his: *Behold your king.* He replies to the renewed excitement of the Jews with a question: Do you really expect me to crucify your own king? Thereupon the high priests—for God gives them the terrible privilege of having the last say—officially bow before Caesar and thereby actualize Zechariah's vision of the priest-king. Then Pilate goes away. A nonchalant gesture—an official decision: the Saviour is given up to be crucified.

Come near now. And pray. Have you noticed the clear *distinction* which the smitten Saviour is still able to make? In the presence of a whole college of judges, none of them disposed to make clear distinctions, He discriminated fastidiously and distinguished well. He had said to Pilate: I do indeed hold you responsible, but those who delivered me into your hands are guilty of the greater sin. He makes a sharp distinction: God be praised. A judge must be able to discriminate, but if he fails to do so, one must take recourse to the priest. Inasmuch now as Christ, the Priest-King, is surrounded by the furies, after whose name I myself also am called, His perfect gift for discrimination *comforts* me. He places Pilate's responsibility over against the Jews in the proper light. Not for one moment may He obscure the distinction between the spheres of general and of special grace. He is very terrible. The most gruesome evil does not make Him lose His penetrating gift of discrimination. Lord, Thou searchest me, and Thou knowest my heart, and Thou knowest that what I think is not to Thy honor. I need Thee, Lord, cleanse me, me in particular, with hyssop. Thou knowest with what penetration the sun's rays have beat upon me.

He makes distinctions.

Thus He takes upon Himself at last the perfecting of the vicious circle, of Annas, of Caiaphas, of Pilate, and now also of the people called by the name I bear. Pilate wanted to excite their sympathy. Ah me, he wanted to compensate for the suffering which takes its position at the very central point of world history by means of sympathy which, he supposed, could succeed in obliterating the line which describes the course of that vicious circle. He said *ecce homo*, for he again wished to cleanse the time by means of time, the visible by means of the visible, the heart by means of the heart. *Ecce homo*—Saviour, Master, forgive him for he knew not what he said. Lord, I mean forgive me, for I do not know what I am saying. *Ecce homo*—if that is proclaimed *from above* it is the very essence of truth; but if it is proclaimed *from below* it is the very essence of insult. Then it casts Thee into the vicious circle, the very circle which Thou hadst already conquered by means of the Word.[1] Didst Thou hear it, Saviour? A satyr just pronounced the words: *ecce homo*. And this was his commentary of it: Do not fear him. Hereafter thou shalt see the lost son of man descend in the weakness of His flesh down to the very pit of hell in which the living damned abide. By means of the *ecce homo*, they tried to excite pity for Thee, Jesus. Alas, that was turning the gospel topsy-turvy. Thou dost not want to be the *object* of my pity, but it is Thy will to be afflicted in my affliction. The angel of my countenance may not comfort Thee. That is why the offensive *ecce homo* represents a negation of Thy priesthood. Yet when Pilate pronounced these words, Thou didst reply: What thou doest do quickly, for I see God standing in this place. And that reply, my Saviour, is my redemption. Thou didst place Thy blood in the Father's sacrificial basin.

Keep my tongue in check, I pray, lest it too quickly and too bravely proceed to sing psalms out of a book. I should be very eager to sing songs about Thy golden crown, and about Thy sharp sickle, and I should be very eager to put into rhyme the songs of Paul who taught me that on the Friday of the Passover feast Satan did indeed make a public exhibition of Jesus, but that on the same day Jesus also publicly made a spectacle of Satan and his whole tribe.[2] Master, hold my tongue in check, for I must first confess that *I* have publicly made a spectacle of Thee, that *I* am Pilate, that *I* am the high-priest, and court servant, the scum of the people, and Barabbas also. *I* have said concerning Thee: I dare to condemn Him. I am no better than Pilate, Lord. He sacrificed Thee to protect himself. On this very day my *flesh* would do the same.

Lord, my God, it is impossible for Thee to be tempted now; the pity of the people which to this day is aroused by Pilate and his

---

1. See Chapter 7.
2. Colossians 2:15.

æsthetic family, can not tempt Thee any more. But forbid that I should do Thee injustice. What a terrible day. I may not even sympathize with Jesus. Sympathy He calls negation; He calls it saying *ecce homo,* and saying it from below. He calls it saying *ecce homo* with Pilate's inflection. To say it thus is to ignore Him in His triumph of justice. It represents opposing Him even as He is in the idea. Hence, I must keep silence before the people and must raise a hymn of praise and must excite love in my heart in the power of the Lord. The power of the Lord—those are great words—but it requires omnipotence to teach me how to sing a hymn of praise here. I hear good tidings. A voice comes to me from Dordrecht, which answers me as I stand here at Gabbatha unable to sing but summoned to sing. The voice comforts me: Omnipotence is operative; there is such a thing as *regeneration,* an almighty, an irresistible deed of Christ's Holy Spirit. *Veni, Creator Spiritus,* and teach me His hymn now. It seems to me that He needs me, He needs a comforting hymn. But I see Him ever shaking His head. He would also be forsaken of me; He needs no comfort now after the temptation He has just withstood.

Nevertheless, I want to say what I see in Him as He limps to the cross, and I want to say it before my eyes are dimmed with tears. I want to tell Him that I see Him as great here as He was in the wilderness. In the wilderness He was first tempted, tempted by Satan. Satan wanted Him to shun the way of suffering, wanted Him to accept His glory without taking this terrible digression which He is taking today. Today He—be quiet, people; in the name of peace just look—today He is being *tempted* again. In the last moment He is being tempted, terribly tempted. He is being tempted in the moment of the general repetition, of the painful recapitulation to which we alluded above. When Pilate's tender voice very movingly pronounced the *ecce homo,* and when a few women nodded approvingly, and when a few people began to blush in shame, and when the crowd was at the point of reconsidering, then Satan whispered into Jesus' ear the temptation: Take advantage of this hour, and all will yet be well. Pilate was giving Him the floor and Jesus might have spoken. Even Pilate would have been moved to tears by a perturbing story.

But Jesus held His peace.

He did not answer. He did not profit from the occasion. He was only profited by, He was made sin. His last pronouncement was: *I see God standing*. Jesus, now I know that Thou didst withstand the temptation even in the last moment in which it was possible for Thee to do something.

They are all going on their way, Saviour. It will take place, it is sure to happen, they are telling each other that it will happen this very day. I stand alone on this court square, and Thou dost not even look at me. Perhaps Thou thinkest that he would not have a good word for me unless it were given him from above. And where would Simon be? I see him nowhere near here to help me; I mean only that he is not helping Thee, that he is leaving Thee alone. I think that Simon is just like me: he does not dare to express any sympathy; he is ashamed, and he is afraid of Thy eyes, I think; I have seen those eyes, seen them when the *ecce homo* was spoken. But I am wandering from the subject: I simply wanted to say, Master, that when Thou wast tempted in the wilderness the angels came to succor Thee, the beasts to greet Thee, and there was a Paradise, be it a very small one, in the form of a great promise. Now Thou art being tempted again, and now Thou hast triumphed anew. But there are no angels here; the wild animals could not possibly come here—their eyes are too faithful to be tolerated by the people and not to shun Thee. As for Paradise, what shall we say of that? Why bring that beautiful word into this discussion? The cross is coming.

Jesus, Thou goest Thy way alone. Would I dare to accompany Thee? But what shall *I* do now? Can it be that I am the substitute for angels or for beasts? Why should *I* follow Thee? The wild beasts have faithful eyes but *I* have just now condemned Thee. Lord, save Him, for He perisheth. Lord, save me, for I perish. Lord, my God, Thou hast spoken to me today. And the burden of Thy message was this: He that justifies the wicked and condemns the just, even they both are an *abomination* to the Lord. *He* knows that text already. Oh, wonderful thing. He quoted the text, and sought me with His eyes. His eyes were tender. I cannot withstand. I am going outside . . . outside . . .

The sun kept on shining. It was very warm. A Jew hurried past, muttering a curse between his teeth. It was hot at high noon. He was sweating freely. The soldiers found the way rather heavy. How long it was, they said to each other, how long it was and how far.